Deke McClelland's

Look & Learn™
Dreamweaver®

version 4

by Glenn Weadock

A Type & Graphics Book

Hungry Minds™

Best-Selling Books • Digital Downloads • e-Books • Answer Networks • e-Newsletters • Branded Web Sites • e-Learning

New York, NY • Cleveland, OH • Indianapolis, IN

Deke McClelland's **Look & Learn™ Dreamweaver 4°**

Published by:
Hungry Minds, Inc.
909 Third Avenue
New York, NY 10022
www.hungryminds.com
www.dummies.com

ISBN: 0-7645-3507-2

Library of Congress Control Number: 2001092067

Printed in the United States of America

10 9 8 7 6 5 4 3 2 1

IO/QW/RR/QR/IN

Distributed in the United States by Hungry Minds, Inc.

Distributed by CDG Books Canada Inc. for Canada; by Transworld Publishers Limited in the United Kingdom; by IDG Norge Books for Norway; by IDG Sweden Books for Sweden; by IDG Books Australia Publishing Corporation Pty. Ltd. for Australia and New Zealand; by TransQuest Publishers Pte Ltd. for Singapore, Malaysia, Thailand, Indonesia, and Hong Kong; by Gotop Information Inc. for Taiwan; by ICG Muse, Inc. for Japan; by Intersoft for South Africa; by Eyrolles for France; by International Thomson Publishing for Germany, Austria and Switzerland; by Distribuidora Cuspide for Argentina; by LR International for Brazil; by Galileo Libros for Chile; by Ediciones ZETA S.C.R. Ltda. for Peru; by WS Computer Publishing Corporation, Inc., for the Philippines; by Contemporanea de Ediciones for Venezuela; by Express Computer Distributors for the Caribbean and West Indies; by Micronesia Media Distributor, Inc. for Micronesia; by Chips Computadoras S.A. de C.V. for Mexico; by Editorial Norma de Panama S.A. for Panama; by American Bookshops for Finland.

For general information on Hungry Minds' products and services please contact our Customer Care department; within the U.S. at 800-762-2974, outside the U.S. at 317-572-3993 or fax 317-572-4002.

For sales inquiries and resellers information, including discounts, premium and bulk quantity sales and foreign language translations please contact our Customer Care department at 800-434-3422, fax 317-572-4002 or write to Hungry Minds, Inc., Attn: Customer Care department, 10475 Crosspoint Boulevard, Indianapolis, IN 46256.

For information on licensing foreign or domestic rights, please contact our Sub-Rights Customer Care department at 212-884-5000.

For information on using Hungry Minds' products and services in the classroom or for ordering examination copies, please contact our Educational Sales department at 800-434-2086 or fax 317-572-4005.

Please contact our Public Relations department at 212-884-5163 for press review copies or 212-884-5000 for author interviews and other publicity information or fax 212-884-5400.

For authorization to photocopy items for corporate, personal, or educational use, please contact Copyright Clearance Center, 222 Rosewood Drive, Danvers, MA 01923, or fax 978-750-4470.

 is a trademark of Hungry Minds, Inc.

About the Author

Glenn Weadock is President of Independent Software, Inc. (ISI), a computer consulting firm he cofounded in 1982. ISI provides Web design services, technical education, intranet-based training, technical support management consulting, and multimedia services to clients such as Ernst & Young, Lucent Technologies, and the U.S. Army.

For the last 15 years, Glenn has been designing and presenting technical seminars throughout the United States, Canada, and the United Kingdom. He has also created several popular computer videos. Since 1995, Glenn has written 15 books published in 4 languages, including *Intranet Publishing For Dummies*. These books have received praise from well-known journalists Jim Seymour, Fred Langa, and Jerry Pournelle, who called *Exploding the Computer Myth* "the most important business computer book of the decade."

Glenn experienced 15 seconds (not minutes) of fame as a consultant and expert witness in the *U.S. vs. Microsoft* antitrust trial. He is presently a technology mentor for *Inc.* magazine's Web site, *www.inc.com*, and a member of various corporate advisory boards. Glenn lives in Golden, Colorado, with his wife Emily and daughters Carina and Cecily.

About the Illustrator

Emily Sherrill Weadock is an award-winning graphic artist, author, animator, and illustrator whose talent ranges from technical illustration to broadcast-quality 3D animation and Web site design. She has illustrated nearly 20 books and written 2, *Flash 5 Quick Reference For Dummies* and *Creating Cool PowerPoint 97 Presentations*. Before trading brushes for mice, Emily enjoyed success as a mixed-media construction artist. She studied art at SMU and Baylor University.

Production Credits

Series designer: Deke McClelland

Series editor: Amy Thomas Buscaglia

Project editor: Kelly Ewing

Acquisitions editors: Michael Roney, Tom Heine

Technical editor: Derren Whiteman

Editorial manager: Rev Mengle

Project coordinator: Nancee Reeves

Layout and graphics: Kelly Hardesty, Shelley Lea, Shelley Norris, Laurie Petrone, Kathie Schutte, Janet Seib, Rashell Smith,

Index art and layout: Barb Obermeier

Proofreaders: Andy Hollandbeck, Carl Pierce, Linda Quigley

Indexer: Sharon Hilgenberg

Special Help: Diana R. Conover

Acknowledgments

A book like this represents the collaboration of many hardworking, creative, intelligent professionals. (Not *this* book, you understand, but a book *like* this.) I'd like to thank Deke McClelland for designing a value-packed, reader-oriented, and visually beautiful series format, and for giving me the honor of being the second author ever to write a *Look & Learn* book. Thanks also to Amy Thomas Buscaglia, who had the patience, dedication, and good humor to guide me to a clear understanding of the series concept; her commitment to getting the details right and her willingness to listen to others' ideas are the marks of a real pro. Derren Whiteman, our sharp-eyed technical editor, did an excellent job, so I forgive his ill-considered comment about Canadian beer being better than American beer.

The folks at Hungry Minds, including (but not limited to) Mike Roney, Rev Mengle, Kelly Ewing, and Kevin Shafer, have all been great to work with, and I owe Mike special thanks for bringing me together with Deke and Amy on this project. Leona Lapez at Macromedia was most helpful, as usual, providing me with more material than I could ever fully digest. Thanks go as always to my longtime literary agent, Mike Snell. And many, many thanks go to my wife-slash-illustrator, Emily, whose support and enthusiasm never flagged even as a 3-month project turned into a 6-month project.

I had planned to thank Acme Cognac for permission to use their Web site in the book's many examples, but then the bribe fell through. So I'll close by acknowledging that I can't stand the stuff. When it comes to cognac, it's Courvoisier, baby, all the way.

Instant Information

Look & Learn™

That Sticks In Your Head

There are lots of ways to teach **computing** and **electronic design**. Books, videos, online courses, live seminars—I've done (and continue to do) them all. But while each method appeals to a specific learning style, none works so well as the inevitable training device of the future: a syringe to the brain. One day, you'll plunk down **$19.99** at your local InfoMart and receive a cylinder of pure knowledge. Poke it in, push the plunger, and **zap!** You've upgraded your head.

Sadly, I got a C in chemistry. (One experiment in particular caught on fire, but that's another story.) So I'm hardly qualified to invent the **information elixir**. But it got me thinking. How can I accomplish **the next best thing**?

The answer is a book. A highly **visual book** that conveys information «FAST» by showing it. A relatively short book «CONCISE» that you can absorb in a few sittings. A book that remains affordable by **maximizing** «EFFICIENT» page space. A book that page after page «COMPLETE» teaches the **most reliable techniques** in the business, and does so as **instantaneously** as humanly possible. A «LOOK & LEARN» book where you **look** at a page and, without delay, **learn** precisely what you need to know.

Fast   concise   efficient   complete.

These are the watchwords for **Look & Learn**, a new series of computer training guides designed for the visual mind.

How does it work? For starters, every word on every page relates to a graphic. This means **features and steps appear in context**, so you can see how they work. It also permits you to hone in on the stuff you're most keen to learn. See an option, read the explanation, and you're ready to get back to work.

To speed your learning, dictionary-like **thumbtabs** show you where chapters start and stop. Each chapter gets a **unique icon**, so you know where you are in a flash. Contents @ A Glance (page vii) uses the thumbtabs to show you where to go.

Tips and insights **tip** are **clearly labeled** and highlighted. Commands, options, and other literal software text appear in bold type. **Color-coded callouts** reference related information within a discussion. And when I decide to refer you to another section, I tell you the **exact page number** to go to. (Shouldn't every book?)

Finally, when you're in a hurry to find information about a specific topic, turn to Look It Up & Learn (page 293), the only index that uses both words and pictures to point you toward the answers you need most.

Throw in **step-by-step tutorials**; succinct, no-nonsense writing; and unflinching discussions of even the most complex topics, and you have what I consider to be the best training value on the market. I hope you'll agree with me that no reference provides so much, so quickly, and so clearly as **Look & Learn**.

Contents

@ A Glance

Detailed Contents *with steps*

Detailed Contents with steps

Detailed Contents

with steps

Detailed Contents with *steps*

chapter

Get To Know Dreamweaver

Welcome to **Dreamweaver 4!** Dreamweaver is a *Web design* program: Its role in life is to help you create Web pages (and whole Web sites) from text, graphics, and multimedia source material. Dreamweaver is the fastest-growing Web design program around. In its fourth generation, the program's design is mature and sophisticated.

This chapter provides a bird's-eye view of the Dreamweaver landscape for those new to the program (or at least new to Version 4). Most of the chapter explains the different parts of the Dreamweaver user interface: what the different windows, menus, and panels do and how you make them do it.

Although Dreamweaver looks and works similarly on a Windows PC and on a Macintosh computer, differences do exist, mainly because of the separate traditions of these platforms. I'll point out those differences here (and in future chapters) by using the shorthand notation **Win** for Windows and **Mac** for Macintosh.

1

The Dreamweaver Desktop, Windows

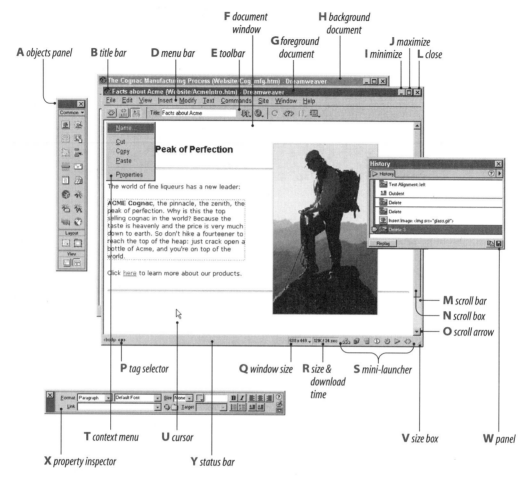

F *document window*

H *background document*

G *foreground document*

J *maximize*

I *minimize*   **L** *close*

A *objects panel*   **B** *title bar*   **D** *menu bar*   **E** *toolbar*

M *scroll bar*

N *scroll box*

O *scroll arrow*

P *tag selector*   **Q** *window size*   **R** *size & download time*   **S** *mini-launcher*

T *context menu*   **U** *cursor*   **V** *size box*   **W** *panel*

X *property inspector*   **Y** *status bar*

A objects panel

This widely used window offers icons for inserting images, frames, layers, tables, Flash text, and other page elements. It's actually many panels in one: You can click the pop-up menu at the top to display different sets of objects.

B title bar (Win)

On the PC, the name of an application typically appears at the top of its window. In Dreamweaver, you see not only the program name in the *title bar*, but also, just before it, the name of the loaded document and its file path. An unsaved document appears as **Untitled** followed by a number. Each document has its own standalone window. Drag the title bar to move

a document window around; click a title bar to make that document window active.

C title bar (Mac)

On the Macintosh (at least up to and including OS9), the title bar for each open document contains the name of the document and the file path, but not the program name, which appears in the upper-right corner of the Macintosh desktop.

D menu bar

To display a list of commands—that is, a *menu*—click a menu name in the menu bar. To select a command, click it. Most commands take effect right away, but a command followed by three dots—such as **Open**—displays a window of options called a *dialog box*.

The Dreamweaver Desktop, Macintosh

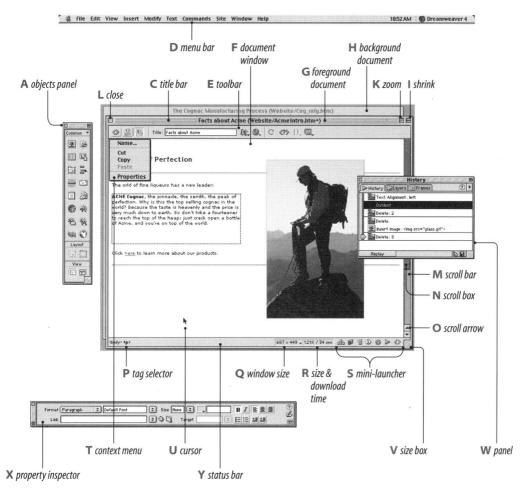

D menu bar

F document window

H background document

G foreground document

A objects panel

C title bar

E toolbar

K zoom   **I** shrink

L close

M scroll bar

N scroll box

O scroll arrow

P tag selector

Q window size

R size & download time

S mini-launcher

V size box

W panel

T context menu

U cursor

X property inspector

Y status bar

E toolbar

The *toolbar* appears just below the menu bar on a PC (just below the title bar on a Mac) and contains icons you click to change the current view of the document: check documents in and out (on multiuser projects); preview the current document in a browser; and a few other common commands. Hide or display it with the **View➥Toolbar** command.

F document window

The current document (that is, a Web page) appears in the document window. Load a document with the **File➥Open** command, close it with **File➥Close**, or create a new document with (you guessed it) **File➥New**.

G foreground document

If you have multiple documents open at one time, one of them must be the *foreground*, or *active*, document. Click anywhere in a document to bring it to the foreground so that you can work on it. Alternatively, you can open the **Window** menu and scroll to the bottom of it, where the currently open documents are listed, and click the one you want to make active.

H background document

A *background* document is simply any open document that is not currently the foreground document. To edit a background document, click anywhere on it (such as its title bar) or choose its name in the **Window** menu.

I minimize (Win)/shrink (Mac)

If you use Windows, click the *minimize* button in the title bar (B) to hide the foreground document window. (If you have background document windows, or the **Site** window, open, they become visible on the screen.) The window you minimized will appear on the Windows taskbar; click it to bring it back up onto the screen. Press **shift+F4** to minimize all windows at once.

On the Mac, each window title bar (C) sports a *shrink* icon. When you click this icon, you collapse the window, and only its title bar remains visible; you can click the icon again to restore the image to its original size.

J maximize (Win)

The *maximize* button in the title bar (B) fills the display with the foreground document window. (If you want to bring the window back to its original size, click the *restore* button, which is the second of the three buttons on the right side of the title bar.) If you have several documents open, you can maximize one, none, or all of them.

K zoom (Mac)

On the Macintosh, click the *zoom* icon in the document title bar (C) to fill the display with the foreground document window. To restore the window to its original size, you can simply click the zoom icon again.

L close

Click the *close* button in the document window title bar to close an open document. If you've modified the document since you last saved it, Dreamweaver prompts you to save or discard the changes.

> *tip* On the Windows platform, if the window you close is the only open window, then closing it exits the Dreamweaver program. This behavior may catch you off guard because it differs from other Windows programs, and also from the Macintosh version of Dreamweaver, which stays loaded even if you close all open windows.

M scroll bar

Any document window that cannot display the entire document includes one or two *scroll bars*. Keep in mind that you only see a horizontal scroll bar if the document window is narrower horizontally than the widest element on the page, so most of the time in Dreamweaver, you'll only see a vertical scroll bar if you see one at all. You can click inside the scroll bar to pan the page inside the document window and show parts of the page that were formerly hidden. Or you can click above the scroll box (N) in the vertical scroll bar to pan up, click below it to pan down; the horizontal scroll bar works similarly. You can also use **shift-page up** or **shift-page down** to scroll vertically.

N scroll box

Drag the *scroll box* to pan the page inside the document window. For example, drag the scroll box in the horizontal scroll bar to the right to pan the page to the right.

O scroll arrow

Click a scroll arrow to pan the view of the page just a little bit.

P tag selector

Dreamweaver is a generator of HTML code, and the *tag selector* shows you the HTML tags that apply to the currently selected object in the foreground document window. You don't have to use the tag selector to create Web pages, but it's powerful; see The Status Bar, on page 21, for more details.

Q window size

The *window size* pop-up menu lets you resize the foreground window to one of several presets. You can create your own window sizes, too, and save them for easy access later.

R size & download time

Dreamweaver reports the size in kilobytes and estimated download time for the foreground document here. The displayed download time depends on the assumed connection speed, which you can view or set by choosing Edit➡Preferences and clicking the Status Bar category in the list at left.

S mini-launcher

You can open various handy Dreamweaver panels from the *mini-launcher*, the contents of which you can modify; see The Launcher, on page 20, for more info.

T context menu

Windows 95 popularized the concept of *context menus*, sometimes called *shortcut menus*, and Dreamweaver uses them extensively. Under Windows, right-click an object to display the context menu, which lists the commands you're most likely to use in the context of that kind of object (paragraph, image, table, and so on). Most Macintoshes don't have a right mouse button, and if yours doesn't, you must press the **control** key and click the mouse in order to display a context menu. When working in a panel (W), you can also activate the context menu by clicking an arrow at the panel's upper-right corner.

When in doubt as to what operations you can perform on a given object on a Web page, bring up the context menu. Also know that you often can't see the full range of possibilities until you choose **Properties** on the context menu.

U cursor

The *cursor* is the on-screen indicator of your mouse's position. Move the mouse and the cursor moves, too. The cursor's appearance indicates what Dreamweaver expects or intends to do next. For details, see Mouse & Cursor on page 6.

V size box

Drag the lower-right corner of the foreground window to change its size. You can usually do this even when a size box isn't visible; for example, panels (W) don't have size boxes, but you can still resize them by dragging their lower-right corners.

W panel

A *panel* is simply a handy window, hosting frequently used commands or features, that you can leave open on the screen while you work. Earlier versions of Dreamweaver referred to these as *palettes*. See the Panels section, on page 18, for the full lowdown.

X property inspector

You may not be familiar with *property inspectors* even if you're a seasoned computer user. These windows, which you can display and hide at will, let you adjust settings that pertain to a specific kind of object. That is, the **Text** property inspector offers different options than the **Image** property inspector. The idea of these windows is to help you see the things you can do with a particular object without using trial-and-error with the menu system. If the property inspector feature is on, clicking different objects in the document window causes the property inspector to "morph" into the type that's compatible with the clicked object. You'll normally leave this feature on at all times.

Y status bar

The status bar is the bottom part of the document window and hosts the tag selector (P), window size menu (Q), size and download time field (R), and mini-launcher (S). See The Status Bar, on page 21, for more details.

Mouse & Cursor

Dreamweaver 4 makes more extensive use of the mouse than any previous version. You can select objects and move them with the mouse, just as in other programs. But in Dreamweaver, you also use the mouse to draw tables, frames, and layers; to create hyperlinks; to reorganize files and folders; and to juggle the various windows, panels, and inspectors. Of course, anything you can do with a mouse, you can do with various mouse substitutes: trackballs, touchpads, tablets, virtual reality helmets, and so on.

> **tip** Your choice of pointing device matters more when working with a graphic design program like Dreamweaver than with word processing, spreadsheet, or database software. If you're using a generic mouse, consider upgrading to a high-resolution, optical, and/or cordless unit—and pick up a low-friction mouse pad, such as Everglide or 3M, while you're at it. You'll appreciate the added precision and comfort when mousing around the Dreamweaver document window.

The cursor does two things for you: It shows you where on the screen the mouse is pointing at any moment and (by its shape, which changes automatically) what Dreamweaver expects or intends to happen next. The cursor changes shape whenever you pass it over a displayed element that you can act upon, for example, with a click. The figure at right shows some common cursor types in Dreamweaver.

A arrow

This arrow is the default shape of the cursor. You can choose a menu command or toolbar button with the arrow cursor; you can also move windows, panels, and inspectors around by clicking and dragging their title bars. The Windows cursor is white (with an optional drop shadow in some versions of Windows), and the Macintosh cursor is black.

B crosshairs

The crosshairs cursor means that you're about to draw something, such as a table, table cell, or layer. The

⬚	**A** *arrow*	⊘	**G** *action denied*
+	**B** *crosshairs*	✋	**H** *touch*
✛	**C** *reposition*	I	**I** *text*
↕	**D** *vertical resize*	✎	**J** *eyedropper*
↔	**E** *horizontal resize*	↘⊕	**K** *point-to-file*
↗	**F** *diagonal resize*	⧖	**L** *wait*

drawing technique is to place the crosshairs cursor at one of the four corners of the rectangle you want to draw and then click and drag to the opposite corner.

C reposition

The reposition cursor displays arrows pointing north, south, east, and west. Typically, you see this cursor when you're about to move something, such as a layer. Click and drag when the cursor has this shape in order to move an object without resizing it.

D vertical resize

Click and drag when the cursor has this shape in order to resize an object in the vertical dimension while leaving the horizontal dimension alone. Note that it's not generally wise to resize images within Dreamweaver; that's an activity better undertaken with an image-editing program.

E horizontal resize

Click and drag when the cursor has this shape in order to resize an object horizontally, leaving the vertical dimension alone.

F diagonal resize

Click and drag when the cursor looks like this to resize an object in both horizontal and vertical dimensions at the same time. Holding the shift key down when doing a diagonal resize constrains the object to keep its original aspect ratio (that is, horizontal-to-vertical proportion) during the resize operation.

G action denied

The good old international "NOT" symbol means that whatever you're trying to do, you can't do it right here. For example, if you try to create a table where a paragraph of text already exists, you will see the cursor of denial.

H touch

The hand with a pointing index finger generally appears when you position the cursor over an icon that represents a command. For example, you see the touch cursor when you move over the icons in the objects panel.

I text

The text cursor, also known as the "I-beam" or "insertion point," means that you can type text that will appear at the current cursor position. You can also click and drag the text cursor to select text for editing or formatting, for example, to change the text's color.

J eyedropper

This cursor appears when you've told Dreamweaver you want to "grab" a color from somewhere else on the page. For example, you could use the eyedropper to select a color from a graphic image, and use that color for a paragraph of text on the same page.

K point-to-file

You won't see this cursor much outside of the Dreamweaver program. It appears when you click and drag a point-to-file icon (for example, in a property inspector) to select a file, say, from the **Site** window. You can use this method to create hyperlinks.

L wait

The hourglass (or, on the Mac, the wristwatch) indicates that Dreamweaver is doing something that is so compute-intensive that you can't use the program for anything else. Dreamweaver 4 is much faster than its predecessor, so if you're a veteran of Version 3, you won't see this cursor as much as you have in the past.

Common Mouse Operations

Mousing around has its own vernacular. Here's what I mean in this book when I use the following terms:

Click

Press and release the left button (or, on a one-button mouse, the only button) quickly. "Click" is synonymous with "left-click" if your mouse has two or more buttons.

Right-click

Press and release the right mouse button quickly. If you use a Macintosh with a single-button mouse, hold down **control** while clicking to simulate a right-click.

Double-click

Click twice quickly. For example, double-click in a text section to select an entire word. You can set the double-click speed with your operating system's mouse control panel if the speed setting is not the right sensitivity for you. Depending on the type of object, double-clicking may open a separate application; for example, if you set Fireworks as your default image editor, double-clicking an image opens Fireworks and loads the image for editing.

Click and drag

Press the left (or only) mouse button, hold it down, move the mouse, and then release the button. This is the most common method of moving objects around in Dreamweaver.

<Key>-click

Hold down the specified key, click, and then release the key. For example, **shift**+click lets you select multiple adjacent objects (such as files in the site window). **Ctrl**+click (Win) and **command**-click (Mac) let you select multiple nonadjacent objects.

Hover

Move the cursor over an object of interest (say, a toolbar button) and leave it there a second or two to display the icon's name.

Mouse-over

Move the mouse over an object (such as a rollover button) to see the object immediately change appearance.

The Document Window

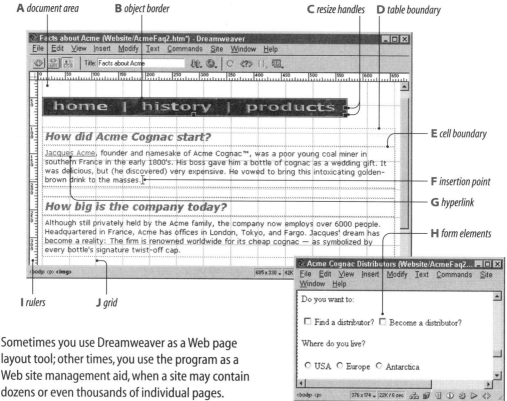

A *document area*   **B** *object border*   **C** *resize handles*   **D** *table boundary*

E *cell boundary*

F *insertion point*

G *hyperlink*

H *form elements*

I *rulers*   **J** *grid*

Sometimes you use Dreamweaver as a Web page layout tool; other times, you use the program as a Web site management aid, when a site may contain dozens or even thousands of individual pages. Normally, you're doing one thing or the other, and Dreamweaver offers a primary workspace for each activity.

The document window is the primary workspace for page layout, and the **Site** window is the primary workspace for site management. This page looks at a few (although certainly not all!) key aspects of the document window; Chapter 10, Manage Your Site, takes a closer look at the **Site** window. More detail on how particular Web objects appear in the document window will appear in future chapters that deal with those types of objects.

> *tip* The Dreamweaver document window does not display all content exactly as it will appear in a browser window. Therefore, use the document window as a *guide* to what your page will look like in a browser, but not as an exact representation.

A document area

The document area is the entire space within the document window borders. You can change the size of this area by clicking the window size pop-up menu on the status bar (Q, page 5), or by dragging the size box at the lower-right corner.

> *tip* Some Web objects, such as text paragraphs, can be set to automatically change shape when a user resizes a browser window, so that the objects remain fully visible. Dreamweaver mimics this behavior in the document window.

B object border

The *object border* is the solid rectangle that appears around a selected object. When an object is selected, you can typically move it, resize it, delete it, or modify its properties in the associated property inspector (see Property Inspectors on page 17).

C resize handles

If you select an object, such as an image, you may see *resize handles* appear on the object border. You can click and drag any of the resize handles to change the object's size.

D table boundary

If your page uses HTML tables, Dreamweaver outlines them with a dotted line in standard view and a solid line in layout view.

E cell boundary

HTML tables consist of one or more *cells*. Cell boundaries appear with a distinctive crosshatch pattern in standard view. In layout view, they appear with solid lines that change color when you mouse over them to indicate an active selection.

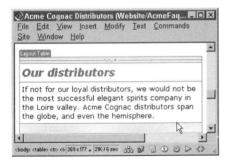

F insertion point

The *insertion point* is the current cursor location and where the next word that you type, or object that you insert, will go on the page. Reposition the insertion point in a text area by moving the cursor and clicking once.

G hyperlink

The one aspect of Web pages that everyone learns first is the *hyperlink*, or simply *link*. Linked words or phrases appear in the document window as underlined and in a different color, just as they do in a browser window. (You can't immediately see links that are associated with graphics or image maps, although such links do appear in the property inspectors for those objects—see page 17 for more on property inspectors.)

H form elements

If you've built a page that uses form elements, such as check boxes and radio buttons, those elements appear in the document window much as they would in a browser window.

I rulers

Rulers (one horizontal and one vertical) provide a reference for your page's physical dimensions. Display them with the **View➥Rulers➥Show** command. You can change the units to pixels, inches, or centimeters by choosing an option on the **View➥Rulers** submenu.

> **tip** Rulers are somewhat less useful in Web design than in (say) print design, so you may decide to leave them off for most of your day-to-day work.

J grid

The *grid* is a set of crosshatching lines that helps you place objects on the page. Show the grid (which does not appear in a browser window) by choosing **View➥Grid➥Show Grid**. You can modify the grid settings with **View➥Grid➥Edit Grid**, which brings up the following dialog box.

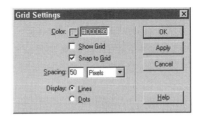

> **tip** Make objects (such as table boundaries) snap to the gridlines by choosing **View➥Grid➥Snap to Grid**. As you position or resize an object or an object's boundary near a gridline, Dreamweaver places it exactly on the gridline, helping you create perfectly aligned objects for a sharper-looking page.

The Objects Panel

The most common window you'll use in Dream-weaver is the *objects panel.* The objects panel's purpose in life is to help you accomplish common tasks with a single click.

Future chapters examine individual functions of this handy window in detail, but here are its main features. I like to leave the objects panel on screen whenever I'm working in the document window. But if it gets in your way, you can hide the objects panel by choosing **Window➞Objects** or by pressing **ctrl+F2** (**command-F2** on the Macintosh).

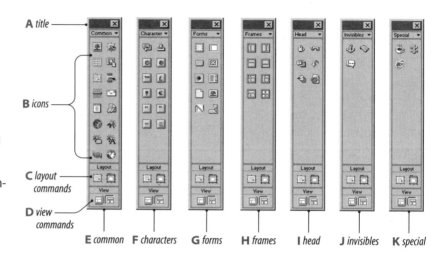

A *title*
B *icons*
C *layout commands*
D *view commands*

E *common* **F** *characters* **G** *forms* **H** *frames* **I** *head* **J** *invisibles* **K** *special*

A title

The *title* tells you which of the objects panels is presently displayed. Click it to display a pop-up menu that lets you select a different objects panel.

B icons

The *icons* on the objects panel generally perform a common command, such as **Insert Image**. The icons change when you choose a different objects panel in the title menu (A).

C layout commands

No matter which objects panel you're using, these icons let you add tables and cells if you're working in layout view.

D view commands

Choose *standard view,* where you do most of your work, or *layout view,* where you can design tables conveniently and quickly.

E common

The panel contains the most frequently used commands: **Insert Image**, **Insert Table**, and so on.

F characters

Insert special characters onto your Web page here.

G forms

The **Forms** panel contains the most common elements used to build an HTML form.

H frames

Frames divide up the space on a Web page to contain different chunks of content. This panel provides the most-used commands.

I head

Here you can add *head elements* that, for example, can help search engines know how to categorize your site.

J invisibles

You can't see some Web page elements, like *named anchors,* in a browser window. Add them with this panel.

K special

Here's where you can add Java applets, ActiveX controls, and Netscape plug-ins to your page.

Reference Guides

A handy addition to Version 4 is the collection of online O'Reilly & Associates *reference guides* for HTML, JavaScript, and CSS (Cascading Style Sheets). The best part of this feature is that it's context-sensitive: Select the item of interest and then activate the reference guide to go right to the relevant information. On this page, I discuss mainly the HTML reference guide; the other ones work similarly.

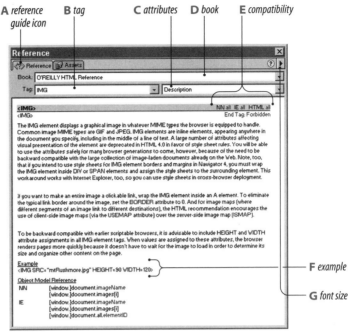

A *reference guide icon* **B** *tag* **C** *attributes* **D** *book* **E** *compatibility*

F *example*

G *font size*

A reference guide icon

To use the HTML reference guide, select a tag (for example, from the tag selector on the status bar) and then click this icon on the toolbar. If the **Reference** panel isn't already open, Dreamweaver opens it and navigates to details about the selected tag. You can also select the tag and then choose **Help→Reference** or press **shift-F1**. (This select-then-open method doesn't always work, so you need to know about the **Tag** field, too [B]).

B tag

Click in the **Tag** field to display a pop-up menu of HTML tags listed in alphabetical order; choose one to display reference information about it. (In the JavaScript reference guide, the **Tag** field becomes the **Object** field, and in the CSS guide, it becomes **Style**.)

C attributes

This pop-up menu lists all the attributes, or modifiers, that you can use with the selected tag (B). Choose an attribute in this list to see details about it in the reference guide's main window. The default choice is **Description**, which isn't an attribute but lets you read about the tag itself.

D book

Here's where you can manually switch between the HTML, JavaScript, and CSS reference guides.

E compatibility

At the upper right, view the tag or attribute's compatibility with different browsers and HTML versions, as well as whether an accompanying end tag is optional or required with the selected tag. (**NN** is short for Netscape Navigator, and **IE** is short for Internet Explorer.)

F example

Scroll to or look at the bottom of the details window to see an example code snippet using the selected tag (B) and/or attribute (C).

G font size

Click the arrow at the upper-right corner to choose a different display font size for the reference guide.

Menus & Commands

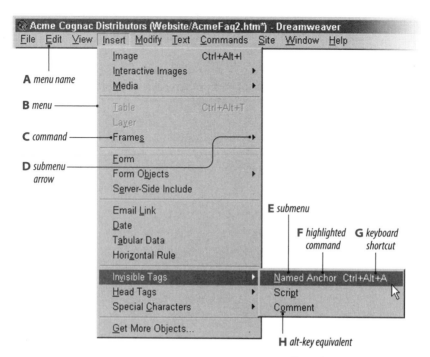

A *menu name*

B *menu*

C *command*

D *submenu arrow*

E *submenu*

F *highlighted command* **G** *keyboard shortcut*

H *alt-key equivalent*

C command

A command is a choice you can make from a menu. This book puts menu commands like **Named Anchor** in boldface.

D submenu arrow

If the commands on a menu are too numerous for a single list, you see one or more arrows that point to submenus branching off the primary menu.

E submenu

A submenu is a menu that branches off another menu. Submenus, which typically contain related commands, are helpful for avoiding really long main menus. In this book, I use the ➡ symbol to indicate the path to a command. For example, if I ask you to choose **Insert➡Invisible Tags➡Named Anchor**, that means click the **Insert** menu, slide down to **Invisible Tags**, and go over to the submenu to click **Named Anchor**.

F highlighted command

The command that your cursor presently hovers over is the highlighted command, which appears on screen in inverse video (light text on a dark background).

G keyboard shortcut

Most Dreamweaver commands also have keyboard shortcuts, a combination of keys that you can press instead of mousing over to a menu command. For example, the **Insert➡Image** command has the shortcut **ctrl+alt+I** (Win) or **command-option-I** (Mac). Under Windows, press and hold the **ctrl** and **alt** keys and simultaneously press **I**; on the Mac, press and hold **command** (the cloverleaf key) and **option** and simultaneously press **I**.

Macromedia is working hard to free you from having to use menus and commands, but some actions have no graphical counterparts on property inspectors and panels—and besides, some people prefer to use the menus, especially while learning what all the individual graphical hieroglyphics mean! This page and the next one explain how menus and commands work and summarize the main menu categories Dreamweaver uses.

A menu name

Each menu has a name, which appears on the menu bar and identifies the menu's contents. For example, you can correctly infer that the **File** menu is where you'll open and save files. However, menu identification can be a little arbitrary. For example, if you want to modify some text, you use the **Text** menu (N), not the **Modify** menu (M).

B menu

When you click a menu name, you see a menu, a list of choices that drops down from the menu name.

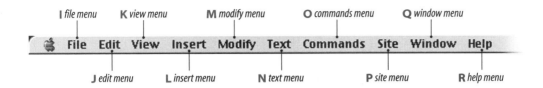

I file menu   K view menu   M modify menu   O commands menu   Q window menu

J edit menu   L insert menu   N text menu   P site menu   R help menu

H alt-key equivalent (Win)

Windows offers another way to activate menus: Press the **alt** key along with the underlined letter in the menu name. Then press the underlined key associated with the specific command you want. Or, you can use the keyboard's arrow keys to move down to the command you want and press **enter**. To navigate to a submenu, use the right- and left-arrow keys.

> **tip** Windows 2000, unlike previous versions of Windows, doesn't show underlined menu letters unless you activate the feature. Do so by opening the **Display** control panel, clicking the **Effects** tab, and clearing the check box labeled **Hide keyboard navigation indicators until I use the alt key**.

I file menu (alt+F, Win)

This menu contains commands for opening, saving, and printing files; performing import, export, and convert operations; checking links; and previewing the current file. It also lists recently opened documents.

J edit menu (alt+E, Wind)

Here's where you undo and redo recent actions; cut, copy, and paste objects; select objects; perform find and replace operations; format HTML code; and set program preferences (as explained in Chapter 16, Personalize Dreamweaver).

K view menu (alt+V, Win)

The **View** menu contains commands to switch between code and design views when tweaking HTML and between standard and layout views when making tables. You can also turn various visual aids, such as rulers and grids, on and off.

L insert menu (alt+I, Win)

Here, you can insert just about anything you may want on a Web page: images, movies, frames, forms, anchors, symbols, and so on.

M modify menu (alt+M, Win)

The **Modify** menu is for changing stuff you've already created, including pages, tables, frames, links, and even animation timelines.

N text menu (alt+T, Win)

This menu lets you add, edit, align, color, resize, and spell-check your text.

O commands menu (alt+C, Win)

Macromedia should've named this one "Miscellany" because that's what it contains: commands to clean up HTML code, optimize graphics, commands you download from the Web, and various other actions that don't fit neatly anywhere else.

P site menu (alt+S, Win)

Here's where you create and modify site files, check files in and out (if you work collaboratively with others), produce site-wide reports, and perform site-wide link checking.

Q window menu (alt+W, Win)

The commands here let you display or hide panels and inspectors, one at a time or en masse.

R help menu (alt+H, Win)

This one's your ticket to Dreamweaver's help system (see Dreamweaver Help on page 22), which is handy if you misplace this book!

Keyboard Shortcuts, Windows

One of the characteristics that distinguishes a professional-quality program from a beginner's program is the availability of *keyboard shortcuts* that can speed up workflow for those who use the program daily (and who don't mind memorizing some key combinations). Mousing around is great for some tasks, but often you can do something faster using the keyboard, and occasionally the keyboard is the *only* way to accomplish a certain task.

This page and the next one offer an introduction to your keyboard and how Dreamweaver generally uses various special keys. For more details on the keyboard shortcuts Dreamweaver provides, see Chapter 18, Essential Shortcuts.

A function keys

Function keys do lots of different things in Dreamweaver. For example, **F1** brings up the **Using Dreamweaver** help system, **F2** opens the **Layers** panel, **F3** performs a **Find Next** command, and so on. **F1** is traditional for help in most programs, but the other function keys don't exhibit any logic. (In fact, some of them—specifically **F6**, **F7**, and **F9**—don't do anything.) You can reprogram function keys with the **Edit➡Keyboard Shortcuts** command (see Chapter 16, Personalize Dreamweaver). Dreamweaver also uses the function keys in combination with other keys; for example, **shift-F7** performs a spell-check.

> *tip* As I write this, both the program manual and the online help system contain errors on the use of the function keys. For example, they state in certain places that **F8** doesn't do anything (it opens and closes the **Site** window). The function key shortcuts listed next to menu commands do seem accurate, however.

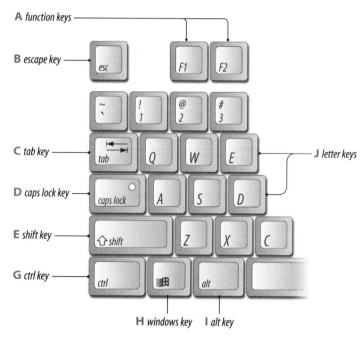

A *function keys*
B *escape key*
C *tab key*
D *caps lock key*
E *shift key*
G *ctrl key*
H *windows key*   I *alt key*
J *letter keys*

B escape key

The **esc** key provides a quick way of closing a dialog box without applying any of the settings in that dialog box. It's the equivalent of clicking the **Cancel** button.

C tab key

You can use **tab** to indent lines of code when you're working in code view. (You can control the number of spaces in a tab via **Edit➡Preferences**.) This key also lets you navigate table cells and cycle through options in a panel or dialog box.

D caps lock key

You can use this key when typing a lot of capital letters, but be mindful of Webiquette (Web etiquette, a subset of "Netiquette"), which states that USING ALL CAPS IS THE EQUIVALENT OF SHOUTING and therefore somewhere between impolite and obnoxious.

E shift key

Aside from its normal function in capitalization, many shortcuts use **shift** as a "modifier" in combination with other keys to create new command shortcuts. For example, **shift-F1** opens the **Reference** panel. (See also G and I for details on the other modifier keys.)

Keyboard Shortcuts, Macintosh

F control key (Mac)

You'd think that the Macintosh **control** key (**ctrl** in Windows) would work just the same as it does on the PC side, but that would be too easy. The truth is that the Mac's **control** key serves only one function in Dreamweaver, but it's a very important one: When combined with a click, it generates the equivalent of a right-click and displays a context menu.

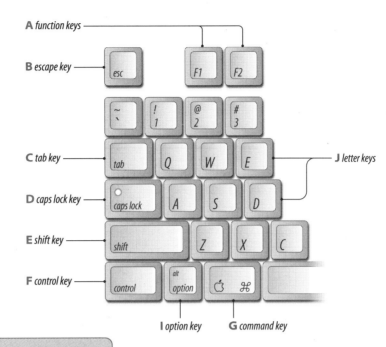

A *function keys*
B *escape key*
C *tab key*
D *caps lock key*
E *shift key*
F *control key*
J *letter keys*
I *option key*
G *command key*

> **tip** PCs with Windows keyboards typically provide a context menu key on the right side of the keyboard. Press the key, and a context menu appears, no mouse required. (Of course, you must have the cursor placed over the object of interest.)

context menu key

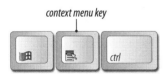

G ctrl key (Win)/command key (Mac)

The **ctrl**, **shift** (E), and **alt** (I) keys are the triumvirate of modifier keys on the PC, with **ctrl** perhaps the most often used. Use **ctrl+B** to make text boldface, **ctrl+F2** to display the objects panel, and so on. The equivalent key on the Macintosh is not **control** but rather **command**, identified by both the Apple logo and the cloverleaf (but, confusingly to newbies, not the word "command").

H windows key (Win)

Tap the **windows** key, and the **Start** menu appears. If you press this key by accident, tap **esc** to make it go away and click the Dreamweaver icon in the taskbar to return to work.

I alt key (Win)/option key (Mac)

The **alt** and **option** keys are modifiers that help define shortcuts. For example, **ctrl+alt+I** (Win) and **command-option-I** (Mac) are shortcuts to the **Insert Image** command. The **alt** key has another important function on the PC: You can use it in combination with an underlined letter in a menu or dialog box to open a menu, choose a field, or click a button.

J letter keys

The letter keys let you enter text on documents and in dialog boxes, of course, but they also let you "jump" up and down in a list of files. For example, in the **Assets** panel or the **Site** window, click at the top of the file list and then press **R** to jump to filenames beginning with the letter **R**. In combination with modifier keys, the letter keys offer a world of shortcuts, such as **ctrl+Z** (Win) or **command-Z** (Mac), the lifesaving **Undo** command.

Dialog Boxes

A *pop-up menu* B *field* C *radio button* D *check box* E *button*

F *scroll bar*

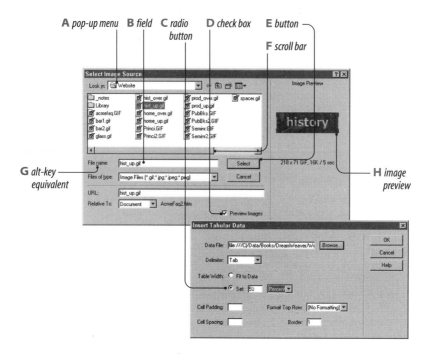

G *alt-key equivalent*

H *image preview*

C radio button

Like the mechanical buttons on old car radios, dialog box *radio buttons* let you choose one, and only one, option from two or more possibilities.

D check box

Check boxes are yes-or-no questions. Checking a box means yes; clearing it means no. When multiple check boxes appear together, you can choose as many or as few as you like, unlike radio buttons.

Despite the name, *dialog boxes* typically exist to get information from you rather than provide information to you. If you haven't worked with Windows or Macintosh programs before, you should get familiar with some of the typical elements you will see in Dreamweaver dialog boxes. Dialog box styles vary somewhat between Macintosh and PC platforms—one reason why I include examples of both in every chapter.

A pop-up menu

If you see an arrow (Win) or a double arrow (Mac) to the right of an item, click it to display a *pop-up menu* of further options.

B field

Fields let you enter numbers or text. The **tab** key moves you forward from one field to the next, while **shift-tab** moves backwards. Fields are sometimes called *option boxes*.

> *tip* On the PC, the **tab** key can actually cycle you through all the elements of a dialog box.

E button

Typically, a *button* is simply what you click to accept or cancel the information you provide in a dialog box. However, some special-purpose buttons are common in Dreamweaver, such as the **+** and **−** buttons that add or remove items from a list.

F scroll bar

Sometimes you have to scroll left, right, up, or down to see the full contents of a data area (such as a list).

G alt-key equivalent (Win)

Under Windows, you can activate some options by holding down the **alt** key while pressing the underlined character in the option's name. If an option doesn't have an underlined letter, there is no **alt**-key equivalent.

H image preview

Previews are handy when you're hunting for images, looking at fonts, and so on. You usually have to activate them with a check box (D).

Property Inspectors

A *move bar*

B *help icon*

C *quick tag editor icon*

D *object name*

E *expander arrow*

Menus don't always tell you what actions make sense for a particular kind of selected object. For example, you could select an image and then go to the menu system and apply a font type to that image with the **Text▸Font** command. Chances are that you don't really want to do that, and you're less likely to make such a mistake if you use a *property inspector*—a window that simultaneously shows you the properties of a selected object and lets you modify those properties. In my example, the **Image** property inspector doesn't have an icon for applying a font.

So property inspectors—which you display by choosing **Window▸Properties** or by pressing **ctrl+F3** (**command-F3** on the Macintosh)— help you work with fewer dead-ends and false moves. Also, like the objects panel (see The Objects Panel on page 10), property inspectors let you accomplish common tasks with a single click; most of the time, changes you make with a property inspector take effect immediately and show up in the document window. Future chapters explore individual property inspectors in detail, but this page shows you some of their common features.

A move bar

Relocate a property inspector by dragging its move bar. Unfortunately, you can't combine, or dock, property inspectors like you dock panels (see next page).

> **tip** If you have a dual-monitor setup, you may find it convenient to move the property inspector, objects panel, and any other relevant panels onto one monitor, leaving the other monitor to display the document window.

B help icon

Get context-sensitive help for the property inspector by clicking this question-mark icon.

C quick tag editor icon

Click this icon, if present, to open the **quick tag editor**—a mini-window that lets you modify the snippet of HTML code associated with the selected object. The quick tag editor is often a faster way to make a code change than switching the document window to code view. See The Quick Tag Editor on page 32 of Chapter 2 for details.

D object name

It's always good practice to name every object you create on a Web page; the inspector shows you the name, typically on the upper-left portion of the window. You must name an object if you intend to reference it later in a script or manipulate it with a JavaScript behavior.

E expander arrow

Some inspectors contain a subsidiary panel of additional information that you may not always need. Display (and hide) such subsidiary panels by clicking the *expander arrow* in the lower-right corner.

Macromedia designed property inspectors this way to reduce screen clutter, which is fine as long as you remember the expander arrow when you're hunting for a setting that doesn't seem to exist. And don't be alarmed when you encounter some property inspectors with expander arrows that display a blank, gray space: Not all inspectors have additional options.

> **tip** Dreamweaver remembers the expander arrow setting from one computing session to the next.

Panels

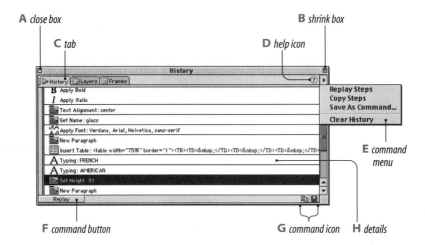

A *close box*

C *tab*

B *shrink box*

D *help icon*

E *command menu*

F *command button*

G *command icon* **H** *details*

panel to move it from one set of panels to another. (The notable exception is the objects panel.) Drag and drop a tab onto any nonpanel area to break it out on its own and create a new panel containing only that tab.

D help icon

Click the question mark icon to open the help system to a page most relevant for that panel or tab. (This is called *context-sensitive* help.)

Panels (called *palettes* in previous versions of Dreamweaver) are little special-purpose windows that, unlike dialog boxes, can stay on the screen while you work and that, unlike property inspectors, don't have a tight association with a particular type of object. Open panels from the **Window** menu, or with their keyboard shortcuts (**F11** for the **Assets** panel, **shift+F10** for the **History** panel, and so on).

> (tip) Press **F4** to hide all open panels. Press **F4** again to bring them back.

A close box

Click the close box to close the panel. The close box is at the upper right on a PC, upper left on a Mac.

B shrink box (Mac)

Click the shrink box (a.k.a. *collapse* box) on a Macintosh to reduce the panel to its smallest size; click it again to restore the panel to normal size. This box is not available on PCs.

C tab

A panel may contain one or more tabs; click a tab to make it active. Drag and drop a tab onto another

E command menu

The arrow at the upper right opens a menu of commands that make sense within the context of a specific panel. These commands typically duplicate the functions of command buttons (F) and icons (G).

F command button

A command button is just a text- or image-labeled button at the bottom left of a panel that performs some relevant action.

G command icon

A command icon is a graphic at the bottom right of a panel that performs some relevant action. If there is any rhyme or reason to how Macromedia decided to make certain commands buttons and others icons, I haven't figured it out.

H details

The details window of the panel is where you see data specific to the open document or site. For example, the details window of the **History** panel lists recent actions, which you can undo by moving the slider upwards in the list. Different panels organize their details window very differently.

The Main Toolbar

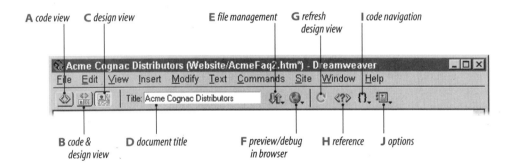

A *code view*   C *design view*   E *file management*   G *refresh design view*   I *code navigation*

B *code & design view*   D *document title*   F *preview/debug in browser*   H *reference*   J *options*

The *toolbar* appears just below the menu bar in the document window or the **Site** window. I discuss the **Site** window toolbar in Chapter 10, Manage Your Site, so this section focuses solely on the document window toolbar.

The idea of the toolbar is to collect in one place commands that affect the view of the document, plus various other commands (such as **Preview In Browser**) that pertain to the document as a whole. (Commands that pertain to individual objects, as opposed to the document itself, typically reside on the objects panel or on the various property inspectors.) Display or hide the toolbar by choosing **View→Toolbar** or by pressing **ctrl+shift+T** (**command-shift-T** on the Macintosh).

A code view
This button instructs Dreamweaver to show you only the underlying HTML code that defines the Web page in the foreground document window. Dreamweaver lets you tweak the code to your heart's content, preserving any manual edits that you perform.

B code & design view
Click this button to display a split-screen, with HTML code in one half and the page's design in the other half. For more details on code and design views, see Create, Design, & Split Views on pages 26 and 27 in Chapter 2.

C design view
This button changes the display so that only the design of the page, and no underlying HTML code,

appears. For many Dreamweaver users, the design view is the only view you'll ever use; in other words, you may never need to manually modify HTML code, which may be good news to you.

D document title
This field shows you the page's title, if you have defined one. You can also change the title by clicking in this field and modifying the text.

E file management
This button activates a pop-up menu containing commands appropriate for a multi-user environment: **Get**, **Check Out**, **Put**, **Check In**, and so on. It also lets you open the **Design Notes** dialog box, for posting messages that others can see. For more on these features, see Chapter 10, Manage Your Site.

F preview/debug in browser
This button opens a menu letting you preview or debug your page in the browser that you choose. The reason is that although Dreamweaver's design view is reasonably accurate, it does not provide a perfect representation of how the page will look in any particular browser or browser version. The **Edit Browser List** command lets you change the list of browsers that appears in this menu.

G refresh design view
Use this command if you paste HTML code from an external source into your Web page and then want to see its content reflected in your document's design view.

H reference

This icon opens the **Reference** panel, a collection of three online guides from O'Reilly and Associates (see Reference Guides on page 11 for details).

I code navigation

Another pop-up menu appears when you click the **Code Navigation** icon. Use this menu for setting or removing breakpoints in your custom code. (If you're not a Web programmer, you may never need this feature.)

J options

What you see in this pop-up menu depends on whether you're in design view or code view. In design view, you can control the display of various visual aids—ruler, grid, borders, and so on. In code view, you can control the display of line numbers, invalid syntax highlighting, whether automatic indenting is on or off, and so on. The choices on the options menu are duplicated on the menu bar's **View** menu (choose the command **View➤Visual Aids** and **View➤ Code Options**).

The Launcher

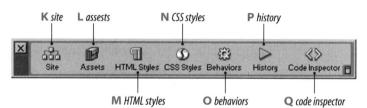

K site   L assets   N CSS styles   P history

M HTML styles   O behaviors   Q code inspector

The *launcher* is sort of a secondary toolbar (display it by choosing the command **Window ➤ Launcher**) that lets you "launch" key Dreamweaver windows. You can modify the list with the command **Edit ➤ Preferences ➤ Panels**, but the default icons include the following:

K site

The **Site** window is where you manage files for the entire site. (See The Site Window on pages 154-157 in Chapter 10.)

L assets

The **Assets** panel lists and organizes reusable content (images, templates, and so on) that you can share among pages across your entire site. (You can read The Assets Panel on pages 164 and 165 of Chapter 10 for details.)

M HTML styles

This panel lets you view any HTML styles you've created for common combinations of attributes. (See The HTML Styles Panel on page 49 in Chapter 3.)

N CSS styles

The **CSS Styles** panel helps you manage advanced formatting specifications for Version 4 and higher browsers. (See The CSS Styles Panel on pages 220 and 221 of Chapter 14.)

O behaviors

This panel lets you assign JavaScript behaviors to objects on your Web pages. (See The Behaviors Panel on pages 192 through 194 of Chapter 12.)

P history

You can see a list of your recent actions—and undo one or more of them—with this panel. Be careful: If you undo some actions and then perform a new action in the document window, you can't redo the undone actions.

Q code inspector

The **Code Inspector** is a separate window that lets you edit HTML code directly. (See The Code Inspector on page 27 in Chapter 2.)

> **tip** You can change the launcher's orientation from horizontal to vertical by clicking the little orientation icon in the lower-right corner.

After you've memorized the icons used in the launcher, close it to reduce clutter and use the *mini-launcher* on the status bar instead (see next page).

The Status Bar

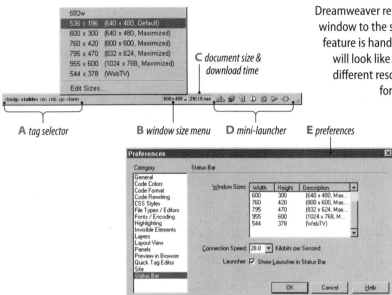

C *document size & download time*

A *tag selector*   **B** *window size menu*   **D** *mini-launcher*   **E** *preferences*

The *status bar* at the bottom of the active document window provides at-a-glance details about the currently loaded document and the HTML code at the cursor's current location. Dreamweaver uses this bit of screen real estate very effectively, but the status bar is easy to overlook—so I want to call special attention to it here.

A tag selector

Here's a cool feature that shows you the HTML code tags that affect the object at the cursor's current location. By clicking different tags in the tag selector, you can select different parts of the object; for example, clicking **<tr>** or **<td>** selects a table cell, while clicking **<table>** selects the whole table. If you right-click a tag and choose **Edit Tag**, you pull up the quick tag editor, which lets you edit a snippet of HTML code. You can remove a tag by right-clicking it and choosing **Remove Tag**. I don't know of a faster way to learn HTML tags than by tinkering with the tag selector as you build your Web pages.

B window size menu

Click this area to display a pop-up menu listing various predefined window sizes; click one, and

Dreamweaver resizes the current document window to the specified dimensions. This feature is handy for seeing what your page will look like on different systems, and at different resolutions, but it's no substitute for previewing the page in a browser window.

C document size & download time

A good Web site designer is ever mindful of performance, so this informational window subtly reminds you of your current document's size in kilobytes and estimated download time at the connection speed specified in the **Preferences** dialog box (E).

D mini-launcher

Like the launcher, but smaller, the mini-launcher bar has just possibly made the full-size launcher window redundant, at least once you've become accustomed to the meaning of the icons, which appear in the mini-launcher without explanatory text. What you see in the mini-launcher are the same icons that you see in the full launcher window.

E preferences

You can modify the look and functionality of the status bar with the **Edit➥Preferences➥Status Bar** command. Specify custom document **Window Sizes** here, and they'll appear on the window size menu (B). Change the **Connection Speed** value to make Dreamweaver refigure its estimated download time for the document (C). Clear the **Show Launcher In Status Bar** check box if you find the mini-launcher more distracting than useful. And, just as with the big launcher, choose **Edit➥Preferences➥Panels** to change which icons appear in the mini-launcher.

Dreamweaver Help

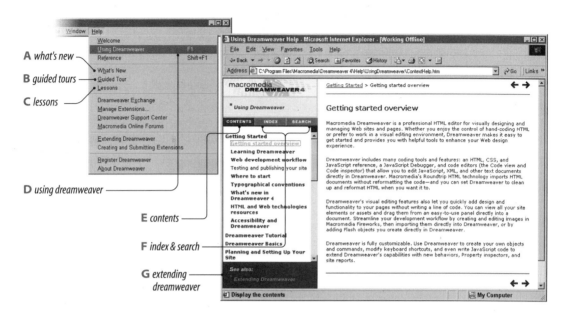

A *what's new*

B *guided tours*

C *lessons*

D *using dreamweaver*

E *contents*

F *index & search*

G *extending dreamweaver*

Dreamweaver's built-in help system is a great adjunct to this book, and much more thorough than help systems in many other applications. Nearly the entire printed user manual is online via the help system. The help system requires a Version 4 browser, with Java enabled, to work properly.

A what's new

This command presents a summary of features new to Dreamweaver 4. If you're already familiar with Version 3, go through this section carefully.

B guided tours

The **Help➞Guided Tour** command provides six mini-lessons on big-picture issues: getting started, planning your site, designing Web pages, adding content, adding interaction, and publishing your site.

C lessons

Help➞Lessons is more detailed than the guided tours and covers procedures like creating an image map and building a page with frames. These lessons are worth doing at least once.

D using Dreamweaver

Choose **Help➞Using Dreamweaver** or press **F1** to bring up the main help file in a browser window. You must have JavaScript enabled in your browser.

E contents

The **Contents** button presents a hierarchical topic list in the left window and explanatory text and graphics to the right. Click a topic in the left window to display its contents and subtopics (if any).

F index & search

These buttons help you find help based on one or more keywords. Watch out: The **Case Sensitive** check box in the **Search** dialog box forces an exact match based on capitalization, which you'll rarely want!

G extending Dreamweaver

Help➞Extending Dreamweaver offers help for advanced users who want to extend Dreamweaver by writing programs. The window works just like the **Using Dreamweaver** window. In fact, you can flip back and forth between the two by using the **See Also** section in the lower left.

chapter 2

Build & Edit HTML

HTML (HyperText Markup Language) is the language of the Web. Browsers read and interpret the HTML code that defines a Web page in order to know how that page should look and act.

One of the things I like best about Dreamweaver is that it lets you deal with HTML as much, or as little, as you prefer. If you're a casual Web designer, you may rarely need to "tweak the code," and you can let Dreamweaver insulate you from HTML's complexities. If you're a pro who knows HTML already, Dreamweaver gives you full and convenient access to it. And if you're a student, I know of no better way to learn HTML than to see how Dreamweaver creates it.

Whichever category describes you, you'll need to edit the underlying HTML at least occasionally. This chapter teaches you what you must know to do so with the tools Dreamweaver provides.

steps Create A Link

This section looks at how you can build the most fundamental HTML object, the *link* (short for *hyperlink*). The "H" in HTML stands for hypertext, and what makes hypertext hyper (and the Web like a web) is the link. Links are also a great way to begin a discussion of HTML *tags*, the special codes in angle brackets that let HTML transcend text.

In this example, I assume that you have created (and opened) a medium-long text document with two sections, and you want to do the user a favor by letting her "jump" down to the second section from the top of the document without scrolling through the first section. The procedure requires two steps: creating a named anchor and creating a link.

1 place insertion point

Scroll down to the beginning of your document's second section and click once where you want to let the user "jump" to. In Dreamweaver, before you insert an HTML object, you generally place the insertion point and then select the object.

2 open objects panel

The command is **Window➡Objects**. The objects panel contains buttons that let you insert many different HTML objects onto your page. When you insert an HTML object, Dreamweaver automatically builds the HTML code for you behind the scenes.

3 choose invisibles

Click the pop-up menu at the top of the objects panel and choose **Invisibles**. The object you want to insert at this point is a sort of bookmark called a *named anchor*. The user can't see it, but it marks a destination where a link can transport the user.

4 click named anchor icon

The upper left icon in the **Invisibles** objects panel looks like an anchor, and when you hover the cursor over it, you see the legend **Insert Named Anchor**, confirming your suspicion. Click it, and the **Insert Named Anchor** dialog box appears. (If you prefer working with menus to working with panels, the command **Insert➡Invisible Tags➡Named Anchor** replaces steps 2, 3, and 4.)

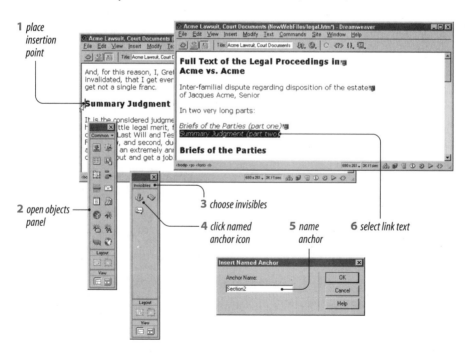

1 *place insertion point*

2 *open objects panel*

3 *choose invisibles*

4 *click named anchor icon*

5 *name anchor*

6 *select link text*

5 name anchor

Enter a unique anchor name with no spaces and click **OK**. (The example uses **Section2**.)

> **tip** You can link to other things besides named anchors. You can link to other documents, to named anchors in other documents, and to files, images, movies, sounds, and just about anything. Also, links don't have to be text; Chapter 4 shows you how to make images into links. Finally, this example just shows you one way to create a link, by typing it; you can create links in other ways, too—for example, by clicking the folder icon in the property inspector to select a file in a dialog box. You'll see that Dreamweaver typically gives you two or three different ways to do the same thing; that makes the program harder to learn, but, over time, easier to use.

6 select link text

Now, scroll to the top of the document and select the text you want to appear with an underline, so that when the user clicks it, the display rockets to the named anchor location. Select the text with a click-and-drag operation; if it's a single word, double-click it.

7 open property inspector

Open the **Text** property inspector by choosing **Window→Properties**.

8 type link target

In the **Link** field of the **Text** property inspector, type the name you chose (5) with a leading pound sign (#), like this: **#Section2**. (You should keep the capitalization just as you entered it in step 5, even though some browsers forgive capitalization discrepancies.) The pound sign tells Dreamweaver that what follows is a named anchor in the current document. (Stuff like that you just have to memorize.) When you're done typing, press **enter** (Win) or **return** (Mac) or just click anywhere else in the document window. Behold, Dreamweaver underlines your new link. It's built an HTML object for you.

9 open context menu

Now, to see the HTML that Dreamweaver just created, just right-click (Win) or **control**-click (Mac) the text you just made into a link, and you see the object's context menu. The context menu works on many kinds of HTML objects and shows you what you can do with that particular object.

10 choose edit tag

Choose the **Edit Tag <a>** command from the context menu. You'll see the HTML code that Dreamweaver built just above the link; it should look something like **<a href="#Section2">**. This HTML *tag*, or code, specifies that the text that follows should link to the named anchor **Section2** in the current document. You didn't have to know the **<a href>** tag ahead of time; you just needed to know to type a value into the **Link** field of the **Text** property inspector.

> **tip** You may be thinking "Huh, **<a href>** isn't that hard to memorize." Let me assure you that HTML tags can get fairly complex, especially when you start working with fancy stuff like frames and layers. Believe me: Using the property inspectors and panels is a lot easier than coding the HTML by hand.

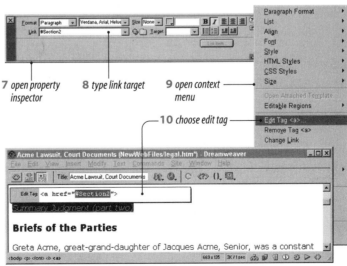

7 open property inspector

8 type link target

9 open context menu

10 choose edit tag

Code, Design, & Split Views

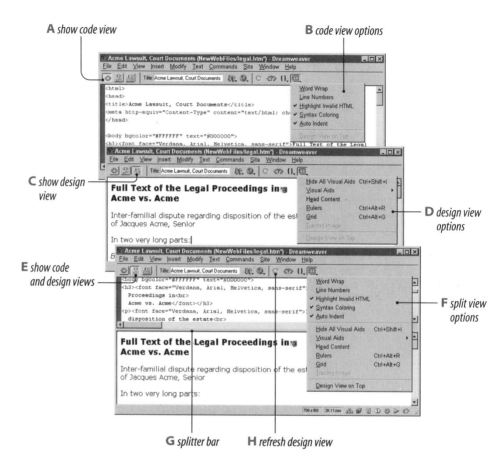

A *show code view*

B *code view options*

C *show design view*

D *design view options*

E *show code and design views*

F *split view options*

G *splitter bar* **H** *refresh design view*

One of the coolest aspects of the Dreamweaver workspace is the one-click access to code view, design view, and split view (the last is my term, not Macromedia's; it calls split view "Code and Design View"). The toolbar icons let you jump immediately from page layout to HTML code; you can even use the split view to divide your screen into two parts, one showing the design and the other the corresponding code.

> *tip* You need at least a 17-inch monitor to really work effectively with split view.

A show code view

Click the **Show Code View** toolbar icon to change the document window so that it shows only the HTML code underlying the current page.

To see the **Show Code View** toolbar icon, as well as the **Show Design View** and **Show Code & Design Views** icons, you must have the Dreamweaver toolbar showing; if it's absent, choose **View⟶Toolbar**, or **ctrl+shift+T** in Windows or **command-shift-T** on the Mac, to bring it to life.

> *tip* When you jump to code view from design view after having selected an object in design view, Dreamweaver selects the same object in code view. The reverse is also true. Nice touch!

B code view options

Click the **View Options** icon in Code View to see options that pertain specifically to that view. (The Code View Options section on page 28 goes into detail on what these options actually do.)

C show design view

Click **Show Design View** to go back to the document layout window that approximates how your page will look in a user's browser.

D design view options

Click **View Options** in design view to see a different set of options, including visual aids and ruler and grid settings. I discuss these settings further in The Document Window on pages 8 and 9 of Chapter 1.

E show code and design views

The **Show Code And Design Views** icon splits your screen, with code at the top and layout at the bottom. I call the resulting view "split view."

F split view options

Click **View Options** in split view to see both the design view options and the code view options, separated by a horizontal rule.

> *tip* If you want to reverse the default positioning of the code and layout panes in split view, choose **View⟶Design View On Top** from the main menu, or **Design View On Top** from the **View Options** menu. This command only appears when you're actually using the split view.

G splitter bar

If you don't like what you see, you can click-and-drag the splitter bar to change the relative size of the code and design view window panes.

H refresh design view

When you make a change in the code view part of a split screen, or in pure code view, your change may not appear immediately when you switch to design view. You can force the design view to refresh (that is, update) itself by simply clicking anywhere in the document after you switch to design view. Another option is to click the **Refresh** icon on the toolbar (the shortcut is **F5**).

If you have the property inspector turned on via **Window⟶Properties**, Dreamweaver displays a handy window as soon as it detects that you've made a manual code change; you can click **Refresh** there, too, as shown.

The Code Inspector

Okay, now you know what code view is, but as you peruse the Dreamweaver manual or online help, you see many references to the **Code Inspector**. What the heck is *that*?

Macromedia wins the Confusing Terminology Award with this one. As it turns out, the **Code Inspector** is nothing more than the code view, but in a separate window! The command to fire up the **Code Inspector** is **Window⟶Code Inspector**, or just press the mercifully short shortcut **F10**. Alternatively, you can click the **Code Inspector** icon on the launcher bar or the mini-launcher at the lower right of the document window. You can also bounce back and forth between the document window

and the **Code Inspector** window with **ctrl+tab** (Win) or **option-tab** (Mac).

Why would you ever use the **Code Inspector** if you have code view and split view only a toolbar click away? One reason would be if you have multiple monitors. When I'm working on a design project, I like to have the **Code Inspector** (and most of the panels) on one monitor, and the current document in design view on the other monitor. (You can't easily use split view in this situation.) Note that multiple monitor support is built right in to Windows 98, Windows Me, Windows 2000, Windows XP, and the Mac; all you need is an extra graphics card and monitor. Highly recommended!

Code View Options

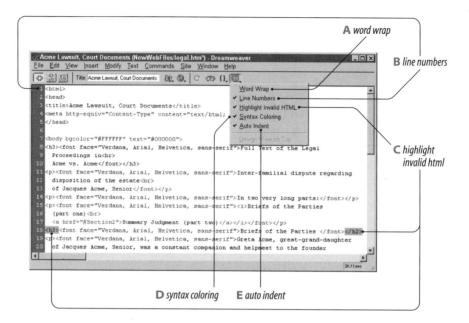

A *word wrap*

B *line numbers*

C *highlight invalid html*

D *syntax coloring*   E *auto indent*

You can customize certain aspects of Dreamweaver's code view by using the **View Options** button on the toolbar (or by choosing the menu command **View→Code View Options**, which opens an identical submenu of choices). Note that code view options only appear when you're actually in code view (or the **Code Inspector**). You should also note also that each option is a toggle; that is, if the option has a check mark next to it, it's on, and you can clear the check mark (turning the option off) by choosing the item from the menu. Conversely, choosing an unchecked item checks it and turns it on.

A word wrap

The **Word Wrap** option wraps long lines within the code view or **Code Inspector** window, deactivating the horizontal scroll bar. This option doesn't change the HTML code at all; it's purely for your viewing convenience. I find that using this option can be a little confusing if you have complex HTML code with several levels of indentation; a better option may be to get a bigger monitor or switch to a higher resolution.

B line numbers

When on, the **Line Numbers** option places a vertical bar along the window's left edge showing line numbers in a light-on-dark pattern. I normally leave this option off for everyday use. This can be very handy when previewing your page results in an error on a particular line. By turning on **Line Numbers**, you can easily move to a specific line to examine what might be causing the error.

C highlight invalid html

The **Highlight Invalid HTML** option is for code view and **Code Inspector** windows only. (Invalid HTML always appears highlighted in design view.) This option makes HTML code that Dreamweaver either doesn't understand or doesn't support appear in yellow highlight. You might have invalid HTML on a Web page, for example, if you hand-coded a tag incorrectly, if you opened a page that someone else created and hand-coded incorrectly, or if you opened a page created in a different program that uses special nonstandard tags or tag attributes. I suggest you leave this option turned on at all times.

Keep in mind that Dreamweaver doesn't automatically delete HTML code that it thinks is invalid; after all, you never know— the code may have some validity in another program, such as an external code editor. Dreamweaver's ability to work with HTML code without disturbing tags it doesn't understand is a key part of what Macromedia calls *roundtrip HTML*.

D syntax coloring

Dreamweaver color-codes HTML tags and scripts to make reading and editing code easier and faster; **Syntax Coloring** is on by default. You can change the colors Dreamweaver uses by choosing the **Edit➡Preferences** command, as discussed in Chapter 16 on page 256 in the section Preferences, Code Colors.

E auto indent

You can make your code indent automatically with the **Auto Indent** option. This feature is a major timesaver! Again, you can control the extent of your indent, as well as which tags activate auto indenting, by choosing **Edit➡Preferences**; choose the **Code Format** category.

Major HTML Tags

You may be the type of designer who wants to know as few of the underlying details as possible, but even so, you should know at least a few major HTML tags by sight. Here are some to get you started; if you want to go further, you can't do much better than the built-in HTML reference panel (**Window➡Reference**, or **ctrl+shift+F1** on Windows, **command-shift-F1** on the Mac; choose **O'Reilly HTML Reference** from the **Book:** pop-up menu).

<a>
The **<a>** tag stands for anchor. Depending on what follows it, this could be a text link (such as **<a href=#Section2>**) or a named anchor (such as **<a name="Section2">**).

<p>
The paragraph tag pair tells the browser to stop wrapping text at the end of the paragraph and put some extra white space onto the page right after it. I say "tag pair" because the text paragraph is enclosed by two tags: **<p>** at the start of the paragraph, and **</p>** at its end. The latter is called the *closing tag*; not all tags have a corresponding closing tag, but many do.

**
**
This tag inserts a line break, for those occasions when you want to force a line to stop but you don't want all the intervening white space that the **<p>** tag would introduce. No closing tag is needed here; a line break is just a point object.

<i> and <b>
The **<i></i>** tag pair denotes italics for the enclosed text, and the **<b></b>** pair denotes boldface. These are text formatting tags.

<h1> through <h6>
The heading tags use a combination of font size and bold to make a line of text into a heading with white space following. These require a corresponding closing tag.

<img>
The Web can thank the **<img>** tag for its many pictures. The typical form of this tag is **<img src="filename">**, and it can have modifying *attributes*, too, such as in this example: **<img src="filename" align="left">**. The **align** portion is the attribute. Many HTML tags have attributes that specify details about the tag's appearance, function, or both.

<head> and <body>
These tag pairs denote the start and end of a document's head content and body content, respectively. These tags are the two main structural divisions of an HTML page. You can find out all the details in the section, Viewing & Adding Head Content on page 35.

<!— comment —>
Browsers don't process comments; you can insert them (via the **Invisibles** objects panel) to remind yourself why you coded a page a certain way. Dreamweaver uses certain specially formatted comments to perform automatic updating of pages that use common elements, such as library items.

Edit Menu Commands

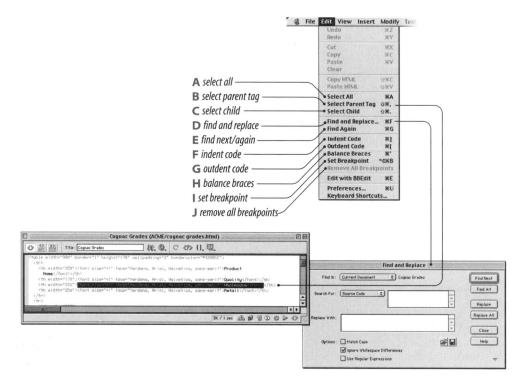

A *select all*
B *select parent tag*
C *select child*
D *find and replace*
E *find next/again*
F *indent code*
G *outdent code*
H *balance braces*
I *set breakpoint*
J *remove all breakpoints*

The **Edit** menu offers several commands beyond the basic cut, copy, and paste directives that may be useful to you in both design view and code view. When you're in code view, the **Edit** menu grows several new options that can help further as you manually fine-tune your HTML code.

I discuss the **Copy HTML** and **Paste HTML** design view commands in Chapter 15, Work With Other Programs.

Keep in mind that many of the **Edit** menu commands appear on an object's context menu when you right-click (Win) or **control**-click (Mac) the object. As you work with Dreamweaver, you'll probably discover that the context menu is quicker than the **Edit** menu, although context menus aren't quite as convenient on the Mac because you must go to the keyboard to open them.

A select all

This command (shortcut: **ctrl+A** in Windows, **command-A** on the Mac) selects all the objects in the body of the current document. You would use this command, for example, if you wanted to copy an entire HTML page to another program (follow **Select All** by **Edit→Copy**) or if you became so disgusted with a page you'd designed that you wanted to start all over again (follow **Select All** by **delete**).

> *tip* Careful: The **Select All** command doesn't really select all the HTML that defines a page. Everything that you set via the **Modify→Page Properties** command, including head content, background color, and document title, remains in place after you choose **Select All** and then **delete**. Edit the HTML code directly, or make changes in the **Page Properties** dialog box, to delete those items.

B select parent tag

One of the bugbears of hand-coding HTML is mis-matched tags. Many HTML tags require a corresponding closing tag with a slash in it, such as **</p>** to close a paragraph. Dreamweaver is pretty good about inserting closing tags for you if you forget, but even so, it's only a matter of time before you bump into an unbalanced tag situation.

The **Select Parent Tag** command is handy in these situations; it highlights the first tag pair around the current insertion point. If a tag pair is missing, this command selects a lot more code than you expect.

> *tip* Choose **Select Parent Tag** repeatedly to keep moving outward in the tag nesting hierarchy and selecting more and more code, each time within a matching tag pair.

C select child

This command, which incidentally is supposed to work in code view but which I can only get to work in design view, is the converse of the **Select Parent Tag** command (B). In other words, this command selects the next tag pair inside the current selection. You can execute this command repeatedly until you run out of children.

D find and replace

This command is very handy for locating specific text and (optionally) for changing all occurrences of a specific text snippet or HTML tag to something different. I discuss this command in detail in the Find & Replace section on page 50 in Chapter 3. The keyboard shortcut is **ctrl+F** (Win) or **command-F** (Mac).

E find next/again

Finds the next occurrence of a search target you've specified with a **Find And Replace** command (D). The shortcut is **F3** (Win) or **command-G** (Mac).

F indent code

Select one or more lines in code view before executing the **Indent Code** command or **ctrl+]** in Windows and **command-]** on the Mac. The indent

distance is a user-changeable setting via **Edit➡ Preferences**.

> *tip* Dreamweaver's auto indent feature is on by default, but you can disable it via the **View Options** icon on the toolbar.

G outdent code

The opposite of indent is outdent, so if you want to undo some indenting in code view only, this command is the one you'll want to use. The keyboard shortcuts are simply **ctrl+[** in Windows and **command-[** on the Mac.

H balance braces

The **Balance Braces** command (shortcuts: **ctrl+'** in Windows, **command-'** on the Mac) in code view works a lot like the **Select Parent Tag** command (B) in that it helps you find unbalanced punctuation. The difference is that **Balance Braces** is for scripts, whereas **Select Parent Tag** is for straight HTML. As with **Select Parent Tag**, if you run **Balance Braces** repeatedly, Dreamweaver highlights script code within the next outlying brace pair.

I set breakpoint

A *breakpoint* is a place in a script (JavaScript or VBScript) where you want Dreamweaver to pause during debugging. By using a breakpoint, you're able to see what's happened up to that point.

It doesn't make sense to place a breakpoint in plain HTML, although Dreamweaver lets you do so, so don't use this code view command unless your page includes one or more scripts. The keyboard shortcuts are **ctrl+alt+B** (Win) and **command-option-B** (Mac), which, incidentally, are the same shortcuts you'd use to remove a breakpoint if the current insertion point is on a previously defined breakpoint.

J remove all breakpoints

This code view command, which unfortunately has no keyboard shortcuts, removes all breakpoints you may have set for your convenience in debugging any embedded scripts.

The Quick Tag Editor

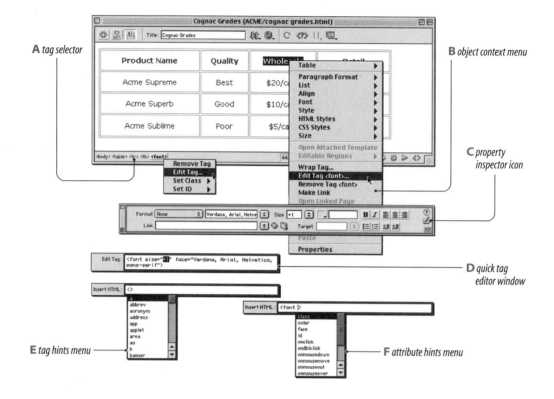

A *tag selector*

B *object context menu*

C *property inspector icon*

D *quick tag editor window*

E *tag hints menu*

F *attribute hints menu*

Use the quick tag editor to perform a tiny bit of HTML surgery. It just pops up a little editing window where you can view or modify the code for a single HTML tag.

A tag selector

The tag selector at the bottom left of the document window displays the tags that apply to the currently selected object or the object surrounding the current insertion point. To activate, right-click (Win) or **control**-click (Mac) a tag here and choose **Edit Tag** from the context menu. Or click the tag and then press **ctrl+T** (Win) or **command-T** (Mac).

B object context menu

Another way to fire up the quick tag editor is to right-click (Win) or **control**-click (Mac) an object in the document window and then choose **Edit Tag** from the context menu. You can't pick the tag, but Dreamweaver usually guesses correctly. Or choose

Insert HTML from the context menu to add HTML at the insertion point, activating "insert mode."

C property inspector icon

Click an object in the document window and click the quick tag editor icon in the object's property inspector.

D quick tag editor window

Just type code into the white area.

E tag hints menu

Press a left angle bracket (<) and hover your mouse over it to see a list of known HTML tags. Choose one by double-clicking it; dispel the menu with **esc**.

F attribute hints menu

Type a space after a tag and hover the cursor over it to see an attribute list that's specific for the tag. Choose one by double-clicking it. The quick tag editor even fills in proper syntax.

 **Modify A Single Tag**

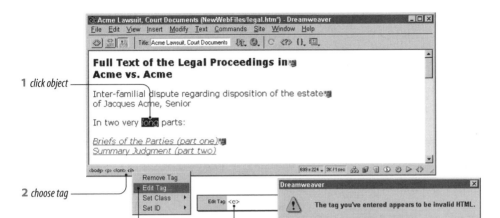

1 *click object*

2 *choose tag*

3 *choose edit tag* 4 *make change*

5 *say you're sorry*

6 *make change correctly*

The example on this page walks you through making a change to a single HTML tag using the quick tag editor. Specifically, you'll change an italics tag (**<i>**) to a bold tag (**<b>**). I purposely include an error in this example to show you what happens if you goof up.

1 click object

Click the object in the document window that you want to change—in this case, an italicized word.

2 choose tag

Hop down to the tag selector at the bottom left of the document window and right-click (Win) or **control**-click (Mac) the tag you want to modify; Dreamweaver displays the tag context menu. The reason I dig the tag selector is that you can choose exactly which tag you want to view or edit. The tags appear in order, with the leftmost tag being the outermost one that applies to the clicked object, and the rightmost tag being the innermost one (closest to the object).

3 choose edit tag

Select **Edit Tag** from the context menu to bring up the quick tag editor window.

4 make change

Now replace the **<i>** tag with a **<b>** tag, but make a mistake on purpose and type **<c>** instead of **<b>**. Press **enter** (Win) or **return** (Mac) to close the quick tag editor window.

5 say you're sorry

If you enter some HTML that Dreamweaver doesn't recognize, such as the fake **<c>** tag, you see a diplomatic error message. Click **OK** to close the dialog box; Dreamweaver discards your changes, and you're primed to try again.

6 make change correctly

Enter the HTML correctly this time, perhaps with the help of the **Reference** panel (click the **Reference** icon on the toolbar), and you won't see the error message. When you press **enter** (Win) or **return** (Mac), Dreamweaver updates the design view to reflect your change. Remember to save your document.

The Modify Page Properties Command

A *title*

B *background image & color*

C *text*

D *links*

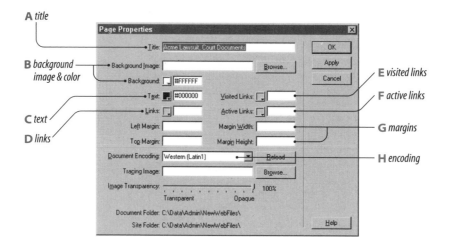

E *visited links*

F *active links*

G *margins*

H *encoding*

HTML pages have two structurally separate areas: the *head* area and the *body* area. (The tag pairs **<head></head>** and **<body></body>** delineate these areas in the code.) Typically, the head area contains the page's title, scripts (such as code for rollover buttons and Dreamweaver behaviors), styles, and character set encoding (for foreign language support). The body area contains the page's text and image content, including frames, tables, layers, background color (if any), background image (ditto), text and link colors, and margins.

The hodgepodge of head and body settings that don't make up the page's actual text and image content live on the **Page Properties** dialog box. That's handy, because you don't have to remember the exact syntax, or even which attributes go into the head section and which into the body section. Get to this dialog box via **Modify▸Page Properties**, or by bringing up the context menu (right-click in Windows, **control**-click on the Mac) over any empty document space and choosing **Page Properties** from that menu.

A title

The **Title** is part of the head content and is the page title that will appear in the user's browser's title bar.

Leaving the title unchanged means that the user will see "Untitled Document," which to me always signifies a sloppy (or overworked!) Web page designer. You should title every page you create. Having said that, typing in the **Title** field on the document window toolbar is certainly easier and faster than firing up the **Page Properties** dialog box. You can also view and change the page title from the head content bar (see Viewing & Adding Head Content on page 35).

> *tip* The HTML title can, and usually should, differ from the filename you use to save the page on disk.

B background image & color

The **Background Image** field lets you specify a graphic Dreamweaver should use as the page's bottom layer. Click the **Browse** button to find an image or directly type the file's path. Dreamweaver automatically tiles the background image to fill the current window. If you don't want an image but you do want a background color, pick it by clicking the color picker box next to the **Background** label or enter the hexadecimal code directly in the white box.

C text

Enter or pick a color you'd like default text (text you haven't set to a different color) to use on your page.

D links

Specify a color you'd like unclicked links to use. The color works in tandem with the underline attribute to make links easy for users to spot.

E visited links

Pick a color for a link that the user's already visited. Making this color different from (D) helps users avoid unintentionally visiting the same link twice.

F active links

This one's a bit subtle: It's the color the link turns when you actually click it. (After you've clicked it, it turns into the visited links color.) I generally don't bother with this setting, as some browsers ignore it.

> *tip* You may be able to save some time by using **Commands➡Set Color Scheme** and setting your background, text, and link colors in a dialog box that shows you the entire "look" in advance. Nice concept, although many of these preselected color schemes don't work well in practice; in particular, the visited links color is often too dim.

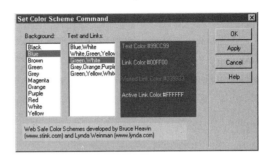

G margins

Set page margins with the **Left**, **Top**, **Width**, and **Height** fields. Careful here: Many users have small screens. If you make your margins too wide, such users will have to scroll to see page content.

H encoding

Specify a character encoding standard for the page if you intend it for a foreign audience. For North American users, leave the default setting of **Western (Latin 1)**. The tracing image settings are covered in Chapter 8, page 135, The Tracing Image Commands.

Viewing & Adding Head Content

The **Modify Page Properties** dialog box doesn't show you everything you may want to see in your document's **<head>** area. For example, you can't see scripts or styles. However, you don't have to drop into code view to see normally hidden head content. You can stay in design view and just use the menu command **View➡ Head Content** (shortcuts: **ctrl+shift+W** in Windows, **command-shift-W** on the Mac). You'll see a new horizontal bar appear at the top of your document, containing an icon for every object in the head area.

If you then open the property inspector (**Window➡ Properties**), you can click on each head area icon to see its properties and change them, if you like. You can also

fire up the Quick Tag Editor from the property sheet and edit the object's HTML code directly. Caveat: You can't use the context menu to work with the icons in the head toolbar; you have to click them and then work with them via the property inspector and **delete** key.

So how do you add your own objects to the invisible head area? One way is via the **Head** objects panel. Open the objects panel with **Window➡Objects** and then click **Head** from the pop-up menu at the top of the panel. You can now click any of the icons to add a generic **<meta>** tag, a keyword **<meta>** tag, a description **<meta>** tag, a refresh **<meta>** tag, a **<base>** tag, or a **<link>** tag.

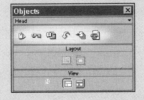

The View Invisible Elements Command

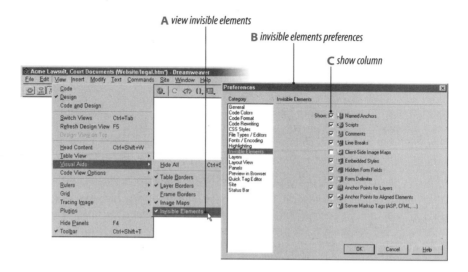

A *view invisible elements*

B *invisible elements preferences*

C *show column*

Dreamweaver is a *WYSIWYG* (What You See Is What You Get) HTML editor, meaning that it shows you your Web page pretty much as it will look in a user's browser. However, many HTML elements don't show up in a browser, the *named anchor* (HTML tag **<a name>**) being one of many examples. Dreamweaver lets you see icons representing these invisible elements in design view, if and when you choose. (I view them when tweaking the code but choose to hide them when I'm judging a page's look and feel.) You can click an invisible element's icon and view or modify its property inspector; look its usage up by clicking the **Reference** icon on the toolbar; edit it in the quick tag editor; or just delete it.

A view invisible elements

The actual menu command is **View➡Visual Aids➡Invisible Elements** (no shortcut). This command acts like a toggle; select it repeatedly to turn it off and on.

B invisible elements preferences

Here's where you can tell Dreamweaver precisely which invisible elements you'd like to see when you've told the program to display them (A).

Get here by choosing **Edit➡Preferences** (**ctrl+U** in Windows, **command-U** on the Mac) and clicking the **Invisible Elements** category to the left.

C show column

Check the boxes to indicate which invisible objects you want to "see" in design view; clear boxes by objects you don't care to see. Dreamweaver's defaults are close to the settings I prefer, but I like to see any forced **Line Breaks** (HTML tag **
**), so I check that normally cleared box. You don't usually need a symbol to show you a client-side image map, because you can see the image, and its hotspots indicate that you've made it into a map.

> **tip** The **Embedded Styles** icon only applies to CSS styles, not HTML styles. Furthermore, it only applies to CSS styles that appear in the *body* of the document; because Dreamweaver places CSS styles into the head section, this icon won't be much use for documents created in Dreamweaver. (For the lowdown on CSS styles, please refer to Chapter 14, Create & Use Style Sheets.) Similarly, the **Scripts** icon only applies to JavaScript or VBScript code in the document's body section. To see styles and scripts in the head section, see the sidebar Viewing & Adding Head Content on page 35.

Clean Up HTML

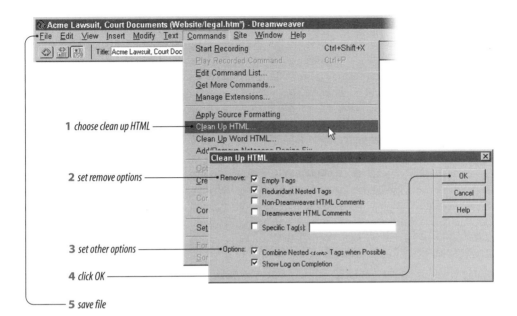

1 *choose clean up HTML*

2 *set remove options*

3 *set other options*

4 *click OK*

5 *save file*

If you're not yet a completely confident HTML jockey, you may find that your code editing adventures sometimes produce less than elegant results. In other cases, you may be opening HTML files created by others, and those files may contain syntactical or formatting errors. Enter the **Clean Up HTML** command.

1 choose clean up HTML

Choose **Commands➡Clean Up HTML** to display the **Clean Up HTML** dialog box.

2 set remove options

Although the default settings are usually appropriate, I'm allergic to the idea of removing comments, whether added by Dreamweaver or not. The **Remove Dreamweaver HTML Comments** option is especially risky, as it destroys the automatic update feature of templates and library items (see Chapter 9). In the **Specific Tag(s)** field, you can name a tag you want Dreamweaver to nuke, such as a nonstandard tag used by the code editor that created the original HTML file.

3 set other options

Normally you want to go ahead and combine nested **<font>** tags for more concise code; doing so

shouldn't change the look of your page. **Show Log On Completion** lets you see what Dreamweaver did to your page.

4 click OK

Dreamweaver cleans up your HTML. (If you chose to see a log of the results, you'll see that next.)

> *tip* Unfortunately, Dreamweaver doesn't offer a batch mode whereby you could clean up a whole bunch of pages in one fell swoop. Do it one page at a time. That's not all bad, though; you usually want to double-check the results to make sure the program didn't inadvertently injure some formatting.

5 save file

If you're the cautious type, save the document with a different name (**File➡Save As**). Later, when you're completely sure it looks and works as it should, you can delete the original file. Compare the file sizes to see how much space you saved by getting your code into shape; I've often seen space reductions of 5 percent to 10 percent, and every little byte helps.

The Clean Up Word HTML Command

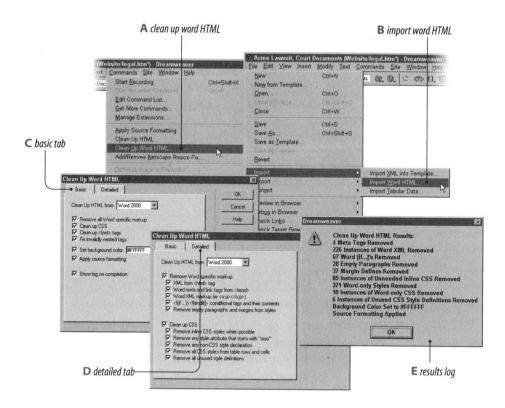

A *clean up word HTML*

B *import word HTML*

C *basic tab*

D *detailed tab*

E *results log*

Microsoft Word has a **Save As Web Page** command that saves a Word document in HTML format. However, the HTML code that Word generates may include a bunch of formatting information that you'd only need if you ever opened the HTML document in Word again. If the document was created with Word 97 or later, Dreamweaver can strip that information out.

A clean up word HTML

If you open a Word HTML file the way you'd open a Dreamweaver HTML file (that is with **File→Open**), Dreamweaver may create a corrections log file and then display the document. Your next move would be to choose **Commands→Clean Up Word HTML**.

B import word HTML

Another way to open the Word HTML file is with the command **File→Import→Import Word HTML**,

so that Dreamweaver opens the **Clean Up Word HTML** dialog box for you.

> *tip* Always keep your original DOC file, because Word won't like what Dreamweaver does to the HTML document.

C basic tab

I normally leave all the options checked; the online help can give you details on each setting.

D detailed tab

Go here for details about what Dreamweaver does to your Word HTML files. Click **OK** to clean up the Word HTML code.

E results log

If **Show Log On Completion** was checked on the **Basic** tab (C), you'll see a list of what Dreamweaver did.

Create & Edit Text

Creating text usually consists of three steps: placing, formatting, and (later) editing.

Dreamweaver lets you place text precisely using tables, layers, or both. The program's layout view is handy for creating tables and cells that will locate your text, visibly or invisibly, on the page.

Formatting placed text is easy with the **Text** property inspector. Use standard HTML paragraph formats and text attributes to get your text looking sharp and save common combinations of attributes as reusable HTML styles. To create text that displays with a specific font, use the new Flash text feature.

Finally, editing existing text goes beyond merely changing formatting options with the property inspector. You can perform search, search-and-replace, and spell-checking operations, too. Dreamweaver isn't yet a word processor, but it's getting closer!

Insert & Place Text

You can insert and place text that you create on the spot, or you can grab text from some external source and bring it into your Web page. The following steps show how to do both:

1 select text

Whether your text source application is on a PC or a Mac, the usual procedure is to click and drag to highlight the text.

2 copy text

You can do this by choosing **Edit→Copy** or by pressing **ctrl+C** (**command-C** on the Mac).

3 set layout view

Open Dreamweaver (the program opens an untitled document for you, which is fine for your purposes) and switch from standard view to layout view by clicking the **Layout View** icon in the objects panel. If you see a descriptive dialog box telling you about layout view, read it and click **OK**. Click the check box labeled **Don't show me this message again** if you don't feel you'll need the information again later.

4 select draw layout cell icon

Click the **Draw Layout Cell** icon in the objects panel to select it. This action tells Dreamweaver you're

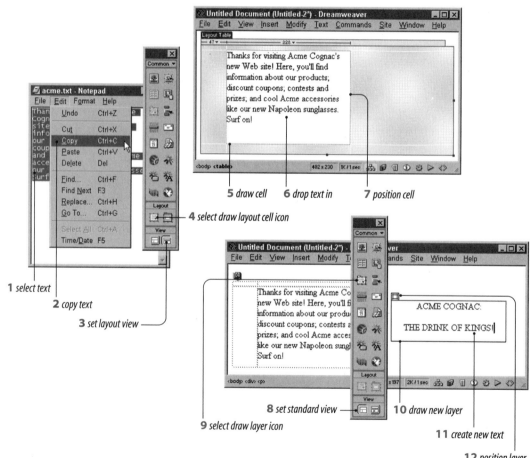

5 *draw cell*　6 *drop text in*　7 *position cell*

4 *select draw layout cell icon*

1 *select text*

2 *copy text*

3 *set layout view*

8 *set standard view*　10 *draw new layer*

9 *select draw layer icon*

11 *create new text*

12 *position layer*

about to draw a table cell. Dreamweaver creates the table structure automatically when you choose to draw a cell before you create a table (for more details, see Chapter 5, Design Tables).

5 draw cell

Click and drag to draw a rectangular cell in the document window, roughly where you'll want your text.

6 drop text in

The text insertion point should be blinking in the cell you just drew. Now, perform a paste operation, either by choosing **Edit➥Paste** or pressing **ctrl+V** (**command-V** on the Mac). Your text should appear within the confines of the cell you created.

7 position cell (optional)

To change the position of the cell on the page, click any of the four bright-blue sides and drag the cell up, down, left, or right.

8 set standard view

Now, use a layer to add a second chunk of text to the page. To add a layer, you must first switch to standard view, by clicking the **Standard View** icon in the objects panel.

9 select draw layer icon

Click the **Draw Layer** icon in the objects panel (or choose **Insert➥Layer**, which automatically inserts a layer and makes step 10 unnecessary).

10 draw new layer

You can click and drag in the document window to draw a rectangle that will become your page's second layer. You can start the layer's upper-left corner wherever you want, giving you positioning flexibility.

> *tip* If you might want to use Version 3 browsers, don't let your layers overlap (see Tables Versus Layers For Placement, **below**).

11 create new text

Type your new text inside the rectangle.

12 position layer

Moving your new layer around is as simple as moving a table cell (7); just move the cursor over the rectangular layer border until you see a four-arrow cursor. (It's easier if you use the layer handle at the upper left.) Then click and drag.

Tables Versus Layers For Placement

You can place text on a Web page by creating tables on a single layer and typing text into one or more cells, or by creating multiple layers and typing the text into a table (or tables) on each layer. Which method is best?

Because layers are only supported by Version 4 and higher browsers, it may seem obvious that you would use one or more tables on a single layer if you wanted maximum compatibility. However, Dreamweaver can convert a layered document to one without layers, using the **File➥Convert➥3.0 Browser Compatible** command. (See Chapter 8, Make & Manipulate Layers, for details.) So, if you're more comfortable working with layers, you can still create Version 3 browser-compatible pages later. Just remember to choose **Modify➥Arrange➥Prevent Layer Overlaps** before you start adding layers, because Dreamweaver can't create a Version 3-compatible table from overlapping layers. I say "before you start adding layers" because

Dreamweaver's **Prevent Layer Overlaps** feature doesn't work retroactively.

Another issue to consider is whether you want to use any of the special capabilities that layers afford, such as *animation*, *stacking*, and *hiding*. Chapter 8 deals with these features in detail, but in a nutshell, if you want text to move around on the page, or if you want to selectively hide and show different chunks of text based on system events or user actions, use layers.

Text Inspector

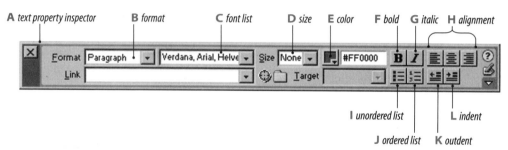

A *text property inspector* B *format* C *font list* D *size* E *color* F *bold* G *italic* H *alignment*

I *unordered list* J *ordered list* K *outdent* L *indent*

As usual in Dreamweaver, your primary tool for formatting text is a property inspector. (Keep in mind, however, that a few infrequently used text-related commands don't appear on the property inspector, but show up on the **Text** menu instead.) The other handy tool for working with text is the **Characters** objects panel, which duplicates the function of the **Insert**➥**Special Characters** command.

Note that the size, color, bold, and italic attributes (D through G) can apply to whole paragraphs or just to selected words or characters.

A text property inspector
Display the **Text** property inspector (if it isn't already open) by clicking any text element and choosing **Window**➥**Properties**.

B format
This pop-up menu presents the traditional options for categorizing HTML text: **None**, **Paragraph**, **Heading 1** through **Heading 6**, and **Preformatted**. For details, see The Paragraph Format Commands on page 44.

C font list
Choose the *font list* you want to use or choose **Edit Font List** to create your own. A user can only view your page with the fonts installed on her system. A font list instructs the user's browser to try the first font listed, and if that one's not installed, try the second one, and so on. Fonts in a list generally look similar, which helps you preserve the look and feel of your site.

> **tip** Avoid Times Roman as a primary choice in a font list. Many browsers default to this typeface, and experienced Web surfers got burnt out on it years ago.

D size
Your choices here are absolute (1 through 7) and relative (+1 through +7, -1 through -7). The default, or norm, is 3, so an absolute value of 5 would be the same as a relative value of +2 (that is, 3+2=5). Users can change what "3" means by varying the point size for the default font size in their browsers.

E color
Click here to pop up the color picker, which presents a grid of Web-safe colors. Move the eyedropper cursor off the grid to pick a color anywhere on the screen.

F bold
The menu command is **Text**➥**Style**➥**Bold**.

G italic
The menu command is **Text**➥**Style**➥**Italic**. If you want strikethrough, or other formatting options, you must use the **Text** menu.

H alignment
Set a block of text to be left-aligned, centered, or right-aligned. (You don't have the option to justify text so that it is both right- and left-aligned.)

I unordered list
An *unordered list* is just a bulleted list. Click this with text selected and make a list from the text; click it without text selected and start a new list. See The List Commands on page 45 for more on creating lists.

Characters Objects Panel

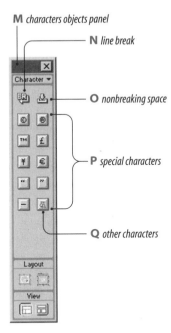

M *characters objects panel*

N *line break*

O *nonbreaking space*

P *special characters*

Q *other characters*

J ordered list

An *ordered list* is Webspeak for a numbered list.

K outdent

This command scoots a text block's left margin out to the left.

L indent

This command scoots a text block's left margin in to the right (in HTML: **blockquote**). In a list, indenting creates a nested list.

M characters objects panel

To display, choose **Window➡Objects** and select **Characters** from the pop-up menu.

N line break

Clicking here inserts a line break (**
** in HTML), which you can also do by pressing **shift+enter** (Win) or **shift-return** (Mac).

O nonbreaking space

Use a nonbreaking space (** **) instead of hitting the space bar if you need to string two or more spaces together or to make sure that a browser doesn't break a line at the space. The equivalent menu command is **Insert➡Special Characters➡Non-Breaking Space**, and the shortcut is **ctrl+shift+spacebar** (**command-shift-spacebar** on the Mac).

P special characters

Insert common HTML *special characters* (such as the copyright and Euro symbols) by clicking here, but test the page in your target browser to ensure compatibility.

Q other characters

Click to see a bunch of other, less common special characters, such as accented vowels.

> *tip* A given browser is more likely to display special characters properly if you specify the **Western (Latin 1)** encoding with **Modify➡ Page Properties**.

HTML Styles Versus CSS Styles

Styles are ways to combine text characteristics that you frequently use together. When you define a text style, you can then assign that style to a chunk of text and make several format settings in one fell swoop.

You can define two kinds of styles: *HTML* (for *HyperText Markup Language*) and *CSS* (short for *Cascading Style Sheet*).

HTML styles work in pre-Version 4 browsers. CSS styles require Version 4 (or higher) browsers.

HTML styles are embedded into the current page. CSS styles can exist in an external document that applies to multiple pages; updating the style updates all attached pages, automatically. (CSS styles can also exist as a page-level, or embedded, style.)

You can mix and match HTML styles on the same page.

Manual HTML formatting overrides any HTML or CSS styles that would otherwise apply.

The Paragraph Format Commands

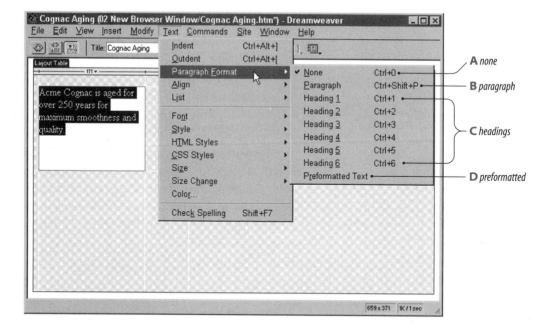

Paragraph formatting applies standard HTML types, such as paragraph, headings, and "preformatted," to blocks of text. You can access the various paragraph formatting options by choosing commands from the **Text** menu as shown in the figure, or from the **Format** pop-up menu in the **Text** property inspector (A, page 42). Select the text of interest and then choose a format. The other option is to choose a format first and then start typing.

A none
Choose this option to remove any previous paragraph format.

B paragraph
This vanilla format performs word wrapping and automatically puts a carriage return both above and below the paragraph.

C headings
These special formats organize blocks of text. Smaller numbers mean larger type. Different browsers interpret headings differently, so you don't see them as much as you used to.

D preformatted
This format lets you insert multiple spaces in a row (normally, HTML only permits one at a time). It defaults to a monospaced font and doesn't automatically wrap to the next line, although you can insert line breaks manually by pressing **shift+enter** (Win) or **shift-return** (Mac).

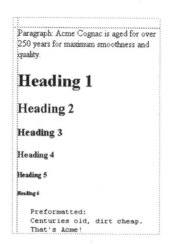

The List Commands

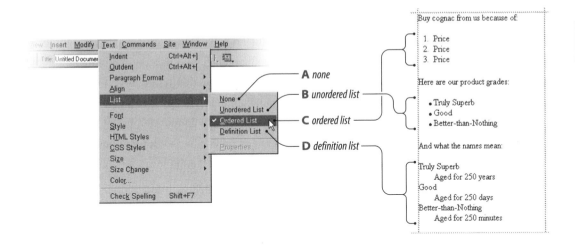

A *none*

B *unordered list*

C *ordered list*

D *definition list*

Lists are handy when you want to present a series of items without making the user wade through a prose paragraph. You access the **List** commands from the **Text** menu, or from the **Text** property inspector by clicking the **Unordered List** or **Ordered List** button (I & J, pages 42 and 43). (The **Definition List** isn't available on the property inspector.) Select paragraphs and then choose a **List** style, or choose the style first and start typing. To end a list, press **enter** (Win) or **return** (Mac) twice in a row.

A none
Choose this option to remove any previous list format.

B unordered list
Choose this option to create a bulleted list. Click anywhere inside an unordered list and choose **Text**➞**List**➞**Properties** to display the **List Properties** dialog box and change the **Style** from round to square.

C ordered list
Choose this option to create a numbered list. Click in an existing ordered list and choose

Text➞**List**➞**Properties** to display the **List Properties** dialog box. Use the **Style** option to choose a numbering scheme: **Arabic**, **Roman Small**, **Roman Large**, **Alpha Small**, or **Alpha Large** numbers. If you want to start your list at a number other than 1, enter that number in the **Start Count** field.

tip Click inside a list (don't select it) and choose **Text**➞**List**➞**Properties** to change the default style for an ordered or unordered list.

D definition list
Use this kind of list for items in pairs (such as word+definition, product+price, and so on). **Definition Lists** don't have properties you can change.

If you find yourself charged with dressing up the text that some artistically challenged engineer thought looked good five years ago, such as the page shown, then this section's for you.

1 set layout view

With your page loaded, switch to layout view by clicking the **Layout View** icon in the objects panel or by choosing **View**➡**Table View**➡**Layout View**.

2 select draw table layout icon

If (as here) the text is not already in a table, click the **Draw Table Layout** icon in the objects panel.

3 draw table

Click and drag a new table below the text you want to beautify. Not only does placing text in a table give you

more precise control over the text's layout, but it looks better as well. (You could also create the table in a new layer.)

4 select draw layout cell icon

Click the **Draw Layout Cell** icon in the objects panel.

5 draw cells

Click and drag a rectangular cell inside the table you just created. Repeat, depending on how many discrete text groupings you want. The example here uses four—one for each heading and one for each content paragraph.

6 copy & paste text

Select the original text, group by group, and copy and paste it into the cells. The shortcuts are **ctrl+C** (Win)

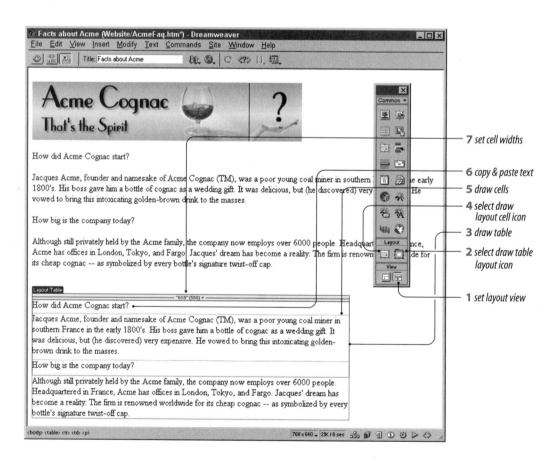

7 *set cell widths*

6 *copy & paste text*

5 *draw cells*

4 *select draw layout cell icon*

3 *draw table*

2 *select draw table layout icon*

1 *set layout view*

and **command-C** (Mac) to copy, and **ctrl+V** (Win) and **command-V** (Mac) to paste.

> *tip* To quickly select an entire paragraph, click in the paragraph and then click the **<p>** tag on the tag selector (at the lower left of the document window). The same trick works for headings and lists—just click the appropriate tag.

7 set cell widths

You may notice two numbers centered on the top edge of the layout table. Those numbers mean that some cells are wider than others. You can make them the same by clicking the numbers and choosing **Make Cell Widths Consistent**.

8 set standard view

Switch to standard view by clicking the **Standard View** icon on the objects panel. In standard view, you can resize and move your table more easily.

9 reposition table

Position the cursor over a table edge until it becomes a four-arrow pointer. At that point, drag and drop the table up or down on the page. If you'd like, you can also resize the table by clicking its top-left corner to select it and then moving the size handles on the right and bottom edges.

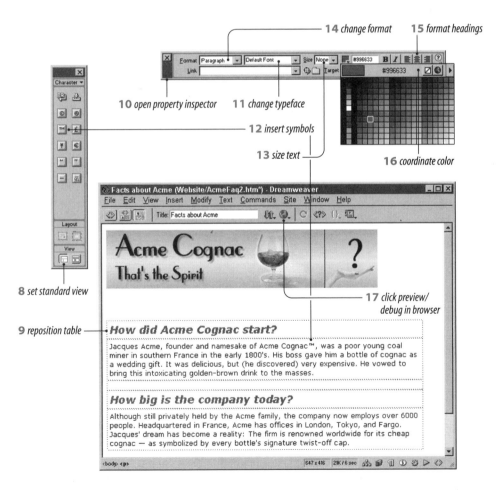

14 *change format*   **15** *format headings*

10 *open property inspector*   **11** *change typeface*

12 *insert symbols*

13 *size text*

16 *coordinate color*

8 *set standard view*

9 *reposition table*

17 *click preview/ debug in browser*

10 open property inspector

Choose **Window→Properties** if the **Text** property inspector isn't already open.

11 change typeface

Select each text element and set the font list you want.

12 insert symbols

Choose **Characters** from the objects panel's pop-up menu (it normally says **Common**) to see the characters you can add. Click where you want the symbol and then click the character in the panel.

13 size text

Select a paragraph and click the **Size** drop-down list in the property inspector to adjust text size to taste.

14 change format

Although not required, headings should probably use a heading format. Select them one at a time and set a heading format using the **Format** pop-up menu on the property inspector.

15 format headings

Select the first heading and then choose **Align Center** from the **Text** property inspector. (If that doesn't look good, choose **Align Left**, as shown here.) Apply italics by clicking the **Italic** button on the inspector.

16 coordinate color

Show some sophistication and pick a color from the page's main graphic to use as the text heading color. Select a heading and then click the **Text Color** box on the property inspector to display the color picker. Move the cursor (now an eyedropper) to the page's main graphic and pick a color you think will look good. In the example, I picked a rich golden-brown from the glass of cognac at the top of the page.

> **tip** If you want to make sure that the color you choose is Web-safe, click the right arrow at the upper right of the color picker display and make sure **Snap To Web Safe** is checked.

17 click preview/debug in browser

After you complete your handiwork, you should look at it in a browser window to see what your users will see. Click the **Preview/Debug in Browser** button on the main toolbar. If you have multiple browsers installed, select the one you want to view, and Dreamweaver opens a new browser window for you. If you see anything that needs adjusting, close the browser window and tweak it. For example, you may want to fine-tune your table cells to account for the way browsers interpret headings. If you can't get them the way you want, you can convert the headings to paragraph format and set their type size and other characteristics manually.

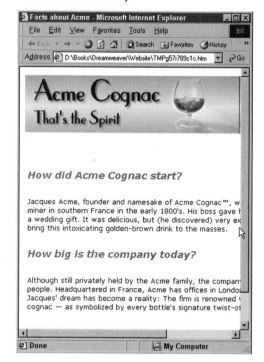

> **tip** One common problem is that a table of text fails to resize automatically when the user resizes the browser window. Easy to fix: Just go into layout view, click the column heading, and choose **Make Column Autostretch**.

The HTML Styles Panel

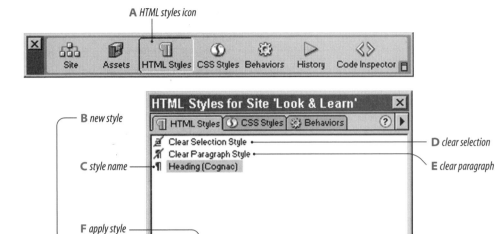

A *HTML styles icon*

B *new style*

C *style name*

D *clear selection*

E *clear paragraph*

F *apply style*

G *auto apply*

H *delete style*

HTML Styles for Site 'Look & Learn'

Clear Selection Style
Clear Paragraph Style
Heading (Cognac)

Apply

The **HTML Styles** panel is a handy time-saver when you want to apply the same combination of formatting attributes several times within a document.

A HTML styles icon

Click the **HTML Styles** icon in the launcher bar or the mini-launcher or choose **Window→HTML Styles** to display the **HTML Styles** panel.

B new style

Click the **New Style** button on the lower right of the **HTML Styles** panel or choose **Text→HTML Styles→New Style** to create a new style. If you click inside a text element first, Dreamweaver uses the attributes of that text element to define the style.

C style name

After you create a style, its name appears in the style list. To edit a style, double-click its name to display the **Define HTML Style** dialog box. Then make your changes and click **OK**. You must manually reapply the style after changing it.

D clear selection

Click this style and click the **Apply** button (F) to remove HTML formatting in preselected text. Or if the **Auto Apply** option (G) in the lower-left corner is checked, click the style.

E clear paragraph

Click this style and click the **Apply** button (or simply click the style if the **Auto Apply** box in the lower-left corner is checked) to remove HTML formatting in the current paragraph.

F apply style

If the **Auto Apply** box at the lower left is checked, click a style name (C) to apply that style to the current text selection; otherwise, click the style and then click **Apply**.

G auto apply

Check this box to have Dreamweaver apply a style as soon as you click it, without your having to click the **Apply** button.

H delete style

Click the trash can button to remove a selected style from the list.

Find & Replace Text

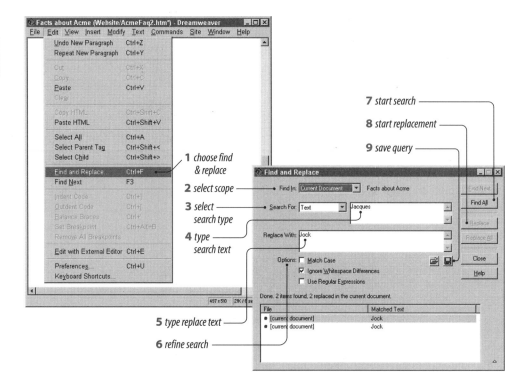

7 *start search*

8 *start replacement*

9 *save query*

1 *choose find & replace*

2 *select scope*

3 *select search type*

4 *type search text*

5 *type replace text*

6 *refine search*

Dreamweaver is all about saving time, and one of the best ways to save time when working with text is to perform automated find-and-replace operations. (The "replace" part is optional, which is handy because sometimes you just want to perform a simple find.) This section first runs through a simple content find-and-replace operation; the concluding tips describe fancier capabilities.

1 choose find & replace

Choose **Edit➡Find and Replace** or press **ctrl+F** (**command-F** on the Mac). These commands work whether you're in design view or code view, and display the **Find and Replace** dialog box.

2 select scope

The *scope* of a find operation specifies where you want Dreamweaver to look. If you have a page loaded as the current document, you can choose **Current Document**. You can also choose **Entire Local**

Site, and if the current site isn't the one you want, you can choose another one in the **Site** window toolbar (not shown). **Selected Files In Site** lets you select a group of files in the site window. Finally, **Folder** lets you select a folder by clicking the (you guessed it!) folder icon. In this example, I selected **Current Document**.

3 select search type

Dreamweaver gives you four types of search operations: **Source Code**, **Text**, **Text (Advanced)**, and **Specific Tag**. The first two look and act very similar, with the main difference being that **Text** ignores HTML code such as tags inside angle brackets, and **Source Code** doesn't. I chose **Text** because I wanted to replace every occurrence of **Jacques** with **Jock** in the visible content.

The **Text (Advanced)** search type lets you find text inside a specific HTML tag, or, alternately, *not* inside a specific tag. The following figure displays a search for **Jacques** within a level 3 header that is center-aligned.

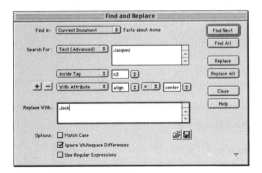

The **Specific Tag** search type lets you find particular HTML tags with certain attributes and replace them. For example, the next figure replaces any **<table>** tags that have a cellpadding attribute lower than 10 with a **<table>** tag having a cellpadding attribute equal to 10. The attributes are supposed to match the tags, but sometimes you need to reselect a tag in order to get Dreamweaver to display the correct attribute list. Also, Dreamweaver warns you if you're about to perform an action (say, on unopened documents) that the program will not be able to undo.

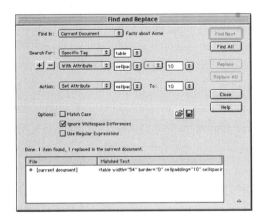

4 type search text
Enter the text you want to find in the **Search For** field.

5 type replace text (optional)
If you want to replace the text you're searching for with alternate text, enter the replacement text in the **Replace With** field. Otherwise, leave it blank.

6 refine search (optional)
You can tell Dreamweaver that you only want it to find matches with the exact same upper- and lower-case punctuation by selecting **Match Case.** Tell the program to treat all white space as a single space by selecting **Ignore Whitespace Differences**. And if you want to get *really* fancy, check **Use Regular Expressions** to embed special codes into your search string. (For the meaning of these codes, see the table "About Regular Expressions" in the *Using Dreamweaver* help file).

7 start search
If you're just doing a find, click the **Find Next** button or press **F3** (**command-G** on the Mac) to find the next occurrence of the search string in the selected scope, or click the **Find All** button to generate a list of "hits" in the dialog box's lower half.

8 start replacement (optional)
If you're doing a find and replace, click **Replace** or **Replace All**. The latter generates a list of "hits" in the dialog box's lower half. (The buttons are dimmed in the figure because Dreamweaver's already done the search.)

> **tip** If you click either **Find All** or **Replace All**, and your search produces one or more hits, you can double-click the hit, and Dreamweaver zips you right over to the specific document and highlights the relevant text—even if the document isn't already open. Cool.

9 save query
Here's a useful option if you tend to perform certain find or find-and-replace operations repeatedly. Click the **Save Query** button to save your search pattern; later, click **Load Query** to retrieve a saved pattern. FYI, find queries end in .DWQ and find-and-replace queries end in .DWR.

steps Check Spelling

After you have your text placed and formatted so that it looks great, you need to make sure that you spell-check it so that a mistake doesn't undermine all that hard work. Macromedia has kindly provided a command to take some of the drudgery out of spell-checking.

1 place cursor

If you want to spell-check the entire document, click at the top of the document's text area; that's where Dreamweaver will begin its spell-check of the page. (Alternatively, you can highlight a chunk of text that you want to check.)

2 choose check spelling

Choose **Text→Check Spelling** or press **shift-F7** to initiate a spell check. If Dreamweaver finds a word it doesn't understand, it presents the **Check Spelling** dialog box.

> *tip* Don't rely on the spell checker too heavily. In my example, it wanted to change "Jacques" to "Jaycees" and "Fargo" to "Cargo." Use the same healthy skepticism you've learned with word-processing grammar checkers.

3 add valid words

When Dreamweaver doesn't know a word and you want the program to remember it next time, click **Add To Personal**.

4 ignore others

If you want to leave a flagged word the way it is, but you don't want to add it to your personal dictionary supplement, click **Ignore** (to skip it this one time) or **Ignore All** (to skip it for the whole document).

5 fix mistakes

If Dreamweaver catches you in an actual error, click **Change** (to fix it this one time) or **Change All** (to fix it in the entire document).

> *tip* The spell checker doesn't process HTML tags (thank goodness).

1 *place cursor* **2** *choose check spelling*

3 *add valid words*
4 *ignore others*
5 *fix mistakes*

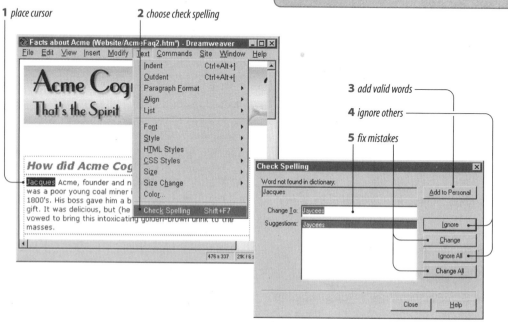

Insert Flash Text

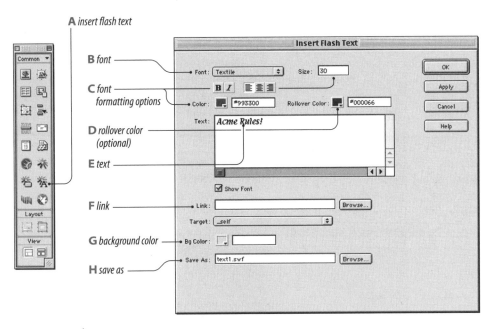

A *insert flash text*

B *font*

C *font formatting options*

D *rollover color (optional)*

E *text*

F *link*

G *background color*

H *save as*

Since the dawn of time (well, since 1994), Web designers have felt handcuffed by the fact that the fonts they can use must be installed on viewers' computers. The font list feature (C, page 42) helps, but doesn't satisfy the stubborn artist who just *has* to use Friz Quadrata for that particular heading. So, many designers turn to bitmap graphics for presenting such text—a technique that looks great but, for users with slow connections, adds significantly to download times.

Enter *Flash text*, which lets you create a text-only Flash movie using whatever the heck font you want to use. Flash text is typically smaller than a bitmapped image but gives you a lot of design freedom, making for an appealing compromise. And now that the Flash player is nearly ubiquitous, browser compatibility is high—although you should consider the possibility that any given user may not have the Flash player and perhaps provide a convenient link on your site for such an eventuality.

A insert flash text
You display the **Insert Flash Text** dialog box by clicking this icon on the objects panel. As with several

Dreamweaver features, you must have a *saved* document open before clicking it. (You should also place the cursor approximately where you want the Flash text to appear, although moving the text around later is no big deal.) Choosing **Insert➥Interactive Images➥Flash Text** also works, although the command is misnamed. (Flash text doesn't have to be interactive.)

> *tip* Once placed on the page, Flash text acts more like an image than like regular text. That is, you can't use the **Edit➥Find and Replace** command with Flash text, nor can you check spelling with **Text➥Check Spelling**.

B font
Pick any TrueType font on your system from the **Font** pop-up menu. (PostScript fonts don't work, bummer.) Flash text transforms the characters into a vector drawing, so the user doesn't need to have the font in order to see the text as you intend it to be seen. Vector graphics are typically smaller than bitmap graphics, so Flash text downloads more swiftly than GIFs.

C font formatting options

The **Size**, **Bold**, **Italic**, and alignment buttons all work as you'd expect. The **Color** button does, too; it activates the by-now-familiar Dreamweaver color picker with its nerdy six-digit hexadecimal codes.

D rollover color

If you want your text to change color whenever the user passes the mouse cursor over it, here's where you choose that color.

Change your mind? In the color picker pop-up, click the white box with the red diagonal if you chose a rollover color earlier and now you don't want the text to roll over after all.

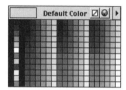

E text

This one is easy to figure out: Just type the text into the **Text** field.

F link

If you want your Flash text to take the user somewhere, you can set up the link in this area. Just be advised that the link should be either absolute or document-relative, not site-relative.

There's no rule against using both a link and a rollover (D). In fact, that's a common use for Flash text. (On a related note, you can create rollovers that *don't* use Flash text by choosing the menu command **Insert→ Interactive Images→Rollover Image**.)

G background color

Why this option isn't right up there with the font color (C) and rollover color (D) is anybody's guess. If you leave this choice unselected, you effectively create "floating" text.

H save as

You can enter a name for your file here. The default extension is .swf, which you should leave alone. It stands for ShockWave Flash, because the program that the browser calls upon to "render" Flash text is the ShockWave Flash Player. Many designers nowadays have thankfully shortened that name to simply "Flash Player."

Add & Edit Graphics

With Dreamweaver, you can specify how your graphics lay out on the page and what (if anything) they do when clicked. An image can be inline with text or floating on the page. It can host a link to another location or host multiple such links (in which case it becomes an *image map*). Dreamweaver provides good tools for making your images do just what you want them to do.

However, Dreamweaver isn't an image editor. If you want to create your own graphics, modify the look of graphics you already have, or optimize images for the Web, you must do so in an external image editor. Macromedia happens to sell one called Fireworks, and Dreamweaver works well with that program; for example, you can easily "jump" from Dreamweaver to Fireworks to optimize an image's quality for the Web. But you can also set up Dreamweaver to work with other image editors, such as Photoshop.

Image Insertion Methods

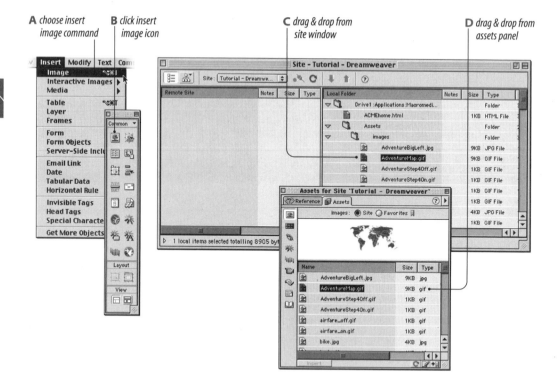

A *choose insert image command*　　**B** *click insert image icon*　　**C** *drag & drop from site window*　　**D** *drag & drop from assets panel*

You can insert an image onto a Web page several different ways. Some ways may seem a little odd, but they can save you some serious time if you design a lot of Web pages.

A choose insert image command

This one's the most straightforward: Just choose **Insert➞Image** or press **ctrl+alt+I** (Win) or **command-option-I** (Mac). The **Select Image Source** dialog box appears, from which you can navigate to the file you want.

B click insert image icon

This one's the fastest: Click the **Insert Image** icon on the **Common** objects panel. Again, the **Select Image Source** dialog box appears.

C drag & drop from site window

If you happen to have the **Site** window open (press **F8** if it's not), you can drag and drop an image file

from it onto the precise point in the document window where you'd like the image to appear.

D drag & drop from assets panel

You can drag and drop an image file from the **Assets** panel (display it with **F11**) onto the document window. You can also select an image in the **Assets** panel, click the **Insert** button at the bottom of that panel, and Dreamweaver will add it to your document at the current insertion point.

> **tip** Alas, dragging and dropping from the desktop or a file manager onto a document window doesn't work consistently, either on a PC or on a Macintosh (for example, you can drag and drop if you choose to copy the file to your site folder, but not otherwise). The best practice in Dreamweaver, therefore, is to gather your files onto your site folder, and then you have full drag and drop capability.

 **Place An Inline Image**

An *inline image* is a graphic whose position on a Web page depends on two factors: where you insert the image relative to other text or graphic elements and how you align the image with those elements. (Inline images are distinct from floating images, which you place independently—for example, in a table, or on a separate layer.)

1 click page
Clicking in the document window tells Dreamweaver where you plan to insert the image.

2 click insert image icon
Click the **Insert Image** icon on the objects panel (you can either be in layout view or standard view) to display the **Select Image Source** dialog box. Alternately, choose **Insert➡Image** or press **ctrl+alt+I** (Win) or **command-option-I** (Mac).

3 check preview images (optional)
By checking the **Preview Images** box, you direct Dreamweaver to display a thumbnail of the selected (clicked) image in the righthand part of the **Select Image Source** dialog box. Using previews helps you locate the right image quickly.

4 choose path type
In the **Relative To** pop-up menu, choose either **Document** or **Site Root**. Normally, you would choose **Document**, so that your page's HTML code refers to the image's location with respect to the HTML file's location. If you choose **Site Root**, then your HTML code refers to the image's location with respect to your site's root folder (that is, with a *root-relative path*).

> *tip* If you choose a document-relative path, then when you move the HTML file that links to an image, you must also move the image file itself. That way, the image file's location relative to the HTML page remains constant. If you choose a root-relative path, then you can relocate your HTML file without updating the image link; but if you move the image file, then you must update all root-relative links that refer to that image file.

5 find file
Use the **Look in** pop-up menu (Win) or the folder list (Mac) to navigate to the folder that contains your desired graphic and then click the filename to select it. The image file can be anywhere, but if you specify a location outside the site root, you'll see a dialog box

1 *click page*

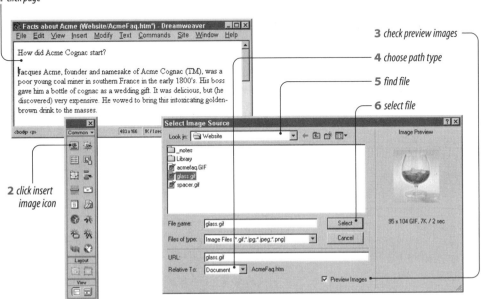

3 *check preview images*
4 *choose path type*
5 *find file*
6 *select file*

2 *click insert image icon*

such as the following, in which Dreamweaver offers to copy the file into your site root folder—an excellent idea to avoid broken links when you upload your site to a Web server!

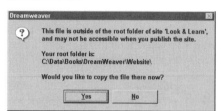

6 select file

Click **Select** (Win) or **Open** (Mac) to choose the image you want. The **Select Image Source** dialog box vanishes, and the image appears in the document window.

7 align image

Right-click (Win) or **control**-click (Mac) the image to display its context menu. Select **Align** and then choose from the options. **Browser Default**, **Baseline**, and **Bottom** generally all mean the same thing: The bottom of the image lines up with the bottom edge of the line of text (see below). **Absolute**

7 align image

Bottom uses *descenders* (like the straight part of a lowercase "q") to determine the bottom edge.

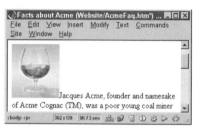

Top aligns your image to the top of the tallest text or image in the current line, while **Text Top** uses the tallest text character for alignment. The result is *not* "word wrap" as you're used to seeing it, as the following figure shows.

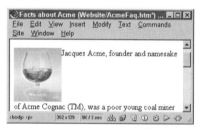

Middle looks like **Top** but with the current line in the middle of the image instead of at the top of it; **Absolute Middle** considers descenders in determining the middle of the line. **Left** puts your image on the left margin, pushing text to its right; notice also the image tag symbol that Dreamweaver places into the document window (assuming that you have Dreamweaver set to display invisible elements). Finally, **Right** puts the image on the right margin, pushing text to its left.

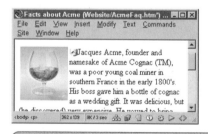

> *tip* Frequent saves are smart. As soon as you have your image where you want it, save the page.

🄢 Place A Floating Image

If the constraints of inline images and their alignment options stifle you, you can place images whose location doesn't depend on surrounding text. First, you can create a table (see Chapter 5, Design Tables) and then drop an image into a table cell. However, Dreamweaver won't let you create a table on top of existing images or text. To create a *floating image* (Version 4 and higher browsers only) that's independent of other page elements and that can even overlap them, put it on a new layer.

1 set standard view
To add a layer, you must first switch to standard view by clicking the **Standard View** icon in the objects panel.

2 select draw layer icon
Click the **Draw Layer** icon in the objects panel or choose **Insert➠Layer**.

3 draw new layer
Click and drag in the document window to draw a rectangle that will be your page's second layer. You can start the layer's upper-left corner wherever you want, giving you positioning flexibility. Make it large enough to contain the graphic you want to insert. (You can always resize the layer later.)

4 insert image
Click the **Insert Image** icon in the objects panel or choose **Insert➠Image** or press **ctrl+alt+I** (Win) or **command-option-I** (Mac). Find and select your image as described in steps 3 through 6 on pages 57 and 58.

5 position layer
Move the cursor over the rectangular layer border until you see a four-arrow cursor. (It's easier if you use the layer handle at the upper left.) Then click and drag.

> 🅣🅘🅟 A special kind of graphic is the *page background*. Choose a background image with the **Modify➠Page Properties** command (see The Modify Page Properties Command on page 34 in Chapter 2). If the browser window is larger than the background image you choose, Dreamweaver *tiles* the image in a repeating pattern. Many graphics programs come with collections of images that are suitable for seamless tiling. Make sure that your background doesn't clutter the page or interfere with the user's ability to read text; subtle, unobtrusive backgrounds usually work best.

6 preview page
Test your page by clicking the **Preview/ Debug In Browser** icon on the document window toolbar, or choosing the **File➠ Preview in Browser** menu command. (What you see in the document window isn't always what you get!) Resize the browser window a few times to make sure that your floating images never unintentionally obscure text or other page elements.

1 *set standard view*

2 *select draw layer icon*

3 *draw new layer*

4 *insert image*   **5** *position layer*   **6** *preview page*

Facts about Acme (Website/AcmeFaq.htm*) - Dreamweaver

File Edit View Insert Modify Text Commands Site Window Help

Title: Facts about Acme

How did Acme Cognac start?

`<body> <div>`   502 x 232   8K / 3 sec

The Image Property Inspector

A *thumbnail* B *size* C *name* E *source*

D *width & height* F *link* G *align* H *alt*

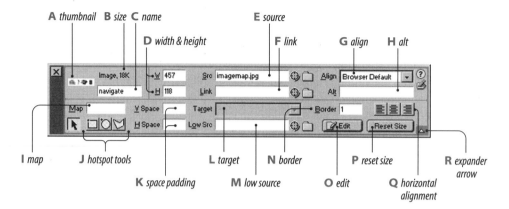

I *map* J *hotspot tools* L *target* N *border* P *reset size* R *expander arrow*

K *space padding* M *low source* O *edit* Q *horizontal alignment*

The **Image** property inspector is a convenient one-stop shop for editing image characteristics. Display the **Image** property inspector (if it isn't already open) by clicking an image and choosing **Window➞Properties**. You can also right-click (Win) or **control**-click (Mac) the image and choose **Properties**. If you're a shortcut kind of person, click the image and press **ctrl+F3** (Win) or **command-F3** (Mac). If you want to see the entire **Image** property inspector but only the top half appears, click the expander arrow (R) at the lower right or double-click anywhere on the inspector.

A thumbnail

Here's a too-tiny-to-be-useful image preview whose main function is to remind you that you're looking at the **Image** property inspector.

B size

Dreamweaver shows you the image's size in kilobytes (K), always an important stat to keep in mind when considering download performance.

C name

Give each image in your Web site a unique, descriptive name. Note that this can be different from the actual filename on disk. You can get by without naming your images, but you won't be able to refer to them from a scripting language, such as JavaScript, so it's good practice to name every HTML object you create.

D width & height

The dimensions of the rectangle that Dreamweaver will reserve for the image appear here, in pixels. These values default to the image's original dimensions. You should normally resize images in an image editing program like Fireworks or Photoshop, rather than in Dreamweaver's document window; for more details, see Edit & Update A Placed Image, on pages 69 and 70.

> **tip** If you manually resize the image from its original dimensions, the width and height numbers appear in boldface. You can restore the image to its original dimensions by clicking the **Reset Size** button (P). To reset the width or height value independently, click the **W** or **H**, respectively.

E source

This box shows the name of the image's source file. The **Point-to-File** icon at the right lets you drag and drop the icon to a different file location, for example, in the **Site** window or **Assets** panel — a convenient way of selecting a file if either of those windows happens to be open. (This icon is a fairly unusual one, so you should practice with it to get the hang of how it works.) Or, click the folder icon to the right of the **Point-to-File** icon to browse for a file with the **Select Image Source** dialog box. Both methods are preferable to entering the name directly into the **Src** field, because you can't make an accidental spelling mistake.

F link

Enter a URL in this field to specify a hyperlink for the image. Or, drag and drop the **Point-to-File** icon at the right to a different file location in the **Site** window or **Assets** panel. Finally, you can click the folder icon to browse via a dialog box. (See Create An Image Link, on page 64, for details.)

G align

Use the **Align** pop-up menu for aligning inline images with other items on the same line. For details, see Place An Inline Image, on pages 57 and 58.)

H alt

I always like to make sure that every image has an **Alt** tag (that's short for alternative text), a word or phrase that describes the image.

Some users (especially those using dial-up connections) set their browsers to download only the images they specify, and the **Alt** tag gives a clue about the value and content of the image. Furthermore, people with visual disabilities use speech software to "read" a Web page—they can't see your image, but they can listen to an **Alt** tag description. Finally, most modern

browsers display the Alt text at the tip of the cursor when a user hovers that cursor over an image.

I map

If the graphic contains an image map, its name appears here. Image maps let you define different regions on the image that link to different targets when clicked.

The map name must be unique among all map names in the site. You should always create a name for image maps you create. (For more information, see Create An Image Map, on pages 65 and 66.)

J hotspot tools

The arrow, rectangle, oval, and polygon tools help you create and edit image map "hotspots" that users can click to perform different actions (again, see Create An Image Map, on pages 65 and 66, for details).

K space padding

Here's a cool feature for helping you place images in an esthetically pleasing way. If you want a bit of empty space on the left and right of your image, enter a number of pixels in the **H Space** field. Similarly, enter a number in the **V Space** field to pad the

---

Image Formats

Dreamweaver can display in the document window the two most common Web graphics formats, .GIF and JPEG. It also works with .PNG, which Macromedia's Fireworks image editor uses as its default format.

GIF

GIF, or *Graphics Interchange Format*, does a good job compressing non-photographic images such as clip art. It supports 256 colors only. The original definition (developed by Compuserve) has seen several evolutions, and you can now create GIFs with simple "flipbook" animation, a single designated transparency color, and interlacing (which lets an image appear

gradually in a browser window, instead of all at once).

JPEG

JPEG, or *Joint Photographic Experts Group*, does a good job compressing photographic images and images without much regularity or pattern. It supports true color files with millions of colors, but the tradeoff is that JPEG files are generally larger than GIF files for a given number of pixels. You can adjust the quality versus size equation, for example, in Fireworks.

PNG

PNG (*Portable Network Graphics*) is a format you may consider as a GIF

alternative, although PNG improves on GIF by supporting true color and by permitting the inclusion of vector data as well as bitmap data.

PNG files support transparency, as GIF files do, and PNG uses a lossless compression technique, again similar to GIF. PNG requires Version 4 browsers (4.04 and up with Netscape) and even then, some PNG files don't display properly.

If you work with Fireworks, consider using PNG for your "original" images, but exporting them in the GIF or JPEG format for Web publishing purposes.

---

image on the top and bottom. You can think of this space padding as a force field around the image, into which no other page elements may intrude.

L target

If the image has a link associated with it (F) and if the current document uses frames, then the **Target** field specifies where in the current document the linked file should load.

The pop-up menu presents all named frames that exist in the current document, plus some special pre-defined names: **_blank** (opens a new browser window), **_parent** (the parent frameset of the frame hosting the link), **_self** (the frame that hosts the link), and **_top** (fills the entire browser window and nukes any existing frames). Chapter 7 goes into all the details you'll need to create frames and framesets with Dreamweaver.

> **tip** If you don't see a frame that you think should appear in the list, then you may not have named it yet.

M low source

Use the **Low Src** field to specify a low-resolution version of your graphic that you would like to download first, giving the user something to see while the full-resolution image works its way down the electron pipe.

You can create a *low source* file in a variety of ways, but the most common is to create a simple black-and-white version of the file, for example, by using an image editor's *threshold* feature.

N border

Enter a value in this field to specify how many pixels wide you'd like the image border to be. A value of 0 means no border. The border color defaults to the same color as the text surrounding the image, if the image is unlinked; the border color defaults to the link color specified in the **Page Properties** dialog box, if the image is linked. You can't change the border color independently of these other colors. (For details on colors, Web pages, and Dreamweaver, see the Web-Safe Colors sidebar, on page 63.)

> **tip** If your low source file isn't at least 50 percent smaller than the full-res file, don't bother. Also, don't bother creating low source files for small images that download pretty quickly anyway.

O edit

This button fires up whatever external image editor you have set up in the **Preferences** dialog box. (Remember, Dreamweaver doesn't do image editing.) Use the image editor, save the file, and exit back to Dreamweaver. For details, see Edit & Update A Placed Image, on pages 69 and 70.

P reset size

Click this button to simultaneously reset the width and height dimensions of the graphic (D) to their original values.

Q horizontal alignment

These horizontal alignment buttons act on the image in a logical way that is nevertheless a little hard to understand.

If you place an inline image that is tied to a line of text, the **Left**, **Center**, and **Right** alignment buttons align the *combined* entity consisting of the image and the line of text.

So, the image itself won't be centered if you click **Center**, but the image plus the text that it goes with will be centered as a grouped element. (If that's too obscure to follow, experiment a little until you get the hang of these buttons.) Note that these options differ from those in the **Align** drop-down list (G); experiment with them all to get the look you're after.

R expander arrow

This little arrow jumps you back and forth between the **Image** property inspector's full view (top and bottom halves) and limited view (top half only). You'll notice that most Dreamweaver property inspectors use the expander arrow, although in some cases the lower half of the inspector doesn't contain anything useful!

> *tip* You can also jump back and forth between views by double-clicking any gray area in the inspector.

Web-Safe Colors

A common mistake for a newbie Web designer is to assume that you have at least 256 colors to work with on an 8-bit display for a PC or Macintosh. It turns out that only 216 of these colors are truly "Web-safe" in that they look the same on these two platforms with both Navigator and Internet Explorer. These colors contain only the hexadecimal codes 00, 33, 66, 99, CC, and FF in their HTML representations. That is, #FF0033 is a Web-safe color, but #AEF50A is not.

Therefore, when you create images for publishing on the Web, you may want to force your image editing program to use only these 216 colors—the language you'll see will be something like "dither to Web palette" or "Web 216 palette." You may need to perform an export of a true-color file in order to convert it to a Web-safe palette, or you may be able to change the image's mode from RGB or CMYK to indexed color and specify a Web palette then.

You can stick with true-color images (JPEG or PNG only) if you prefer, but they may not look great when viewed on a PC or Mac that has its video mode set to 256 colors (also known as "8-bit color"). It's not a bad idea to preview your pages on such a machine, if possible, before uploading them to your Web server.

When you create your own colors in Dreamweaver, for example for the page background, you'll usually click a color box that displays Dreamweaver's "color picker." You can choose a color by clicking it with the cursor, which appears as an eyedropper. (You can also choose a color from the open document, for example, from an image.) The context menu at the color picker's upper-right corner determines the colors you see in the main part of the color picker.

For example, if you choose either the **Color Cubes** or **Continuous Tone** palette, shown here, the colors that appear are all Web-safe. The only difference between these palettes is how the colors are laid out.

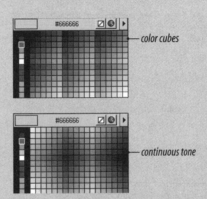

color cubes

continuous tone

If you choose **Windows OS**, or **MacOS**, or **Grayscale** in the context menu, then Dreamweaver displays the 256 colors native to that operating system when it is operating in 8-bit mode. The Windows and Macintosh 8-bit system palettes are quite different. Someof these colors are not Web-safe, but you can choose **Snap to Web Safe** in the context menu to have Dreamweaver choose the nearest Web-safe colors. (UNIX systems use an altogether different color palette. Dreamweaver doesn't give you a "UNIX-safe" palette.)

Finally, you may notice the little color wheel icon at the upper right of the color picker, just left of the context menu arrow. If you click this icon, Dreamweaver displays the *system color picker*, which looks different dependingon the operating system you're running. In Windows, the system color picker is a fairly confusing affair that lets you choose colors based on RGB numbers or on HSL (hue, saturation, and lightness) numbers. On the Mac (OS9), the system color picker is a more intuitive dialog box that lets you use CMYK, Crayon, HSL, HSV (hue, saturation and value), HTML, and RGB scales. The only "Web-safe" system color picker is the HTML scale on the Mac platform.

steps Create An Image Link

You may want to take the user somewhere when she clicks on an image. If you want your image to sport a single link to a file or anchor, this page shows you how; if you want your image to host multiple links, then see Create An Image Map, on pages 65 and 66; and if you want your image to link to a target location in a frameset, check out Build A Simple Frameset, on pages 112 and 113 in Chapter 7.

> **tip** When you use images as links, consider whether their linked nature will be obvious to the user. The user can always tell if an image is a link by mousing over it, but if there's no obvious reason to do that, the user may never know an image "does" something unless you provide a clue.

1 choose make link
Right-click (Win) or **control**-click (Mac) an image to display its context menu and choose **Make Link**. The **Select File** dialog box appears.

2 choose link type
In the **Relative To** drop-down list in the **Select File** dialog box, choose either **Document** or **Site Root**. Normally, you would choose **Document**, so that your page's HTML code refers to the linked file's location with respect to the HTML file's location. For more, see the Tip on page 57.

3 find target
If you want the image link to take the user to a different file, use the **Look In** pop-up menu (Win) or folder list (Mac) to navigate to the folder that contains the target file and then click the filename to select it. If you specify a location outside the site root, Dreamweaver offers to copy the file into your site root folder.

4 specify anchor (optional)
If you want your image to point to a named anchor within the chosen document, type the name of that anchor (with its leading pound sign #) in the **File Name** field, right after the filename. In my case, for example, if I wanted to point to an anchor named **paragraph3**, the target would be **AcmeFaq2.htm#paragraph3**. See page 24 in Chapter 2, Create A Link, for more on anchors.

> **tip** You can also use the **Image** property inspector to create a link to an anchor by dragging the **Point-to-File** icon to the right of the **Link** field onto the desired anchor in the document window. See The Image Property Inspector on pages 60 through 63 for details.

5 select target
Click **Select** (Win) or **Open** (Mac) to choose the link target you want. The **Select File** dialog box vanishes, and the image appears in the document window.

> **tip** Once you've created a link, you can change it at any time. Right-click (Win) or **control**-click (Mac) the image and choose **Change Link**. This menu also lets you choose **Remove Link**.

1 choose make link

2 choose link type *3 find target* *4 specify anchor* *5 select target*

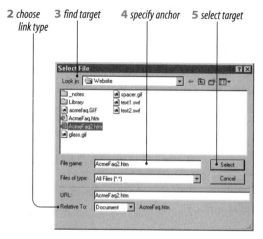

An *image map* hosts multiple links, so that your page takes the user different places depending on which part of the image (that is, which *hotspot*) he clicks. Image maps download more slowly than ordinary text hyperlinks, but they're higher on the coolness scale, and they can be both more fun and more friendly. For example, the different parts of the image can guide the user as to what happens when clicking them. Also, image maps can help internationalize your site because they don't rely as much on words for navigation. Just make sure that you let the user know when you use an image to host an image map, for example, by providing a line of text adjacent to it.

1 select image

The usual way is to click it. When selected, the image appears with a border and resizing handles.

2 open image property inspector

Choose **Window→Properties** if the **Image** property inspector isn't already open. Or right-click (**control**-click on the Mac) the image and choose **Properties**.

3 expand inspector

You need to work with the **Image** property inspector's lower half in order to create an image map. If that lower half isn't already on display, click the little expander arrow in the inspector's lower-right corner.

4 name map

Type a name in the **Map** field. Make sure that it's different from any other image maps you have named.

5 pick hotspot creation tool

The hotspot creation tools appear just below the **Map** field, and they number three: *rectangular, oval,*

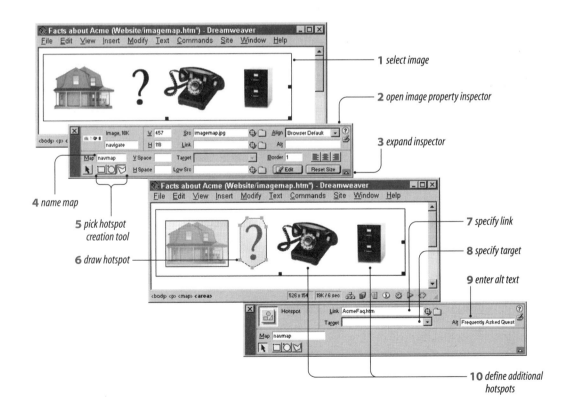

1 *select image*

2 *open image property inspector*

3 *expand inspector*

4 *name map*

5 *pick hotspot creation tool*

6 *draw hotspot*

7 *specify link*

8 *specify target*

9 *enter alt text*

10 *define additional hotspots*

and *polygon*. (That last one should be "polygonal," but you get the drift.) Click the tool that most nearly matches the shape of the first hotspot you want to create.

6 draw hotspot

The drawing technique varies depending on which tool you chose in step 5. If you clicked the rectangular or oval tool, you draw the hotspot with a click-and-drag technique. If you clicked the polygon tool, you click once at each vertex (point) of the polygon. Don't worry if your hotspot isn't perfect, because you can edit its position, size, and shape using the arrow tool. You move a hotspot by clicking inside its border and dragging the hotspot to a new location. You move a hotspot precisely 10 pixels by holding down **shift** and pressing an arrow key; omit the **shift** key to move 1 pixel at a time. Resize or reshape a hotspot by clicking it and then clicking and dragging any of its resize handles.

7 specify link

You have three options: type the name of the linked file in the **Link** field, click the folder icon to browse for a file using the **Select File** dialog box, or click and drag the **Point-to-File** icon to point to a file in the site window or to a named anchor in any open document window. (If you can't see named anchors but you think they should be there, check the setting of **View**➡**Visual Aids**➡**Invisible Elements** and make sure that it has a check mark by it.)

8 specify target (optional)

If the linked file uses frames and has multiple named windows, type the name of the window in the **Target** field of the Hotspot property inspector or choose a frame from the pop-up menu. If the menu doesn't show frames that you think should exist, you may not have named them, in which case you should do so (see Chapter 7 for details).

9 enter alt text (optional)

This step is optional, but recommended, because some browsers display a *tooltip* containing the alt (alternative) text when the user points the cursor over a hotspot.

10 define additional hotspots

Repeat steps 5 through 9 until no more spots remain for you to make hot. Consider that users can become confused if an image map contains any "cold" spots. Even if part of the image is supposed to be "dead," consider attaching a behavior to the hotspot that displays a pop-up message saying "This part of the image doesn't do anything." Chapter 12 explains behaviors and how to associate them with links.

> **tip** You can apply *behaviors* to hotspots (see The Behaviors Panel on pages 192 and 193 in Chapter 12), for example, to create a disjoint rollover (a pop-up graphic that appears when you mouse over the hotspot). In this sense, hotspots act just like separate images.

Client-Side Versus Server-Side Maps

Image maps come in two flavors: *client-side* and *server-side*. When you make a client-side image map, all the information needed to present and process the links is in the HTML file, and the browser does the work of interpreting the user's click. A server-side image map uses a separate map file, stored on a Web server, to define the links; the server, not the browser, interprets the user's click.

Which type is better? Client-side image maps are generally faster because they require less network communication. Client-side image maps do require a Version 2 or later browser, but that's not too restrictive.

When you create an image map with Dreamweaver, it's a client-side image map; if you want a server-side map, you have to code it manually. If you do so, Dreamweaver won't disrupt your HTML, and it's okay to use both types of image map on the same page.

Make A Navigation Bar

A *navigation bar* is a horizontal or vertical graphic with discrete sections that take you to different pages when you click the sections. Each section acts like a button: It has a label and an associated action. Navigation bars can be interactive, too, with each section changing appearance when you mouse over it or click it.

Navigation bars often look like a single image that's been sliced into sections. In fact, you can make them in exactly that way, by slicing an image into separate files (say, in Fireworks) and using Dreamweaver to reassemble those files into the navigation bar. This method has an advantage over creating multiple hotspots on a single image: The image slices download one at a time, making the download "feel" like it's occurring more quickly. Dreamweaver's built-in navigation bar command uses the each-section-is-a-separate-file method.

1 select insert navigation bar

This icon appears on the objects panel. You can also choose **Insert➡Interactive Images➡ Navigation Bar** from the menu. Either way, the **Insert Navigation Bar** dialog box appears.

2 name element

An *element* of a navigation bar is a collection of one or more images representing different states of the same button (unclicked, clicked, and so on). You can define each element, one at a time, in the order that you want them to appear. Give the first element a name that describes its link function, such as *home*. The name should be unique in the site.

3 select up image

The **Up Image** is the graphic as it appears before the user clicks the button. This is the only mandatory state for a navigation bar as the swapping of one image for another is optional. Click **Browse** to navigate to the correct image file (which you've already created in Fireworks or some other image editor).

4 set other image states (optional)

The **Over Image** is the graphic that appears when the user places the cursor over the button. The **Down Image** is the graphic that appears when the user clicks it. The **Over While Down Image** is the graphic that appears when the user has already clicked the button and then mouses over it later. If your button links the user to a different page, you would not use an **Over While Down Image**.

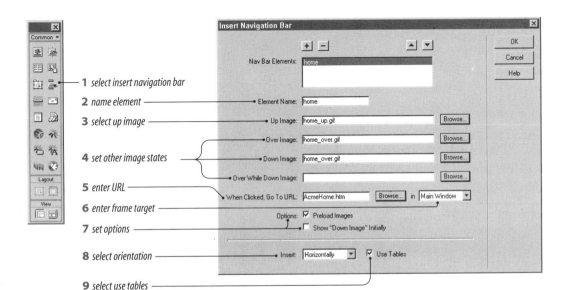

1 *select insert navigation bar*
2 *name element*
3 *select up image*
4 *set other image states*
5 *enter URL*
6 *enter frame target*
7 *set options*
8 *select orientation*
9 *select use tables*

Make the **Over Image** brighter or more intense than the **Up Image**, to let the user know that the button is "armed." Similarly, make the **Over While Down Image** duller or less intense to let the user know that clicking the button again doesn't do anything useful.

5 enter URL

Key in a URL for the linked file manually or click the **Browse** button to navigate to the file.

6 enter frame target (optional)

If your page uses frames, specify the frame in which you want the file specified in step 7 to open.

7 set options

You normally check **Preload Images** so that the images all download when the user opens the page to prevent delays when the user interacts with the navigation bar. Tell Dreamweaver to "push" the button when it first appears, indicating that the user is already at that location, by checking **Show "Down Image" Initially**.

8 select orientation

Use the **Insert** pop-up menu to specify whether you want the navigation bar to appear **Horizontally** or **Vertically** on the page.

> Most sites use a horizontal navigation bar along the top edge of the home page. If you go vertical, make sure that your navigation bar doesn't extend so far down that part of it may not show up in a typically sized browser window.

9 select use tables (optional)

Normally, tell Dreamweaver to make the navigation bar using the table format by checking the **Use Tables** box. Doing so makes the navigation bar easier to modify later.

10 add another image

Click the **+** button at the top of the dialog box and repeat steps 2 through 7 until done.

11 click OK

The navigation bar appears in the document window. You can edit your navigation bar at any time with **Modify→Navigation Bar**. You can copy it to other pages with **Edit→Copy** or make it a feature of every page by adding it to a template.

10 *add another image*   **11** *click OK*

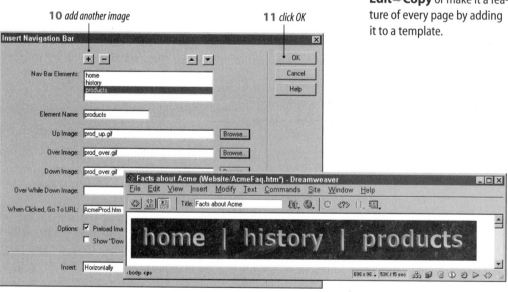

Edit & Update A Placed Image

Dreamweaver is many things, but an image editor isn't one of them. However, Dreamweaver 4 has made life a little easier for the beleaguered Web designer. You still have to jump back and forth between Dreamweaver and the image editor of your choice if you want to edit the images you put onto your Web pages, but with Dreamweaver 4, you don't have to jump quite as far.

In this section, I demonstrate how to tell Dreamweaver what image editor you want to use with which types of image files, and then I show how the edit-update-save-return cycle actually works in practice. (The same basic technique also works for specifying a text editor, if you don't like Dreamweaver's built-in **Code Inspector**, but that discussion appears in Chapter 15.)

1 choose preferences

Choose **Edit➞Preferences** or press **ctrl+U** (**command-U** on the Mac) to display the **Preferences** dialog box.

2 select file types/editors

The **Preferences** dialog box is a many-splendored one whose right side changes depending on what you click in the category list at the left. For my purposes here, click **File Types/Editors** in the category list.

3 choose extension

In the **Extensions** column, choose the file type for which you'd like to specify a preferred external image editor. (Yes, you can specify one program for GIFs and another for JPEGs!)

4 add editor

Click the + sign above the **Editors** column to display the **Select External Editor** dialog box and navigate to the program you'd like to use with the file type you specified in step 3.

5 add alternate editor (optional)

You can repeat step 4 if you'd like the option to use more than one editor with a given file type.

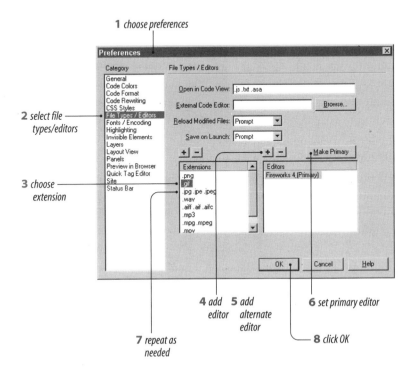

1 choose preferences

2 select file types/editors

3 choose extension

4 add editor *5 add alternate editor* *6 set primary editor*

8 click OK

7 repeat as needed

6 set primary editor

If you specified more than one editing program, pick which one you want to use when you double-click an image file in the Dreamweaver document window.

7 repeat as needed

Repeat steps 3 through 6 for as many file types as you use regularly. (Normally, you'd specify a maximum of three, for GIF, JPEG, and PNG.)

8 click OK

This action closes the **Preferences** dialog box and saves your settings to disk so that Dreamweaver will use them from that point forward. Now, you'll see how this feature works in real life.

9 activate image

In the document window, with a page open containing at least one image, press and hold **ctrl** (Win) or **command** (Mac) and double-click the image. Alternatively, you can click the image and then click the **Edit** button in the **Image** property inspector.

10 edit image in external editor

Dreamweaver fires up the external editor you specified as the primary editor for the file type of the image you activated and loads the image into the

editing window. Here, you can make whatever changes to the image you want to make, such as applying a filter, changing the palette, resizing the image, and so on. The Dreamweaver program remains loaded in memory while you're using the external image editor. Therefore, using this technique may require more system memory than using the programs serially.

> *tip* If you specified more than one image editing program in the **Preferences** dialog box (6), you can right-click (Win) or **control**-click (Mac) the image and choose the program you want from the context menu. Note that the context menu works with many Web page objects in Dreamweaver, and the commands it offers depend on the actions that you can perform with that type of object (hence the name "context menu").

> *tip* If the procedure described in step 10 seems like a lot of effort just to resize a graphic when you can stretch or shrink the image within Dreamweaver, by selecting it and manipulating the resize handles, be aware that you're better off resizing images in an image-editing program. The image will look better and be smaller if you use a tool such as Fireworks or Photoshop. These programs have more sophisticated algorithms for resampling the pixels in a resized image so it looks more like the original.

11 click done

In my example, Fireworks presents a **Done** button that saves the edited image and closes Fireworks, returning you to Dreamweaver (which has remained in memory). Other image editors may simply require you to save the file and exit as you would normally.

> *tip* If you're using PNG graphics, clicking **Done** in Fireworks updates both the PNG source file and the JPEG or GIF file used by Dreamweaver for the Web page.

9 *activate image*

10 *edit image in external editor*

11 *click done*

Insert Fireworks HTML

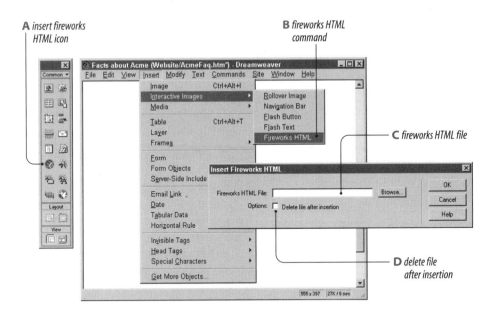

A *insert fireworks HTML icon*

B *fireworks HTML command*

C *fireworks HTML file*

D *delete file after insertion*

Fireworks, Macromedia's Web-oriented image editing program, has the capability of generating its own HTML code. For example, you (or a colleague) may have used Fireworks to create images in HTML tables or to create image maps with associated hotspots. The **Fireworks HTML** command makes bringing such HTML-enriched images into Dreamweaver a piece of cake—handy if you'd rather not spend time re-creating those tables or image maps in Dreamweaver.

> *tip* The **Fireworks HTML** command also brings in any JavaScript programming associated with a Fireworks HTML file.

A insert Fireworks HTML icon

The **Insert Fireworks HTML** icon on the **Common** objects panel is the fastest way to display the **Insert Fireworks HTML** dialog box.

> *tip* You'll find that you generally want to leave the objects panel open at all times so that these handy icons are at the ready. You can even modify the objects panel's appearance and functionality, as Chapter 16 explains.

B Fireworks HTML command

You can also use the menu command **Insert➥ Interactive Images➥Fireworks HTML**. No corresponding keyboard shortcut exists. (Note that there's not necessarily anything interactive about a static table of images, so don't let the menu command confuse you.)

C Fireworks HTML file

The **Fireworks HTML File** field is where you specify the file you want to insert. You can type the location here or click the **Browse** button to navigate your computer's file system. Generally, I suggest using the button, because it eliminates the possibility of typographical errors.

D delete file after insertion

The **Delete File After Insertion** check box instructs Dreamweaver to get rid of the original Fireworks HTML code after bringing it into Dreamweaver, although Dreamweaver leaves the original PNG file or files alone. (Keep in mind that typically, when you insert Fireworks HTML, the original Fireworks file uses the PNG format, even though the HTML file that Fireworks generated from the PNG file uses GIF or JPEG images.)

✎steps Optimize Graphics With Fireworks

One of the more important activities any Web designer performs is optimizing graphics for the right compromise between beauty, size, and download time. Gorgeous images that dominate the page may look great once downloaded, but a busy or impatient dial-up user who leaves your site after waiting "too long" will never see them. And at the rate that DSL and cable modem providers are going bankrupt, assuming that everyone has access to a broadband Internet link may be a hasty generalization.

Even images that are small in pixel size—such as a 100x100 continuous-tone JPEG file with a very high-quality setting—can occupy many kilobytes and take a while to download over a slow link. Conversely, larger images can still be fairly small in terms of kilobytes if carefully optimized through file format choice, palette control, and quality settings.

Dreamweaver makes image optimization a simple and convenient chore if you happen to use Fireworks as your graphics editor. Fireworks has evolved into a competent program, and you may already have it if you purchased the "Dreamweaver/Fireworks Studio" bundle. You can still perform optimization with a different graphics editor, such as Adobe Photoshop; you just have to navigate manually to the relevant dialog boxes in that editor.

1 select image

In the document window, click the image you want to optimize. You'll see a border appear around the image as well as the resize handles (which you shouldn't, in general, use!).

2 choose to optimize image

The specific command to use is **Commands➡ Optimize Image in Fireworks**; no keyboard shortcut exists. Dreamweaver launches Fireworks, loads the image into Fireworks, and pulls up the **Optimize** dialog box—all automatically. (Again, using Fireworks and Dreamweaver together like this puts greater demand for memory on your system; if the computer seems to bog down significantly, consider adding RAM. Dreamweaver uses a lot of memory, and Fireworks does as well.)

3 click 4-up

I usually like to see four different optimizations so that I can compare the effect of different palette choices. You could click the **2-up** button if that feels like too much information.

4 choose palettes

By tweaking the palettes in the pop-up menus for each image, you can see how the image changes visually, and you can see how the file size and estimated download times change, too. For example, the upper-left image looks fairly ratty compared to

1 select image

2 choose to optimize image

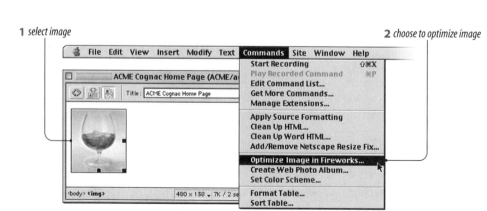

the lower-right image, but the file size difference is only that between 4.06K and 6.49K.

5 change file format (optional)

You can change the file format from GIF to JPEG (or vice versa) in the **Format** pop-up menu to the left. This command changes the data in the active image preview window.

6 set image dimensions (optional)

If you want to resize the image — for example, because none of the palette optimizations you perform in step 3 gets the download speed as quick as you want it — click the **File** tab, where you can rescale the image.

7 adjust other settings

Set the other options at the left of the dialog box as you want them. For example, you could tweak the

quality of a JPEG file or add a bit of lossy compression (**Loss** field) to a GIF file. (Lossy compression is compression that degrades the quality of the image to some degree.)

8 select best preview

When you're done experimenting with optimization settings, click the image preview you like best.

9 click update

Click the **Update** button to save the image with your new settings, update the file in your Dreamweaver site folder, and return to the Dreamweaver document window. You can now see how the changes you made affect the look of your Web page. (Click the **Preview/ Debug in Browser** button on the toolbar to get a more accurate look, though.)

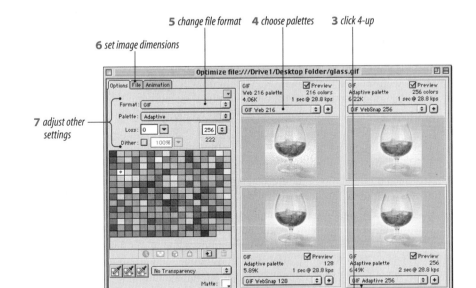

5 *change file format*   **4** *choose palettes*   **3** *click 4-up*

6 *set image dimensions*

7 *adjust other settings*

8 *select best preview*

9 *click update*

The Create Web Photo Album Command

A *create web photo album command*

B *title*

C *subheading*

D *other info*

E *source folder*

F *destination folder*

G *thumbnail size*

I *columns*

J *thumbnail format*

K *photo format*

M *navigation page*

H *filename toggle*

L *scale*

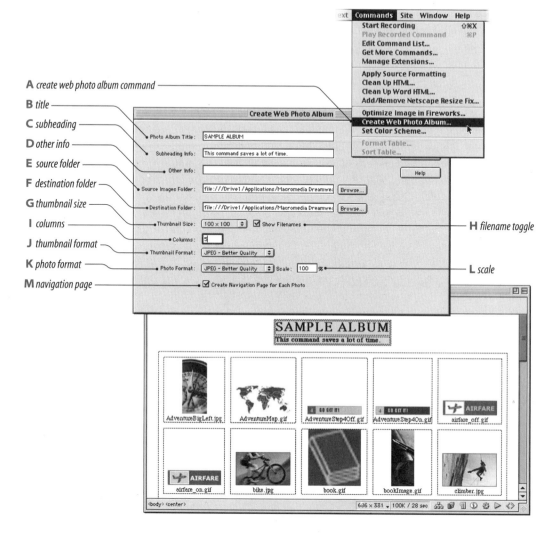

Presenting a collection of photos in a user-friendly way on a Web page is no small task. The considerate method is to create thumbnails (small versions) of each photograph and then set the thumbnail to link to a larger version of the photo when the user clicks the thumbnail. Laborious? Yes, but Dreamweaver 4 takes away some of the pain.

Macromedia has added a **Create Web Photo Album** command to Dreamweaver

to semi-automate the process of creating such a page. This command requires that you have Fireworks installed on your computer as well as Dreamweaver; Fireworks handles the image manipulation, and Dreamweaver (with a little help from JavaScript) handles the Web page creation.

A create web photo album command
Sorry, shortcut fans, by default this command's only available on the menu, via **Commands➡Create**

Web Photo Album. If you really must have a keyboard shortcut for it, then you can create one by choosing **Edit➡Keyboard Shortcuts** and defining one there; Chapter 16 provides all the gory details.

B title

Give your album a name in the **Photo Album Title** field; Dreamweaver will display the title at the top of your thumbnail page.

C subheading

You can add a line that will appear directly beneath the title, in the **Subheading Info** field. Dreamweaver and Fireworks handle the formatting, although you can change it after the fact if you like.

D other info

If a subheading just isn't enough description for you, add a second line, in the **Other Info** field.

E source folder

Specify the folder containing your source images in the **Source Images Folder** field. Dreamweaver expects you to have all your original images in a single folder, ready to go, by the time you issue the **Create Web Photo Album** command. Web photo albums work best if your original images are all the same size, and square (or nearly so).

> **tip** You may only use GIF, JPG, JPEG, PNG, PSD, TIF, or TIFF files with this command. However, all files in the source folder need not be the same type.

F destination folder

Specify the target folder where the modified images and their related HTML Web page files will go, either by keying its location into the **Destination Folder** field or by clicking the **Browse** button next to that field and navigating to the folder in the **Choose A Folder** dialog box. If this folder you specify doesn't already exist, Dreamweaver will create it for you.

> **tip** To avoid all risk of overwriting existing files, create a new destination folder each time you make a Web photo album.

G thumbnail size

Specify the dimensions (in pixels) of the thumbnail images that the script will create, using the **Thumbnail Size** drop-down list. Your choices are **36x36**, **72x72**, **100x100**, **144x144**, and **200x200**. If your original images aren't square, Fireworks will scale them proportionally so that they fit within the square thumbnail space.

H filename toggle

Decide whether you want Dreamweaver to display filenames and set the **Show Filenames** check box accordingly. I usually clear this option to reduce clutter. Selecting it can also cause confusion, in that you see the original filenames, even though the Web photo album may have changed their formats (for example, from GIF to JPEG).

I columns

In the **Columns** field, specify how many columns your thumbnail page should use. If the results look bad, build a new album with a different number of columns and/or a different thumbnail size.

J thumbnail format

In the **Thumbnail Format** pop-up menu, specify the image format for your thumbnails. Your choices, in order from smallest file size to largest, are **GIF WebSnap 128**, **GIF WebSnap 256**, **JPEG-Smaller File**, and **JPEG-Better Quality**.

K photo format

In the **Photo Format** field, specify the image format for your full-size images. Your choices are the same as for the thumbnail format, but you can choose the two formats independently. The **Create Web Photo Album** command generates new versions of your source images all in the same format, a step that may sacrifice some quality. (It helps to choose a format that matches the majority of your original images.)

L scale

Set a percentage value in the **Scale** field to resize all your original images proportionally for display on the Web. Note that Dreamweaver doesn't let you specify different scale percentages for different images; this is an across-the-board setting.

> *tip* Remember that the script will modify your original images to match the photo format that you select (K). So, even if you specify 100 percent for the scale, the images that Dreamweaver will ultimately publish probably won't look exactly the same as your originals.

M navigation page

If you want your thumbnails to link to a separate page hosting the full-size graphic as well as Home, Next, and Back buttons, select the **Create Navigation Page for Each Photo** check box. Leaving this cleared makes your thumbnails link to a simple page containing the full-size image.

Fireworks Versus Photoshop

So, which is the better image editor—Fireworks or Photoshop? Once you understand some of the key differences between the two programs, you can make your own choices (Of course, these aren't the only two image-editing programs available, but they're the two most likely for Dreamweaver designers to be using.)

Purpose

Macromedia designed Fireworks as a Web graphics tool. Adobe designed Photoshop as a general-purpose graphics tool (although the company has addressed Photoshop's Web graphics shortcomings with a newer program, ImageReady, that now comes bundles with Photoshop). So, you will find Fireworks to be a bit more Web-oriented than Photoshop. If you sometimes create images for print output as well as Web publishing, the Photoshop-plus-ImageReady combo may be more suitable for you. Another alternative is to use Fireworks for Web page graphics work and Photoshop for print work.

Learning Curve

If you already know either of these products, that's a strong vote in its favor. If you don't, you'll find Fireworks significantly easier to learn because its user interface is very

similar to Dreamweaver's. (Macromedia is putting a lot of effort into making the user interface between Dreamweaver, Fireworks, and Flash as consistent as possible.) Photoshop's user interface, while elegant and richly layered, is way different from Dreamweaver's. It also contains many tools and options oriented toward print media.

Add-ons

Photoshop has been around longer than Fireworks, and a wealth of third-party add-ons (mostly filters, for special effects) exists in the marketplace. So, if you want the greatest possible artistic freedom, you should probably use Photoshop, as augmented by these add-on components. Fireworks used to work with Photoshop filters, but as of Photoshop Version 6, Adobe changed the code format for its filters so that they don't work with Fireworks any more. If you have an earlier version of Photoshop, you may want to install it so that Fireworks can have access to the filters. Also, you may want to explore filters that specifically work with Fireworks, such as Eye Candy 4000 and Xenofex from Alien Skin Software.

Inventory

If you already have lots of images in PSD (Photoshop) format, then using Photoshop may be more

convenient; ditto regarding PNG and Fireworks. True, both programs can read both formats, but annoying little incompatibilities may remain.

Synergy

If you're likely to use features such as the **Create Web Photo Album** command, **Insert Fireworks HTML**, **Optimize Image in Fireworks**, and so on, use Fireworks for its superior integration with Dreamweaver. If you don't, and if you don't plan to do a lot of image editing after dropping graphics into your Web site, then choose an image editor based on other criteria.

Editability

Fireworks images are sometimes easier to edit later, because Fireworks uses a vector model for image creation, whereas Photoshop (with certain exceptions) uses a bitmap model. If you expect to do a lot of tweaking to your images, you may find Fireworks' vector-based engine will save you some time down the road. If you go with Photoshop for other reasons, spend time mastering its layers feature to maximize image editability.

Cost

Fireworks is less expensive than Photoshop, especially in a bundle with Dreamweaver (called the Dreamweaver 4, Fireworks 4 Studio).

Design Tables

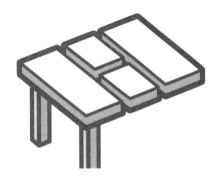

Given the Internet's origins in the scientific and academic communities, the fact that HTML includes extensive support for *tables* comes as no surprise. Tables let you present a set of ordered data in a neat row-and-column format.

Today, designers have adapted tables to serve another purpose: aligning nontabular page elements to look good and be easy to follow. Dreamweaver 4 facilitates this use of tables in its new *layout view*. Layout view is handy, but you have to know when to use it versus the original *standard view*. So, this chapter begins by exploring the two views and then moves to the details of table creation and formatting.

Despite what you may have heard, formatting tables isn't difficult, just tedious. The good news is that nearly all browsers display tables correctly. So, once you master them, you can design pages that look good to a wide audience.

Layout View

A *layout view*

B *standard view*

E *layout table tab*   **F** *column header*

G *column header menu*

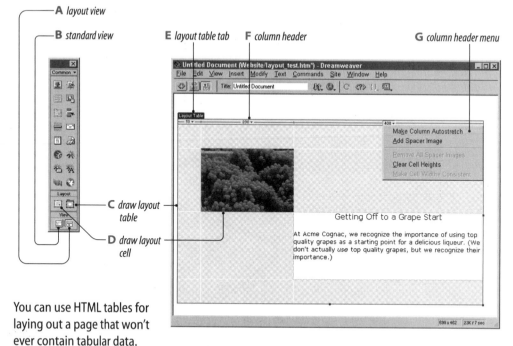

C *draw layout table*

D *draw layout cell*

You can use HTML tables for laying out a page that won't ever contain tabular data. For example, you can use a table to beautify an HTML form (see Enhance A Form With A Table on page 103 of Chapter 6). Dreamweaver 4 introduces *layout view* to hide some of the complexity of HTML tables when a designer wants to use them for page layout.

A layout view

Click this icon on the objects panel to switch to layout view quickly. Alternatively, you can choose **View➡Table View➡Layout View** or press **ctrl+F6** (**command-F6** on the Mac). The first time you select layout view, you see an informative dialog box that you can suppress for the future by clicking a check box.

In layout view, you can draw tables and cells visually, the property inspectors are a little simpler, and you can create *autostretch* columns that automatically change width to fill the browser window. However, you can't perform operations such as splitting and merging cells in layout view, nor can you insert or delete columns and rows.

B standard view

When you need to tweak a table in more detail than layout view permits, click here to switch to standard view. You can also switch to standard view by choosing **View➡Table View➡Standard View** or pressing **ctrl+shift+F6** (**command-shift-F6** on the Mac).

If you need maximum control over table attributes, you can always switch back to standard view with a single click. In fact, you can switch back and forth between the two views as often as you need to. Like most designers, I use layout view to draw my tables and cells and then standard view for any fine tuning. If I'm designing an actual table of data, I find it faster to work in standard view from the outset.

C draw layout table

You can draw the outline of your layout table by clicking this icon, which is only active in layout view, and then drawing a rectangle in the document window. In layout view, the table border is green by default, but you can change that by choosing

Edit→Preferences, selecting **Layout View** in the **Category** list, and specifying a new **Table Outline** color. You can create multiple tables per page, but they can't overlap. You can also create a table within a table—that is, a *nested* table—using this icon, although splitting cells in standard view may be a simpler way to achieve the same effect. The **Draw Layout Table** icon has no menu command equivalent and is not available in standard view.

> *tip* In layout view, you can draw a table only in a new document that contains no content, or at the bottom of a document that does contain content. In standard view, by contrast, you can place the insertion point wherever you want and insert a table with the **Insert→Table** command (a command that's not available in layout view).

D draw layout cell

Click this icon to draw a cell inside an existing table. Cell borders are blue by default, turning red when you pass the cursor over them to indicate you can select the cell by clicking. If no table exists when you draw a cell, Dreamweaver creates one for you that fills the width of the document window. Create a cell wherever you plan to insert content; the gray areas of a layout table do not accept content (although they do if you switch to standard view). The **Draw Layout Cell** icon has no menu command equivalent and is not available in standard view.

> *tip* You don't have to be exact with the mouse if you want a cell to line up at a table's edge. Get within 8 pixels, and Dreamweaver will snap the cell into place. To disable snapping, hold down **alt** (Win) or **option** (Mac) while drawing or moving the cell.

E layout table tab

A nice aspect of working in layout view is the **Layout Table** tab at the table's upper-left corner. Click the tab to select the table. If you find the tabs distracting, you can turn them off with the **View→Table View→ Show Layout Table Tabs** toggle (only available in layout view).

F column header

Another good layout view feature is the *column header*. This feature shows you the width of the column in pixels, or a zigzag line if you've made the column autostretch, in which case the column expands to fill the browser window.

> *tip* You may also see cases in which the column header shows two numbers, one in quotation marks. The number in quotes is the one that the underlying HTML code specifies, but the other number is the true, or *effective*, column width. The effective width could be larger than the HTML column width value, for example, if a cell in the column contains an image that's wider than the HTML value. An HTML table won't crop an image.
>
> Or, you could enter a line of text that's wider than the HTML value and specify the **No Wrap** attribute for that cell; again, HTML tries to display cell content even if it means overriding the specified column width. The column header menu (G) has a **Make Cell Widths Consistent** command that changes the HTML value to reflect reality, at which point the column header only shows one number.

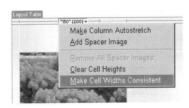

G column header menu

Click a column header (F) to display a menu of choices for common layout operations. (You can access these commands from the property inspector and menu, also. See The Table Property Inspectors on pages 80 through 82 for the complete lowdown.) Note that you can't actually select a column in layout view, even though you can change some of its attributes with the column header menu.

The Table Property Inspector, Standard View

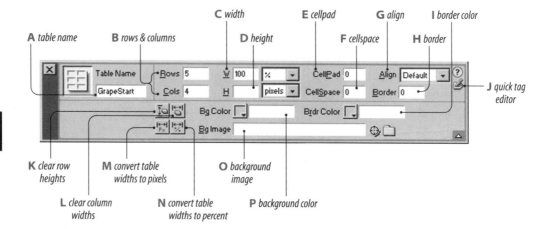

A table name
B rows & columns
C width
D height
E cellpad
F cellspace
G align
H border
I border color
J quick tag editor
K clear row heights
L clear column widths
M convert table widths to pixels
N convert table widths to percent
O background image
P background color

You get two versions of the **Table** property inspector: one for standard view and another for layout view. Macromedia has tried to make each inspector relevant for the tasks appropriate to each view. The following pages take a look at both versions.

The two versions of the property inspector aren't always consistent, and some options don't exactly match the wording of their menu equivalents. Also, be aware that you can sometimes choose a menu command in layout view when the property inspector doesn't give you an icon for that function.

To display the **Table** property inspector in either view, choose **Window→Properties** and select a table in one of the following ways: Click the right or bottom table border; click in the table and then click the **<table>** tag on the status bar; click anywhere in the table and choose **Modify→Table→Select Table**; or click the **Layout Table** tab if you're in layout view.

> **tip** The keyboard shortcut for the **Select Table** command, **ctrl+A** (Win) or **command-A** (Mac), doesn't work as advertised. It selects the *cell* in which you click, not the table. Press the shortcut again, however, and Dreamweaver will then select the table.

A table name

You can name a table only in standard view. If you plan to do anything with the table from a script, give it a unique and descriptive name.

B rows & columns

Available only in standard view, these options let you set the number of rows and columns you want in your table. If you're modifying an existing table, Dreamweaver adds columns at the right and rows at the bottom. You can also add columns and rows to a table with the **Modify→Table** insert commands if you want to place them elsewhere; Dreamweaver will add a column immediately to the left of the currently selected column, and it will add a row immediately above the current row.

> **tip** You can also add a row to the end of a table by clicking in the last cell and pressing the **tab** key.

C width

In standard view, you can only specify width in pixels or as a percentage of the user's browser window width. In layout view, you can specify a pixel width in the **Fixed** field, or you can click **Autostretch** to make a column expand or shrink to fill the user's browser window. Although you would normally want the rightmost column to be the one to autostretch, in a frameset, you may want to make the center column

The Table Property Inspector, Layout View

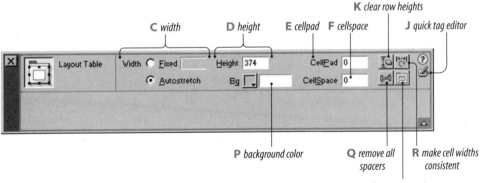

K *clear row heights*

C *width* **D** *height* **E** *cellpad* **F** *cellspace* **J** *quick tag editor*

P *background color* **Q** *remove all spacers* **R** *make cell widths consistent*

S *remove nesting*

autostretch. You can use the *column header menu* (G, page 79) to set a different column as the autostretching column, but only one column per table can autostretch.

> **tip** HTML will expand a column if necessary to accommodate cell content, even if that content exceeds the column's "fixed width."

D height

You can specify your table's height in the **H** field (standard view) or the **Height** field (layout view), or you can just let the browser size it automatically and keep your HTML code a bit cleaner.

E cell padding

Cell padding is the pixel distance between cell content and cell boundary. For example, if you're using a border to highlight cell boundaries, you typically set the **CellPad** field to a positive value to provide some "air" between text and border.

F cell spacing

Cell spacing is the pixel distance between adjacent cell boundaries. Normally you adjust cell padding (E) before entering a value in the **CellSpace** field. You can combine the two values, and different border widths, to achieve various visual effects.

> **tip** You can't change cell padding or spacing on a cell-by-cell basis; these values are global for the entire table.

G align

Available only in standard view, you won't use this field often, because you rarely put a table in the same HTML paragraph as other content. If you do, though, here's where you control how the table aligns itself with such content. Your options are **Default**, **Left**, **Center**, and **Right**.

H border

When you use tables for page layout, you generally don't want a border, so the **Border** field (available only in standard view) would stay at its default of zero pixels. When you create a data table rather than a layout table, borders can make the data easier to read, especially for tables with more than two columns. A cleaner alternative to borders is increasing cell padding (E), but that does require more space.

I border color

In standard view, you can choose the table's border color in the **Brdr Color** field by clicking the pop-up menu square and selecting a color from the Dreamweaver color picker. You can set the border color for individual cells separately by selecting a cell and changing the **Brdr** field in the standard view **Cell** property inspector (see The Cell Property Inspectors on page 83).

J quick tag editor

Click this icon to view or modify the HTML tag for the selected table.

```
Edit Tag: <table width="100%" border="0"
          cellpadding="0" cellspacing="0"
          name="GrapeStart">
```

K clear row heights

Click this icon (or choose **Modify→Table→Clear Cell Heights**) to remove the height attribute for all cells in the table, effectively collapsing table rows to fit the content.

L clear column widths

In standard view, the **Clear Column Widths** button wipes out any column width setting you may have made, and columns resize to the minimum width necessary to display their content, taking any cell padding (E) into account. This icon performs the same function as the **Modify→Table→Clear Cell Widths** command. In layout view, you can execute the menu command, even though no equivalent button exists on the **Table** property inspector in layout view.

> **tip** The **Clear Cell Widths** command is totally different from the **Make Cell Widths Consistent** command in layout view (S). Unfortunately, they're not both available in the same view, so be aware that you may have to switch views to use the one you want.

M convert table widths to pixels

If you've defined column widths as percentage values and would like to change them to pixel values, click this button (available only in standard view) or choose **Modify→Table→Convert Widths To Pixels**. In layout view, you can run the menu command even though the button doesn't exist on the property inspector.

N convert table widths to percent

If you've defined column widths as pixel values and would like to change them to percentage values, click this button or choose **Modify→Table→Convert Widths To Percent**. Remember, the percentage is

of the table width, not browser window width. In layout view, you can run the menu command even though the button is absent from the property inspector.

O background image

In standard view, you can set a background image by typing in the file path and name; by clicking and dragging the **Point-to-File** icon; or by clicking the folder icon and browsing to the image. You can also set a background image for individual rows, columns, or cells by selecting those objects and specifying an image in the inspector's **Bg** field . (Note that background images don't work right in Netscape 4.75 and earlier.)

P background color

Set a table's background color in either view here. As with a background image, you can also set the background color for individual rows, columns, or cells.

Q remove all spacers

When you make a column autostretch (C) in layout view, Dreamweaver adds *spacer GIFs* to the table to control spacing, because otherwise you can't specify exactly how a browser will resize a table when the user changes the browser window's size. If you decide to convert a layout table to a data table, you can remove the spacer GIFs with this button. In layout view, you can also choose **Remove All Spacer Images** from the column header menu (G, page 79).

R make cell widths consistent

This button reconciles the HTML column width value with the effective column width as determined by the widest content in any column cell. If you see two numbers in the column header in layout view, click this button.

S remove nesting

A *nested* table is a table within a table. To simplify a nested table in layout view, click this button, and the parent table assimilates the nested table's cells.

The Cell Property Inspectors

Property inspectors exist for rows, columns, and individual cells. As with the **Table** property inspector, the **Cell** property inspector varies in form between standard view and layout view; the **Row** and **Column** property

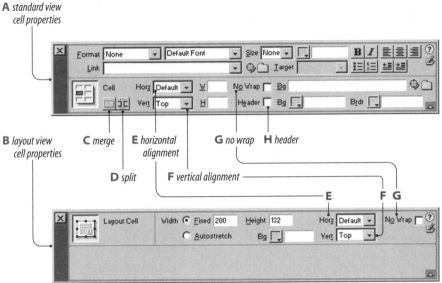

A *standard view cell properties*
B *layout view cell properties*
C *merge*
D *split*
E *horizontal alignment*
F *vertical alignment*
G *no wrap*
H *header*

inspectors are only available in standard view. Row, column, and cell formatting overrides table formatting when two similar settings, such as background or border color, conflict (as long as you format the cell after you format the row or column).

> **tip** To make your HTML code as concise as possible, perform as much formatting at the table level as you can, changing individual rows, columns, or cells only as needed.

To select a cell, click its border in layout view; click in the cell and drag the mouse to the lower right in standard view; or (in either view) hold down **ctrl** (Win) or **command** (Mac) and click inside the cell, or click inside the cell and press **ctrl+A** (Win) or **command-A** (Mac). Select a row in standard view by clicking and dragging across the whole row, or by moving the cursor over the row's left edge until it turns into a selection arrow pointing right and then clicking once. Select a column in standard view the same ways (go to the top to see the arrow).

A standard view cell properties

In standard view, you get a more complete set of properties in the inspector than you do in layout view,

particularly the **Merge** and **Split** buttons and the option to specify both background image and border color.

B layout view cell properties

In layout view, the first three options on the **Cell** property inspector let you adjust the width, height, and background color of the selected cell, just as you would for a table (see C, D, and P on pages 80, 81, and 82). The remaining three options (E through G on the next page) affect the behavior of cell contents.

C merge

In standard view, click this button to merge two or more selected (and adjacent) cells into a single cell. Alternatively, you can choose **Modify→Table→ Merge Cells** or press **ctrl+alt+M** (**command-option-M** on the Mac).

D split

Click here, choose **Modify→Table→Split Cell**, or press **ctrl+alt+S** (**command-option-S** on the Mac) in standard view to split a single cell into two or more cells. The ensuing dialog box lets you choose whether you want to split the cell into rows or columns and how many rows or columns you want to split the cell into. Any cell content stays with the leftmost or uppermost cell after a split.

The Row & Column Property Inspectors

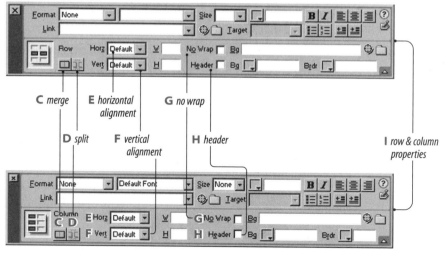

C merge

D split

E horizontal alignment

F vertical alignment

G no wrap

H header

I row & column properties

appropriate column width, given the size of the user's browser window. To force a line of text to stay all on one line, check **No Wrap**.

H header

A *header* row is normally the top row of a table and contains column labels. When you click the **Header** check box in standard view, Dreamweaver center-aligns the text in the selected row, column, or cell and makes it bold.

E horizontal alignment

The **Horz** pop-up menu formats the horizontal alignment of content in the selected row, column, or cell as **Left**, **Center**, **Right**, or **Default**.

F vertical alignment

Use this pop-up menu to specify the vertical alignment of row, column, or cell content. **Middle** is typically the browser default.

G no wrap

Normal table behavior is to wrap lines of text as necessary to achieve what the browser deems is an

I row & column properties

Available only in standard view, the **Row** and **Column** property inspectors contain the same options as the standard view **Cell** property inspector (A). Dreamweaver applies row and column formatting attributes to all cells within the selected row or column, including cells that you have previously formatted. Also note that you can't select rows, columns, or even groups of cells in layout view.

Cut, Copy, & Paste Cells

You can cut, copy, and paste cells easily in Dreamweaver by selecting them and using the **Cut**, **Copy**, and **Paste** commands on the **Edit** menu. (Click in the target cell before pasting.) However, some subtleties exist.

For example, when you cut or copy a cell, you're moving that cell's attributes (such as alignment) as well as its content, whereas when you cut or copy a cell's content, the cell's attributes don't travel with the content. In many cases, you don't really want to copy the entire cell, with all its formatting attributes; you want to copy the content, in which case you should select the content as you would normally select an image or text object and use the **Edit** menu's commands.

Another subtlety is that if you want to cut or copy a group of cells, they must make a rectangle. Selecting a rectangular group of cells is easy in standard view: Just click in the top left cell and drag to the lower left until the cell borders become highlighted. Finally, when you cut every cell in a given row or column, Dreamweaver deletes that row or column. When you perform the paste operation, Dreamweaver will create a new row or column.

The Format Table Command

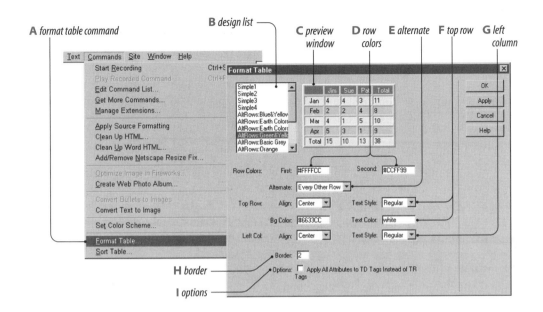

A *format table command*   **B** *design list*   **C** *preview window*   **D** *row colors*   **E** *alternate*   **F** *top row*   **G** *left column*

H *border*

I *options*

The **Format Table** command autoformats your tables to one of several predefined styles.

> **tip** Even if none of the predesigned formats is perfect, choose a close match and then fine-tune the table with the property inspectors or code view.

A format table command
Choose **Commands⇒Format Table** to display the **Format Table** dialog box.

B design list
Here are the available designs.

C preview window
Here's a sample of the selected design (B).

D row colors
You can specify background colors for the first row and the second row. Enter these colors by using the six-character hexadecimal notation. (In case you haven't memorized them all, you can easily get to Dreamweaver's color picker via the **Table** or **Cell** property inspector's **Bg** field.)

E alternate
Choose whether, and how, you'd like the row colors you specified (D) to alternate: **<do not alternate>**, **Every Other Row**, **Every Two Rows**, **Every Three Rows**, or **Every Four Rows**. I especially recommend alternating row colors with wider tables, which are harder to traverse than narrow ones.

F top row
You can use this area to set text alignment, style, color, and a special background color that can differ from the colors you specify in the **Row Colors** section (D).

G left column
Dreamweaver lets you format this column separately from all the others, both in alignment and text style.

H border
Here you can specify the border's pixel width, which should be 0 if you don't want a border at all.

I options
There's only one: **Apply All Attributes to TD Tags Instead of TR Tags**. The option applies attributes to each cell (the **<td>** tags), which adds to the size and complexity of the HTML code.

⬭steps⬭ Build A Table In Layout View

This section presents the main steps involved in creating a *layout table* — that is, a table you create to align or position page elements such as text blocks and images. You can rough out a page much faster in layout view than in standard view, because you draw the layout just as you would draw rectangular areas in a paint program. This example assumes that you're starting with a blank document.

1 set layout view

Click the **Layout View** icon on the objects panel. Alternatively, you can choose **View➡Table View➡Layout View** or press **ctrl+F6** (**command-F6** on the Mac). If you see a dialog box with info about working in layout view, click OK to dismiss it.

2 draw layout cell

Click the **Draw Layout Cell** icon on the objects panel (no menu equivalent here) and then draw a rectangle by clicking and dragging in the document window. (You can draw the table first if you want, but

if you draw a cell, Dreamweaver automatically builds a table around it, saving time.) By default, your cell appears with a blue border; the surrounding table has a green border, and noncontent areas appear gray (You can change these colors in the **Layout View** category of the **Preferences**). Repeat this step for as many layout cells as you think you need.

3 make column autostretch (optional)

Layout view lets you designate one (and only one) column to *autostretch* — that is, expand or contract to fill the user's browser window no matter what size that window may be. Click the column header menu and choose **Make Column Autostretch**. (You can also click the **Autostretch** radio button in the **Table** property inspector.)

4 choose spacer image (optional)

The reason this step is optional is that the dialog box doesn't appear if a) you didn't create an autostretch column in step 3 or b) you've already chosen or

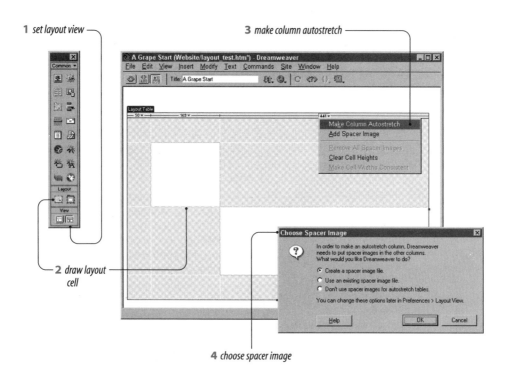

1 *set layout view*

3 *make column autostretch*

2 *draw layout cell*

4 *choose spacer image*

created a spacer image for a given site. If this is the first layout table you've created within the current site, however, you'll see the **Choose Spacer Image** dialog box, and you must tell Dreamweaver what to do. I normally let Dreamweaver create one for me and save it in the site folder with the default name of **spacer.gif**.

A spacer image is nothing more than a single-pixel transparent GIF graphic file that Dreamweaver uses to maintain the dimensions of your layout table. Browsers won't collapse a column that contains a graphic, so your fixed-width columns stay fixed.

5 insert content

Put whatever content you want into the cells you've drawn. The procedure is the same as adding content to a nontabular Web page, with the exception that you click inside the target cell first. If you insert an image that's larger than the cell, Dreamweaver automatically expands the cell to fit the image and adjusts other cells to accommodate the change.

6 move & resize cells (optional)

You can do some fine-tuning by moving and/or resizing the cells you've drawn. Select a cell by mousing over its border until the border turns bright red and then clicking. You can drag the cell to a new position, or resize it by dragging the resize handles. (I *love* this feature of layout view.) Or, after selecting the cell, you can use the arrow keys to move it in one-pixel increments. Hold down **shift** while using the arrow keys to move the cell 10 pixels at once.

7 save & preview

Save your work with **File➡Save** and preview the results with the **Preview/Debug In Browser** icon on the toolbar. Resize the browser window to see how your table behaves under different circumstances. You can switch to standard view to adjust table properties that layout view doesn't offer, such as borders and background images.

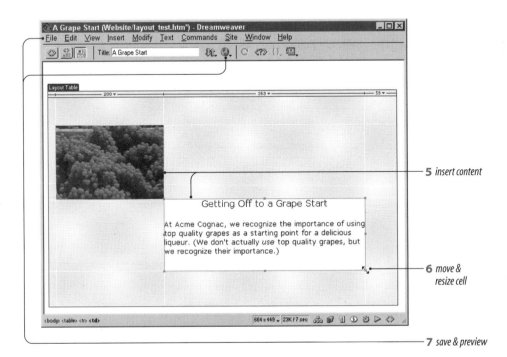

5 *insert content*

6 *move & resize cell*

7 *save & preview*

 # Build A Table In Standard View

You'd create a new table in standard view if you're designing a *data table* — that is, a table you create for the purpose of providing information in an ordered row-and-column format. Standard view is faster here, because you can use a single dialog box to build a table structure with any number of uniform rows and columns. As in the preceding example, this one starts with a fresh, blank document.

1 place insertion point

Click in the document window to position the insertion point at the spot where you want the table to appear.

2 set standard view

Click the **Standard View** icon on the objects panel. Alternatively, you can choose **View⇒Table View⇒Standard View** or press **ctrl+shift+F6** (**command-shift-F6** on the Mac).

3 click insert table icon

This icon lives on the objects panel. Alternatively, you can choose **Insert⇒Table** or press **ctrl+alt+T**

(**command-option-T** on the Mac). Any which way, you get the **Insert Table** dialog box.

4 set rows & columns

Specify the number of rows and columns you wish to create by entering numbers in the **Rows** and **Columns** fields. (You can always add or delete rows and columns later, with the **Modify⇒Table** commands. For example, I start by creating a table that's three by three, but will add a column in step 10.)

5 set width

Express the desired width of your table as a percentage of the user's browser window width or as an absolute pixel value. Note that even if you set an absolute pixel value, the table will still resize proportionally when the user resizes the browser window. If you want a truly fixed-width column, use layout view and spacer GIFs (see Build A Table In Layout View on page 86).

6 set padding & spacing (optional)

The default cell padding is 1 pixel; the default spacing is 2 pixels. You can change these values to taste; for details on padding and spacing, see E and F on page 81. By the

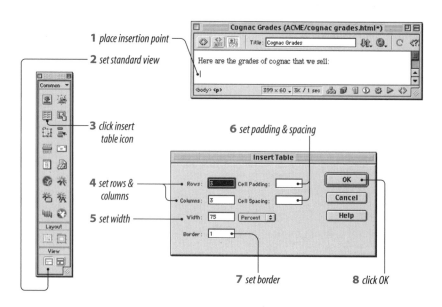

way, Dreamweaver doesn't display the cell padding and spacing values unless you enter your own.

7 set border (optional)

Enter the desired border width, or 0 if you don't want a border at all. If you're using a table for the standard presentation of data, then you'll probably want to have your borders set to 1 or above, so that the table retains a visible shape. If you're using a table to separate a column of text from an image, then you'll probably want to set its border value to 0, so the borders don't detract from your text and so the image will appear to float beside, or above, what you've written.

8 click OK

Or press **enter** (Win) or **return** (Mac) to close the **Insert Table** dialog box. Dreamweaver draws your new table.

9 insert content

Put whatever content you want into the cells you've created, just as you would add any content to your page. Images larger than the cell will automatically expand the cell size.

10 adjust rows & columns (optional)

You can adjust the size of rows and columns by mousing over their boundaries until you see a resize cursor and then clicking and dragging the boundary to a new location. If you get your table hopelessly muddled, you can always clear row heights and column widths using the commands on the **Modify➡Table** submenu and start over. Additionally, you can add a column with **Modify➡Table➡Insert Column** if you find that you forgot one (as I did) back at step 4; you can do the same with rows.

11 save & preview

Choose **File➡Save** to save your work and then click the **Preview/Debug In Browser** icon to see how the table looks in a browser. You can fine-tune the table further using the **Table** property inspector in standard view, as explained in The Table Property Inspector, Standard View on page 80.

9 *insert content*

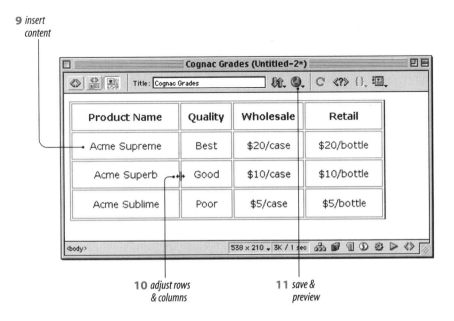

10 *adjust rows & columns*

11 *save & preview*

steps Sort Table Data

Nothing drives Web visitors crazier than having to wade through lots of information, but one thing comes close, and that's having to wade through lots of *disorganized* information. Organize your tables by sorting them in the manner most convenient for most users. Dreamweaver makes the process a piece of cake.

> **tip** If you're designing a complex table that your users may want to sort in more than one way, you can design multiple pages that use the same data but different sort criteria. Putting a link in the column header cell has become the accepted way to let visitors re-sort a Web table on that column; the link can take the visitor to a different page that is identical to the first one except for the sort column. (In database-enabled Web sites, the link typically runs a script that recreates the page's table from the back-end database, using the revised sort criterion.)

1 set standard view

You can only sort a table in standard view, so if you're in layout view, click the **Standard View** icon on the objects panel or choose **View⇒Table View⇒ Standard View** to change views.

2 select table

Select the table with any of the various methods: click the table's upper-left corner, click the right or bottom edge, click in the table and then click the **<table>** tag on the status bar, or click in the table and choose **Modify⇒Table⇒Select Table** or press **ctrl+A** (**command-A** on the Mac) *twice*. (Contrary to the user manual, pressing the keyboard shortcut once just selects the cell, not the table.)

> **tip** If the table you select contains any merged cells, you can't sort it. If you don't want to create a new table, you must split apart the merged cells, perform your sort, then remerge the cells to their original condition.

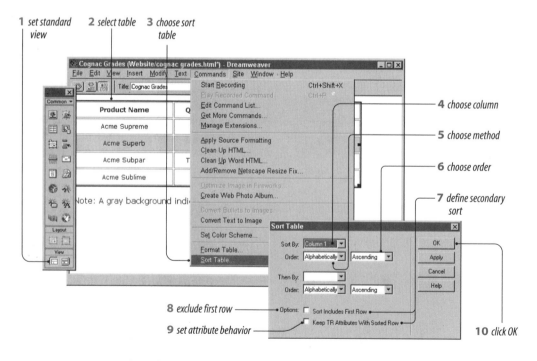

1 *set standard view*   2 *select table*   3 *choose sort table*

4 *choose column*

5 *choose method*

6 *choose order*

7 *define secondary sort*

8 *exclude first row*

9 *set attribute behavior*

10 *click OK*

3 choose sort table

Choose **Commands⇒Sort Table** to display the **Sort Table** dialog box.

4 choose column

Select the column you wish to sort by, in the **Sort By** drop down list.

5 choose method

The **Order** option actually contains two settings, method and order. The method can be **Alphabetically** or **Numerically**. (Note that in an alphabetical sort, "10" comes before "2.")

6 choose order

The choices here are **Ascending** and **Descending**.

7 define secondary sort (optional)

If two or more table rows have the same value in the specified column, you can specify a *secondary sort* to determine the order in which Dreamweaver will display those rows. The fields are the same as in steps 4, 5, and 6.

8 exclude first row

Most tables have a header row as the first row, including column titles. You don't normally want to sort the header row; it should remain at the top. Clear the **Sort Includes First Row** check box to exclude the first row from the sort operation; check it to include it.

9 set attribute behavior

You may have set a particular property, such as the background color, for one or more rows in your original, unsorted table. That property is an attribute of the **<tr>** tag ("table row"). Now, you may have set that property because of the row's *position* (for example, every tenth row has a blue background), or because of its *content* (every row describing an item with a price under $10 has a blue background).

If position was the criterion, then you want the colored rows to stay in the same place after the sort, so you'd clear the **Keep TR Attributes With Sorted Row** check box. If content was the criterion, as in my example, then the color should go with the content, and you'd check the box. The figure on this page shows before-sort and after-sort snapshots.

10 click OK

Or press **enter** (Win) or **return** (Mac) to close the **Sort Table** dialog box and perform the sort. Alternatively, you could click **Apply** to sort the table but leave the dialog box open.

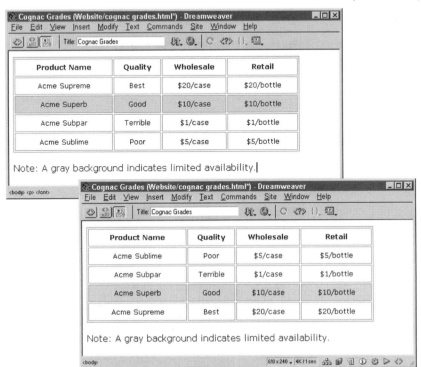

Export Data To Other Programs

You may need to move data from a Web page table into some other application, such as a spreadsheet or database program. Dreamweaver makes that process simple, but you first must determine which characters your intended application can use as *delimiters* for the purpose of importing data.

A delimiter is a character that separates items in a list. For example, in a database program, the delimiter for a database record is typically a line break, and the delimiter for fields within the record is typically a comma or tab character. Dreamweaver lets you set different values for record delimiters (which Dreamweaver calls line breaks) and field delimiters (which Dreamweaver simply calls delimiters).

1 click in table

In either standard or layout view, click inside any table cell.

2 choose export table

Choose **File➡Export➡Export Table**, which displays the **Export Table** dialog box.

3 set delimiter

Your choices are **Tab**, **Space**, **Comma**, **Semicolon**, and **Colon**. Choose a delimiter that your target application supports; tabs and commas are widely supported.

4 set line break

Usually, within an operating system, the line break character is a constant, so Dreamweaver simply asks you to specify the operating system (**Windows**, **Mac**, or **UNIX**) you use.

5 click export

Click the **Export** button when you're happy with the delimiter and line break settings. Name the target file and choose a location for it in the **Export Table As** dialog box. You must supply the suffix, but the result is always a text file.

> *tip* If you need to import data from another program into a Web table, check out Chapter 15, Work With Other Programs.

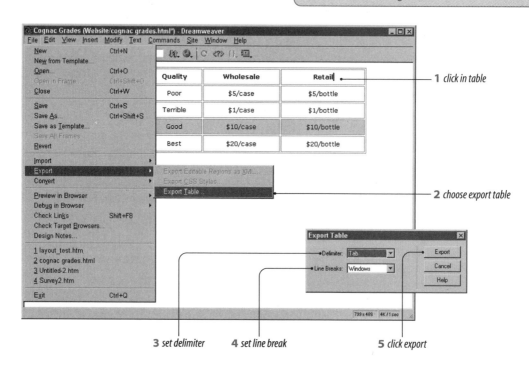

1 *click in table*

2 *choose export table*

3 *set delimiter*   4 *set line break*   5 *click export*

Assemble Forms

Title ▢ ▼
◎ Region

If you want to interact with your Web site visitors, the easiest way to proceed is to design a *form*. *HTML forms* are special pages or page fragments that provide places for the user to enter information right into the browser window.

HTML doesn't enable you to specify precisely what to do with that information; an external program, typically a *CGI (Common Gateway Interface)* script, does that. HTML collects the information, passes it along to the script, and then displays any information the script sends back.

Dreamweaver offers you all the standard HTML form elements: buttons, check boxes, text boxes, and so on. The program's WYSIWYG (What You See Is What You Get) design makes form design a matter of dragging and dropping. Dreamweaver even provides a mechanism for you to validate form content on the client side.

The Insert Form Objects Commands

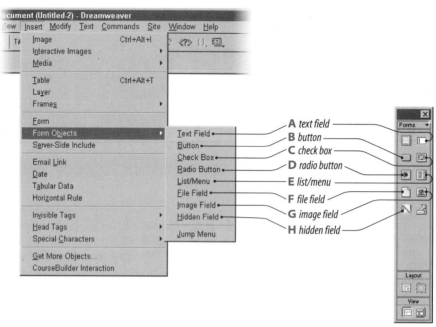

The **Insert→Form Objects** submenu gives you a choice of eight form objects to place onto your Web page at the insertion point's current position in the document window. (A ninth item, the *jump menu*, appears set apart on the same command submenu, but you're more likely to create a jump menu in the context of a frameset, so I refer you to the Create A Jump Menu section on page 117 of Chapter 7 for details on that animal.)

> **tip** You must have a form on your page (that is, the **<form>** tag pair) before you can insert a form object. Dreamweaver has an **Insert→Form** command and an equivalent **Insert Form** icon on the **Forms** objects panel, but I never use either. As soon as you tell Dreamweaver to insert a form object, the program asks whether you want to create a form first. If you check the **Don't Ask Again** box, then the program assumes henceforth that when you direct it to insert a form object, it should automatically create the **<form>** and **</form>** tags for you first. Handy.

The **Forms** objects panel provides equivalents to the menu commands for those who prefer icons

over menus. Display the **Forms** objects panel by choosing **Window→Objects** (**ctrl+F2**; **command-F2** on the Mac). Next, click the pop-up menu at the top of the panel and choose **Forms** from the list.

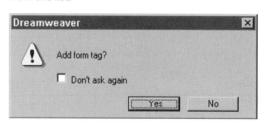

A text field

Text fields, which let the user enter text for uploading to the Web server, can be *single line*, *multi-line* (in which scroll bars appear), or *single-line password* (in which the browser displays asterisks when the user enters text). You can validate certain types of text entry to trap errors; see Validate A Form on page 105 of this chapter for details.

What's your email address?

B button

The traditional HTML form contains two buttons at the bottom: *submit*, for sending the data to the Web server for processing, and *reset*, for resetting the form and all its objects to their default (unmodified) state. The submit button is required, but the reset button is optional. You can create your own text for these buttons, and you can even create a graphical submit button using an *image field* (G).

C check box

Use *check boxes* when you want the visitor to choose one or more items from a list of related items. Each check box functions independently of any other check boxes.

D radio button

Use *radio buttons* when you want the visitor to choose exactly one item from a list of related items. As soon as the visitor clicks one radio button, the other ones clear automatically; that is, radio buttons are mutually exclusive.

E list/menu

Lists and menus are similar, but have the distinction that a list lets the visitor choose multiple items, whereas a menu lets the visitor choose only one item. You don't see lists as often as menus, because a list requires that a user understand how to select multiple items (for example, by shift-clicking), a procedure that many computer users don't know.

F file field

This one consists of a blank text field coupled with a Browse button. If you want a visitor to be able to upload a file to your Web server as part of the form, use this field, but be sure that your server administrator has set up the server to accept anonymous uploads.

G image field

The main use for the image field object is to create a submit button that uses an image instead of a boring gray button.

H hidden field

Your form can include one or more *hidden fields* that the visitor doesn't see. For example, you may have created multiple pages hosting identical forms. A visitor would navigate to a specific page by clicking one of several links, and you could include a hidden field that would identify the page from which the user submitted the form. In a different scenario, you may want to use a CGI script that can take submitted form data and send it to you in the form of an e-mail. That script may require certain fields, such as your e-mail address, that your Web site visitor doesn't need to see, so you'd put your e-mail address into a hidden field.

The Text Field Property Inspectors

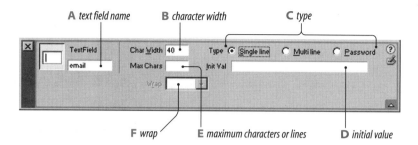

A text field name   **B** character width   **C** type

F wrap   **E** maximum characters or lines   **D** initial value

Dreamweaver doesn't give you just one **Forms** objects property inspector, it gives you several, each of which reflects the characteristics of a particular form object. This section looks at the property inspector for the three types of form text objects: single line, multiple line, and password. Place these objects by clicking **Insert Text Field** in the **Forms** objects panel.

> **tip** As usual, you can choose the command **Window⟶Properties** to display the property inspector window, but with form objects, you can also double-click the object to display the inspector.

A text field name
Common to the single-line text and multiple-line text fields, here's where you name the forms object. Make sure that you never duplicate an object name within a site; any behaviors that you attach to objects won't work if you do. Also, don't use spaces or other special characters.

B character width
Also common to single-line and multiple-line fields, **char width** specifies the width of the text object, in—what else?—characters. In a multiple-line field, you can enable wrapping and define the maximum size of the field independently of character width.

C type
Your choices are **Single line**, **Multi line,** and **Password**. Remember that **Password** is a single line field in which the browser displays only asterisks (Windows) or round bullets (Mac) as the user types.

D initial value
The *initial value* (**Init Val**) field lets you put example text into the field. Different schools of thought exist on whether to use initial values, because sometimes visitors don't know to change them; you be the judge.

E maximum characters or lines
The text field property inspector for single-line and password text lets you define the maximum number of characters the visitor can enter. Leave this blank, and the user can drone on and on. The multi-line text field property inspector lets you specify a maximum lines, rather than characters. Again, blank means no limit.

F wrap
Your wrapping options in a multi-line field are **Default**, **Off**, **Virtual**, and **Physical**. The first two turn wrapping off. **Virtual** means the user sees word wrapping, but the submitted data that the server-side script sees doesn't contain any actual line breaks. **Physical** means the line breaks are visible both to the user and to the script.

Radio Button & Check Box Property Inspectors

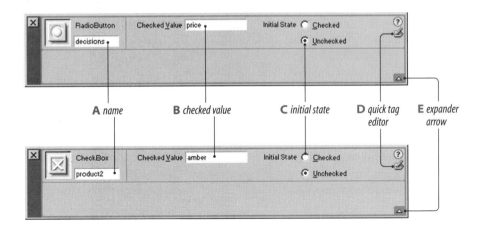

A name   **B** checked value   **C** initial state   **D** quick tag editor   **E** expander arrow

Radio buttons and check boxes are popular with both users and designers because they're unambiguous and easy to process. The property inspectors for these two kinds of Forms objects are similar, with one key difference: Radio buttons go together in groups of at least two buttons, whereas check boxes can stand on their own. You can create a group of logically related check boxes, but each still behaves as an independent entity.

> *tip* When laying out radio buttons and check boxes on the page, keep the buttons and boxes and their captions far enough apart so that the visitor can quickly see which caption goes with which button or box.

A name

The **Name** field works differently with check boxes versus radio buttons. Each check box must have its own unique name. However, radio buttons *within the same group* must all have the same name (but different checked values; see B) in order for the browser to know which radio buttons to clear when the user selects one from the group. If you have multiple groups of radio buttons, the group names must be unique.

> *tip* Names are case-sensitive, so **decisions** will not be considered the same as **Decisions**.

B checked value

The **Checked Value** field works similarly with check boxes and radio buttons. This field contains the data you want to pass to your server-side script if the user selects the check box or radio button. For example, if a radio button group has the name **decisions**, and a specific button has the checked value **price**, then if the user selects that button and clicks the Submit button on the page, the browser sends the data **decisions=price** to the server for subsequent processing. Like the **Name** field (A), the **Checked Value** field is case-sensitive.

C initial state

This field specifies how the check box or radio button appears when the page first loads. Your choices are **Checked** and **Unchecked**, logically enough. Set the initial state to the most likely value for most users, to minimize the work they must do in filling out the form. Note that if you set the initial state of a check box to **Unchecked**, and the user does not click the check box, the browser sends no form data for the check box to the server upon form submission.

D quick tag editor

Click this icon to see or modify the HTML code constituting the form definition.

E expander arrow

This arrow displays additional options in other inspectors, but not this one.

Button & Image Field Property Inspectors

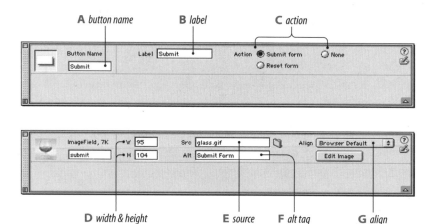

A button name   **B** label   **C** action

D width & height   **E** source   **F** alt tag   **G** align

You've got four kinds of forms buttons: *regular submit*, *graphical submit*, *regular reset*, and *do-nothing*. The usual practice is to place one regular submit and one reset button at the bottom of your form. The Submit button sends the form data to a Web server for processing; the Reset button clears form fields to their initial default states. You'd use a graphical Submit button to jazz up the page (but you can't make a graphical Reset button). A do-nothing button expects you to attach a JavaScript behavior (see Chapter 12) to make it do something.

A button name

Behaviors and scripts use the **Button Name** field, which must be a unique name. (Users don't see the button name.) A Submit button (regular or graphical) must have the reserved name **submit**, and a Reset button must have the name **reset**. You can give a do-nothing button any name you want.

B label

You can put whatever text you want in the **Label** field; this is the text that a visitor sees on a regular submit, reset, and do-nothing button. (The **Label** field does not exist for the graphical submit button type.)

C action

Your choices for a regular button are **Submit form**, **Reset form**, and **None**. When you choose an action,

Dreamweaver automatically sets the **Button Name** field (A). (Keep in mind, though, that if you choose **None**, the name is Button, which you should definitely change!).

D width & height

If you create a graphical Submit button, for example, by using the **Insert Image Field** icon on the **Forms** objects panel, then its width and height will automatically reflect the source image's dimensions.

E source

The **Src** field specifies the image file you selected for a graphical Submit button, after clicking **Insert Image Field**. You can change the file either by typing a path name or clicking the folder icon to browse to a new file.

F alt tag

The optional **Alt** tag for a graphical Submit button includes text that would appear in a text-only browser or that would appear at the cursor tip when the user mouses over the image.

G align

Your choices for a graphical Submit button are **Browser Default**, **Top**, **Middle**, **Bottom**, **Left**, and **Right**. These graphics work just as with "normal" images (see page 57, the Place An Inline Image section, in Chapter 4 for details).

Menu & List Property Inspectors

A type   B height   C selections

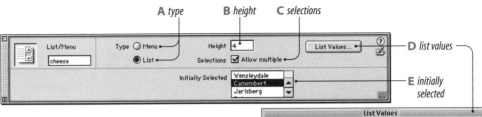

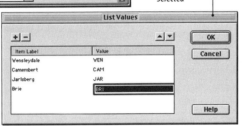

Menus and lists are kissing cousins, inserted with the same command (**Insert List/Menu** on the **Forms** objects panel), and their property inspectors are similar. How do you decide which to use? Use a menu if you're tight on space and you don't need to let the user choose multiple items. Use a list (sometimes called a *list box*) if you've got a bit more room, or if you want to let the user choose more than one item. If you've got a lot of room, or a relatively small number of choices to present, don't use either a list or a menu—use a group of check boxes or radio buttons.

> **tip** A *jump menu* is a special type of menu that designers often use to control navigation or the display of content in a frameset. For details on how to create this special type of menu, see Create A Jump Menu on page 117 in Chapter 7.

A type

Your choices are **Menu** and **List**. The first paragraph on this page explains when to use which.

B height

Specify how many lines tall you want the list to appear. If the number of list items is greater than the height value, the browser presents a scroll bar.

C selections

The **Allow multiple** check box lets the user choose multiple items from the list (for example, with **shift-**click) when you check it. Clear it, and the list works like a menu, except that it can show more than one item at a time on the form. If you allow multiple selections, consider explaining the keystroke combinations on the page, remembering that the Windows and

Macintosh platforms select non-adjacent items differently (**ctrl-**click versus **command-**click).

D list values

Click this button to display the **List Values** dialog box, where you click the + button to add new list or menu items. Each item has an associated **Item Label** and **Value**; the **Item Label** is what the user sees, the **Value** is what the server-side script sees. (If you leave the **Value** fields blank, the browser will submit the item labels as values.) Select an item label or value and click the – button to delete the row.

> **tip** You don't have to click the + button multiple times to enter multiple list or menu items. Once you're working in the main part of the **List Values** dialog box, the **tab** key will move you from column to column and from row to row. Use **shift-tab** to move in the opposite direction (left and up).

E initially selected

Here, choose which list or menu option you want the user to see when the page first loads into the browser window.

> **tip** Always use the **File➡Preview In Browser** command to verify that your menus and lists work like you want them to.

The Forms Property Inspector

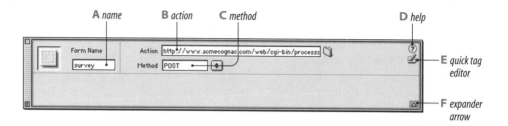

A *name*   B *action*   C *method*   D *help*   E *quick tag editor*   F *expander arrow*

The Forms property inspector is small, but critically important. In it, you specify the form's name, the target location of the script that will process the form's data when it arrives at the Web server, and the posting method. If the property window feature is active, you can display the Forms property inspector by clicking anywhere along the red dashed line of the form's boundary or by clicking the **<form>** tag on the document window's tag selector.

A name

Label your form with a unique and descriptive name in this field.

B action

The **Action** field is where you tell Dreamweaver the location of the script that acts on the form's data once submitted. (Such scripts also go by the name of *form handlers*.) This field also specifies where user-uploaded files should go, if you use the *file field* object.

You can either type in the URL in the text area or click the folder icon and locate it with the usual file selector dialog box. This field is required if you want your form to activate a server-side script upon submittal.

> *tip* Form handlers typically live in a Web server folder named **CGI-BIN**, which stands for Common Gateway Interface binaries.

C method

HTML lets you specify that form data be submitted in one of two ways: the **GET** or **POST** command.

The GET method puts form data at the tail end of a Uniform Resource Locator (you've probably seen some of these long, complex URLs in your browser's address window when surfing). Problem is, this method limits you to 8,192 characters, the maximum length of a URL. If your form should contain more data than that, which can happen easily with long or complex forms, anything past character 8,192 doesn't survive, and the user will be submitting an incomplete form to your server.

The other method, POST, is suitable for longer forms (and is required if you use the *file field*, which lets users upload a file to your Web server). POST sends the form values in a message that's separate from the URL. This command doesn't have a size limit, and it's also more secure than GET.

> *tip* You can set the **Method** field to **Default** and let the browser decide. I don't generally recommend doing so; browsers often default to GET rather than POST.

D help

As usual in property inspectors, click the question mark icon to view context-sensitive help.

E quick tag editor

Click this icon to see or modify the HTML code constituting the form definition.

```
Edit Tag: <form name="survey" method="post"
action="http://www.acmecognac.com
/web/cgi-bin/processsurvey.exe"
enctype="multipart/form-data">
```

F expander arrow

You can expand this property inspector by clicking the arrow at the lower right, but nothing new appears.

steps Build A Simple Form

You can use HTML forms for many purposes, including customer feedback, user surveys, and product selectors. In this example, I built a simple form that the Acme Cognac marketing department will use to get a better handle on its customers' consumption and buying habits—with the incentive of a contest prize to inspire participation.

1 place insertion point

Open an existing document or create a new one and place the insertion point in the document window where you want the form to begin. Note that you can't insert a form into another form. (You can put two forms on a page if the tags don't overlap, but that can get confusing for the user.)

2 insert form object

The first field is an e-mail address, so click the **Insert Text Field** icon on the **Forms** objects panel (or choose the menu command **Insert➧Form Objects➧Text Field**).

Dreamweaver detects that you haven't defined a form yet and asks whether you want to do so. Click the **Yes** button, and Dreamweaver creates the form tag pair and then immediately inserts a text field.

tip Dreamweaver displays a dotted red line showing you the form's boundary. If you can't see it, choose **View➧Visual Aids➧Invisible Elements**.

3 enter prompt

The *prompt*, or *descriptor*, is normally just a line of text telling the user what to do with the adjacent object. Type the text with the insertion point just to the left of the text field. Format it to taste with the Text property inspector (see Chapter 3's section Text Inspector on page 42 for details).

4 set field properties

Double-click the text field to open the Text Field property inspector. Here, as I'm setting the first field to be

1 *place insertion point*   2 *insert form object*   3 *enter prompt*   4 *set field properties*   5 *click end & enter/return*

6 *repeat*

7 *insert submit button*

8 *save file*   9 *preview in browser*   10 *define action*

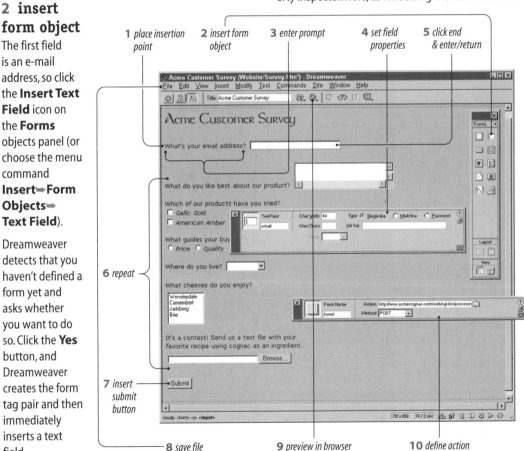

an e-mail address, I make sure that the **Type** is **Single line**. Always give the form object a name, too.

5 click end & enter/return

Press the **end** key to move the insertion point to the end of the e-mail field, and press **enter** (Win) or **return** (Mac) to create a new line.

6 repeat

Perform steps 1 through 5 for as many form objects as you need. Remember that when you create a group of radio buttons, the button name must be the same for each button in the group. Also remember that **shift+enter** (Win) or **shift-return** (Mac) creates a line break rather than a paragraph break, if your form is beginning to look a little too "spaced out."

7 insert submit button

Place the insertion point at the bottom of the form and click the **Insert Button** icon on the **Forms** objects panel. Dreamweaver defaults to making your

button a Submit button, so you don't have to change any properties unless you want to.

> **tip** If you want to take your form design one step further and format your form objects with a table, refer to page 103, Enhance A Form With A Table.

8 save file

Choose **File➧Save** to save your form to disk.

9 preview in browser

Choose **File➧Preview In Browser** to see how your form elements work in real life.

10 define action

Finally, back in the document window, click the **<form>** tag on the status bar's tag selector and specify a script URL in the **Action** field of the property inspector. (You can't actually test the script processing until you upload your site to a *bona fide* Web server.)

How Forms Really Work

This chapter goes over how to create the client side part of a form, but that's only part of the process. For a form to be useful, it has to do something, and most of the time, that "something" occurs at a Web server. Here's how the process normally works.

First, the visitor fills out the form fields on the page you've designed in Dreamweaver. (You can tell Dreamweaver to perform some rudimentary error-checking at the client side; see the Validate A Form section on page 105.) When the visitor is happy with the data and your validation criteria are all satisfied, she clicks the Submit button.

Dreamweaver then sends the form data to the server-side script whose URL you've specified in the form's **Action** field of the **Forms** property

inspector. The script, called a *CGI (Common Gateway Interface)* script, is a program (it can be Perl, Java, C, VBScript, JavaScript, Pascal, or almost anything) that does something useful with the form data. (CGI is not a programming language itself; rather, it's an interface defining how a server moves data between an HTML form and some other program.)

Scripts can be simple or complex. A complex one might evaluate the data that the user has provided, consult a back-end database of products that your company sells, and make a recommendation about the specific product that would be most appropriate for the user. Dreamweaver won't help you write scripts, but you can get "canned" scripts from many public Web sites, or you can learn to write your own.

The final step in the process is typically for the CGI script to return an HTML page to the user, presenting the results of the processing.

As a variation on the theme, you can leave the **Action** field blank if you want to write a JavaScript code function in your document's **<head>** section and perform some pure client-side form processing. Attach the **Call JavaScript** behavior to the Submit button (see Chapter 12 for more on behaviors) and specify the function you want to execute. You might see such a client-side form on a mortgage broker's Web site in the form of a monthly payment calculator, for example. Client-side processing is fine in cases where you don't need to keep the results of the processing.

◆steps◆ Enhance A Form With A Table

The default alignment of form objects and descriptors isn't always pretty, but you can make a form look a lot sharper by placing those page elements inside a table, where you can lay them out and align them any way you want. You can even use a nested table if appropriate. (For the lowdown on table layout, see Chapter 5, Design Tables.)

I normally lay out my form elements first and then create a blank table inside the form and populate the table cells with the form elements using drag and drop. If you create the table first, without creating a form, and then start adding form objects to the table, Dreamweaver creates a new form for every table cell—not what you typically want.

1 create form

Build your form with all the necessary form objects, as set forth in the Build A Simple Form section on pages 101–102.

2 place insertion point

Click anywhere inside the form to position the insertion point. (I usually click at the top left of the form.) Your table must reside inside the **<form></form>** tag pair, which Dreamweaver displays on screen with a dashed red line. If you can't see this line, toggle the menu command **View➞Visual Aids➞Invisible Elements**.

3 insert table

Choose **Insert➞ Table** command or press **ctrl+alt+T** (**command-option-T** on the Mac).

tip You can't use Dreamweaver's layout view if you've already created a form that you want to convert into a table. The cursor won't turn into a crosshair unless you position it over an empty area, and when you're inside a form, no area is empty. Furthermore, Dreamweaver doesn't let you resize a form (for example, to create an empty area in which to draw a table).

4 format table

You can set your table's dimensions in the **Insert Table** dialog box. See Chapter 5 for a discussion of the various settings in detail if you need it.

5 drag & drop form elements

You can move your form elements into the table cells. Keep in mind that you'll normally move the text descriptors (such as "Enter your e-mail address") independently of their associated form objects, because you'll want to align the form objects in one or more separate columns.

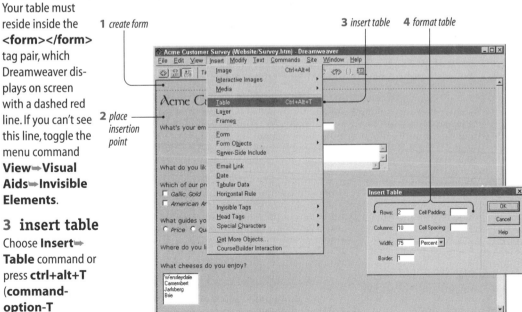

1 *create form*   **2** *place insertion point*   **3** *insert table*   **4** *format table*

6 display property inspector

If the property inspector panel isn't already open, open it with the **Window→Properties** menu command or **ctrl+F3** (Win) (**command-F3** Mac).

7 format columns

For example, if you put your form objects in the right column of a two-column table, you can left-justify them all by selecting the column (position the cursor above the column until it turns into a down-arrow and click) and setting the **Horz** field to **Left** in the table property inspector.

8 adjust columns & rows

Drag and drop column and row borders to get the table looking the way you want.

9 set border

Click the table border, or the **<table>** tag in the status bar, to select the table and display its properties in

the Table property inspector. If you want a border, set its size and color in the inspector's **Border** and **Brdr Color** fields; if you don't want one, set its size to 0 in the **Border** field.

10 set padding

If you want a clean look with no border, you'll probably want to increase the cell padding so that your form elements don't crowd together too closely. With the table still selected, enter a positive value in the **CellPad** field.

11 save page

Choose **File→Save** to store your newly formatted form to disk.

12 preview in browser

Click the **Preview/Debug In Browser** icon on the toolbar and choose the appropriate command to preview in the intended browser.

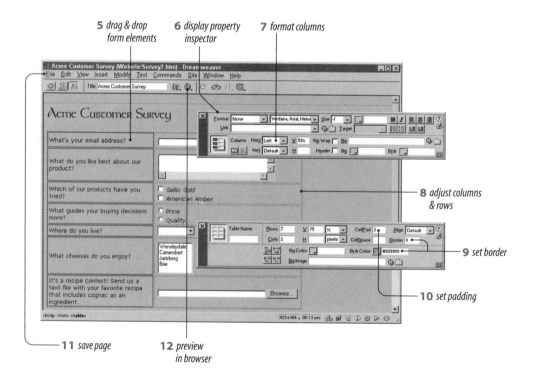

5 *drag & drop form elements* 6 *display property inspector* 7 *format columns*

8 *adjust columns & rows*

9 *set border*

10 *set padding*

11 *save page* 12 *preview in browser*

steps Validate A Form

Dreamweaver includes a JavaScript behavior called *Validate Form* that lets your Web page perform some simple form field validation (such as ensuring that a numeric field contains only numbers) before the user submits the form data to a Web server. You can either validate fields as the user fills them in (which I usually prefer), or all at once when the user clicks the Submit button to send form data to the server.

The validation options are few and simple, but use them when you can. A time-honored software design principle is to trap user errors at the earliest possible time. Doing so reduces unnecessary communications between client and server; reduces server workload (desirable because servers are usually busier than clients); and speeds the process of error notification and user correction.

1 select field
Select the field you wish to validate by clicking it in the document window—in this example, a single-line field for the survey respondent's e-mail address.

2 open behaviors panel
The menu command is **Window➔Behaviors**; the keyboard shortcut is **ctrl+F3** (Win) or **command-F3** (Mac).

3 click +
Clicking the plus sign at the top of the **Behaviors** panel activates the drop-down list of behaviors.

4 choose validate form
Select the **Validate Form** behavior from the list.

5 choose field
Dreamweaver doesn't automatically highlight the field you selected in step 1, so you may have to highlight it again by clicking its

name in the **Named Fields** list of the **Validate Form** dialog box.

6 click required (optional)
If you want to insist that the field contain something, check this box. If you don't care what it contains, as long as it contains something, check this box and choose **Use Anything** as the validation criterion (7).

7 choose validation criterion
In the **Accept** part of the **Validate Form** dialog box, you click a radio button that corresponds to what you want to check. In the example, clicking **Use E-mail** tells Dreamweaver to make sure that the address contains an @ character. **Use Anything** means that the field can contain any characters; **Use Number** validates for numbers only; and **Use Number From** validates the field for a specific number range, which you specify.

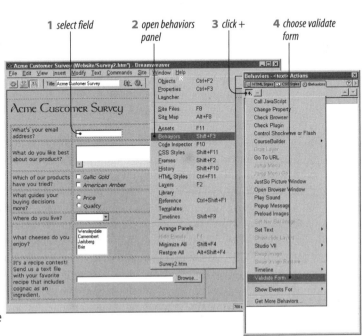

1 *select field*   2 *open behaviors panel*   3 *click +*   4 *choose validate form*

8 click OK

Clicking **OK** closes the **Validate Form** dialog box.

9 set event

Clicking the down arrow in the **Behaviors** panel's **Events** column displays a list of events that you can choose to trigger the field validation behavior.

When performing field-by-field validation, your choices are *onBlur* or *onChange*. Use *onBlur* if you mark the field as required in step 6 because *onChange* only triggers the validation if the user has changed the field's contents.

10 save page

Choose **File➟Save** to save your modified form page.

11 preview in browser

Click the **Preview/Debug in Browser** toolbar icon and preview your page in a browser. In my

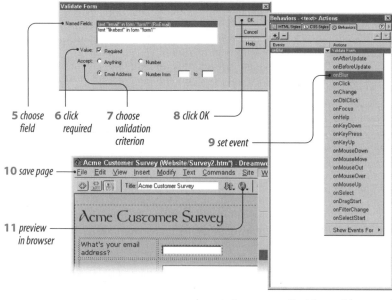

5 *choose field*   6 *click required*   7 *choose validation criterion*   8 *click OK*

9 *set event*

10 *save page*

11 *preview in browser*

example, entering an e-mail address without an @ in it generates the following error:

This demonstrates another reason to name your form fields descriptively: The browser's error message refers to the field's name, as you can see!

Validate An Entire Form

The example in this section shows you how to validate a form one field at a time. This method is normally the way to go because most users get frustrated if they fill out an entire form, submit it, and only then receive notice that they've made an error. However, if you want to validate form fields all at once, when the user clicks the Submit button, Dreamweaver

can accommodate you. Here is what you must do differently:

Attach behavior to <form>

In step 1, instead of selecting the field to validate, select the **<form>** tag itself, before opening the **Behaviors** panel. You'll see the tag on the document window's status bar, in the tag selector area.

Set criteria for fields

To do so, repeat steps 5, 6, and 7 for as many fields as you want to validate.

Use onSubmit

In step 9, instead of choosing *onBlur* or *onChange* as the triggering action, you need to choose *onSubmit*.

Providing a convenient, intuitive way for users to navigate a Web site is one of the designer's biggest challenges. One of the more valuable tools in your belt for meeting this challenge is the *frameset*, a collection of two or more rectangular regions in which one region provides navigation links and another region changes when the user clicks one of those links. These regions are called *frames*, and each frame has its own separate HTML page.

You have other options for navigation, of course. You can create a navigation bar and place it on every page of your Web site, for example. You may find frames attractive because you create the navigation area (the frame containing the links) one time on one page, rather than placing it onto multiple pages. You may also just like the look of framed pages.

Some people may tell you that frames are hard to learn, but they're not really difficult. This chapter tells you how to build, format, and modify them.

The Frames Objects Panel

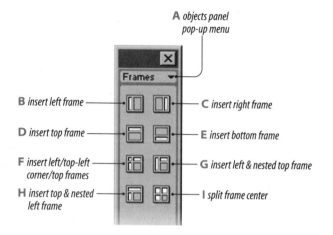

A *objects panel pop-up menu*

B *insert left frame*

C *insert right frame*

D *insert top frame*

E *insert bottom frame*

F *insert left/top-left corner/top frames*

G *insert left & nested top frame*

H *insert top & nested left frame*

I *split frame center*

The **Frames** objects panel helps you create a frameset. It provides graphical icons, which, with a single click, let you create one of several different types of framesets. (Use the icon you want *before* you save the frameset, so Dreamweaver knows you want to build a frameset and not just a single HTML page.) The icons have more descriptive names than the corresponding menu commands.

> **tip** The blue part of each icon represents which frame the current document (if any) will reside in after Dreamweaver creates the frameset. The white part (or parts) represents the new frame(s) Dreamweaver will add.

A objects panel pop-up menu
Display the **Frames** objects panel by first displaying the objects panel (if it isn't already showing) with **ctrl+F2** (Win) or **command-F2** (Mac). Then, click the pop-up menu at the top (which normally says **Common**) so that **Frames** is selected.

B insert left frame
Click this icon or choose **Insert➡Frames➡Left** to create a frameset in which the current document becomes the right frame, and Dreamweaver adds a new, left frame.

C insert right frame
Creates a frameset in which the current document becomes the left frame and Dreamweaver adds a new, right frame. Equivalent to the menu command **Insert➡Frames➡Right**.

D insert top frame
The current document becomes the bottom frame, and Dreamweaver adds a new, top frame. Equivalent to the menu command **Insert➡Frames➡Top**.

E insert bottom frame
The current document becomes the top frame, and Dreamweaver adds a new, bottom frame. Equivalent to the menu command **Insert➡Frames➡Bottom**.

F insert left/top-left corner/top frames
The current document becomes the lower-right frame, and Dreamweaver adds new left, top-left, and top frames. Equivalent to the menu command **Insert➡Frames➡Left and Top**.

G insert left & nested top frame
The current document becomes the lower-right frame, and Dreamweaver adds a new left frame and a new top frame that nests inside the right frame (and therefore doesn't go all the way across the frame). Equivalent to **Insert➡Frames➡Left Top**.

H insert top & nested left frame
The current document becomes the lower-right frame, and Dreamweaver adds a new top frame and a new left frame that nests inside the right frame (and therefore doesn't go all the way up). Equivalent to **Insert➡Frames➡Top Left**.

I split frame center
The current document becomes the lower-right frame, and Dreamweaver adds three new frames to the left, upper left, and top, none of which are nested. Equivalent to **Insert➡Frames➡Split**.

The Frames Panel

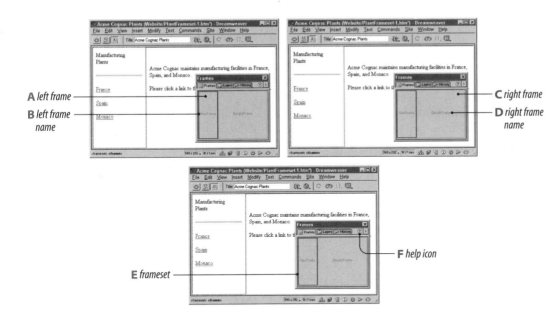

A *left frame*
B *left frame name*
C *right frame*
D *right frame name*
E *frameset*
F *help icon*

One of the secrets to working with frames and not pulling your hair out from frustration is to make appropriate use of the **Frames** panel. Frames and framesets are a little tricky to select from the document window, but they're much easier to select from the **Frames** panel. You can display it by choosing **Window⇒Frames** or by pressing **shift-F2.**

The illustration shows you how the **Frames** panel looks. The **Frames** panel becomes even more useful when you use nested frames, because the relationship between frames is easier to see than in the document window.

A left frame
Click inside the left frame to select it. The **Frames** panel shows a border around that frame. The selected frame also appears surrounded by a dotted line in the document window.

B left frame name
The frame name appears in the **Frames** panel. Note that this name is not the same as the associated HTML

page's title or the associated HTML page's filename. Each frame in a frameset should have a unique name so that you can refer to that frame when specifying link behaviors. You can name your frames in the **Frames** property inspector described on page 110.

C right frame
Click in the right frame in the panel, and Dreamweaver highlights it to show that the right frame is now selected.

D right frame name
The right frame name appears centered in the frame area.

E frameset
Select the frameset by clicking the outer border of the **Frames** panel's display, and a thick black border appears around all the frames in the set. The frameset is the HTML page that holds the individual frames in place.

F help icon
Click the question mark to open the **Using Dreamweaver** help system to the topic of frames.

The Frames Property Inspector

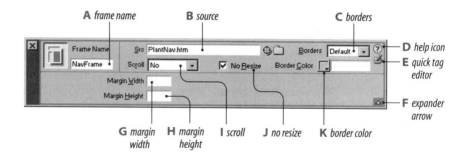

A *frame name* B *source* C *borders* D *help icon* E *quick tag editor* F *expander arrow*

G *margin width* H *margin height* I *scroll* J *no resize* K *border color*

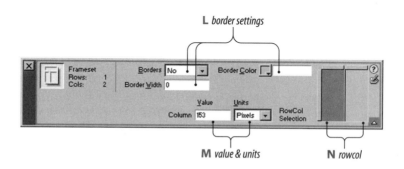

L *border settings*

M *value & units* N *rowcol*

The **Frames** property inspector is the most convenient place to name a frame and define detailed aspects of its appearance. You can toggle the property inspector on or off by choosing the command **Window➡Properties** or **ctrl+F3** (Win) (**command-F3** Mac). To have the property inspector show properties for a frame, you must select a frame by either clicking the frame in the **Frames** panel (see page 109) or by **alt**-clicking (Win) or **option-shift-clicking** (Mac) inside a frame in the document window.

The **Frames** property inspector takes on a different appearance and function if you select a frameset rather than an individual frame. Think of the frameset as the master file that specifies the internal layout of each individual frame; the frameset has its own HTML file.

Select a frameset by clicking the outer frame border in the **Frames** panel or by clicking any vertical

or horizontal frame border in the document window. (If you can't see any frame borders, display them with the command **View➡Visual Aids➡Frame Borders**.) Confirm that you've selected the frameset by checking the tag selector on the status bar for the boldface tag **<frameset>**.

A frame name

Each frame should have a unique name, so that when you create links that display frameset content, you can tell Dreamweaver the frame in which it should display that content. Don't use spaces, hyphens, or periods (underscores are okay), and start each frame name with a letter, not a number.

B source

The *source* is the name of the HTML file on disk containing the content in the selected frame. You can change it by clicking the folder icon and browsing to a different file or by dragging the **Point-to-File** icon onto a file in the site window.

C borders

The choices are **Yes**, **No**, and **Default**. If you don't want borders, you can leave this at **Default** as long as the parent frameset turns borders off.

> **tip** If the parent frameset has borders turned on, then to disable the display of any specific border, you need to set all frames adjacent to that border to **No**.

D help icon

Click the question mark to bring up context-sensitive help.

E quick tag editor

Click this icon to bring up a mini-HTML editing window for the frame tag.

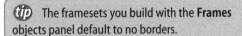

F expander arrow

By default, the **Frames** property inspector doesn't show you margin width (G) or margin height (H). You need to click the expander arrow to see these values. Then you click it again to hide them.

G margin width

In the expanded view of the property inspector, you can see and set **Margin Width**, which is the number of pixels of padding between the left border and the left edge of the content, and between the right border and the right edge of the content. The default value is 0.

H margin height

Similarly, **Margin Height** is the number of pixels of padding between the top border and the top edge of the content, and between the bottom border and the bottom edge of the content. The default is 0.

I scroll

The scrolling choices are **No**, **Yes**, **Auto**, and **Default**. **No** forces scroll bars off, **Yes** forces them on, **Auto**

displays scroll bars automatically (but only if the content doesn't fit completely within the frame), and **Default** lets the browser's own setting take precedence (it's usually Auto).

J no resize

If checked, the user can't drag the frame's border to resize it.

K border color

Here, you set the border color for the current frame (for Version 4+ browsers only). This setting takes precedence over that for the frameset.

> **tip** The framesets you build with the **Frames** objects panel default to no borders.

L border settings

If you select a frameset, then you can make border settings that apply to all frames that don't have their own overriding border settings. Note that if you want to disable borders, you should set the **Borders** field to **No** and the **Border Width** field to **0**, because some browsers key off one value and other browsers key off the other.

M value & units

These two frameset settings work together to let you set a size for the row or column selected in the Row-Col area. If you specify a value of **Pixels**, then the selected column or row has that pixel size at all times. If you choose **Percent**, the selected column or row makes up that percent of the frameset. And if you choose **Relative**, then the column or row will take up all remaining frameset space after any other frames with **Pixels** or **Percent** sizes have been drawn.

N rowcol

This is the selection area where you click the frame you want to size, using both the **Value** and **Units** fields (M).

⬭steps Build A Simple Frameset

Now that you're familiar with the **Frames** panel, the **Frames** objects panel, and the **Frames** property inspector, you're ready to create a frameset in Dreamweaver. This page and the next one describe the most common type of frameset: A two-frame layout in which you create navigational links in the left frame and then add content to appear in the right frame when the user clicks one of the left-frame links.

1 create new document
Choose **File➡New** or press **ctrl+N** (Win) or **command-N** (Mac).

> 💡 **tip** Do not save this page yet! Dreamweaver doesn't yet know it will be part of a frameset.

2 display frames objects panel
If the objects panel isn't already open, press **ctrl+F2** (**command-F2** Mac) to display it. Then choose **Frames** from the objects panel pop-up menu.

3 insert left frame
Click the upper-left icon, **Insert Left Frame**, to create exactly the predefined, two-frame set that you want. You can see the frame borders in the document window. (If they don't appear, choose **View➡Visual Aids➡Frame Borders**.)

4 click in left frame
Click in the left frame to display the text insertion point.

5 enter text for links
Because the left frame will be the navigation frame, type the text that will become the hyperlinks for the content that will appear in the right frame.

6 reposition frame border
You may find that the border between the left and right frames is too far to the left for the link text you want to add. Move the border by simply dragging it to the right. (The joys of visual Web page editing!)

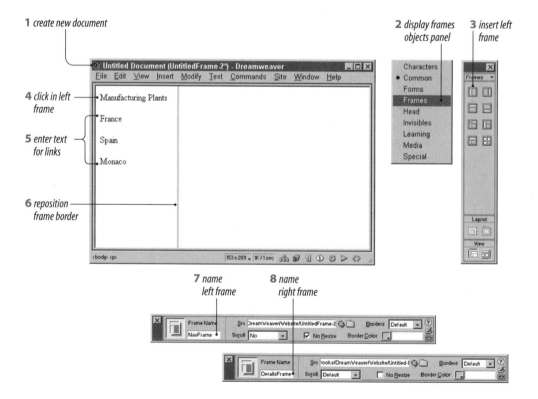

1 create new document

2 display frames objects panel

3 insert left frame

4 click in left frame

5 enter text for links

6 reposition frame border

7 name left frame

8 name right frame

7 name left frame

In the property inspector, select the left frame with an **alt**-click (Win) or **option-shift**-click (Mac) in the left frame area and enter a descriptive name in the property inspector's **Frame Name** field, such as *NavFrame*.

8 name right frame

Select the right frame and enter a descriptive name, such as *DetailsFrame*.

9 save all frames

This is a good time to save the work done so far. Choose **File→Save All** to save all open files at once. My example has three files: an HTML file for the frameset (container file), and one HTML file each for the left and right frames. Dreamweaver prompts you to save each file in sequence. (If you choose **File→Save Frame** or **File→Save Frame As**, you only save a single frame; choose **File→Save Frameset** or **File→Save Frameset As**, and you only save the frameset file.)

10 specify link

Now, go back and select the link text you keyed in at step 5, for example, by double-clicking the word. The

property inspector switches to the **Text** property inspector. Click the folder icon next to the **Link** field and browse to the predefined Web page you want to appear in the right frame when the user clicks the link.

> **tip** Look at the highlighting in the document window to see which file Dreamweaver is about to save, so you can give it an appropriate filename.

11 specify link target

Click the drop-down list arrow by the **Target** field and choose *DetailsFrame* to tell Dreamweaver where you want the file you specified in step 10 to appear in the frameset. (Now you see why you needed to name those frames!) If you don't specify the target, then the linked file will load into the same frame as the link itself, which is not normally what you want to do.

12 preview in browser

Press **F12** to preview your frameset in a browser window. Try the links and see how they work.

9 *save all frames* **10** *specify link* **11** *specify link target* **12** *preview in browser*

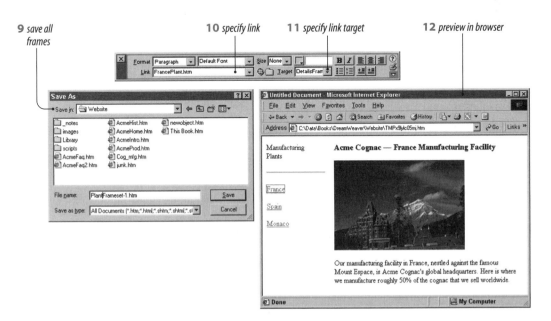

Frame Content Controls

A _blank

B _parent

C _self

D _top

You can control the display of content in a frameset with several different techniques. The simplest is to use a hypertext link, as described in Build A Simple Frameset on pages 112 and 113, and set the link target to a named frame using the property inspector.

Dreamweaver also provides access to four predefined frame identifiers, described here, which appear in the property inspector's **Target** pop-up menu above any named frames. And you don't have to use a simple hypertext link, either: You can use JavaScript behaviors for greater control (see the three Steps sections following this page).

In addition, you can update multiple frames simultaneously. (Typically, when you create a link in a frame that you use for navigation, only one target frame changes its content.) This trick uses the **Go To URL** behavior, which I describe on page 115. (For more on behaviors, please see Chapter 12, Add Interactivity.)

> **tip** Don't use these predefined target names, with or without the leading underscore, as the names of any frames that you create. You could confuse the browser.

A _blank

The **_blank** predefined target opens the linked document in a new browser window. The user can then close that window to return to the original browser window containing the frameset. The effect is akin to that of a pop-up window. You may see this target used in Web-based television program guides to display details about a specific clicked program without overwriting the schedule grid.

B _parent

The **_parent** target tells Dreamweaver to open the linked document in the link's *parent* frameset—that is, the one in which the current frame is nested (see Nested Frames on page 118). You don't see this target used as often as the **_blank** target.

> **tip** To set a different default target for all the links on a given page, add some HTML code to the page's <head> section, after the <title> tag. Select code view and add the tag <base target="framename">, where **framename** is the name of the frame you're setting as the default target. After making this change, you'll still have complete freedom to choose a specific frame as a target with the property inspector.

C _self

This one opens the linked document in the same frame that the hyperlink occupies, overwriting the current frame. That's the default behavior of HTML if you don't specify a target, so this one's even less common than **_parent**.

D _top

This target instructs Dreamweaver to break all the frames and load the results into a single page in a single window, effectively exiting the frameset.

> **tip** Use named frames in your **Target** fields whenever possible so that you don't have to remember the behavior of these predefined targets. When naming frames, don't use spaces or hyphens; it's okay to use underscores, however. As always, use descriptive names rather than names like Frame_1, Frame_2, and so on.

Link Frame Content To URLs

The example on this page shows how clicking a link in the *NavFrame* on the left changes the graphic in *ImageFrame* (upper right) as well as the text in *TextFrame* (lower right).

1 create text for link
Click in the left frame and add the text to which you will attach the **Go To URL** behavior.

2 create null link
Select the text you created in step 1 and, in the property inspector, enter **javascript:;** in the **Link** field to create a null link. (You can't attach a behavior to plain text.)

3 open behaviors panel
The menu command is **Window**➥**Behaviors**. Leave the text selected.

4 click +
This tells Dreamweaver you want to add a behavior.

5 choose action
Choose **Go To URL** from the Actions pop-up menu. This opens the **Open In** list, where you can see all named frames in the open frameset.

6 select first target frame
Choose the first frame whose content you want the link to change—for example, *ImageFrame* or *TextFrame*.

7 specify URL to open
Either browse to the file containing the content you want to appear in the frame or enter a file path directly into the **URL** field.

8 click OK
This adds the behavior to the list.

9 change event type
Change the event type to **On Click** in the Events column of the Behaviors panel by clicking the down arrow. If the **On Click** event type doesn't appear, you may need to choose **Show Events For** in the same drop-down menu and choose **4.0 or Later Browsers**.

Repeat steps 5 through 9 to specify the content you want to change in *TextFrame*. With a single behavior list, you can modify the content of as many frames as you have in the frameset.

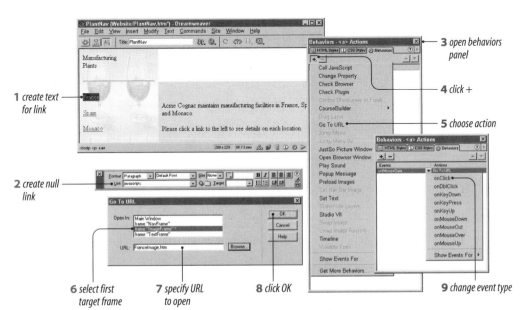

1 *create text for link*

2 *create null link*

3 *open behaviors panel*

4 *click +*

5 *choose action*

6 *select first target frame*

7 *specify URL to open*

8 *click OK*

9 *change event type*

Set Frame Text

Sometimes you want to modify the content of a target frame without reloading its entire HTML page. The **Set Text Of Frame** behavior lets you change the text displayed in a frame dynamically, for example, when the user mouses over a link or clicks a link. As with other behaviors, the procedure is to create a null link in the navigation frame and then associate a behavior with that link. (For more on behaviors, please see Chapter 12, Add Interactivity.)

Repeat steps 1 through 4 on page 115. Then do the following:

5 **choose action**

Choose **Set Text➥Set Text of Frame** from the **Actions** pop-up menu to open the **Set Text Of Frame** dialog box, where you can see all named frames in the open frameset.

6 **select target frame**

Choose the frame whose content you want the link to change from the **Frame** pop-up menu.

7 **click get current HTML**

This button loads the selected frame's HTML code into the **New HTML** window.

8 **add or modify HTML**

Put whatever valid HTML code you want into the **New HTML** window.

9 **click OK**

This adds the behavior to the list.

10 **change event type**

Change the event type to **On Click** (or whatever you want) in the **Events** column of the **Behaviors** panel by clicking the down arrow. If this event type doesn't appear, you may need to choose **Show Events For** in the same pop-up menu and choose **4.0 or Later Browsers**.

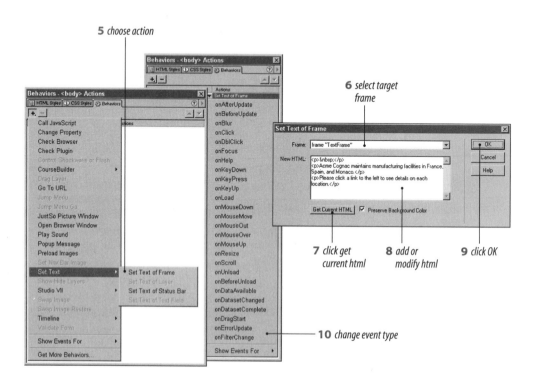

5 *choose action*

6 *select target frame*

7 *click get current html*

8 *add or modify html*

9 *click OK*

10 *change event type*

Spiff up your navigation frame by using a *jump menu* instead of plain hypertext links. A jump menu lets the user "jump" to content in a specific frame, just as she would by clicking a normal hypertext link.

1 insert jump menu

Click this command icon on the **Forms** objects panel or choose **Insert➥Form Objects➥Jump Menu**.

2 enter selection prompt

Type a *selection prompt* (telling the user what to do) in the **Text** field of the **Insert Jump Menu** dialog box.

3 check select first item

The check box labeled **Select First Item After URL Change** tells Dreamweaver to reset the jump menu to display the selection prompt (2) after the visitor has already used the jump menu once.

4 click +

This tells Dreamweaver to add a menu item.

5 enter menu item

Enter text for each menu choice in the **Text** field. (The **Menu Items** field keeps a running list of the items you've added.)

6 specify URL

Specify the Uniform Resource Locator of the document that the jump menu should display when the user selects the menu item.

7 specify frame

Choose the frame where you want the content to display by specifying it in the **Open URLs In** field. (This field acts just like the *target* field for a hyperlink.)

8 name menu

Give the menu a descriptive name.

9 test menu in browser

After repeating steps 5 through 7 for each menu item, click **OK** and press **F12** to preview the page.

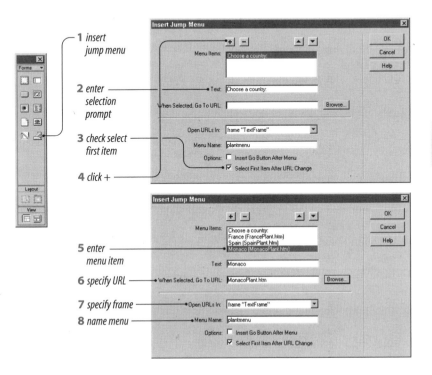

9 *test menu in browser*

Nested Frames

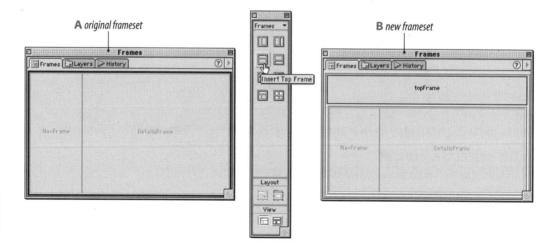

A *original frameset*

B *new frameset*

Insert Top Frame

Frames

Layout

View

A *nested* frame is simply a frame within another frame—although that's where the simplicity ends. The nested frame is called the *child*, and the larger frame within which the nested frame lives is called the *parent*.

> **tip** When you click inside a frame and then insert a new frame, for example with the **Frames** objects panel, Dreamweaver's default behavior is to create the new frame nested inside the frame you clicked, that is, as a child. Conversely, when you click a frame *border* (thereby selecting a frameset) and then insert a new frame, the default behavior is to nest the existing frameset as a child inside a new frameset that also contains the new frame. Try it!

Nested frames give you design options. For example, if you have two frames, one left and one right, and you want a logo or other static graphic to appear at the top of the right frame, you can achieve that result by nesting a new frame at the top of the right frame. Or, if you want your static graphic to appear at the top across both left and right frames, you could nest the current frameset inside a new frameset.

Although nested frames are popular, they make your HTML pages more confusing, so consider whether you can achieve your design goals with other methods.

A original frameset

Here's a simple two-frame set before nesting. Note the way the frameset appears in the **Frames** panel. Three HTML files exist: one for the left frame, one for the right, and one for the frameset container.

B new frameset

By clicking in the right frame and choosing **Insert➡Frames➡Top**, or clicking the **Insert Top Frame** icon in the **Frames** objects panel, you create a new frameset consisting of two frames on the right side: the original frame and the new, nested, upper-right frame. Now, five HTML files exist: the original three, plus the new frame at the upper right, and the new frameset that contains the two right frames.

> **tip** If you want to undo the creation of a frame, the undo command may read **Edit➡Undo Edit Source** or something like **Edit➡Undo Insert Top Frame**, depending on whether you created the new frame inside or outside an existing frame.

Align Frame Backgrounds

One of the problems that some designers have with frames is that they're square—or, more precisely, rectangular.

You can reduce the sensation of choppy blockiness to some degree by turning off frame borders. You can also use transparent GIF images of irregular shapes and sizes to make your frameset appear less "framey."

In addition to these techniques, you can smooth out a frameset's appearance by setting up page backgrounds for side-by-side frames so that the backgrounds mesh perfectly and give the illusion of a single, seamless background.

The example here looks at a tiled background that measures 100 pixels wide by 200 pixels tall; you can apply the same basic technique to nontiled background images. The example uses a simple

side-by-side, two-frame set with borders turned off and assumes that you've already opened the **Frames** panel (choose **Window→Frames**).

1 click in left frame

Click anywhere in the left frame in the document window to tell Dreamweaver that the background you're about to select should apply to the left frame.

2 choose page properties

Choose **Modify→Page Properties** or press **ctrl+J** (**command-J** on the Mac) to display the **Page Properties** dialog box. Here's where you specify the background image. (This is also the dialog box where you can specify a background color, if you aren't using a background image.)

3 select image

Browse to the tiled image by clicking the folder icon or typing the file path into the **Background Image**

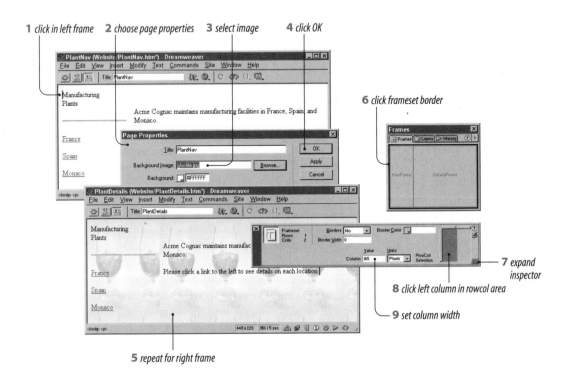

field. Dreamweaver automatically "tiles" the image to repeat within the space that the frame defines.

> **tip** On the subject of tiling, you can use CSS styles to modify Dreamweaver's default behavior. First, create a style that specifies the background image you want. Then specify the style's **Repeat** attribute, which can be **No Repeat**, **Repeat-x** (for horizontal repeating only), and **Repeat-y** (for vertical repeating only). Finally, apply that style to the document's **<body>** tag. (Chapter 14 goes into the nuts and bolts of creating and applying CSS styles.)

4 click OK

This action tells Dreamweaver to make the image the background for the selected left frame document.

5 repeat for right frame

Repeat steps 1 through 4 for the right frame. Unless you created your left frame so that its width is an even multiple of 100, you will see a seam, or discontinuity, between the two frames.

6 click frameset border

Clicking the outer border in the **Frames** panel is the fastest way to select the frameset.

7 expand inspector

If the property inspector isn't open, display it by choosing **Window➡Properties**. If the panel doesn't show the **Column** fields, expand the panel by clicking the small arrow at its lower-right corner.

8 click left column in rowcol area

This action selects the left column so that you can adjust its width in the next step.

9 set column width

Now for the clever bit. In the **Value** field for the column, enter the lowest even multiple of 100 (the background tile image's width) that allows your links to display completely within the frame and set the **Units** field to **Pixels**. This step ensures that the vertical border between frames falls exactly on a tile seam, so that the background looks just as if it were tiled in a single HTML page. By choosing **Pixels**, you make the width of the left frame absolute—that is, independent of any browser resizing the user may perform.

NoFrames Content

A good Web site designer is ever mindful of the case when the user doesn't have a browser capable of viewing any feature outside the bounds of simple HTML. Frames have been around for a while, ever since Version 2 of Netscape Navigator and Version 3 of Internet Explorer, but some users may not have a frames-capable browser. In that case, you can create "noframes content," a chunk of HTML bounded by the **<noframes>** and **</noframes>** tags that users see when they can't see frames.

You don't have to edit the HTML directly to create noframes content. Open the frameset in the document window and choose the command **Modify➡Frameset➡Edit NoFrames Content**. The document window gains a header bar proclaiming "NoFrames

Content," and you can click in the document window to create whatever message you want the user to see (such as a link to an alternative Web page that doesn't use frames). When you're done, choose **Modify➡Frameset➡Edit NoFrames Content** again, and you're back to the original frameset.

Make & Manipulate Layers

A *layer* is simply a box on your page that can hold other HTML objects, such as images, tables, and text (but not frames). The most obvious benefit of layers is positioning flexibility: You can place a layer anywhere on the page. So, for example, you can place an image with pixel precision by giving that image its own layer. You can even "nest" one layer inside another, for still more artistic freedom.

Layers have other charms as well, though. You can achieve interesting overlapping effects. You can hide and show layers based on user actions. You can even change the "stacking order" of layers. And when you've finished this chapter, check out Chapter 11 for details on creating animation effects with layers and timelines.

The sacrifice you make for using layers is compatibility with Version 3 browsers. However, with some restrictions, Dreamweaver lets you work with layers and then convert them to tables that work with older browsers.

The Draw Layer Commands

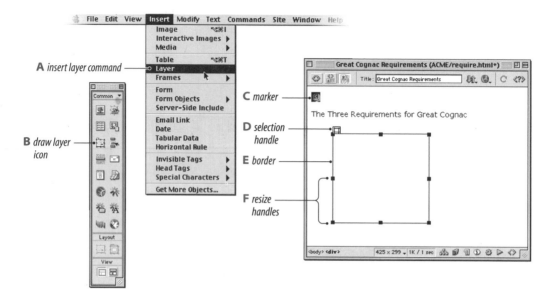

A *insert layer command*

B *draw layer icon*

C *marker*

D *selection handle*

E *border*

F *resize handles*

Creating a new layer on a Web page in Dreamweaver takes longer to describe than to do. However, as you may have come to expect by now, Macromedia gives you more than one way to create a layer.

A insert layer command

One way to create a layer is to choose **Insert→ Layer**. (Oddly, no keyboard shortcut exists for this common command.) Dreamweaver draws a new layer at the current insertion point. The width and height of the new layer are set by values in the **Preferences** dialog box, which you can display by choosing **Edit→Preferences**; see Layer Preferences on page 130 for details.

B draw layer icon

The preferable way for most people to create a new layer is to click the **Draw Layer** icon on the objects panel and then move the cursor to the document window and click and drag to draw a rectangle defining the layer's approximate size and position. (I say "approximate" because you can always tweak the layer's size and position after you draw it.) The

position of the insertion point doesn't matter; you can draw a layer anywhere on the page. Hold down **ctrl** and you can draw multiple layers without having to reselect the icon.

> *tip* If Dreamweaver doesn't seem to want to let you draw the layer where you want it, click in the document window and press **enter** (Win) or **return** (Mac) a few times to insert some paragraph tags.

> *tip* If you draw a new layer with method (B), and that new layer is inside another layer, Dreamweaver will decide whether to *nest* the new layer inside the existing layer based on the status of the **Nesting** check box in the **Preferences** dialog box. You can hold down **alt** (Win) or **option** (Mac) to override the preference setting. If you use the **Insert→Layer** command, Dreamweaver ignores the preference and always nests the new layer! Again, Layer Preferences on page 130 explains.

C marker

Whether you use the **Insert➧Layer** command or the **Draw Layer** icon (A) or the **Insert➧Layer** command (B), Dreamweaver adds a special marker to the page indicating the position of the HTML code defining the layer. If you don't see such a marker—it appears at the insertion point or (for a new document) at the top of the page—then you can toggle its display on by choosing **View➧Visual Aids➧Invisible Elements**.

If the layer marker *still* doesn't appear, you may need to choose **Edit➧Preferences**, click **Invisible Elements** in the category list, and make sure that **Anchor Points for Layers** is checked.

A layer anchor point is the same as a layer marker, incidentally. Consistent terminology is not Dreamweaver's strong suit.

> **tip** Invisible elements like layer markers have the side effect of nudging page elements out of position in the document window, so if you use these, it's a good idea to preview your pages frequently using the **Preview/Debug In Browser** button on Dreamweaver's main toolbar (or its **F12** shortcut). You could also toggle the invisible elements display off occasionally with **View➧Visual Aids➧Invisible Elements**, but that's more work than pressing **F12,** and the browser preview gives you a more accurate rendering.

D selection handle

The layer selection handle at the layer's upper left corner appears when the layer is either *active* (that is, hosting the current insertion point or currently selected object) or *selected* (for example, by having been clicked in the **Layers** panel; see The Layers Property Inspector on pages 126 and 127). You can also click and drag this selection handle to move a layer.

E border

A solid black rectangular border delineates a selected layer. Other layers on the page, if any exist, have a gray border.

If you don't see borders around other layers but you know the other layers exist, toggle on their display by choosing **View➧Visual Aids➧Layer Borders**.

F resize handles

As with images, a selected layer sports eight *resize handles* along its border. You can click and drag these resize handles to change the layer's size. Clicking and dragging a corner resize handle lets you resize a layer in both horizontal and vertical dimensions. If you just want to resize horizontally or vertically, click and drag a middle handle.

If you prefer to resize a layer to precise dimensions, use the **Layers** property inspector (see The Layers Property Inspector on pages 126 and 127).

Layers & Browser Compatibility

Your users must have Netscape Navigator Version 4.0 or higher, or Internet Explorer Version 4.0 or higher, to see layers the way that you build them. Users of earlier browsers should see your layers' content, but without any style sheet attributes of positioning, visibility, and stacking. If you create multiple overlapping layers, there's no telling exactly what a Version 3.0 browser user will see without actually experimenting.

Having said that both Navigator Version 4.0+ and IE Version 4.0+ support layers, I should add that maddening little differences exist between them.

I strongly recommend previewing your layered pages in as many versions of common browsers as you can to be sure that the differences aren't significant. Play around with resizing the browser window when previewing, so that you can see how your layers look in different window sizes and shapes.

Also, be aware that Navigator Version 4.*x* has a particular problem that I discuss in Layer Preferences on page 130.

The Layers Panel

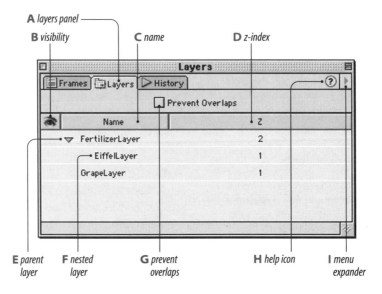

A *layers panel*

B *visibility*   **C** *name*   **D** *z-index*

E *parent layer*   **F** *nested layer*   **G** *prevent overlaps*   **H** *help icon*   **I** *menu expander*

An indispensable tool for dealing with layers is the **Layers** panel. Use it to select layers, rearrange their stacking order by dragging and dropping, rename them, delete them, change their visibility status, and manage nesting relationships.

A layers panel

Press **F2** or choose **Window→Layers** to display the **Layers** panel, which itemizes all layers in the current document with the most recently created layer at the top of the list.

B visibility

Click in this column, under the eye-con (sorry), to control whether a given layer is to be visible or not. You may want to make some layers invisible while you're working on other ones (but don't forget you did so; the visibility status also determines whether a layer will be visible when the page loads in a browser window).

An open eye means the layer is visible; a closed eye means the layer is invisible. By default you don't see either icon, meaning that each layer is visible. No icon for a nested layer (F) means that the visibility status of the parent layer determines whether the nested layer is visible.

> **tip** You can click the eye in the column header to make all layers either visible or invisible in one fell swoop.

C name

A layer is an HTML object and therefore should have a unique and descriptive name. (Choosing the layer you want from a list is a lot easier if you don't have to deal with names like **Layer1**, **Layer2**, and so on.) Change a layer's name in the **Layers** panel by simply double-clicking the name to display a little text-editing rectangle and then typing in your changes.

Activate and select a layer in the **Layers** panel by clicking its name (which is a whole lot easier than selecting it in the document window). Once you've selected a layer, its selection handles appear in the document window, and you can move, resize, or delete it.

D z-index

The *z-index* refers to the layer's place in the stack, if a stack exists, with higher numbers being nearer the top. The **Layers** panel parallels the stack on your page—that is, the topmost layer in the panel is the topmost on the page, and the last one the browser draws. You can reorder layers in the panel by dragging and dropping them. Note also that two or more layers can have the same z-index and the browser will figure out which to draw first, but that's not great design.

E parent layer

Click the – sign (Win) or down-pointing triangle (Mac) to the left of a layer name to hide the child layers nested beneath it (F). Click the + sign (Win) or right-pointing triangle (Mac) to redisplay the nested layers.

F nested layer

By default, nested layers appear indented beneath their parent layer (E). You can unnest a nested layer by dragging its name to a new location.

G prevent overlaps

The **Prevent Overlaps** check box corresponds to the **Modify➥Arrange➥Prevent Layer Overlaps** command. Check this box if you want Dreamweaver to prevent you from creating overlapping layers, for example, because you plan to

convert the document to tables (which can't overlap) for Version-3 browser compatibility.

> **tip** This option is fairly limited. It's not retroactive; it won't unoverlap layers you've already built. It also only works if you add layers with the **Draw Layer** icon from the objects panel (that is, it doesn't work if you use the menu command or if you tweak your page's HTML code in code view). Bottom line: Don't rely on this feature to keep you out of overlap trouble.

H help icon

Click the question mark to open the Using Dreamweaver help system to the topic of layers.

I menu expander

This button is grayed out and therefore inactive. The reason it even appears at all is that all panels in Dreamweaver 4 must have the same basic layout elements, even if the program doesn't always use each one.

Layer Selection Methods

Clicking a layer name in the **Layers** panel is the easiest way to activate and select a layer, but Dreamweaver provides several other methods, too.

First, a bit of terminology. The *active* layer is the one in which you're working; you can make a layer active merely by clicking anywhere inside it. (When you first open a layered page, no layers are active.) However, an active layer isn't necessarily *selected*; for example, you may have most recently selected an image inside the active layer. You have to select a layer before moving or resizing it. When you click the layer name in the **Layers** panel, you simultaneously activate and select that layer.

Click layer border

As long as the layer is visible—that is, *active*—you can click its border to

select it. The cursor turns into a four-arrow pointer (Win) or a hand (Mac) when you mouse over the layer border.

If layer borders are on (check the menu toggle **View➥Visual Aids➥Layer Borders**), you can see the borders of non-active layers as well as of the active layer; non-active layers have a gray border, whereas the active layer has a black border.

If layer borders are off, then you can still mouse over where you think the border of a non-active layer would be and watch for the cursor to change into the four-arrow pointer.

Shift-click inside layer

If a layer isn't active, you can **shift**-click anywhere inside it to select it.

Click layer tag

If you see the **<div>** tag (or **<span>** if you're using that one) on the status bar of the document window, you can click the tag to select the active layer.

Click layer marker

Dreamweaver creates layer markers in the document window when you create a layer. The menu toggle **View➥Visual Aids➥Invisible Elements** must be checked for you to see these markers, which indicate the placement of the layer HTML code. By default, Dreamweaver creates layer markers at the insertion point. (A nested layer's marker appears inside the parent layer.) Click a marker to simultaneously activate and select a layer.

The Layers Property Inspector

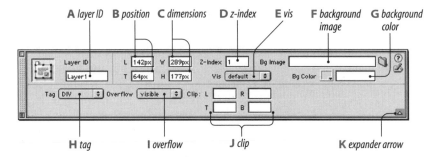

A *layer ID* B *position* C *dimensions* D *z-index* E *vis* F *background image* G *background color*

H *tag* I *overflow* J *clip* K *expander arrow*

The **Layers** property inspector is your primary vehicle for viewing and changing layer attributes in Dreamweaver. To display the **Layers** property inspector, select a layer and choose **Window→Properties** or press **ctrl+F3** (**command-F3** on the Mac).

The **Layers** property inspector is one of the more complex property inspectors in Dreamweaver, but when you study its components one at a time, it's not too difficult to master.

> *tip* You can set properties for two or more layers at a time by selecting multiple layers. See Layer Selection Methods, on page 125, for different ways to select layers.

A layer ID
Despite the different name, this field is the same as the **Name** field in the **Layers** panel (C, page 124) and uniquely identifies the layer. Stick to alphanumerical characters (no spaces, hyphens, and so on) and don't duplicate layer names within a Web site.

B position
The value in the **L** (left) field is the number of pixels between the left margin of the document (or parent layer, if the selected layer is *nested* inside another layer) and the left margin of the current layer. The **T** (top) field contains the number of pixels between the top margin of the document (or parent layer) and the top margin of the current layer.

C dimensions
The layer's width and height live in the **W** and **H** fields. If you enter dimensions that are too small to

display the images and text that the layer contains, Dreamweaver overrides you and automatically increases the layer's size.

> *tip* If you want to use some metric other than pixels for the position (B) or dimension (C) values, you can enter values in inches (**in**), centimeters (**cm**), millimeters (**mm**), picas (**pc**), points (**pt**), or a percentage (%) of the parent object's dimension. Just make sure that you don't put a space between the number and the abbreviation.

> *tip* If you're creating a new layer that will contain only a single image, draw the new layer too small and then insert the image. Dreamweaver automatically sizes the layer to fit the image, leaving you with one less design chore to perform manually.

D z-index
The *z-index* of a layer is a nerdy way of referring to its place in a stack of layers, if a stack exists, with higher numbers being nearer the top. I prefer changing the z-index by dragging and dropping layers in the **Layers** panel (see The Layers Panel on pages 124 and 125), but you can change it here, too, by entering a number.

E vis
The **Vis** pop-up menu lets you specify the layer's initial visibility setting. (I say "initial" because a behavior can change the layer's visibility in response to a user action.) **Default** means the browser determines the setting (typically, this is the same as inherit). **Inherit**

means that a nested layer looks to its parent to determine its visibility; non-nested layers are visible with this setting. The **visible** and **hidden** settings are absolute, regardless of the parent layer's setting.

F background image

If you want a background image for the layer, you can specify it here, either by typing the file path, or by browsing to the image by clicking the folder icon. A layer background image floats above any page background image that you have defined.

G background color

Each layer on a page can have a different background color.

H tag

The **Tag** field specifies which HTML tag Dreamweaver should use to code the layer. For details, see the sidebar CSS Versus Netscape Layers below.

I overflow

What happens if a layer's contents are larger than the layer's dimensions (D)? **Visible** (the assumed setting if you leave this field blank) tells Dreamweaver to relocate the layer's lower-right corner to accommodate the contents. **Hidden** keeps the layer size as specified, meaning that some content won't display; no scroll bars appear. **Scroll** is like **hidden**, but scroll bars always appear, whether you need them or not. **Auto** is like **scroll**, but scroll bars only appear when required.

 Some of these overflow settings behave differently (or not at all) in different browsers.

J clip

The **Clip** area contains four fields, **L** (left), **T** (top), **R** (right), and **B** (bottom). These fields define the *clipping region*, the visible part of the layer. (You can use clipping regions to achieve cool special effects with scripting.) The **L** and **R** numbers represent distances in pixels from the left margin of the layer, and the **T** and **B** numbers are distances from its top margin. Only content between **L** and **R** horizontally, and **T** and **B** vertically, appears.

 If you enter one number, enter all four.

K expander arrow

Click here to show or hide the inspector's lower half.

CSS Versus Netscape Layers

Different browser developers have come up with different implementations of the layer concept. Layers correspond to no fewer than four HTML tags: **<div>**, **<span>**, **<layer>**, and **<ilayer>**. Navigator Version 4.0 supports the proprietary **<layer>** and **<ilayer>** tags, but later versions don't, and Internet Explorer doesn't support them at all, so I don't suggest you use these tags unless you have a compelling reason—and I won't take space in this book to discuss the unique aspects of

Netscape layers. (If you need that information, check out Dreamweaver's online help.) Stick with the **<div>** and **<span>** tags that are part of the CSS (Cascading Style Sheet) specification; both Navigator and Internet Explorer support these.

How do layers relate to style sheets? Just about every attribute of the **<div>** and **<span>** tags are style sheet attributes. Layers draw from a subset of the CSS standard called *CSS-P*, where the "P" stands for

positioning. Dreamweaver's **Layers** property inspector insulates you from the style sheet coding chores, but under the hood, the layer is just another CSS style.

Incidentally, the **<div>** and **<span>** tags differ in that **<div>** uses absolute positioning and is more suitable for block content (that is, content set off like a separate paragraph) while **<span>** uses relative positioning and is more suitable for inline content. Dreamweaver's default behavior is to use **<div>**.

Create A Layered Page

In this example, I'll use the objects panel icon to create two layers. My goal here is to create a mildly interesting visual effect: two images that overlap each other slightly. This will give the user a little visual relief from the rigid blockiness that most Web pages exhibit and present a subtle 3D effect. I'm also going to add a little text into the same layer as each image, so that if I move a layer around later, the descriptive text stays right with the image.

1 click draw layer icon

Click the **Draw Layer** icon on the objects panel. If the objects panel isn't showing, display it by choosing **Window➞Objects** or by pressing **ctrl+F2** (**command-F2** on the Mac).

2 draw first layer

With your document window in design view, place the cursor about where you want the upper-left

corner of the layer to be. Click and drag the cursor to the lower right corner and release the mouse button.

3 insert image

After you create a new layer, the layer is active, and the current insertion point blinks at its upper-left corner, waiting for you to insert some content. Click the **Insert Image** icon on the objects panel and then select the image you want either by typing in its path name or by browsing to it. (For more on inserting images, see Chapter 4, Add & Edit Graphics, pages 56 through 58.)

4 increase layer height (optional)

The image that I've added is bigger than the layer I drew, so at this point the layer is precisely the same size as the image. Because I want to add some descriptive text, I need to increase the layer's height. Do so by clicking the layer's border to select it and typing a higher number in the **H** field of the **Layers** property

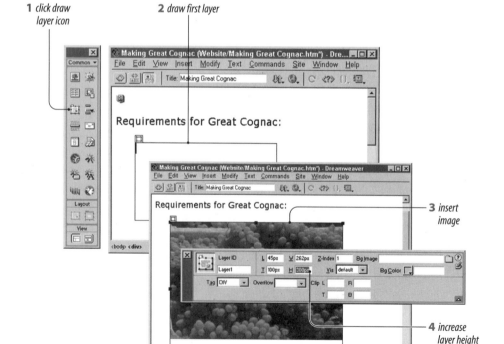

1 *click draw layer icon*

2 *draw first layer*

3 *insert image*

4 *increase layer height*

inspector. (If the inspector isn't visible, make it so with **Windows➡Properties**.) Here's incentive: If you draw the layer big enough, you can skip this step.

5 add text
Now I've got room to add some text below the image. Click the image, press **end** to position the insertion point, press **enter** (Win) or **return** (Mac) to start a new paragraph, and then type in the text you want. Format it to taste, using the **Text** property inspector (see the Text Inspector section on page 42 of Chapter 3).

6 open layers panel
The next layer I want to add will overlap the first one slightly, so I have to make sure that Dreamweaver is set to permit overlapping layers. The setting lives on the **Layers** panel, which you open by choosing **Window➡Layers** or by pressing **F2**.

7 clear prevent overlaps
If the **Prevent Overlaps** check box is checked, click it to clear it. Now, Dreamweaver will let me draw an overlapping layer.

8 draw second layer
Click the **Draw Layer** icon from the objects panel and draw the second layer so that it overlaps the right edge of the first layer.

9 repeat steps 3 through 5
Add the second image, and descriptive text for it, into the second layer.

10 preview in browser
Click the **Preview/Debug in Browser** toolbar button and choose to preview your page in the browser of choice. (The actual list depends on which browsers you've installed onto your computer.)

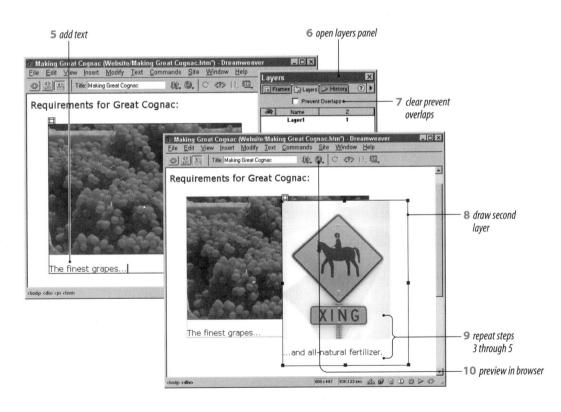

5 add text

6 open layers panel

7 clear prevent overlaps

8 draw second layer

9 repeat steps 3 through 5

10 preview in browser

⑧ **Make & Manipulate Layers:** Create A Layered Page   **129**

Layer Preferences

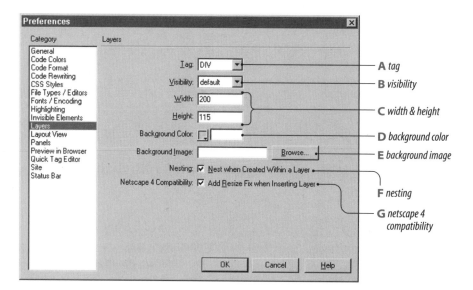

You can tell Dreamweaver to make certain changes to its default layer-related behavior by choosing **Edit➛Preferences** or pressing **ctrl+U** (**command-U** on the Mac). In the **Preferences** dialog box, click the **Layers** entry in the **Category** list at the left to see the layer-specific preferences you can preset. (For other preferences you can set, see Chapter 16, *Personalize Dreamweaver*.)

A tag
Choose the HTML tag Dreamweaver should use when you create a new layer. **DIV** is the default.

B visibility
The default value is (logically) **default**, which depends on the browser. If you specify **inherit**, then the new layer takes its visibility value from its parent—either the layer in which it is nested, or, if it's not nested, the actual document, whose status is always "visible." Specifying **visible** or **hidden** means that newly created layers have that setting regardless of the parent's setting. These settings affect both designer and user.

C width & height
These determine the default size of any layer you create via the **Insert➛Layer** command, as opposed to the **Draw Layer** icon on the objects panel.

D background color
Use the color picker or type the code to specify a default background color for all new layers.

E background image
You can either click the **Browse** button to go find an image file to serve as the background for all newly created layers or enter its path directly.

F nesting
If you check this box, then anytime you draw a new layer inside of an existing layer, Dreamweaver nests it. Override this default preference by holding down **alt** (Win) or **option** (Mac) while drawing a new layer.

G netscape 4 compatibility
When a user resizes a Navigator 4.*x* browser window, layer positioning gets out of whack. The JavaScript code you add with this check box makes the page reload every time the user resizes the browser window. Change the setting for the current page by choosing **Commands➛Add/Remove Netscape Resize Fix** and clicking the **Add** or **Remove** button.

ⓢⓣⓔⓟⓢ Build Nested Layers

You would *nest* one layer inside another if you want to position the inner layer or layers precisely (as you can with a layer on a document), but you also want the inner layer(s) to move with the outer layer, for example because the inner layer content ties to the outer layer content. In the example, the outer (parent) layer has the headline "Plant Locations," and the two nested inner layers contain photos of two manufacturing facilities. You can move the parent layer and the child layers move with it, but you can overlap the two nested child layers for a nice visual effect that you couldn't achieve with a table. On a complex page, you could create two or more sets of nested layers and move them around in logical groups.

> ⓣⓘⓟ You can't convert a nested layer to tables using the **Modify➤Convert➤Layers to Table** command.

1 draw parent layer

Click the **Draw Layer** icon on the objects panel and then click and drag to draw a rectangle in the document window. This will serve as the parent layer, so make it big enough to hold the content you plan to nest inside it.

2 add text

Enter some text at the top of the parent layer that describes the layer's contents; in my example, it's a heading that says **Plant Locations**.

1 *draw parent layer*   **2** *add text*   **3** *set nesting preference*

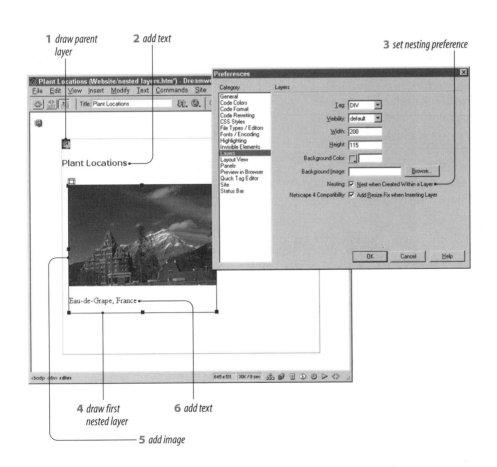

4 *draw first nested layer*   **6** *add text*

5 *add image*

3 set nesting preference

Choose **Edit➥Preferences**, select **Layers** from the **Category** list, and check the status of the **Nesting** check box. For this example, make sure that it's checked, so that Dreamweaver's default behavior is to nest a layer that you draw inside another layer.

(For more on setting layer preferences, see Layer Preferences on page 130.)

4 draw first nested layer

Click the **Draw Layer** icon on the objects panel again and draw the first nested layer completely inside the boundaries of the parent layer. Dreamweaver automatically nests it.

5 add image

Click the **Insert Image** icon on the objects panel to insert a picture, in this example, a photo of the first plant location.

6 add text

Add a bit of descriptive text below the image you added in step 5. If necessary, enlarge the layer to make room by dragging a layer resize handle.

7 draw second nested layer

Click the **Draw Layer** icon on the objects panel and draw the second nested layer completely inside the boundaries of the parent layer but overlapping the right edge of the first nested layer. Again, Dreamweaver nests the layer inside the parent layer. At this point, you've created two layers, both of which nest inside a parent layer.

8 add image & text

Repeat steps 5 and 6 for the second nested layer in my example, using a picture of the second plant location and text describing that facility.

9 confirm nesting

Open the **Layers** panel (**Window➥Layers**) to confirm the relationships of the layers you've created. The parent layer should appear with a plus sign (+), which reveals the two nested layers when you click it.

If you click the parent layer's name to select it, and then move the parent layer by dragging the selection handle in the document window, the nested layers fall neatly and automatically into place.

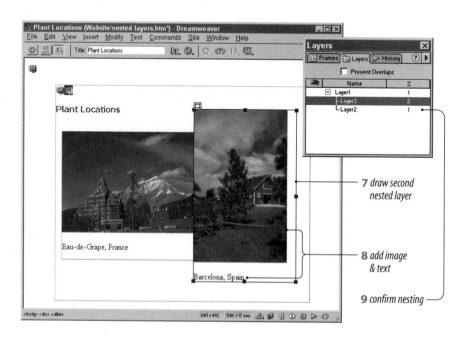

The Convert Commands

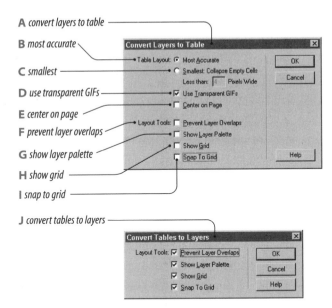

A *convert layers to table*
B *most accurate*
C *smallest*
D *use transparent GIFs*
E *center on page*
F *prevent layer overlaps*
G *show layer palette*
H *show grid*
I *snap to grid*
J *convert tables to layers*

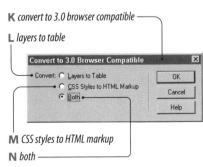

K *convert to 3.0 browser compatible*
L *layers to table*
M *CSS styles to HTML markup*
N *both*

You may find that you like to design pages with layers and then convert those pages to tables as a final step in order to achieve maximum browser compatibility. Or, you may want to make both a layered version and a nonlayered version of a given page available for users, depending on their browser version. Such conversion would be mighty tedious if not for Dreamweaver's handy built-in **Convert** commands.

Two things to bear in mind. First, you can't convert between layers and tables if you've applied a template to your document, or for that matter if you're editing an actual template; see Chapter 9, Use Templates & Libraries, for more on what templates are and how to use them. Second, the conversion dialog boxes are not well designed or worded, so read the descriptions here to understand what their options *really* mean.

Note that the program offers conversion commands on the **Modify** menu and on the **File** menu. The difference is that the **Modify** menu commands don't create a new page (they modify the existing page), but the **File** command does.

A convert layers to table

Choose **Modify➡Convert➡Layers to Tables** to bring up the **Convert Layers to Table** dialog box, where you set your choices for converting a layers layout to a table layout.

B most accurate

If you're more concerned with accurate positioning than with page size, select the **Most Accurate** radio button, which instructs Dreamweaver to create as many table cells as necessary to honor your precise layout.

C smallest

If you're willing to sacrifice some positioning precision for the sake of a smaller download, select the **Smallest** radio button and specify a pixel distance within which Dreamweaver will align layer edges.

D use transparent GIFs

If you check this box, Dreamweaver puts transparent GIF files in the last row of the table to force all browsers to display the table with the correct column widths. The tradeoff here is that you can't later edit column size by dragging column borders.

E center on page

Check this, and the resultant table appears centered; leave it cleared, and the table aligns itself to the left margin.

F prevent layer overlaps

This check box shouldn't be in the **Convert Layers to Table** dialog box (A) at all, because Dreamweaver can't convert layers to a table if the layers overlap, regardless of this setting. In the **Convert Tables to Layers** dialog box (J), check this box to prevent created layers from being overlappable if you move them around later.

> **tip** You also can't convert layers to tables if the layers are nested. You have to manually un-nest any nested layers (for example, using the **Layers** panel) before converting layers to a table.

G show layer palette

What Macromedia means is the **Layers** *panel* (palette is a Dreamweaver 2.0/3.0 term). This check box seems unnecessary to me, but I guess it saves you having to press **F2** if the **Layers** panel isn't already visible.

H show grid

The **Show Grid** option tells Dreamweaver to display the grid after performing the conversion. If you like using the grid, you probably already have it on, but here's another chance to activate it.

I snap to grid

This check box turns on grid snapping, but it doesn't actually snap your layers or tables into place during a

conversion. Think of this setting as saying "Activate snapping so that if I move the layers or tables later, they'll snap to the grid."

J convert tables to layers

If you choose **Modify➡Convert➡Tables to Layers**, you see this dialog box, which includes the same layout settings (F, G, H, and I) that appear at the bottom of the **Convert Layers to Table** dialog box. Anything on the page that isn't in a table will get its own new layer; empty cells only get a new layer if they have a background color. With this command and the **Modify➡Convert➡Layers to Table** command (A), you can alternate between layers and tables as often as you like.

K convert to 3.0 browser compatible

The two dialog boxes that you access via the **Modify** menu (A and J) don't create a new file, but the command **File➡Convert➡3.0 Browser Compatible** does, giving it a name containing *Untitled* (you have to save the new file after the conversion). Otherwise, this command works like the **Modify➡Convert➡Layers to Table** command, with two exceptions: You don't have as much control over the conversion process, and you can also choose to have *all* CSS style coding on the page (not just layer codes) converted to HTML styles.

L layers to table

Click this radio button to convert layers to a table.

M CSS styles to HTML markup

Click here to convert any nonlayer CSS styles to HTML styles that Version 3.0 browsers can understand. If any CSS code doesn't have an HTML style equivalent, Dreamweaver gets rid of it.

N both

Click this radio button to activate both the **Layers to Table** (L) and **CSS Styles to HTML Markup** (M) options.

The Tracing Image Commands

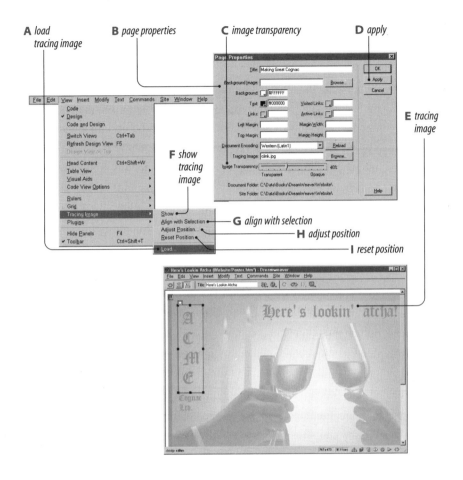

A *load tracing image*

B *page properties*

C *image transparency*

D *apply*

E *tracing image*

F *show tracing image*

G *align with selection*

H *adjust position*

I *reset position*

If you like to design complex Web pages by first creating a mockup in a paint or scanning program, you can use the **Tracing Image** commands in Dreamweaver to help you position layers that correspond to that mockup. The mockup appears in the document window in place of any background color or image you've defined for the document. You can then position your layers precisely over the mockup graphic.

When a user views the page in a browser, any defined background color or image appears, but the tracing image does not; the tracing image exists solely for the designer's use in positioning objects on the page. Those objects are most often

layers, which (unlike images, tables, and text) you can position precisely anywhere on the page. The tracing image commands are mighty handy when a client or boss gives you an image file and says "I'd like my home page to look like *this*." Also, in layout view, you have excellent control for creating tables from a tracing image.

A load tracing image

The command **View➡Tracing Image➡Load** prompts you to select an image, which must be a JPEG, GIF, or PNG file, and then automatically opens the **Page Properties** dialog box (B). Alternately, you can choose **Modify➡Page Properties** and either enter a path in the **Tracing Image** field, or browse to one by clicking the **Browse** button next to that field.

B page properties

This dialog box appears right after you choose an image file, if you begin the loading process by choosing **View→Tracing Image→Load**. The image you've selected appears in the **Tracing Image** field. You can also get here by choosing **Modify→Page Properties**. This dialog box is the only place you can set or change the tracing image's transparency (C).

C image transparency

The **Image Transparency** slider controls how intensely the tracing image appears, with 0 percent meaning you can't see it (completely transparent) and 100 percent meaning you can see it with full intensity (completely opaque). To adjust the value, simply drag the slider tab. You can also click the slider bar to the right or left of the tab to increase or decrease the value in 20-percent increments. Or for more precise adjustments, click the slider tab and then press the left- or right-arrow key to raise or lower the value by one percent.

> *tip* The main reason you make the image faded is to remind yourself that it's not actually part of your page. I typically set the **Image Transparency** value to about 40 percent, but any mid-range value—say, between 30 and 60 percent—should work nicely for most images.

D apply

Click **Apply** after changing the image's transparency (C) to see how it looks in the document window. If you don't like what you see, adjust the amount of transparency and click **Apply** again.

E tracing image

By default, the tracing image appears in the document's upper-left corner, with the transparency level you specified. You can now position one or more new layers at precise places over the mockup file you loaded as your tracing image.

F show tracing image

The **View→Tracing Image→Show** command is a toggle that you can set or clear to show or hide the tracing image. Note that it doesn't hurt anything to leave the tracing image set, and simply hide it when you're done with it. The tracing image does not download with your Web page.

G align with selection

To align the tracing image with an object, such as a layer or image, select the object and choose **View→Tracing Image→Align with Selection**. The upper-left corner of the tracing image will relocate to coincide with the upper-left corner of the selected object in the document window.

H adjust position.

To change the position of the tracing image in the document window, choose **View→Tracing Image→Adjust Position**. The **Adjust Tracing Image Position** dialog box appears, as shown below. You can either enter the exact pixel coordinates in the **X** and **Y** fields (remembering that the upper-left corner is 0,0) or press the arrow keys to move the tracing image in one-pixel increments.

> *tip* Throw in the **shift** key to nudge the image in five-pixel increments.

You can see the results of your changes in the document window, but your new position settings aren't actually put into effect until you click **OK**.

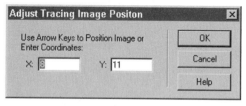

I reset position

Choose **View→Tracing Image→Reset Position** to snap the tracing image's position back to the upper-left corner of the document window after you've moved it (G and H). This command is quicker than choosing **View→Tracing Image→Adjust Position** and entering **0** in both the **X** and **Y** fields.

Use Templates & Libraries

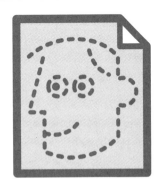

Many Web sites have lots of pages with basically the same layout. You can use Dreamweaver *templates* to make creating and updating such pages faster and easier. A template specifies elements that are common to all similar pages.

Templates save you time in two ways. You can create a new page based on a template, kick-starting the layout. Later, you can update existing template-based pages by editing the template and rippling the edits throughout your site.

Templates are also great for collaborative projects, because you can mark which parts of a page other designers can edit and which are "off limits."

The drawback of templates is that you can't use CSS styles, layer animation, or JavaScript behaviors with them without significant restrictions. However, you can use *library items* to achieve some of the same benefits that templates offer without compromising the usability of these three features.

The Templates & Library Panels

A template icon

C panel name

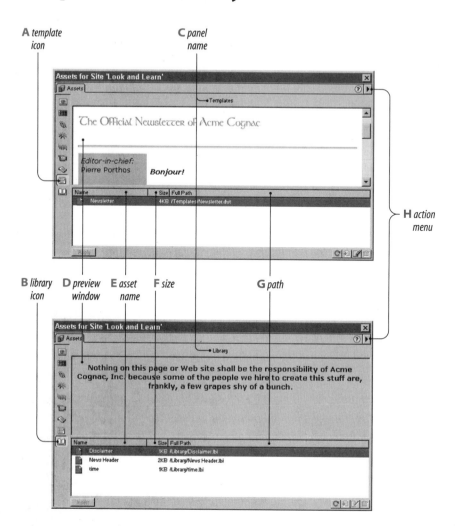

H action menu

B library icon

D preview window

E asset name

F size

G path

The **Templates** and **Library** panels are really specific views of the **Assets** panel, even though each has its own menu command (**Window→ Templates** and **Window→Library**). No keyboard shortcuts exist for these specific commands, although the shortcut to display the **Assets** panel is **F11**. Once the **Assets** panel is open, you can click the template icon (A) or library icon (B) to see the respective panels (See The Assets Panel on page 164 of Chapter 10).

These two panels let you see a list of all the templates and library items that are defined for a

specific site. You can also see a preview of their appearance in these two panels. The action menu (H) for the selected item is a great springboard for performing template and library procedures, such as updating a site to reflect changes to the item.

A template icon

Click here to see the **Templates** panel. (Other panels that fall under the rubric of "Assets" include images, colors, URLs, Flash objects, Shockwave objects, movies, and scripts.)

B library icon

Click here to see the **Library** panel.

C panel name

The name of the currently selected panel appears just above the preview window (D). Good thing, as the **Templates** and **Library** panels are darn near identical.

D preview window

In the preview window for both the **Templates** and **Library** panels, you can see all or part of the asset's content. Scroll bars let you adjust the view, and you can resize the panel (as well as the horizontal divider) to see as much as you need to see.

E asset name

This column contains the names of the assets—either templates or library items—for the current site. Assets for other sites do not appear. You should name your templates and library items descriptively so that you can use the panels effectively.

F size

Dreamweaver displays the size of the template or library item in kilobytes.

G path

Here's the full path specification for the template file (normally these live in the site's **Templates** folder) or the library item file (these live in the site's **Library** folder).

H action menu

Click this arrow to display the action menu for the selected template or library item. This menu is the same as the *context menu* that you display by right-clicking (Win) or **control**-clicking (Mac) the asset name (E). The action menus are nearly identical.

Templates Versus Library Items

Both templates and library items let you create groups of page elements that apply to multiple pages. Both let you change the "master" file and then propagate changes to pages based on that master file. And both are Dreamweaver "assets" that you can reuse within a site as often as you like. So when should you use templates and when should you use library items? I've never seen a great explanation of this issue, so here's my attempt.

Collaboration

First off, if you're going to be working with other people on a Web site,

and you want to specify some parts of a page's layout to be fixed and others editable, use templates. Templates let you specify "editable regions," but library items do not.

Layout control

If you want to constrain the page's overall layout—say, with tables or layers—then again, templates are the way to go. Library items are usually discrete chunks of HTML that you can place anywhere on the page; with a template, you can control the placement of editable and non-editable content. If you don't care where a page fragment goes or

if you might place it differently on different pages, make the fragment a library item. Library items permit greater layout flexibility.

Head content

If your pages need to use CSS styles, JavaScript behaviors, layer animation, or any other features that modify the part of the page's HTML code bounded by the **<head></head>** tag pair, you're almost always better off using library items. With templates, the **<head>** area is normally locked out from modification, with the sole exception of the document's title.

steps Create A New Template

Broadly speaking, creating a new template is a two-step process. First design the page as you would any other and then specify *editable regions* (that is, areas where content can change from page to page).

> **tip** If you've ever created a computer slideshow with a program like PowerPoint, then you can think of the Dreamweaver template as a *slide master* and editable content as the *titles and bullets* that vary from slide to slide.

In this example, I create a template for a company newsletter's main page. My client, Acme Cognac, wants to maintain back issues of the newsletter online, so each month's new issue will use the template. The benefits are twofold: Each newsletter

issue has a consistent look and feel, and creating new newsletter pages is a snap. (Although I do so in this example, you don't have to start from scratch. If you already have an HTML page that you'd like to use as the basis for your new template, you can open it instead of laying out a new page, and skip to step 4.)

1 lay out page

The first step in building a template is to create the page layout. You can do this with layout tables, as discussed in the Build A Table In Layout View section on page 86 of Chapter 5, or with layers, as discussed in The Draw Layer Command on page 122 of Chapter 8. In my example, I use a simple two-cell table as the page's centerpiece.

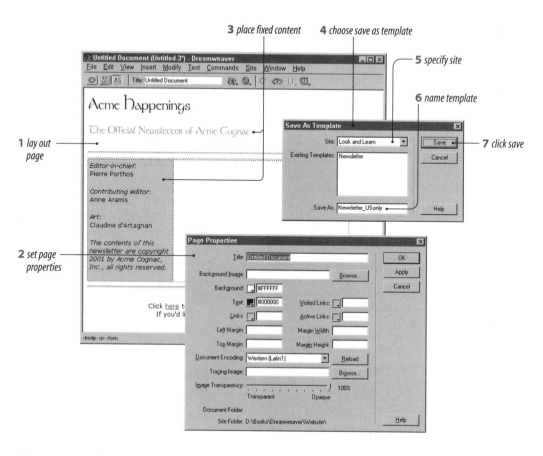

3 *place fixed content*   4 *choose save as template*

5 *specify site*

6 *name template*

1 *lay out page*

7 *click save*

2 *set page properties*

2 set page properties

The command here is **Modify→Page Properties**, and the shortcuts are **ctrl+J** (Win) and **command-J** (Mac). All the properties that you set here, with the sole exception of the page title, will be set in stone for all future pages that you base on the template, unless you modify the template itself.

3 place fixed content

Next, place any fixed content onto your page: images and text that you want to stay the same for all documents you create in the future based on this master design. In my example, the newsletter title and subtitle, a couple of horizontal rules, and some footer lines are all fixed content. In addition, the left table cell, containing the masthead information, will be fixed. The only editable content will be the right table cell.

If you place a link onto a template file, browse to it with the **Point-to-File** icon or by clicking the **Folder** icon. This action ensures that Dreamweaver uses the correct document-relative path.

tip Don't use library items in your template pages if you want your locked regions to be truly locked. If you place a library item into a locked region, other designers can change that locked region by modifying the library item and then choosing **Modify→Library→Update Current Page**. For more on library items, see the sidebar Templates Versus Library Items on page 139, and the last few pages of this chapter.

4 choose save as template

Choose **File→Save As Template** to open the **Save As Template** dialog box. No icon or keyboard shortcut exists.

5 specify site

In the **Site** field, specify the site where you want the new template to live. Templates are site-specific, so you have to choose one. You can copy your template to another site later, using the **Copy To Site** command on the template's context menu in the **Assets** panel.

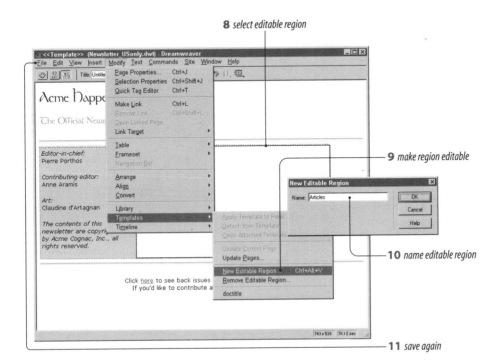

8 *select editable region*

9 *make region editable*

10 *name editable region*

11 *save again*

6 name template

Give your template a descriptive name that doesn't conflict with any that already exist for the site.

7 click save

The **Save** button saves the file as a template, with the suffix **.DWT**. Dreamweaver stores templates by default in the **Templates** folder just under your main site folder. Note that these files are not standard HTML files; they're special files that only Dreamweaver uses. You won't publish the **Templates** folder to your "live" Web server unless you let Dreamweaver include dependent files; this folder exists solely for your convenience in creating new pages.

8 select editable region

Select the part of the page you want to be variable or editable *in documents based on your new template*. (You can always edit everything in the template itself.) In my example, the right table cell contains the titles for that issue's articles, so the right cell must be editable, and I would select it by clicking inside the cell and pressing **ctrl+A** (Win) or **command-A** (Mac).

Note that if you make a layer editable, then other designers can move the layer. If you don't want that,

select only the layer's *content* (for example, click inside the layer and choose **Edit➡Select All**).

> *tip* You can select an entire table or just individual cells to be editable.

9 make region editable

Choose **Modify➡Templates➡New Editable Region**. If you prefer, you can bring up the selected object's context menu, or right-click the selected object (**control**-click on the Mac), and choose **New Editable Region** from the context menu. (You can reverse your decision later with the **Modify➡Templates➡Remove Editable Region** command.)

10 name editable region

Enter a descriptive name into the **New Editable Region** dialog box (remembering that region names must be unique within a template) and click **OK**. Repeat steps 8 through 10 for as many regions as you want to make editable.

11 save again

Save your completed template one more time via **File➡Save** to record your editable region selections.

Templates & Code View

Dreamweaver lets you access a Web page's underlying HTML code with a single click of the **Show Code View** icon on the toolbar. So, can't another designer simply drop down to the code and tweak areas you've identified as non-editable?

Not in Dreamweaver. Click **Show Code View** when working on a document based on a template having locked regions, and you see something like the screen at right. You can tweak the nonhighlighted HTML all you want, because it lives in the editable region or regions; the HTML in locked regions appears highlighted and if you change it, Dreamweaver silently throws your changes away. (If you don't see highlighting, you must have turned off syntax coloring under **View➡Code View Options**.)

The special **#BeginEditable** and **#EndEditable** tags are how Dreamweaver identifies in the page's HTML where the editable regions are. Sure, someone could take a given page and load it into another HTML editor that doesn't understand about these nonstandard tags and edit locked code. So don't take locked regions to be a completely secure solution. However, in most business situations, they don't need to be.

Make A New Page From A Template

Dreamweaver offers a couple of ways to make a new page from an existing template. You can create a new page normally and then drag a template from the **Assets** panel onto the document. Or you can create a new page normally, click a template name in the **Assets** panel, and click the **Apply** button. This page describes the easiest way, though, which is to use the **New From Template** command.

1 choose new from template
The menu command is **File➥New From Template** (no shortcuts), which opens the **Select Template** dialog box.

2 choose site
Your first job is to select the site containing the template you want to apply. The current site appears by default.

3 select template
Next, select the template from the list by clicking its name in the **Templates** list. (Here's where those descriptive names come into play!)

4 choose update option
The check box labeled **Update Page When Template Changes** is normally one you'll leave checked, because one of the main benefits of templates is that you can make a change to the template later and have the change automatically update multiple dependent pages. Clear this check box if you simply want to use the template as a design starting point, but don't want the automatic update feature.

5 click select
Clicking the **Select** button closes the **Select Template** dialog box and formats your new document based on the chosen template.

6 add content to editable region
The insertion point automatically activates at the top of the first editable region. Modify the region (or regions) as appropriate.

7 save document
Save and name your new document with the **File➥Save** command.

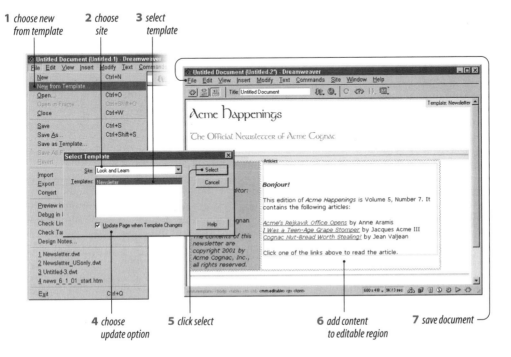

1 *choose new from template* **2** *choose site* **3** *select template*

4 *choose update option* **5** *click select* **6** *add content to editable region* **7** *save document*

Attach A Template

Sometimes you'll want to make an existing page conform to a template that you created later. This process is called *attaching* or *applying* a template.

> **tip** If the template you wish to apply to an existing document has multiple editable regions, you may find it quicker to create a new document with the **File→New From Template** command and then drag and drop sections from the existing document into the new document. The reason is that when you apply a template to a document that has no previous template applied to it, Dreamweaver places the entire body content into a single editable region.

1 open existing document
Use **File→Open** to choose the document to which you want to attach the template.

2 remove unwanted content
Delete anything in the document's body that you don't want after you attach the template.

3 open templates panel
Choose **Window→Templates**, or press **F11** and click the **Templates** icon in the **Assets** panel.

4 select template
Click the template that you want to apply, in the list at the lower part of the **Templates** panel. The preview window in the upper part of the panel helps you confirm that you've chosen the correct template.

5 click apply
Click the **Apply** button or drag and drop the template onto the document window.

6 save document
Save your newly attached document with **File→Save**, or **File→Save As** if you want to give it a new name.

> **tip** If you're designing a new template to replace an old one, keep the editable region names the same for easy migration.

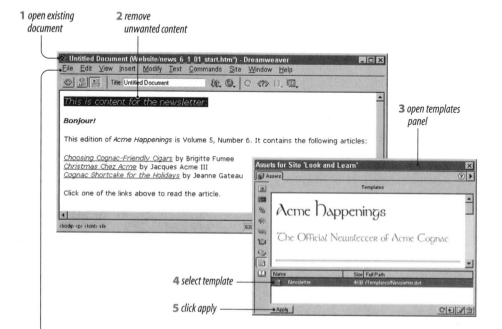

1 *open existing document*

2 *remove unwanted content*

3 *open templates panel*

4 *select template*

5 *click apply*

6 *save document*

Detach A Template

You may occasionally need to sever the link between a document and its associated template, such as when you want to change the document's layout beyond what the template's editable regions permit. This process is called *detaching* a template from a document (or a document from a template), and it has two effects. It makes the document fully editable, and it also makes it unaffected by any future template updates.

1 open existing document

Use **File⇒Open** to choose the document which you want to detach from the template.

2 choose detach from template

Choose **Modify⇒Templates⇒Detach From Template**. You'll notice that the template highlighting and the editable region highlighting disappear from the document window.

tip Keep in mind that a document that you've detached from a template is no different from a document that never had a template applied to it in the first place.

3 edit document (optional)

You can now edit any part of the document, which is presumably why you wanted to detach it from the template. Because it's no longer attached to a template, those edits can include changes that modify head content, such as layer animations and JavaScript behaviors. However, you don't have to edit the document now; you can save it (4) and edit it later.

4 save document

Save your newly detached document with **File⇒ Save**, or **File⇒Save As** if you want to give it a new name.

1 *open existing document*   **2** *choose detach from template*

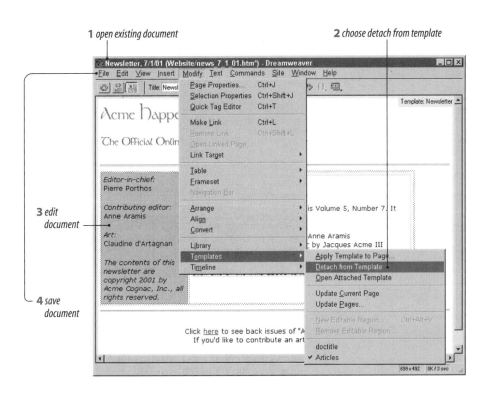

3 *edit document*

4 *save document*

Make A Global Change

For most designers, the big advantage of using templates is that you can make a layout or design change in the template file and automatically update all attached documents. This section shows you how such an update would work. Here, Acme Cognac's president has decided that gold should be the new corporate color, and she wants the newsletter masthead section to have a gold background instead of a green one.

1 open templates panel

You can choose **Window➛Templates**, or you can press **F11** and click the **Templates** icon at the left icon bar of the **Assets** panel.

2 double-click template name

The fastest way to open a template for editing is to double-click its name in the list at the bottom half of the **Templates** panel. However, you can also single-click the template and click the **Edit Template** button at the bottom of the panel.

3 edit template

In this example, the designer highlights the left table cell by clicking inside it and pressing **ctrl+A** (Win) or **command-A** (Mac) and then changes the background color in the property inspector.

4 save template

Choose **File➛Save** or just click the document window's close box and click **Yes** when asked whether you want to save changes.

5 click don't update (optional)

Immediately after saving the revised template, Dreamweaver asks whether you want to update all pages in the site that are attached to the template. If you click **Yes** (or **Update**—Dreamweaver may show one of two different dialog boxes here), the update occurs automatically. In my example, the designer wants to try applying the revised template to a single page first, before applying it sitewide, so she clicks **No** (or **Don't Update**).

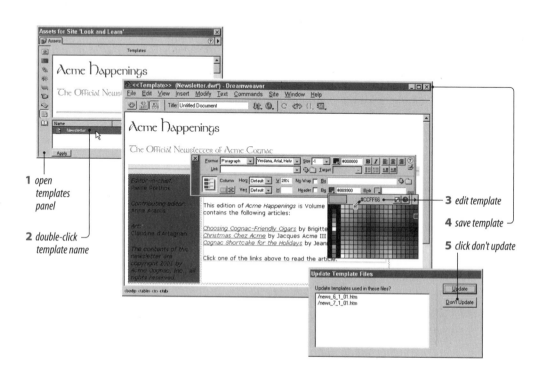

1 *open templates panel*

2 *double-click template name*

3 *edit template*

4 *save template*

5 *click don't update*

6 open sample document

To apply the new template to a single document, first open that document by choosing the command **File→Open**.

7 choose update current page

Choose **Modify→Templates→Update Current Page** (no shortcut). The background color of the masthead should change.

8 update all pages

You can now preview the page in a browser window, print it, and show it to other designers. You finally decide that the change is **OK** to apply sitewide. **Modify→Templates→Update Pages** brings up the **Update Pages** dialog box.

9 specify scope

The **Look In** field lets you specify the scope of the update. Choose **Entire Site** to update every page with every template. Here, choose **Files That Use** in order to limit the update to a single template. Make sure that the **Templates** box is checked; this dialog box can also update files that use library items.

10 click show log (optional)

Check the **Show Log** box if you want a report of the update details.

11 click start

The **Start** button performs the sitewide update and displays the results in the log window.

12 click close

The **Close** button closes the **Update Pages** dialog box.

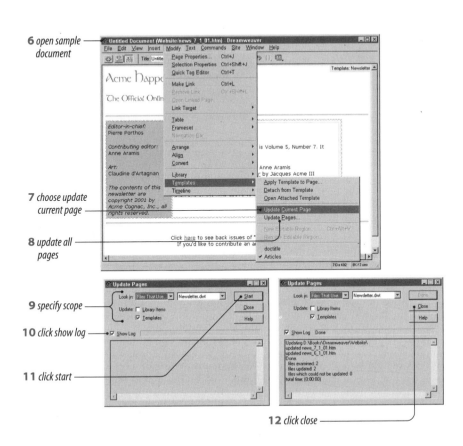

6 open sample document

7 choose update current page

8 update all pages

9 specify scope

10 click show log

11 click start

12 click close

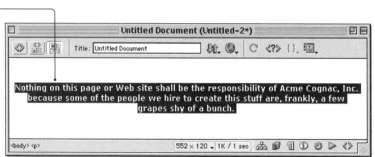 Create A Library Item

Creating a *library item* is simpler than creating a template, in that you don't have to specify any editable regions. (In fact, you *can't* specify such regions in a library item.) Library items are usually snippets of a page, such as headers or footers, so they're often smaller than templates, too.

1 place content

You can start with a blank document and then add the content that you want to make into a library item. Or, you can open an existing page that has the content already laid out, if such a page exists. In my example, I create some text that I'll use as a legal disclaimer on certain Web pages.

> *tip* Library items can only contain HTML code that would live in the body of a page, rather than in the head content. This limitation means that you can't have style sheets or layer animations in a library item.

If you include any images, Flash text objects, or other linked content in the group of objects that you intend to make into a library item, those objects must stay

put in their original file locations or else the library item won't incorporate them. Furthermore, if you edit any such objects, for example in Fireworks, the library item automatically reflects the edits.

2 select content

The simplest way to select the content is to drag and drop the cursor over it, but watch out: You don't want to include the **<head>** content in your selection because it can cause strange behavior down the road. As a result, I generally add a blank line at the top of the page to make it easier to select just the body content I want.

> *tip* Use code view to verify that your selection includes all the necessary HTML elements. For example, when selecting a group of text, it's easy to miss the **<p>** tag pair, which contains the alignment attributes. Reselect the content in code view if you need to.

3 open library panel

Choose **Window➥Library** to open the library view of the **Assets** panel, if it isn't already open.

1 *place content*

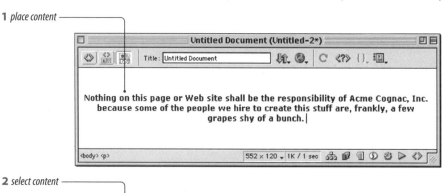

2 *select content*

4 click new library item

The quickest way to add the selected chunk of code to the Library is to click the **New Library Item** icon at the lower right of the **Library** panel. (It has a plus sign over a page.) However, you can also drag and drop the selection from the document window into the list area of the **Library** panel. You can also choose **Modify➡ Library➡Add Object To Library** or press **ctrl+shift+B** (Win) or **command-shift-B** (Mac) to add the selection to the Library.

However you do it, your code fragment appears in the preview pane at the top of the **Library** panel.

5 name item

Dreamweaver automatically adds the new item to the list and places the insertion point under the **Name** column, so you can type in a descriptive name and

press **enter** (Win) or **return** (Mac) when done. The program creates a file with the **LBI** suffix (for **LiB**rary **I**tem, I guess) and saves it in the **Library** folder under your site's root location.

At this point, you can open any page in the site and drag and drop your new library item from the **Library** panel onto the page. If you change the library item, you can have the changes propagate to all pages that use it. (See the Update A Library Item section on page 151.)

> **tip** As soon as you name the library item, Dreamweaver saves it to the **Library** folder. If you created your item content on a fresh new document, you can now close that document without saving it.

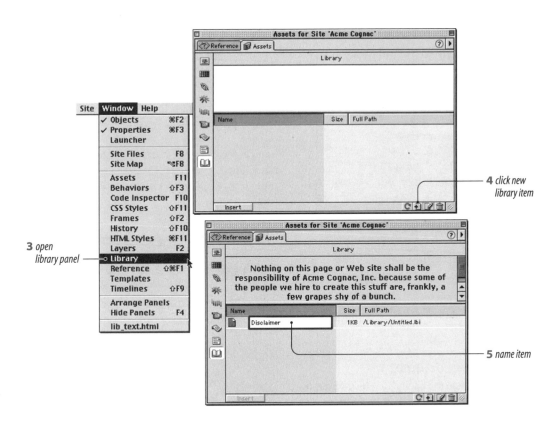

4 click new library item

3 open library panel

5 name item

The Library Item Property Inspector

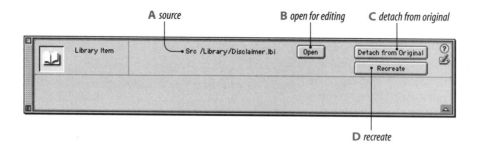

A *source* **B** *open for editing* **C** *detach from original*

Library Item   Src /Library/Disclaimer.lbi   Open   Detach from Original
                                                        Recreate

D *recreate*

Click a library item in the document window, and if the property inspector feature is active— choose **Window→Properties**, **ctrl+F3** (Win), or **command-F3** (Mac), to display it if it isn't— you'll see the **Library Item** property inspector. This little inspector doesn't have many commands, but the ones it does offer can be useful, especially (C) and (D).

A source

This read-only field contains the path and name for the library item's source file. The property inspector won't let you change the item's source; if you want to use a different library item in the current item's place, you must delete the current one and add the new one.

> **tip** The source field only has room for about 24 characters. If your site uses several layers of directories, or if your library items use long names, you may not see the full path or full filename here. View that information by switching to code view or by opening the library item (B) and reading the title bar.

B open for editing

If you want to open the library item for editing, click the **Open** button. A new document window opens up, with the library item's name in the title bar; this window has a gray background to remind you that you're editing a library item and not a regular HTML page.

C detach from original

If you want to change the library item on the specific document, and you want to make sure that your changes aren't reversed (for example, when you or another designer performs a site update via **Modify→Library→Update Pages**), then you have to *detach* the HTML code from the library item. (This action is a lot like breaking a link in a compound document, or detaching a page from a template.)

The **Detach From Original** button lets you do just that. Once detached, you can modify the code on your page that used to be the library item, and any future changes to the original library item (or any future updates) won't affect your page.

D recreate

If you ever accidentally delete a library item, you can use the nifty **Recreate** button to regenerate it, as long as you can open at least one page that was set up to use that item. This command re-creates the original *.LBI file in the **Library** folder under the site root folder.

> **tip** Another option you have is to use the update feature, described on p. 151. But watch out! The **Don't Update** feature doesn't work perfectly. For example, if you use Flash text in a library item and later change the color of the Flash text but choose **Don't Update** after saving the edited library item, all pages that used the library item update anyway. The reason? When you edit the Flash text, you're not really editing the library item, you're editing an object to which the library item links.

steps Update A Library Item

When you change a library item, you have the option to update the pages that use that library item. If you don't perform the automatic update, you can later open selected pages and update them individually, or , if you want, you can perform a sitewide update.

1 open library panel
The command is **Window→Library**. If the **Assets** panel is already open, you can just click the **Library** icon in the left icon bar.

2 double-click item
Double-click the item's name in the list window to open it for editing. Alternately, you can right-click (Win) or **control**-click (Mac) the item and choose **Edit** from the context menu. A new document window appears, with the library item's name in the title bar; this window has a gray background to remind you that you're editing a library item and not a regular HTML page.

3 edit item
In the library item document window, make any changes you like to the item, just as if you were editing a regular HTML page.

4 close document window
The fastest way is to click the close box, but you can also choose **File→Close**. Click **Yes** when Dreamweaver asks whether you want to save your changes, and Dreamweaver displays the **Update Library Items** dialog box.

5 choose update or don't update
Click the **Update** button or the **Don't Update** button, depending on whether you want to update all pages in the site that use the library item. If you decide not to update right away, you can open a single page later and update it with **Modify→Library→Update Current Page**. Then, if you like the way things look, you can choose **Modify→Library→Update Pages** to bring up the **Update Pages** dialog box and perform a sitewide update, just as I describe in the Make A Global Change section on page 146.

1 open library panel **2** double-click item

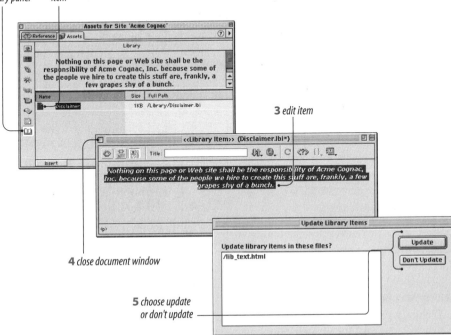

3 edit item

4 close document window

5 choose update or don't update

The Highlighting Preferences Window

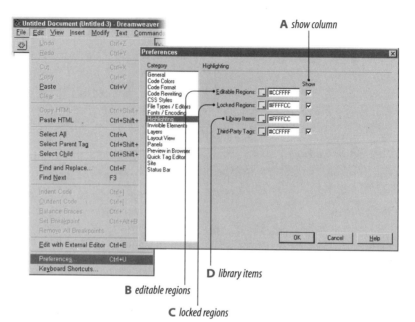

A show column

B editable regions

C locked regions

D library items

You can control whether, and how, Dreamweaver highlights editable regions, locked regions, and library items. Choose **Edit→Preferences** and click the **Highlighting** category in the left window pane to display the highlighting preferences choices.

> *tip* If you've marked highlighting preferences in the **Preferences** dialog box but they're still not showing up, check the menu toggle **View→Visual Aids→Invisible Elements** and make sure that it has a check mark by it.

A show column

The check boxes in the **Show** column indicate which highlight items you want to see in the document window. Clear a check box to hide the item.

B editable regions

Click the color box to open the color picker and choose a color with the eyedropper cursor, or type the hexadecimal value of the color in the white field. The default is #CCFFFF, a light blue. This shade is subtle, and I usually pick a more visible color, such as #99FFFF.

> *tip* This color is visible when viewing the actual template file and the documents attached to the template file.

C locked regions

Dreamweaver marks locked regions with the outline color you choose here. Note that the locked region outline may surround an editable region. The default is #FFFFCC, a pale yellow. Again, you may consider choosing a more noticeable color, such as #FFFF33.

> *tip* This color is only visible when viewing documents attached to the template file. It appears in document view and in code view, just in case another designer is trying to tweak the HTML.

D library items

Library items appear outlines with this color. The default is #FFFFCC. You may want to leave this color at the default setting; it's less important for other designers that may be using your comuter to notice library items as locked regions.

Manage Your Site

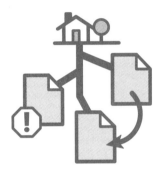

Early HTML editors helped you create Web pages, but you were on your own when it came to file management. No more! Dreamweaver helps you organize your files into *sites*. A site consists of all the HTML pages, images, movies, links, and other assets for a particular URL. You can manage your site as a list of files or as a map that shows you link relationships. An **Assets** panel helps you organize many kinds of reusable site components.

Dreamweaver helps you keep the local version of a site synchronized with the remote "live" version that users see. The program also includes great tools for designers who collaborate with others: the check-in/check-out and Design Notes features. You can test your site for browser compatibility and broken links. Finally, ready-to-run reports can help you optimize your site's code and clean up loose ends.

Dreamweaver doesn't do the dishes for you yet, but I hear that's planned for Version 5.

The Site Window

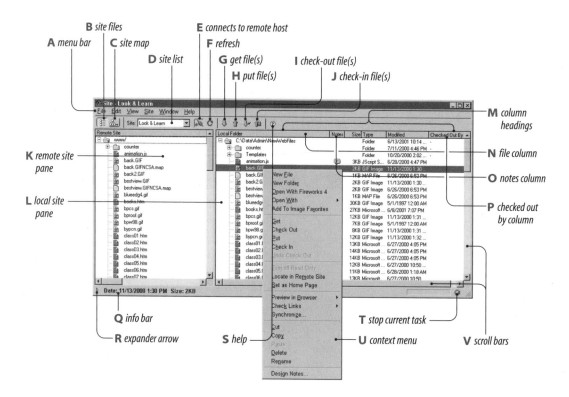

B site files

A menu bar   **C** site map   **E** connects to remote host

D site list   **F** refresh

G get file(s)   **I** check-out file(s)

H put file(s)   **J** check-in file(s)

M column headings

N file column

K remote site pane

O notes column

L local site pane

P checked out by column

Q info bar   **T** stop current task

R expander arrow   **S** help   **U** context menu   **V** scroll bars

Way back in Chapter 1, I told you that I'd take a closer look at the site window in Chapter 10, and here I are. Here's where you'll perform most of your file management chores, create and change your site's folder structure, delete files, and synchronize between your local hard drive and the remote Web server (assuming that those are different machines, as they usually are). Get here via **Window▸Site Files** or **Site▸Site Files** (shortcut **F8**) or the **Show Site** button on the launcher and mini-launcher or, if you want to see a map view, **Window▸Site Map** or **Site▸Site Map** or **alt+F8** in Windows (**command-F8** on the Mac).

> **tip** This section shows you the typical form of the site window, but you can rearrange aspects of it if you like. For the details, see page 258 in Chapter 16, Preferences, Site, for a discussion of the Site Preferences dialog box. Any changes you make there are global for all sites on your computer.

A **menu bar** (Win only)

The site window looks different on the PC and on the Mac in one major respect. On the PC, the site window has its own menu bar (as shown here), but on the Mac, it doesn't; all site-related commands are on the main program menu at the top of the screen. So, you'll have to do a bit more submenu navigation on the Mac. I'll call out the menu commands for each platform as I go along.

Macromedia has put most of the site-related commands on this menu bar for your convenience. (Sorry, Mac-ophiles.)

B **site files**

Click this button if you want to see files only, no maps. For example, you'd click **Site Files** to see the list of files on the remote server in the left pane, while the files for your local site appear in the right pane. If you activate the site window with **Window▸Site Files**, then this is the view you'd see.

C site map

You can click and hold this button to see a submenu with two choices, **Map Only** and **Map and Files**. In either case, Dreamweaver displays a graphical map of the local site in the left pane. If you choose **Map and Files**, the file list stays open in the right pane, and you can adjust the relative size of the map and file panes by dragging the border between them; choose **Map Only** to see a bigger view of the map but no file list.

Note that you must define a home page before map view will work; set the **Home Page** field on the **Site Map Layout** category of the **Define Sites** dialog box, or by bringing up the desired home page's context menu in the site files window and choosing **Set as Home Page**. (If your site uses **INDEX.HTM** or **INDEX.HTML**, then Dreamweaver will automatically take that to be the home page.)

> **tip** If you just click the **Site Map** button and don't hold it down, Dreamweaver assumes that you want to see either **Map Only** or **Map and Files** based on your most recent choice.

You can't see a map for the remote site in the site window. But don't worry: That's not a problem, because the local site should have the same structure as the remote site.

D site list

This drop-down list lists all the sites currently defined on your computer and also gives you the option to jump to the **Define Sites** dialog box. If you want to switch to managing a different site, just choose it from the list. Dreamweaver updates the local site cache, which may take a second or two, and then displays the selected site's files in the site window.

E connects to remote host

Click this button to have Dreamweaver connect to the remote host that serves the "live" version of your site (or, optionally, to a code management system; see page 246 in Chapter 15 for the section Connect To A Code Management System). You can set connection details in the **Preferences** dialog box, as discussed on page 258 in Chapter 16. If you use a dial-up link, you'll have Dreamweaver use FTP, or File Transfer Protocol, for the connection; happily, Dreamweaver insulates you from the details of the FTP command line.

If you see the error message shown here, then Dreamweaver didn't find a physical network link over which to make the connection. For example, if the link to the remote host is via modem, you'll need to establish it separately by dialing up your ISP or corporate network *before* clicking this button.

F refresh

This button updates the local and remote file lists to show you any changes that have occurred since you opened the site window. If you have **Refresh Local File List Automatically** turned on in the site definition dialog box, which is the default, then you'd only need to click this button to display changes on the remote site. If you want to refresh only the local site, you can do that by choosing the menu command **View➞Refresh Local** in the site window (Win) or **Site➞Site Files View➞Refresh Local** (Mac). If you just want to refresh the remote site, choose **View➞Refresh Remote** in the site window (Win) or **Site➞Site Files View➞Refresh Remote** (Mac).

G get file(s)

Click this button to copy the files selected in the active file list to your local site. You could also choose **Site➛Get**, shortcut **ctrl+alt+D** (Win) or **command-option-D** (Mac).

Careful, because the active list may be either local or remote; that is, if the local file list is active, Dreamweaver looks for the files on the remote server with the same names as the selected local files and downloads those remote files. Also, be aware that if you choose this option and you copy any files that already exist on your local drive, Dreamweaver will overwrite them.

> **tip** If your site uses the check in/check out feature, then the **Get File(s)** command copies the files to your local drive but doesn't let you modify them. If you want to modify them, you have to check them out (I).

H put file(s)

Click here to copy the files selected in the active file list to the remote site. (The menu equivalent is **Site➛Put**.) The same caution in (G) applies here: Dreamweaver puts the files you've selected in the active list, be it local or remote.

> **tip** If you use check-in/check-out, putting files doesn't make them available for modification by other users. Use **Check In** for that purpose (J).

I check out file(s)

If you have enabled the check-in/check-out feature via the **Define Sites** dialog box, then you'll see this button, which is equivalent to **Site➛Check Out**. Checking out a file is like getting it (G), with the distinction that when you check out a file, you can edit it, and nobody else can, until you check the file in again.

> **tip** If you check out a file and then change your mind about editing it, you don't have to check it back in; it's a bit faster to choose **Site➛Undo Check Out**.

J check in file(s)

If you use check in/check out, then checking a file in to the remote server is like putting it, except that you're also telling Dreamweaver that other people are free to work on the file by checking it out from the server, and you can no longer modify the local copy of the file. If you create a new file that the remote server doesn't have, check it in rather than putting it (common mistake). The menu equivalent is **Site➛Check In**.

K remote site pane

Normally, when you're not viewing a map, the left pane contains a list of the remote files (assuming that you've connected to the remote site). The columns display file and folder names (N), size, type, modification dates, Design Notes (O) if you use that feature, and checked-out status (P) if you use *that* feature.

L local site pane

Here's where you see the folders and files in your local site. The columns are the same as for the remote site pane (K).

M column headings

The column headings do double duty as buttons, which, when clicked, re-sort the file list according to values in that column. Click the column heading again, and the file list inverts, again using the clicked column as the index. You can change column widths by dragging the lines between the buttons in the column headings.

> **tip** You can change the columns that the site window displays and the order in which they appear (except **Name**). Choose **View➛File View Columns** from the site menu (Win) or choose **Site➛Site Files View➛File View Columns** (Mac). You can also add columns that correspond with specific Design Note types, such as **assigned, due, priority,** and **status** as long as you don't exceed 10 columns total. Check **Share With All Users of This Site** to let others see the column(s) you've added, and clear the **Show** check box to hide a column you may want to use later.

N file column

In the **File** column appear folders and files. In Windows, the folders appear first, alphabetized, and files under them (also alphabetized); the Mac lists files and folders alphabetically together. Add a folder by right-clicking (Win) or control-clicking (Mac) its parent folder, or any file in the same folder where you want the new folder, choosing **New Folder**, and giving the new folder a name. Add a file by dragging it to the site window from Explorer (Win) or the Finder (Mac).

You can move files from one folder to another, and Dreamweaver automatically updates links as necessary to reflect the new location. You can also double-click a file to open the application associated with that file; double-clicking an HTML file opens it in Dreamweaver, for example. Delete a file by highlighting it and pressing the **delete** key. Rename a file by highlighting it, waiting a second, and then clicking on the name again to open the editing text box.

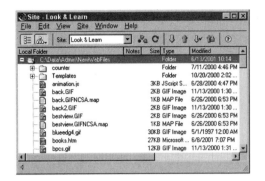

O notes column

If you use Design Notes, any notes associated with a given file show up in the **Notes** column with an icon. Double-click the icon to read the note, even without opening the file.

P checked out by column

If you use check in/check out, this column shows you who has checked out a given file for editing. If you really need to edit that file, you can send that person an e-mail telling him to check the file back in to the remote server so that you can check it out for editing.

Q info bar

As you mouse over files, the info bar at the bottom of the site window displays the file's date, size, and (if it's an HTML file) page title.

R expander arrow

Click the tiny expander arrow in the lower-left corner to shrink the site window down to the just the right pane, as shown here. Do this to unclutter your screen if you don't need to see the map or the remote site files list. Click the expander arrow again to expand the site window back to its dual-pane format.

S help

Click the question mark icon for context-sensitive online help.

T stop current task

The **Stop Current Task** button only shows up (at the lower-right corner) when a file transfer is in process. It's a little red octagon with a white X in the middle. Click here if you discover you've made a horrible mistake; whether Dreamweaver stops before doing any damage is a dice roll, because the operation on the file in transit must finish before Dreamweaver knows to stop. Dreamweaver displays a little progress bar to the left of the button to indicate that a task is under way.

U context menu

The site window's context menu is really handy. Just about every operation that you can do with a toolbar button or menu command lives on the context menu, so try to get in the habit of using it. Right-click (Win) or control-click (Mac) a file to display its context menu.

V scroll bars

Drag the scroll box in one of the scroll bars to see more rows or columns. If you find yourself scrolling around too much, consider resizing individual columns by dragging the vertical line between column headings. (You can also drag the vertical bar between the local and remote panes to the left or right.)

The Site Map

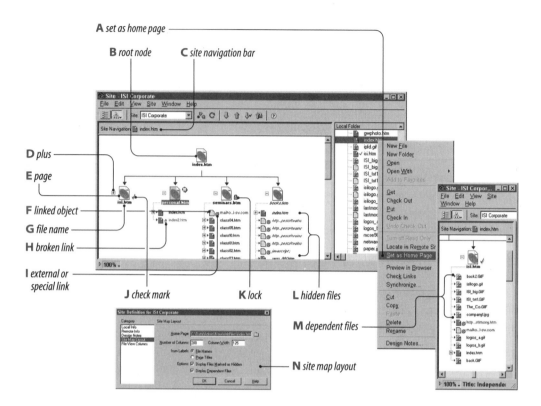

A *set as home page*

B *root node*   **C** *site navigation bar*

D *plus*

E *page*

F *linked object*

G *file name*

H *broken link*

I *external or special link*

J *check mark*   **K** *lock*   **L** *hidden files*

M *dependent files*

N *site map layout*

When you view the site window in map view or map-and-files view, Dreamweaver paints a graphical picture of your HTML pages and their link relationships. It's simple, visual, and fast. You can select files by dragging around them with the mouse, which is faster than shift-clicking adjacent items or control-clicking (Win) or command-clicking (Mac) nonadjacent items. Get to the site map from the document window by choosing **Site➞Site Map** or **Window➞Site Map (alt+F8** on Win, **command-F8** on the Mac). If you already have the site files window open, click the **Site Map** toolbar button.

A set as home page

To use map view, you must set an HTML file as the site's home page. Right-click (Win) or **control**-click (Mac) the file and choose **Set As Home Page**. You

can also select the file and choose **Site➞Set as Home Page** in the site window (Win) or **Site➞Site Map View➞Set as Home Page** (Mac).

B root node

The root node is the page at the top of the site map. In larger sites, you may want to set the root node at a different page; bring up the file's context menu and choose **View As Root**. (The menu commands are **View➞View As Root** on Win and **Site➞Site Map View➞View as Root** on the Mac.) Get back to the original root node by clicking it in the **Site Navigation** bar (C).

C site navigation bar

The **Site Navigation** bar shows the path from the home page to the root node, with arrows between each page. If you change the map view to use a page other than the home page for the root node (B), click any page along the pathway to view that page as the root.

D plus

Click the plus sign next to any file to expand the branch and display pages to which that file links. (The minus sign has the opposite effect, as I bet you guessed.) The site map automatically expands only two levels from the root node by default.

E page

Dreamweaver indicates an HTML page with the Dreamweaver logo, which symbolizes needles and threads.

F linked object

Linked objects that are not HTML pages all have the same icon, a piece of paper with some lines on it.

G filename

Beneath or beside each icon in map view is the object's filename. You can rename it by clicking it, waiting a second, and clicking it again to open a text editing window. Dreamweaver automatically fixes any links that would otherwise be broken by the name change.

> *tip* If you'd rather see the HTML page titles instead of their filenames, choose **View**➡**Show Page Titles** (Win) or **Site**➡**Site Map View**➡**Show Page Titles** (Mac). If you're displaying page titles, you can rename them just as you'd change a filename.

H broken link

If you have any broken links—that is, they point to something that doesn't exist—Dreamweaver displays them in red with a broken chain link icon. Right-click (Win) or **control**-click (Mac) the link and choose **Change Link** to find a file that does exist for the link to point to.

I external or special link

If a link points to a page outside the current site or is an e-mail or script link, it shows up in blue text, listing the full URL, and with a globe icon to the right of a folded sheet of paper.

J check mark

A green check mark, means that you've checked a file out for editing. A red check mark means that somebody else has checked it out.

K lock

A padlock symbol means that you can't modify a file; it has the locked (Mac) or read-only (Win) attribute.

L hidden files

Normally, Dreamweaver doesn't display pages you've marked as hidden with the command **View**➡**Show/Hide Link** (Win) or **Site**➡**Site Map View**➡**Show/Hide Link** (Mac). You can force their display by choosing **View**➡**Show Files Marked as Hidden** (Win) or **Site**➡**Site Map View**➡**Show Files Marked as Hidden** (Mac). Hidden files have italicized icon names. To unhide a hidden file, you first must check the **Show Files Marked as Hidden** toggle and then select the file and choose **Show/Hide Link**.

M dependent files

Objects (such as images, templates, and library items) embedded onto a Web page are dependent files, and the map view normally doesn't display them. You can force their display with **View**➡**Show Dependent Files** (Win) or **Site**➡**Site Map View**➡**Show Dependent Files** (Mac).

N site map layout

Here you can change several site map preferences in one place. Choose **View**➡**Layout** from the site window menu (Win) or **Site**➡**Site Map View**➡**Layout** (Mac). You can also get to this dialog box by choosing **Site**➡**Define Sites**, clicking **Edit**, and clicking the **Site Map Layout** category to the left of the **Site Definition** dialog box.

> *tip* You can save the site map as an image suitable for printing, e-mailing, or framing. Choose **File**➡**Save Site Map** from the site menu (Win) or **Site**➡**Site Map View**➡**Save Site Map** (Mac). From Windows, you can save it as a BMP or a PNG file; the Mac offers PICT or JPEG.

Define A Site

The first thing you should do when starting to work with Dreamweaver is define a site, even if you just want to play around for a while designing test pages that nobody else will ever see. Dreamweaver's grand design revolves around the site concept, and if you just start creating siteless HTML pages that are lost in space, you won't be able to take advantage of some of the program's handier features, such as the site cache, **Assets** panel, site map, automatic relative link generation, and so on.

Defining a new site is a fairly tedious process that would benefit greatly from a *wizard,* a sequence of dialog boxes stepping you through the decisions. I've tried to supply the next best thing in this section of this book! And don't worry if you make a mistake when defining your site; everything's easy to change later. The best news of all is that defining a site is a chore you need to do only once for each site.

1 choose new site

The menu command is **Site➥New Site** (no keyboard shortcut), which plunges you right in to the **Site Definition for Unnamed Site 1** dialog box, starting with the **Local Info** category highlighted in the list at left.

2 name site

Give your site a name in the **Site Name** field. It can be anything you want; users never see it, but you'll see it in the site window and the site list. You should avoid spaces in filenames as a general rule, but you can use them in the site name. This setting is mandatory.

The local root folder is the site's top-level directory, under which all files for the site will reside. This setting is mandatory. You can use an existing folder, for example, if you've inherited a site from someone else, or if you're converting an old site you created before installing Dreamweaver 4. Or you can create a new folder, but not by just typing it. You have to use the folder icon, which lets you browse your computer's file structure.

3 set local root folder

The local root folder is the site's top-level directory, under which all files for the site will reside. This setting is mandatory. You can use an existing folder, for example, if you've inherited a site from someone else, or if you're converting an old site you created before installing Dreamweaver 4. Or you can create a new folder, but not by just typing it. You have to use the folder icon, which lets you browse your computer's file structure.

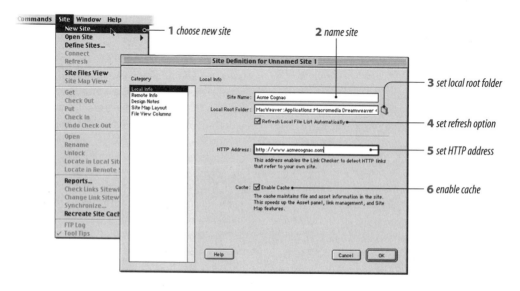

1 *choose new site*

2 *name site*

3 *set local root folder*

4 *set refresh option*

5 *set HTTP address*

6 *enable cache*

4 set refresh option

If you check **Refresh Local File List Automatically**, as I suggest, Dreamweaver will update the site window's file list when you copy files into the site. The only cost is a tiny bit of speed you won't even notice. Clear this box if you don't mind clicking the site window's **Refresh** toolbar button whenever you need it to reflect a file copy operation or if you're working on an unusually large site and find the updates counterproductive.

5 set HTTP address

This is the address users specify to navigate to your remote site. It can be a private intranet address, such as *http://acmecognac.intranet.com/index.htm*, or a public Internet address, such as *http://www.acmecognac.com/index.htm*. You should specify this address in case you use any absolute links in your site, and you want the **Check Links** command to be able to verify them (see The Check Links Commands section on page 170 of this chapter).

6 enable cache

The local site cache requires a check in this box. Without a cache, the **Assets** panel (see page 164) doesn't work, and many other features get really slow. Again,

if you're working on a really large site, these cache updates may begin to get in your way.

7 click remote info

This is another category in the left of the **Site Definition** dialog box.

8 set access type

Your choices are **None**, **FTP**, **Local/Network**, **SourceSafe Database**, and **WebDAV**. I discuss the last two in Chapter 15; you'll typically choose **FTP** or **Local/Network** if you're posting to an intranet server; when you choose a different method, most of the detailed options under the **Server Access** field change. For example, if you choose **Local/Network**, your detailed options are simply **Remote Folder** (where you specify the path to your intranet server) and **Refresh Remote File List Automatically** (where you tell Dreamweaver whether to update the site window's remote file list when you copy files into it).

9 set FTP details

The FTP host, host directory, login name, password, and other FTP details should be provided for you by your Internet Service Provider, and you'd enter them here. On a public server, the host directory usually has a

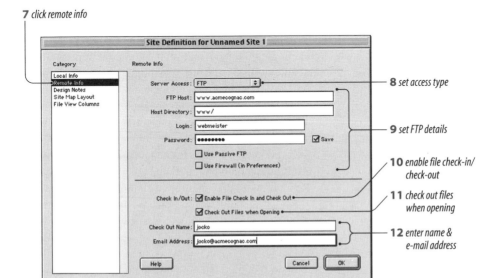

7 *click remote info*

8 *set access type*

9 *set FTP details*

10 *enable file check-in/ check-out*

11 *check out files when opening*

12 *enter name & e-mail address*

name like **WWW** or **Web**. Some ISPs use case-sensitive login names and passwords, so watch for that. If you leave **Save** checked, the computer will remember the password you type; clear this for greater security, but you'll need to enter the password each time you connect to the remote server.

Also, be aware that the remote host directory's sub-structure should parallel your local site's substructure. (You'll usually start with the remote host directory empty and upload your local site to it, so the parallelism occurs naturally.)

10 enable file check in/check out

When you check this box, you enable Dreamweaver's check-in/check-out feature, an option but a near-necessity for sites with multiple designers. The feature helps prevent Abbott from changing a file while Costello is also changing the file; when you both upload your changes, one of you does so after the other and knocks out the other's changes.

The way this feature works is simple: When you check a file out in the site window, Dreamweaver puts a flag on the server that other designers using Dreamweaver

recognize as the signal that somebody's already working on that file. When you check the file back in to the server, other Dreamweaver users can check it out themselves.

> **tip** Check in/check out works transparently, as long as you remember to use the **Check Out** command in the site window instead of the **Get** command when you want to edit a file, and **Check In** instead of **Put** when you're done editing. This feature also requires everybody to be using Dreamweaver, but if a team's working on the same site, each member should certainly be using the same application!

11 check out files when opening

Check here if you want Dreamweaver to check out a file automatically when you double-click it in the site window. If you're learning a new site, you probably don't want to check out files for editing every time you open them, because checking out a file locks out other users from modifying it. However, if you're doing mostly editing, checking this box can save you some steps.

13 *click design notes*   **14** *click maintain design notes*   **15** *select notes for sharing*

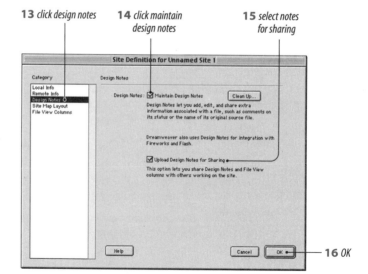

16 *OK*

12 enter name & e-mail address

If you use check in/check out, you have to provide a name (so that others can see when you've checked out a file) and an e-mail address (so that they can send you a message asking you to please check it back in!).

13 click design notes

Click the **Design Notes** category in the left of the **Site Definition** dialog box.

14 click maintain design notes

Check the **Maintain Design Notes** box if you want to enable this optional feature, which enables you to enter comments and attach them to documents, page objects, and even templates. The comments appear as icons that you can double-click in the site window's **Notes** column. This is another feature geared for multi-designer projects, but I've used it even on solo jobs as a way of making sticky-note reminders to myself. ("This page looks top-heavy; fix later.") Also, Dreamweaver uses Design Notes for Fireworks integration to track image source files, so you'd want to enable Design Notes if you work with Fireworks. Dreamweaver saves such notes in a separate file and moves them automatically if you ever move the file, object, or template to which they're attached. For more on Design Notes, see page 166, Create A Design Note.

15 select notes for sharing

You can keep all your notes on your local copy of the site, if you use them solely as reminders on a one-person project, in which case you'd clear this box. Check it if you want other co-workers to be able to see, and add to, your notes.

16 click OK

You can make settings in the Site Map Layout and File View Columns categories

later, if you want; but for now, 16 steps is enough. Click the **OK** button to create your site.

> *tip* If you don't really need to share notes, turn this feature off, and your uploads will go faster.

17 click OK, again

Before Dreamweaver builds your site cache and creates the necessary file structures, it tells you it's about to do some work that could take awhile. Click **OK** to proceed, but click the **Don't Show Me This Message Again** box if you don't feel you need future reminders.

18 edit site

Once Dreamweaver cranks its gears and your site is built, you can edit it later anytime with the **Site→Define Sites** command. In the ensuing dialog box, click the site of interest and the **Edit** button.

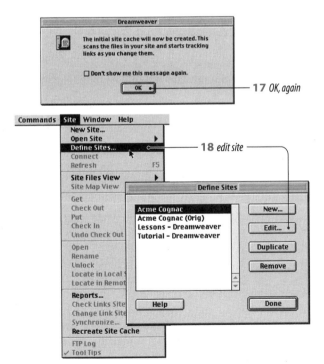

The Assets Panel

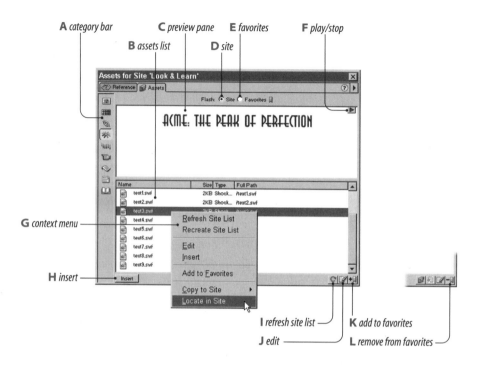

A *category bar*

B *assets list*

C *preview pane*

D *site*

E *favorites*

F *play/stop*

G *context menu*

H *insert*

I *refresh site list*

J *edit*

K *add to favorites*

L *remove from favorites*

As long as you enabled the local site cache in the **Site Definition** dialog box, you can use one of Dreamweaver's handiest features, the **Assets** panel, which you can activate with **Window➡Assets**, **F11**, or the **Assets** icon on the launcher and mini-launcher. This panel lets you organize site assets more conveniently than in the site window alone, for four reaons.

The **Assets** panel shows your site's files by type, wherever those files may reside in the site's hierarchical file structure. If you want to see all your image files, for example, the **Assets** panel shows them to you in a single window pane. Second, you can preview many types of Web objects in the **Assets** panel's preview pane. Third, you can use the **Assets** panel to create a list of "favorite" assets you tend to use frequently, making them easier to get to when you want them next. Fourth, the **Assets** panel shows you objects that don't appear in the site files window at all for the good reason that they aren't actually files, such as colors in your site or URLs (both internal and external links).

tip As handy and helpful as the **Assets** panel may be, it doesn't necessarily know about all the types of assets you may use in a given Web site. One glaring omission is sound files, which the panel doesn't recognize at all, but subtler exclusions apply as well. For example, the Movie category includes QuickTime and MPEG, but not AVI files. So you may still have to use the site window for some asset types.

A category bar

Here's where you click an icon to see assets of a specific type. The categories are **Images** (GIF, JPEG, PNG), **Colors**, **URLs** (external), **Flash** (SWF), **Shockwave**, **Movies** (MOV and MPEG), **Scripts** (JavaScript, VBScript), **Templates**, and **Library Items**.

B assets list

Here, in alphabetical order by default, are the assets for the active site (defined by the currently loaded document, not the site window!) in the category selected in the category bar (A). You can re-sort the list by clicking a column heading. The assets list displays all of the site assets if the **Site** radio button (D) is selected, or only favorite assets if the **Favorites** (E) radio button is selected.

C preview pane

Here's where you see a preview of the selected asset. For certain assets, this pane also contains the **Play/ Stop** button (F). You can change the preview pane's size by dragging the horizontal bar between it and the assets list.

D site

Click this radio button to display all assets in the site for the selected category. If you want to use an asset in a different site, you have to copy it there; assets are site-specific.

> *tip* Keep in mind that you don't see the **Site** button, or the **Favorites** button (E) either, when you've selected **Templates** or **Library Items** in the category bar.

E favorites

Click this radio button to display the assets you've added to the Favorites list for the selected category. (Initially, the Favorites list is empty.) You can right-click (Win) or **control**-click (Mac) a favorite asset and choose **Edit Nickname** from the context menu to give the asset a nickname, if you like. (You can't do this in the site view of the **Assets** panel, though.)

F play/stop

You see the tiny **Play/Stop** button at the upper right of the preview pane (C) only with the Flash, Shockwave, and Movie asset categories. It manifests as a green arrow when the asset's preview is stopped and as a red square when the preview is going.

G context menu

You can activate the context menu by clicking the right arrow in the upper-right corner of the panel, or by right-clicking (Win) or **control**-clicking (Mac) a specific file in the assets list (B). One handy command

on the context menu is **Locate In Site**, which finds the selected asset in the site files window.

H insert

Insert an asset to the open document by placing the insertion point in the document window, selecting the asset in the **Assets** panel, and clicking **Insert**. Or, you may prefer to drag and drop assets into the document window. To apply a color to a chunk of text, simply select the text first and then insert the color asset.

> *tip* When you apply a template asset, it applies to the loaded document rather than to any document object.

I refresh site list

The **Assets** panel does not refresh its contents automatically. Click this button to update the **Assets** panel when you add or remove an asset or save a file containing a new color or new URL.

J edit

Click the **Edit** button to activate whatever program Dreamweaver associates with the selected asset. For example, if you choose a GIF image and you've set Fireworks to be your default image editor via the **Edit➞Preferences** command, Dreamweaver will launch Fireworks. You can also double-click an asset to achieve the same effect.

K add to favorites

This little button adds the currently selected asset to your favorites list. I've seen installations where this button doesn't work, in which case you can use the context menu and choose the **Add to Favorites** command that way. Sometimes having more than one way to execute a command comes in handy!

L remove from favorites

When you're in the Favorites view, you can click the **Remove From Favorites** button to change the selected asset from a favorite asset to a regular old asset.

Design Notes are most useful for collaborative environments, but I find 'em handy for small one-person projects, too. Simply put, Design Notes let you annotate your HTML files with any information you want to share with co-workers or remember yourself. Dreamweaver saves your notes in a separate file that travels with the document and that you can see in the site window's Notes column. You can associate Design Notes with HTML pages, with specific objects on your pages, and with templates.

This procedure shows you how to create a Design Note for an HTML page and add a custom note type. The Define A Site section on page 160 shows how to set up your site for Design Notes.

1 open document
Most often, you'll open the document to which you want to attach a Design Note, so you can be sure that it's the document you have in mind. However, you don't have to do it this way. You can also click the file in the site window.

2 choose design notes
The menu command is **File➡Design Notes** (no keyboard shortcut). Another alternative, if you're using the site window, is to right-click (Win) or **control**-click (Mac) the file and choose **Design Notes** from the context menu. (Yet another method is to double-click the **Notes** column of the site files window.) However you get there, the **Design Notes** dialog box appears.

3 click basic info
The **Basic Info** tab may be all you need for simple Design Notes. Here is where you can set a document's status and key in any uncategorized comments you want to associate with the document.

4 enter status
You can assign the document a status that you can report on later with **Site➡Reports**. Choices are **draft**, **revision1**, **revision2**, **revision3**, **alpha**, **beta**, **final**, and **needs attention**.

1 *open document*   **2** *choose design notes*   **3** *click basic info*

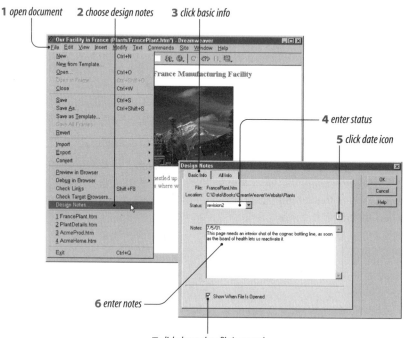

4 *enter status*

5 *click date icon*

6 *enter notes*

7 *click show when file is opened*

5 click date icon

When you click the date icon, you add the current date to the **Notes** window. This action saves you a few keystrokes.

6 enter notes

In this area, you can enter as much text as you like. Just remember that you cannot pull up a report later on any data in the **Notes** area. If you want to report on something other than document status, you must create a new name/value pair via the **All Info** tab (8).

7 click show when file is opened

The problem with Design Notes is that you don't know that they exist when you open a document, unless you open them in the site window. Click **Show When File Is Opened**, and you've solved the problem: Dreamweaver displays the Design Note when you load the document.

> **tip** This only works for notes attached to Web pages, not to objects such as images.

8 click all info

Click the **All Info** tab to enter a custom name/value pair that you can report from later.

9 click plus

The plus button tells Dreamweaver you want to add a name/value pair. Dreamweaver places the text insertion point in the **Name** field (10).

10 enter name

Type the name of the field you want to add. For example, here I type "Importance."

11 enter value

Type the value corresponding to the field name; here, "high." Watch out: These values are case-sensitive, so if you later run a report looking for "High" instead of "high," this note won't show up in the report!

12 click OK

Click the **OK** button to save your Design Note. Dreamweaver saves the data in the folder **_notes** and gives it the filename **<document>.MNO**, where **<document>** is the same as the document's filename.

> **tip** When you're ready to publish your site, you can strip out the Design Notes in the **Site Definition** window by clearing the **Maintain Design Notes** check box and then clicking the **Clean Up** button. Make sure that you have an archive of the site, so you don't lose all the comments!

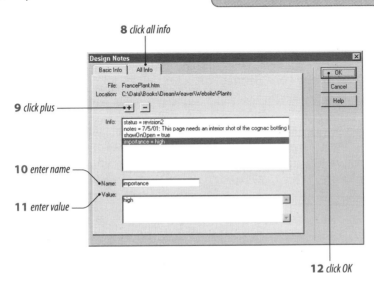

8 *click all info*

9 *click plus*

10 *enter name*

11 *enter value*

12 *click OK*

The Check Target Browsers Command

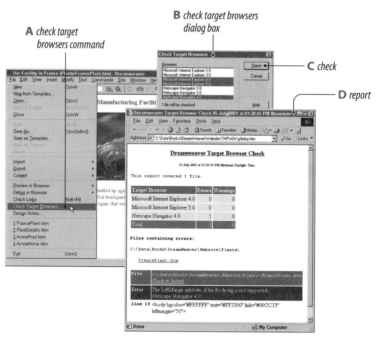

A *check target browsers command*

B *check target browsers dialog box*

C *check*

D *report*

Dreamweaver provides a convenient way to test your site's tags and attributes for compatibility with the browsers that Dreamweaver knows about, namely, Netscape Navigator and Internet Explorer. Based on the report that the program generates, you can decide whether to "dumb down" features that might present a compatibility problem or live with a more limited audience and perhaps create an alternate page.

A check target browsers command

Choose **File➥Check Target Browsers** to check the currently loaded page (save it first!). If you have the site files window open and you select multiple files or a folder, then the **Check Target Browsers** command acts on the selected objects. To check the entire site, click the site's root folder before performing the command.

B check target browsers dialog box

Pick one or more browsers to check the selected file or files against for compatibility. You're allowed to select multiple browsers in this dialog box. Use

shift+click to select adjacent browser names, and ctrl+click (Win) or **command**-click (Mac), to select nonadjacent ones. The ensuing report will combine the results; you'll have to decide whether that's more convenient or more confusing!

C check

Click the **Check** button when you're ready to run the report. It may take a few seconds on a large site with many different browser types and versions selected.

D report

Dreamweaver presents its report in your primary browser window. The errors and warnings that the program presents indicate the specific tag or attribute that isn't supported and which of the browsers you selected doesn't support it. Many of these warnings apply to code that Dreamweaver uses internally, which won't present any problems for site users. Save the report by choosing **File➥Save**.

> **tip** The browser compatibility check doesn't cover any scripts that you or Dreamweaver may have written, for example, to perform behaviors associated with specific browser events.

The Change Links Sitewide Command

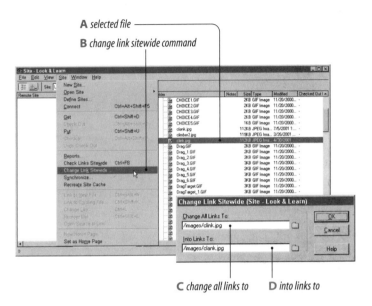

A selected file

B change link sitewide command

C change all links to **D** into links to

When you want to delete a file that other pages point to with links, you have a dilemma. Deleting the file may break several (or several hundred) links, which you could then repair but which would take a lot of time and effort. The approach I suggest is to change all those links first to point to a different file and then delete the orphaned file you no longer need.

In other situations, you may have some time-sensitive links ("Today's Prices") that point to one file today but that you need to point to a different file tomorrow. The answer to both situations is the **Change Links Sitewide** command.

> 💡 Make sure that you have the correct site selected before executing this command. The current site is not necessarily the same as you might assume by looking at the document window; let the Site window be your indication as to which site Dreamweaver considers the current one.

A selected file

Highlight the file that is currently the target of the links you want to change. Click the file in the site window's files list.

B change link sitewide command

Choose the menu command **Site➤Change Link Sitewide** from the site menu (Win), or **Site➤Site Files View➤Change Link Sitewide** (Mac). Unfortunately, this command doesn't have a keyboard shortcut. It does, however, bring up the **Change Link Sitewide** dialog box.

C change all links to

This field displays the path of the file you selected (A), so you shouldn't need to change it, but you can—for example, if you want to change an e-mail, null, or script link. (Keep in mind that you can't select those graphically in the site files window.)

D into links to

This text box is where you specify the new link target you want Dreamweaver to substitute for the old file that you want to archive or delete. You can simply type the path in directly, or you can click the folder icon to browse for it. (If the field titles feel confusing, put 'em together, like this: "Change all links to <old file> into links to <new file>.")

The Check Links Commands

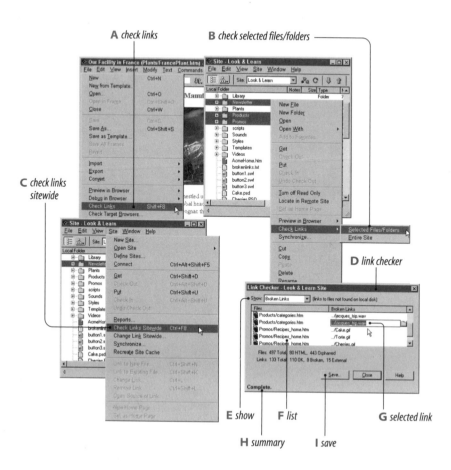

A *check links*

B *check selected files/folders*

C *check links sitewide*

D *link checker*

E *show* F *list* G *selected link*

H *summary* I *save*

Broken links are links that point to a file or Web site that no longer exists, or a path that is no longer valid because one of the folders in the path has been moved or deleted. Dreamweaver's automatic site management system does a great job of minimizing the chance of links breaking, because whenever you move or rename a file in the site window, the program updates all relevant links for you. (This is why you should use the site window for file management, rather than Windows Explorer or the Mac Finder.) However, as long as designers have access to the underlying HTML code and the operating system's file management utilities, links can break. Dreamweaver provides three commands for checking links, depending on whether you want to check a single file, a handful of files, or an entire site.

A check links

When you have a file loaded in the document window, you can check any links that it contains with the **File➞Check Links** command (shortcut **shift+F8**), which runs a check and displays the **Link Checker** dialog box.

> *tip* If you open a document that belongs to a different site than the one you have open, Dreamweaver gets confused, and the **Link Checker** dialog box doesn't ever finish processing. (That **Stop Current Process** icon in the lower right stays there forever.) The fix is to choose **Site➞Open Site** and open the site containing the document that's currently loaded.

B check selected files/folders

If you have the site window open, you can select multiple files and/or folders, bring up the context menu for any of the selected items (right-click in Windows, **control**-click on the Mac), and choose **Check Links→Selected Files/Folders**. (You can also choose **File→Check Links** after selecting the files and folders.)

C check links sitewide

To check all links for a site, choose **Site→Check Links Sitewide** or **ctrl+F8** in Windows (**command-F8** on the Mac). Dreamweaver runs the check and displays the Link Checker.

> *tip* The sitewide check provides a report category that the other types (A and B) don't: *orphaned files*—that is, files that are present but not linked to by any page in the site. You can see why only a sitewide check could identify such files, for Dreamweaver must check each page to determine which files are orphans. Consider deleting or relocating any orphan files the sitewide check discovers.

D link checker

Whichever report you run (A, B, or C), Dreamweaver displays the results in the **Link Checker** dialog box. The remaining sections explore the components of this dialog box, which, incidentally, you can't minimize.

E show

You can show three categories of reports: **Broken Links**, **External Links**, and (in a sitewide check only) **Orphaned Files**. External links are links to files, pages, or graphics that are outside the site; Dreamweaver does not check external links for validity; it only lists them.

> *tip* Save the External Links report to a disk file and then open it in a program (such as Microsoft Word) that recognizes URLs and formats them as hyperlinks. Then, establish an Internet connection, and you can easily check your external links one by one by clicking each link.

F list

Here's where you can see the broken links, external links, or orphaned files, depending on what you choose in the **Show** menu (E). Dreamweaver gives you the file and link for the first two reports, and just the filename for the third. You can delete orphaned files in the list by clicking them and pressing the **delete** key.

G selected link

The **Link Checker** lets you fix a broken link without navigating to any other command or window. Click a link in the list window, and Dreamweaver pops up a folder icon you can click to browse to where the correct link really is. Once you find and choose it in the **Select File** dialog box, press **enter**, and if any other broken links identical to the one you just fixed are out there, Dreamweaver asks you whether you want to fix 'em all. (If you have check in/check out turned on and the program can't check out one or more files to modify them, it lets you know so you can modify them manually later.)

If you prefer to see some context for the correction, double-click in the **File** column. Dreamweaver both opens the offending file and highlights the offending link, which you can then correct in the property inspector.

> *tip* If you don't see the offending link in the property inspector, but you do see a null or script link (like **javascript:;**), you may have attached a behavior to the highlighted object, and the behavior is trying to link to the missing file. Open the **Behaviors** panel and see whether that's the case by double-clicking behaviors in the list until you find the culprit.

H summary

File and link count totals show up in the summary lines at the bottom of the dialog box.

I save

Click to create a plain text, tab-delimited file that you can open in a text editor, spreadsheet, or database program.

The Reports Command

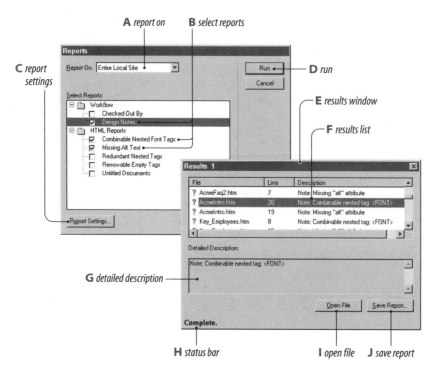

A *report on* **B** *select reports*

C *report settings*

D *run*

E *results window*

F *results list*

G *detailed description*

H *status bar* **I** *open file* **J** *save report*

Dreamweaver's **Check Links Sitewide** command reports on broken links, external links, and orphaned files. You can create several other useful site management reports with the **Site➡Reports** command, however, and you can even design your own reports if you use Design Notes.

> *tip* Consider running the **Commands➡ Clean Up HTML** command on your site's pages before running the **Reports** command. The **Clean Up HTML** process fixes most of the problems that would show up in Dreamweaver's HTML reports. (In fact, some have criticized the reporting module for basically duplicating the **Clean Up HTML** code.) Having said that, you may find it a more efficient use of your time to run the reports first and then just run **Clean Up HTML** against any pages for which you find problems, because Dreamweaver doesn't provide a way to run **Clean Up HTML** across the entire site in one fell swoop.

A report on

Select your report's scope in the **Report On** drop-down list. Use the **Entire Local Site** option when you think you're done with your site and you want to check all files for problems before you upload the site to the remote server.

B select reports

Click a check box to select the corresponding report. Note that you can choose multiple check boxes, and Dreamweaver will combine the results into a single report. The dialog box sorts reports by two categories, **Workflow** (which may require check in/check out or Design Notes to be active for the site) and **HTML Reports** (which run on any site).

C report settings

This button is only active for the two workflow reports; it appears dimmed for the HTML reports. Use **Report Settings** to specify the user name for the **Checked Out By** report and to specify the Design Notes selection criteria in the **Design Notes** report.

(For more on the **Design Notes** report, see the sidebar, Report Types, on the following page.)

D run

Click **Run** to run the report. Dreamweaver will prompt you for more information if you haven't saved the current document for a document report or selected a folder for a folder report or one or more files for a file report. The program also fusses if you try to run a report without first fully defining the site; you'll have to go back and finish the site before you can proceed.

E results window

Here's where you see the results of your report. The results window may not float to the top of the desktop, so you may need to minimize or move one or more foreground windows to see enough of the results window to click it and bring it to the surface. Dreamweaver labels the windows **Results 1**, **Results 2**, and so on so that you can see multiple reports at once.

> *(tip)* While a report is running, the Results window displays a **Stop Current Task** icon in its lower right corner; it looks like a Stop sign. Click it to cancel the currently running report.

F results list

This lists all pages that correspond to the report criteria you chose. Dreamweaver provides the filename, line number in the code (where relevant), and a summary description in the results list. You can click the column headings to sort report items by that column. You can also double-click an item in the list to mimic the behavior of the **Open File** button (I).

G detailed description

Click an item in the results list (F), and you'll see a detailed description here, although most of the time it won't contain any information that the description column in the results list contains.

H status bar

The lower left of the **Results** window shows you filenames as it processes them, and the word **Complete** appears when the report is done.

I open file

Click this button to open the file in the currently selected results list. Dreamweaver opens the file into the document window, switches to code view, and highlights the problematic tag, so you can edit it! You can double-click a result in the list to open the file a bit faster. If you prefer letting Dreamweaver do the editing for you, you can choose **Commands⇒ Clean Up HTML** instead of making correction to the HTML yourself.

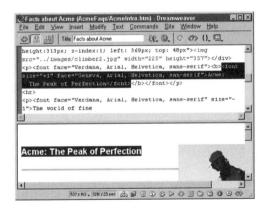

J save report

Click this button to save the report to disk. Dreamweaver saves reports as XML files, and that's presently the only option. As a practical matter, you would need to design a template into which to import the XML file and then export the data if you want to work with it in a spreadsheet or database.

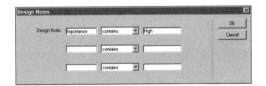

Report Types

So what do the various reports actually do? Here's a summary.

Checked Out By

Displays all the files that have been checked out by a specific user, whose name you input.

Design Notes

Lets you specify a criterion list by note type. For example, you can run a report to list all documents whose status is "beta." You can specify up to three criteria in the **Design Notes** dialog box, each criterion consisting of a Design Notes field name (such as status), operator (such as contains), and value (such as beta). Available operators are **contains, does not contain, is, is not**, and **matches regex**. What's a regex? It's a *regular expression*, a way for you to specify a pattern you want the report to match. You can use regular expressions to specify special characters that you can't normally key into the value field; for example, **\t** indicates a tab, **\r** a carriage return, and so on. You can even indicate logical operations; for example, **bob|robert** performs an "or" search that returns matches for either **bob** or **robert**. Check out the online help using the search phrase "about regular expressions" for details.

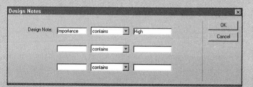

Combinable Nested Font Tags

Sometimes HTML code contains multiple **<font>** tag pairs, each with a different attribute.

For example:

```
<font size="3"><font color="#FF00FF">Welcome to
Acme!</font></font>
```

After you run a report and identify the nested tags, you can edit them manually (the Results list lets you double-click the item to open code view) or use Dreamweaver's **Clean Up HTML** command to combine them into a single tag for more efficient code, as follows:

```
<font size="3" color="#FF00FF">Welcome to Acme!</font>
```

Missing Alt Text

This report lists all **<img>** tags that don't have any alternative text defined. It's a good idea to supply alt text for images, first because for large images, it gives the user something to read, second because some users set their browsers to download images manually, and they need to know what an image is to decide whether to download it, and third because some speech synthesis tools read the alt text for the benefit of visually impaired visitors. Note that all text is not the same as the image's HTML name.

Redundant Nested Tags

Redundant nested tags occur when you have the same attribute specified twice for a given chunk of HTML text. Usually this occurs when you make a single word in a paragraph bold or italic and then decide to make the whole sentence or paragraph bold or italic; you no longer need the tag pair that you inserted originally in this scenario.

For example, this report would flag the following code:

```
<b>Welcome to <b>Acme!</b></b>
```

which you could then repair manually as follows:

```
<b>Welcome to Acme!</b>
```

Note that this report does not flag combinable nested font tags, even though technically they, too, are "redundant nested tags."

Removable Empty Tags

Sometimes, when you get rid of an HTML object while editing your HTML directly in code view, you forget to remove all the tags that used to surround that object in the code. (This doesn't happen when you delete objects in design view.) The Removable Empty Tags report lists such empty tags, which don't do anything useful but which do add to the size and complexity of your page.

Untitled Documents

This report finds any documents that have no title (empty or missing **<title>** tag pair), the default Dreamweaver title ("Untitled Document"), and a title that's duplicated in the site by one or more other documents. Good Web design practice mandates a unique and descriptive title for every page. Add or change the document title via the **Title** field in the document windows's toolbar or by choosing **Modify➡Page Properties**.

chapter

11

Add Animation

For a long time, at least in Internet years, all Web pages were static. You visited a page, looked at the text and images, and then you visited another page. Today, you have several options for making your pages more animated. These options range from relatively simple rollover buttons to fancier Flash buttons to complex layer animations with sophisticated timelines.

Some forms of Web page motion are beyond Dreamweaver's scope. Dreamweaver, for example, doesn't create animated GIF graphics or QuickTime movies. However, once you see what Dreamweaver _can_ do, especially in Version 4-and-up browsers that support Dynamic HTML, you may decide to implement certain animated effects right in the HTML instead of by dropping in movies from an outside program.

You'll want to be sure to read Chapter 12, Add Interactivity, as well as this one. When you master both timelines and behaviors, you can create some _very_ slick special effects.

175

The Insert Rollover Image Command

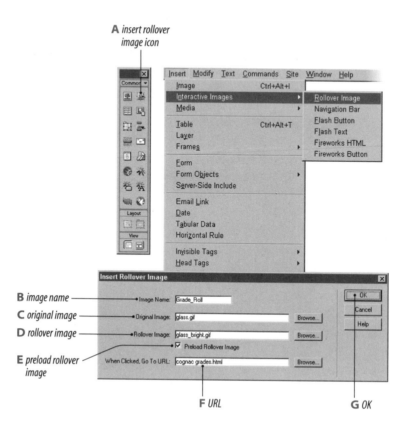

A *insert rollover image icon*

B *image name*

C *original image*

D *rollover image*

E *preload rollover image*

F *URL*

G *OK*

A simple but effective tool to apply interactivity to a Web page is the *rollover image*, an image that changes its appearance (actually switching to a different image) when you pass the cursor over it. Most of the rollover images you see on the Web are hyperlinks, but they don't have to be.

A insert rollover image icon

The fastest way to insert a rollover image at the current insertion point (that is, cursor location) is to click the **Insert Rollover Image** icon on the objects panel (which you can display with **Window➠ Objects**). You can drag and drop the icon, too. An alternative method is to choose the menu command **Insert➠Interactive Images➠Rollover Image** (no keyboard shortcut here). Any of those methods open the **Insert Rollover Image** dialog box.

B image name

Enter a descriptive name for your rollover, even if you've already given names to the two individual images you plan to use. The rollover object will have its own name independent of those two.

C original image

Here's where you specify the image that you want your rollover to display *before* the user rolls the mouse over it. You can type the path to the file or (better) click the **Browse** button and navigate to it.

> *tip* If you haven't yet saved your document, Dreamweaver prompts you to do so. To avoid such annoyances, save your document right after you click **File➠New**.

D rollover image

Here, specify the image you want the user to see as she rolls the mouse over it. Again, the **Browse** button is the preferred method.

E preload rollover image

You'll usually want to make sure that the **Preload Rollover Image** box is checked, because it instructs Dreamweaver to download the two image files into the browser's memory when the page loads. If you don't preload the rollover images, users could see a delay when mousing over the original image (C) before they see the rollover image (D). On a slow dial-up connection, the delay could be long enough to negate the interactive effect, because the user may mouse away from the image before it has a chance to change.

F URL

In the **When Clicked, Go To URL** field, specify the destination to which the link should take the visitor when she clicks the rollover image.

> *tip* You're allowed to leave this field blank, if you're using a rollover image for some nonlink purpose.

G OK

As usual, when you're happy with your choices, click the **OK** button. Dreamweaver closes the **Insert Rollover Image** dialog box, and you can preview the effect in your browser with the **File➡Preview In Browser** command.

For some different kinds of rollovers, check out the following sidebar.

Swap Image Behaviors

If you want to peek under the hood of a rollover image you've created, click it and open the **Behaviors** panel with **Window➡Behaviors**. You'll see something like the following window, with two behaviors listed: **Swap Image** and **Swap Image Restore**.

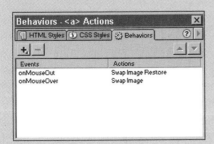

When you become adept with the **Behaviors** panel (which Chapter 12 discusses in detail), you can fine-tune how Dreamweaver's "canned" interactions, such as the rollover image, behave. For example, if you double-click the **Swap Image** behavior, you'll see the dialog box shown at the right.

Clear the check box labeled **Restore Images onMouse-Out** and click **OK**. You'll see the **Swap Image Restore**

behavior disappear from the **Behaviors** panel. Now, when you preview your rollover in the browser window, the image changes when you mouse over it, but it doesn't change back when you mouse away.

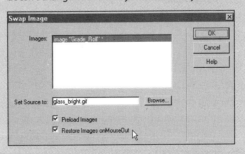

You can use the **Behaviors** panel to create yet another variation on the rollover theme: the *disjoint rollover*, which is a rollover image that makes something else happen on the page. For example, you could draw a new layer on the page and add two new behaviors using the **Set Text of Layer** action and the **onMouseOver** and **onMouseOut** events, to make a message appear and disappear at the layer location at the same time the rollover image changes. Read through Chapter 12 and then try this out!

The Insert Flash Button Command

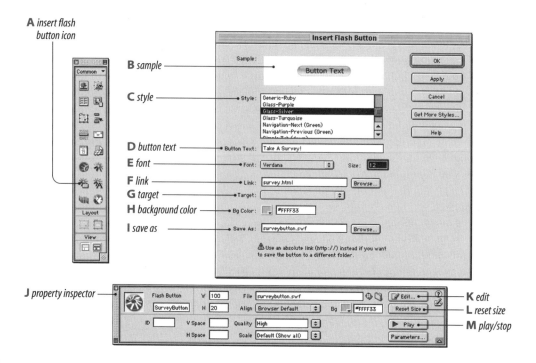

A *insert flash button icon*

B *sample*

C *style*

D *button text*

E *font*

F *link*

G *target*

H *background color*

I *save as*

J *property inspector*

K *edit*

L *reset size*

M *play/stop*

One more piece of evidence that demonstrates the continuing integration of Dreamweaver and Flash is the **Insert Flash Button** command. Flash buttons are little Flash animations that Macromedia has prefabricated for you so that you can add some cool interactive effects to your page without knowing how to program in Flash. They typically act like rollovers but they may include behavioral wrinkles, such as fade-in effects.

> *tip* Dreamweaver's going to insist that you save a new document before it will let you add a Flash button.

A insert flash button icon

Add a Flash button at the current insertion point in design view by clicking the **Insert Flash Button** icon on the objects panel (which you can display with **Window→Objects**) or by dragging and dropping that icon into your document. Another method is to choose the menu command **Insert→Interactive**

Images→Flash Button (no shortcut). Dreamweaver opens the **Insert Flash Button** dialog box.

> *tip* These buttons are cool, but they do require the Flash Player plug-in. A user who lacks the plug-in must download it before he can use Flash buttons (or Flash text or Flash movies). Most browsers come with Flash support nowadays, so this requirement is becoming less of an issue.

B sample

The **Sample** window shows you a preview of the selected style (C). This window lets you preview the button's animation effects for **onMouseOver** and **onClick** states. You can also preview button behavior with the **Play/Stop** command on the property inspector (M), or via **File→Preview in Browser**.

C style

Choose from one of several predefined button types in the **Style** area. Click a style to see its preview in the **Sample** window (B).

D button text

Enter the text you want your button to show. Note that this text typically appears before a mouse-over, during a mouse-over, and during a click.

E font

Pick the font you want your button text to use. I favor buttons that use the same main font the page uses, for design continuity. As long as the user has the Flash Player, the user doesn't have to have the font on his system (unlike regular browser text).

F link

If you want your button to be a hyperlink, specify the destination document in the **Link** field by typing in the path and filename or by using the **Browse** button.

G target

If the destination document you specify in (F) has a named frame you want the user to go to, specify it.

H background color

If you want the Flash button to appear against a particular color background, as you may if you use something other than white as your page background color and you want the button to appear to "float," set an optional background color here. You can click the color box to bring up Dreamweaver's color picker or enter a hexadecimal color value directly.

I save as

The **Save As** field is where you name the file defining your customized Flash button. It should have the SWF extension and should live in the same folder as the page's HTML file according to Macromedia, although many people prefer to use a "media" or "images" folder.

J property inspector

After you've created a Flash button, you can see its properties by opening the property inspector (**Window→Properties**) and clicking the button. The settings you're most likely to use are **Edit**, **Reset Size**, and **Play/Stop** (K, L, and M).

K edit

Click the **Edit** button to bring up the **Insert Flash Button** dialog box to change any of the button's defining characteristics. (You can also just double-click the button in the document window to achieve the same effect.)

L reset size

One of the useful things about Flash animations (and buttons are really mini-animations) is that, unlike bitmap images, you can resize them and maintain a fairly good level of quality. If you resize a Flash button (by clicking and dragging the resize handles) and then decide you want to go back to the original size, click the **Reset Size** button.

M play/stop

You don't have to execute the **File→Preview in Browser** command to see how your Flash button behaves when you mouse-over it and click it; just click the **Play** button on the property inspector, and you can interact with the button in the document window. Click the button again (it'll say **Stop** now) when you're done.

The Timelines Panel

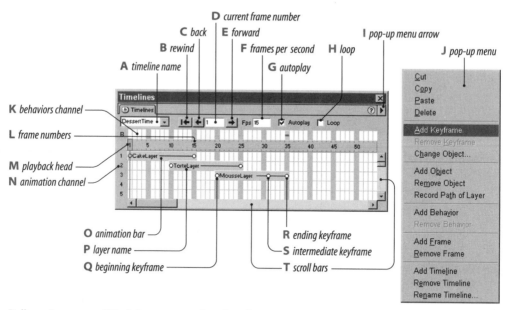

D current frame number
C back
E forward
B rewind
F frames per second
H loop
I pop-up menu arrow
A timeline name
G autoplay
J pop-up menu
K behaviors channel
L frame numbers
M playback head
N animation channel
O animation bar
P layer name
Q beginning keyframe
R ending keyframe
S intermediate keyframe
T scroll bars

Rollover images and Flash buttons are all well and good, but if you want to do some really sophisticated animations with dynamic layers, and you're willing to limit your browsing audience to Version 4.0 browsers and higher, then you'll want to get intimate with the **Timelines** panel. Activate it with **Window⟶Timelines** or the keyboard shortcut **shift-F9**.

The first time you look at this panel, the blood may drain from your face, but don't worry; it's not as complex as it looks. This section breaks it down element by element, and the sections that follow show you how to put it to work.

A timeline name

The name that appears in this area is the current timeline loaded in the panel. You can have multiple timelines on the same page (see Multiple Timelines per Page on page 190 for more), in which case you can click the arrow by the timeline name to see a pop-up menu of all the timelines defined for the page.

You name a timeline by clicking and typing in this area.

B rewind

This button sets the timeline to the starting point and causes all animated layers to assume their starting positions in the document window. (Note that timelines animate layers, not images or paragraphs. If you want to animate an image, put it into a layer first.)

C back

Click this button once to move one frame to the left in the timeline, causing all animated layers to assume their positions at that frame.

Incidentally, a frame, indicated by a single rectangle in the timeline grid, is a point in time at which the animation has a discrete, defined position.

> **tip** You can hold down the **Back** button, and the timeline will play in reverse. Change the speed of your keyboard repeat feature to change the speed at which this occurs.

D current frame number

Frames start numbering at 1 and increase to the right. The unnamed field between the **Back** and **Forward** controls shows you the number of the currently selected frame. Note that it's possible to have a behavior defined after the end of the animation; the **Loop** behavior (H), for example, lives at the last-plus-one frame.

E forward

Click here once to move one frame to the right, or into the future. As with the **Back** button (C), you can hold down the **Forward** button, and the animation will play in the document window. (Macromedia documentation calls this the **Play** button, but that's inaccurate because it doesn't act like a VCR's Play button, which you click once and don't have to hold down.)

F frames per second

This value indicates how many frames per second the animation should try to play; the default is 15. You should view this figure as an upper limit, because the user's browser may not be able to realize the specified frame rate.

Unlike most multimedia viewers, browsers don't drop frames if they aren't able to play an animation at its rated speed; they just slow down.

> *tip* Assuming that the browser can handle the frame rate you specify in the **FPS** field, you can calculate the duration of an animation using the formula *seconds = frames divided by FPS*. In any case, you can be sure that the animation will never play in *fewer* seconds than the formula indicates.

G autoplay

Click this check box to make the timeline play automatically upon loading of the page into the user's browser. The **Autoplay** feature associates the **Play Timeline** action with the **onLoad** event for the **<body>** tag (which may all mean more to you after you've read Chapter 12).

H loop

Be very careful with this one, which causes your animation to loop endlessly. Looping animations can quickly move from dazzling to irritating. This command adds a behavior to the B channel (K) invoking the **Go To Timeline Frame** action at the end of the animation, much like a "goto" command in a

programming language. When you click this box, you get a message from Dreamweaver telling you how to modify the action after you've added it.

> *tip* You wouldn't know it to look at the Loop check box, because check boxes are generally all-or-nothing propositions, but you can control the number of loops in a layer animation. Double-click the cell in the **Behaviors** channel at the last-plus-one frame and then double-click the line in the **Behaviors** panel to display the following dialog box. Maybe Dreamweaver 5 will make this a bit simpler by putting an "...X times" field next to the **Loop** field in the **Timelines** panel.

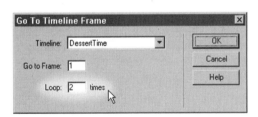

I pop-up menu arrow

The arrow at the panel's upper right is your gateway to most timeline-related commands.

J pop-up menu

This menu appears when you click the context menu arrow (I). I find this menu much handier than **Modify➡Timeline**. Note that when you cut, copy, or paste an animation channel (N), you must use the commands on the context menu as opposed to the ones of the same names on the **Edit** menu. Note also the command **Change Object**, which lets you apply an existing animation to a different layer on the same page.

K behaviors channel

A *channel* is just a row in the **Timelines** panel. The **Behaviors** channel is the part of the panel where you can specify that a specific action should occur at a specific point in time.

Sometimes, as with the **Loop** command, Dreamweaver adds behaviors to the timeline automatically. However, preferably after looking over Chapter 12, you can add your own behaviors manually, simply by double-clicking the cell in this row that sits at the point in the animation sequence where you want something to happen, and adding one or more behaviors in the **Behaviors** panel.

L frame numbers

Dreamweaver provides a helpful ruler with frame numbers on it in this row.

M playback head

The **Playback Head** indicates what point in the animation the current state of the document window represents. When you click the VCR-like motion buttons **Rewind** (B), **Back** (C), and **Forward** (E), you move the **Playback Head**.

N animation channel

This is the row in which an animation bar (O) can exist. It's perfectly legal to have multiple objects in the same animation channel, one after another, although for visualization purposes, you may find it cleaner to put each layer into its own channel. The one thing you're not allowed to do is have the same object (layer) showing up in two or more different animation channels at the same frame number.

O animation bar

When you drag and drop a layer to the **Timelines** panel, you create an animation bar that consists of the layer name (P), beginning keyframe (Q), and ending keyframe (R).

Dreamweaver creates the bar with an arbitrary length; you can extend the bar by dragging the ending keyframe, making the animation longer.

P layer name

By default, Dreamweaver names the animation channel after the layer whose animation it represents. It's smart to give your layers descriptive names before you add them to the **Timelines** panel.

Q beginning keyframe

A *frame* is an animation cell for which a specific position is defined for each object in the animation, and a *keyframe* is a special frame that you use to place objects. All animations have at least a beginning keyframe, shown here by a circle, and an ending keyframe (R).

Click the beginning keyframe and reposition the layer that you're animating to its starting position. Drag the beginning keyframe to make the animation start at a different time in the timeline (but drag the animation channel if you don't want to change the length of the animation).

R ending keyframe

The last frame in the animation channel has a circle indicating that it's the ending keyframe. Drag this to the right to make the animation longer and smoother.

S intermediate keyframes

You can add intermediate keyframes if you want to refine the motion in your animation. For example, if you have an object moving in a straight line, and you'd like it to move in a curved motion, you could add one or more keyframes between the beginning and ending keyframes.

Just click in the animation channel at the frame you want to make a keyframe, click the pop-up menu arrow (I), and choose **Add Keyframe**. Then, click the keyframe and reposition the layer in the document window to where you want it to be at that point in the animation sequence; Dreamweaver fills in the intervening frames.

Another way to add a keyframe is to **control**-click (Win) or **command**-click (Mac) the frame of interest.

> *tip* Don't manually add a lot of keyframes to create a complex path; there's an easier way, described in Make A Curved Path Animation on page 188.

T scroll bars

If your animation is long or contains many channels, you can navigate with the scroll bars, although you may want to try resizing the **Timelines** panel first so that you can see more of what's going on. As usual with Dreamweaver windows, you resize the **Timelines** panel by dragging its lower-right corner.

Timelines & Dynamic HTML

The **Timelines** panel is Macromedia's user interface for the layer animation capabilities of *Dynamic HTML (DHTML)*, which is technology supported by Version 4.0-and-higher browsers. In order for layer animation to work, the user's browser must also support JavaScript (and have JavaScript processing turned on), because Dreamweaver puts the timeline code into the head of the HTML document into JavaScript functions named **MM_initTimelines** and **MM_timelinePlay**. Check out your document in code view and see what I mean.

When you use the **Timelines** panel to place behaviors into the **B** channel and make certain things happen at specific times, you're also using JavaScript, because that's the language Dreamweaver uses to implement the behaviors feature. For example, **MM_showHideLayers** is the JavaScript function Dreamweaver writes to make layers appear and disappear; **MM_control Sound** is the JavaScript function that plays a sound file; and so on. For lots more info on behaviors, see Chapter 12.

If you think the **Timelines** panel is complicated, I can't disagree with you. It's the most complex panel in the whole program. However, here's something you should do to put its complexity into perspective. Run through the Make A Timeline Animation exercise on the following pages and then look at your document in code view and check out the HTML that Dreamweaver builds. It's a lot more horrifying than what you had to go through with the **Timelines** and **Behaviors** panels. Imagine writing that HTML from scratch!

⟨steps⟩ Make A Timeline Animation

This section puts the **Timelines** panel to work creating a simple but effective layer path animation. Three dessert images (each in its own layer) will automatically "fly in" from off the page and take their position as the banner collage for a page of recipes. Layer animation works in browsers that don't have the Flash Player plugin, as long as the browsers are Version 4 or higher. At the end of the animation, a fourth layer appears, proclaiming the page's title.

This example illustrates how you can use layers that start a motion path outside the browser window, and how you can add a behavior to make an event occur at a specific frame within a timeline.

> ⟨tip⟩ This animation changes layer position. You can also create animations that change the visibility, size, and stacking order of layers.

1 draw layer
Click the **Draw Layer** icon on the objects panel and draw a layer on the page. Make it smaller than the image you plan to insert into it, so that the layer will automatically expand to the exact dimensions of the image. (You have to put the images into layers because you can only animate layers, not stand-alone images.)

2 insert image
Click inside the layer you just drew and click the **Insert Image** icon on the objects panel. Select the first graphic you want to "fly in" to your page's banner area.

3 show invisible elements
Choose **View➞Visual Aids➞Invisible Elements** if it's not already checked. This command displays layer anchors, which you'll need because the layers will be off the page when their animations begin.

4 open property inspector
Choose **Window➞Properties** to display the property inspector. You'll use it to monitor the layer's positioning coordinates.

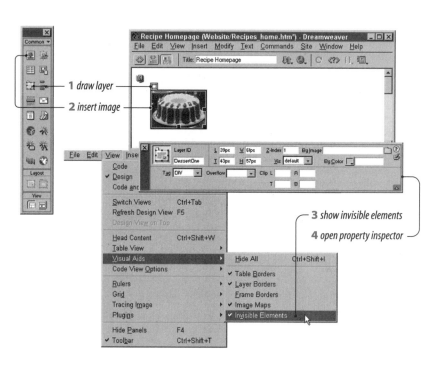

5 click layer

Click the layer's upper-left corner to select it. (Select the layer, not the image.)

6 move layer to start

Move the layer with the arrow keys to set its vertical position. You want it to slide in from off the page, moving left to right, so once you have the vertical position correct, use the left arrow to move the layer until you can't see it any more. You'll notice a negative number in the inspector's **L** field.

7 open timelines panel

The command is **Window→Timelines**, and the shortcut is **shift+F9**.

8 drag layer anchor

Now you need to add the layer to the timeline. You can't see the layer because it's off-screen, so drag the layer anchor instead. Drop it into Channel 1 on the **Timelines** panel so that the left part of the animation bar sits in the first column (frame 1). (You could also just click the anchor and choose **Modify→ Timeline→Add Object to Time-line**.)

You'll see the layer in the timeline as a colored bar with the layer name on it.

(You may also see an educational dialog box when you drop the layer into the **Timelines** panel.)

9 click ending keyframe

Now, tell Dreamweaver where the layer should be at the end of its animation. Click the last keyframe of the layer object in the **Timelines** panel; it'll have a circle on it indicating that it's a keyframe.

10 click layer anchor

Click the layer anchor to select it.

11 move layer to end

Hold down your right arrow key to move the layer to the right, or hold **shift**-right arrow to move 10 pixels at a time, until it's where you want it to be at the end of its

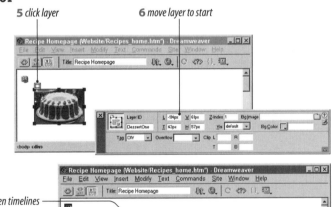

5 click layer *6 move layer to start*

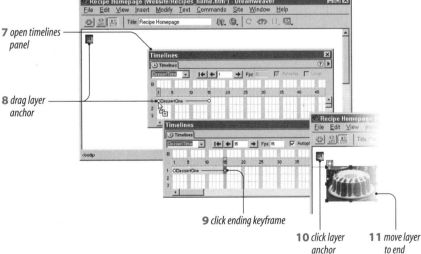

7 open timelines panel

8 drag layer anchor

9 click ending keyframe

10 click layer anchor *11 move layer to end*

animation. You'll see a trailing horizontal line behind the layer as you move it, indicating the animation path.

12 click play

Click and hold the **Play** icon (a right arrow) on the **Timelines** panel to watch the animation you just created play back in the document window.

13 add layers 2 & 3

Repeat steps 1, 2, and 5 through 12 to add and animate the second and third image layers. Place the starting point for layer 2 a little lower than for layer 1, and for layer 3 lower than for layer 2. Also, make the endpoints a bit farther to the right for layer 2, and another bit farther right for layer 3. The result will be a nice overlapping effect.

> *(tip)* It's easy to muck up your carefully crafted timelines accidentally. If a layer gets out of synch, you can always re-create its animation by clicking the keyframe in the **Timelines** panel and then moving the layer to where it should be at that keyframe.

You can get two different effects by having the three layers overlap a little in time, as opposed to each layer

starting only after the previous layer has finished. Create an overlap effect by clicking and dragging the animation bars in their channels. When you move an entire animation bar, you change the animation's start time, but nothing else.

14 tweak start & endpoints

Experiment with different start and endpoints by dragging keyframes horizontally in the **Timelines** panel. Again, click and hold the **Play** icon for a preview.

15 check autoplay

The **Autoplay** check box tells Dreamweaver to start the animation upon loading the page into the user's browser.

16 preview in browser

Click the **Preview/Debug in Browser** icon on the toolbar and choose your target browser. The animations should execute automatically. Having fun?

17 save document

At this point, you've done a lot of work, so do a **File➡ Save**. All that remains is to add the fourth layer, the page title, and make it appear at the end of the timeline.

18 draw title layer

Click the **Draw Layer** icon on the objects panel and draw a fourth layer on the page. Place this one to the right of the three dessert images' final position.

19 insert text

Click inside the new layer and add some text to act as the page title.

20 hide layer

You want this layer to be invisible initially and to appear only when the third dessert image has finished zooming in. Make the fourth layer invisible by clicking its

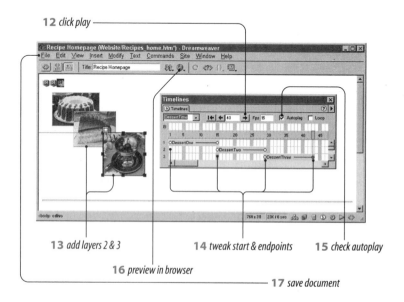

12 click play

13 add layers 2 & 3   *14 tweak start & endpoints*   *15 check autoplay*

16 preview in browser

17 save document

selection handle (upper left corner) and choosing **Hidden** in the **Vis** field of the property inspector.

21 place behavior

Double-click the cell in the **B** (for Behaviors) channel of the **Timelines** panel that corresponds vertically with the final frame of the layer animation. (If you see a didactic dialog box, read it and click **OK** to proceed.) Dreamweaver opens the **Behaviors** panel.

22 click add action

It's the + button in the **Behaviors** panel. Chapter 12 discusses this panel in much more detail, so I walk through only the necessary steps in this example.

23 choose show-hide layers

When you select the **Show-Hide Layers** action, Dreamweaver opens the **Show-Hide Layers** dialog box. While you're here, notice all the other actions you can choose.

24 choose layer

Click the fourth layer containing the banner text (it should show up in the **Layers** list).

25 click show

This action tells Dreamweaver to make the layer visible at the final frame of the animation, as you specified in (21).

26 click OK

Close the **Show-Hide Layers** dialog box. Incidentally, you can use the **Show-Hide Layers** action to do many useful things on your page, including displaying a "Loading . . ." layer that obscures the entire page until all the elements have downloaded.

27 close behaviors panel

But before you close it, notice the action that you just added, with the "OnFrame *n*" event, which tells Dreamweaver when to perform the action, (*n* being the number of the animation's last frame).

28 preview in browser

Choose **File→Preview in Browser** to view your completed animation. If it's gone haywire, go back to Dreamweaver and re-create the part that isn't working. Timeline work is ticklish so if you have to go back and repeat some steps, it's no shame.

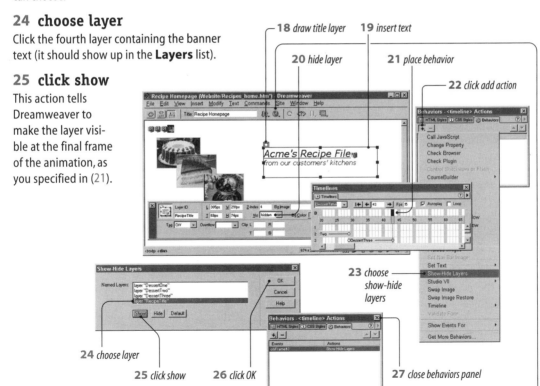

18 *draw title layer*   19 *insert text*

20 *hide layer*   21 *place behavior*

22 *click add action*

23 *choose show-hide layers*

24 *choose layer*

25 *click show*   26 *click OK*

27 *close behaviors panel*

28 *preview in browser*

⑪ **Add Animation:** Make A Timeline Animation   **187**

✏️ steps Make A Curved Path Animation

The previous example used a simple horizontal path with only two keyframes. You can create more complex animation paths in one of two ways: Make an initial animation with start and end points and then add intermediate keyframes with the **Add Keyframe** command, or draw the path yourself and let Dreamweaver figure out the keyframes. This example uses the latter method.

> 💡 **tip** The effectiveness of dynamic layer path animation depends greatly on the speed of the user's Internet connection and computer CPU. Choose small images and relatively short motions, and if necessary, extend the length of the animation bar in the **Timelines** panel by dragging the end keyframe. To create *really* smooth path animations that include larger images or lots of complex motions, consider building them in Flash and using the **Insert Flash** icon on the objects panel. The Chapter 15 section Import a Flash Movie, on page 236, provides details.

1 draw layer
Click the **Draw Layer** icon on the objects panel and draw a layer on the page. Make it smaller than the image you plan to insert.

2 insert image
Click inside the layer and click **Insert Image** on the objects panel. Select the graphic you want to animate.

3 move layer to start
Move the layer to its initial position by dragging its selection handle at the upper-left corner.

4 open timelines panel
Choose **Window➥Timelines** or press **shift+F9**.

5 choose record path of layer
The menu command is **Modify➥Timeline➥ Record Path of Layer** (no shortcut).

6 draw path
Drag the layer in the path you want to create, releasing the mouse button only when you reach the endpoint. You'll be able to see the object in the **Timelines** panel with the keyframes Dreamweaver created. You can now tweak the animation using the panel.

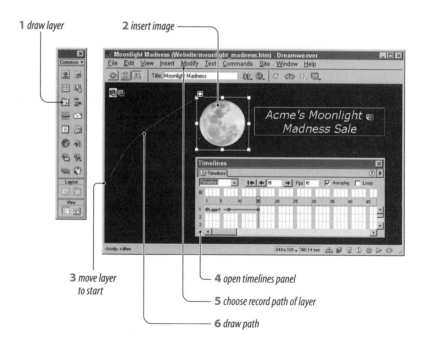

1 *draw layer*

2 *insert image*

3 *move layer to start*

4 *open timelines panel*

5 *choose record path of layer*

6 *draw path*

Copy A Layer Animation

You've created a dynamite layer animation, and your boss wants you to duplicate it on existing pages of the French and German versions of your Web site. Thankfully, you don't have to re-create the animation from scratch; Dreamweaver allows you to copy it from one document to another. You can also copy animations from one timeline to another on the same page; see Multiple Timelines Per Page on page 191 for details on when you might use multiple timelines.

The main thing to remember when you copy a layer animation from one document to another is that if your target document contains layers with the same names as the layers in the animation, Dreamweaver applies the animation to those layers in the target document, rather than copying the original layers to the target document. If you want

Dreamweaver to copy the original layers over, make sure that the target document doesn't contain any layers with names that match the layers in the original document's animation. And if you want to copy an animation sequence but apply it to a different layer in the target document, follow these steps and then use the Change Object command in the **Timelines** panel's context menu to change the object to which the animation applies.

1 open timelines panel
The command is **Window→Timelines**, and the shortcut is **shift-F9**.

2 click animation bar
Click the animation bar that you want to copy.

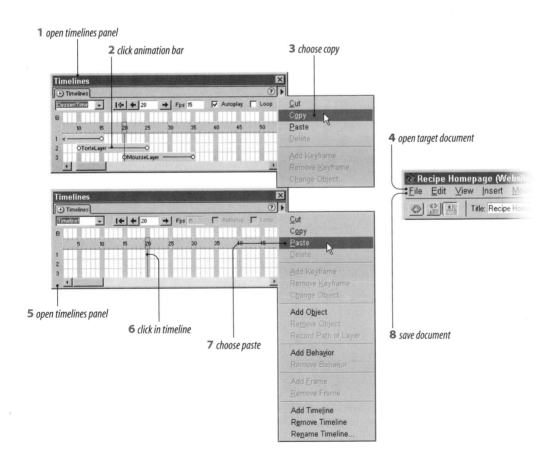

1 *open timelines panel*

2 *click animation bar*

3 *choose copy*

4 *open target document*

5 *open timelines panel*

6 *click in timeline*

7 *choose paste*

8 *save document*

> **tip** If you want to select multiple animation bars at once, **shift**-click to select additional bars after you click the first one. If you want to select all the animation bars in the **Timelines** panel, use **ctrl+A** (Win) or **command-A** (Mac)

3 choose copy

Careful here. You have to choose the **Copy** command from the pop-up menu of the **Timelines** panel (the arrow at the panel's upper right), not from the main menu bar's **Edit** menu.

4 open target document

The target document can be an existing one, as in this example, or a new document that you create with **File➡New**.

5 open timelines panel

Choose **Window➡Timelines** or press **shift-F9** in the target document, because you'll paste the animation bar into the **Timelines** panel for the target document.

6 click in timeline

Click the frame in the timeline where you want to paste the animation. You're allowed to paste it at a frame location that's different from where the animation existed in the originating document.

7 choose paste

Again, choose the **Paste** command from the **Timelines** panel's pop-up menu, not from the main toolbar's **Edit** menu.

> **tip** Make sure that the animation bar you're pasting doesn't overlap another existing animation bar for the same layer. If it does, Dreamweaver will automatically kick the pasted bar to the right until no conflict exists.

8 save document

Until you save the target document, the animation may not work correctly, and you may see any images in the pasted layers as broken links. Once you save the document (with **File➡Save**), Dreamweaver rebuilds the page and properly updates the images, replacing the broken links with the images.

> **tip** In yet another weird idiosyncrasy, you may not be able to set the **Fps**, **Autoplay**, or **Loop** characteristics of the timeline in the target document until you actually close that document and re-open it. (Don't ask me how long it took me to figure *that* one out when I was beta-testing the program.)

Multiple Timelines Per Page

If you're getting creative and doing some extensive animating, and your **Timelines** panel is getting cluttered, be aware that Dreamweaver allows you to create multiple timelines on the same page. You choose the current timeline from the drop-down menu at the upper left of the panel.

You must create multiple timelines when you want different animations to occur when the user performs different actions. For example, you may associate the **Play Timeline** action with three different hyperlinks on the page, each time activating a different timeline animation. Chapter 12 provides details on how to associate an action with a page object and a specific browser event.

Give your timelines descriptive names when you use more than one timeline on a page. You can use **Modify➡Timeline➡Rename Timeline** for this purpose, but it's easier just to click in the name field of the Timelines panel and change the name there. Don't change the name in code view, because it crops up multiple times and your animation probably won't work anymore.

Create a new timeline with the command **Modify➡Timeline➡Add Timeline** or by choosing **Add Timeline** from the panel's pop-up menu (the right arrow at its upper right). If you want to delete a timeline you're no longer using, the command is **Modify➡Timeline➡Remove Timeline**, which also exists on the panel's pop-up menu.

Add Interactivity

This chapter deals with *interactivity*: getting the user involved with the Web page.

Interactivity isn't the same as animation, although it can surely involve animation. The key to interactivity is the user performing some sort of operation with the mouse or keyboard that produces some sort of result from the browser. The most basic interaction is clicking a hyperlink to display different content. However, you can get much fancier than that with Dreamweaver 4!

Dreamweaver implements interactivity by means of little prebuilt JavaScript programs called *behaviors*. A user triggers a behavior by doing something that the browser registers as an *event*. A behavior, then, is the combination of an event and its subsequent action. Different browsers generate different events, and not all actions work in all browsers, so take care that your interactive elements work with your target audience.

191

The Behaviors Panel

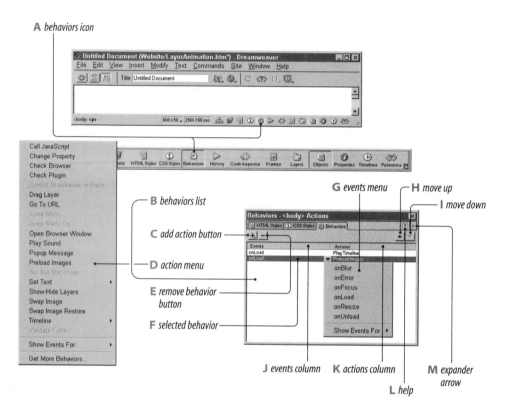

A behaviors icon

B behaviors list

C add action button

D action menu

E remove behavior button

F selected behavior

G events menu

H move up

I move down

J events column

K actions column

L help

M expander arrow

Your primary vehicle for dealing with behaviors (as with layers, frames, and so on) is a free-floating panel that you display via the **Behaviors** icon on the mini-launcher or launcher, the **Window→ Behaviors** command, or the shortcut **shift+F3**. The **Behaviors** panel lets you associate new behaviors with existing tags, edit existing behaviors, and (for tags that sport multiple behaviors) change the sequence in which the behaviors execute.

> *tip* Behaviors go with tags, which means you can associate a behavior with an image that has a tag (**<img>**), or a link (which has an **<a>** tag), or even the **<body>** tag of the document (for example, if you want a sound to play when the page itself loads). Not all tags support behaviors, but all behaviors must be associated with a tag. If you want to associate a behavior with a chunk of text, see page 200 in Attach A Behavior To Text.

A behaviors icon

I find it quickest to open the **Behaviors** panel by clicking the cogged-wheel icon on the mini-launcher. You can also use the big-daddy launcher if you prefer.

B behaviors list

The main part of the panel, with a white background, lists the behavior or behaviors associated with the tag you selected in the document window.

C add action button

This button is the first step to adding a behavior to the behaviors list. I call this the **Add Action** button, although Macromedia documentation refers to it sometimes as simply the **Action** button.

D action menu

The **Action** menu appears when you click the **Add Action** button (C). The menu contains a list of actions that Dreamweaver can perform, assuming the user's browser has JavaScript enabled.

> **tip** The **Action** menu is a bit like Mystique from the movie *X-Men*, changing its form depending on circumstances—specifically, the selected tag. The menu dims actions that Dreamweaver doesn't support for that tag. You can see this effect for yourself: Compare the menu when you have a layer anchor selected, as opposed to an image.

E remove behavior button

Click the minus-sign or **Remove Behavior** button to remove the currently highlighted action from the list. (The **delete** key works just as well.) In case you're wondering why the minus-sign is **Remove Behavior** but the plus-sign is **Add** *Action*, the reason is that Macromedia's implementation of adding behaviors is, well, a little goofy.

First, you click **Add Action** and pick an action from the **Action** menu, which creates an entry in the behaviors list. If the wrong event is listed in the **Events** column, then you need to pick the correct event from the **Events** menu (G). Once you have the right event selected, the entry in the behaviors list is truly a behavior (remember, behavior = event + action). It would have made more sense for the **Add Action** button to prompt you for the correct event after picking the action, in which case I could properly call it the **Add Behavior** button.

> **tip** You can remove only one action at a time. The usual technique of shift-clicking in a list to select multiple adjacent items doesn't work in the **Behaviors** panel. Right-clicking (Win) or **control**-clicking (Mac) a behavior doesn't bring up a context menu, either.

F selected behavior

When you click a behavior in the behaviors list, you select it, and it appears in inverse video. The selected behavior acquires an arrow at the far right of the

Events column that, when clicked, pops up the **Events** menu (G).

If you double-click a behavior in the **Behaviors** panel, Dreamweaver displays a dialog box that lets you change the settings for the specified action. For example, if the action is **Play Sound**, the dialog box lets you play a different sound file. The settings in the dialog box vary, depending on the action. If you want to change the action rather than the action's settings, delete the behavior and start over.

G events menu

Here's where you choose the event that you want to trigger the action in your behavior. The list of events is highly browser-dependent, and you can select to limit your choices by browser type using the **Show Events For** submenu, shown here. Generally, newer browser versions support a wider variety of events, and IE supports more events than Navigator. (For some strange reason, the **Show Events For** submenu also appears off the **Action** menu.)

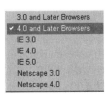

> **tip** If you want events for Netscape 6, download Dreamweaver 4.01 from www.macromedia.com. It's a free update.

You can change a behavior's event by activating the **Events** menu after selecting the behavior. Notice, however, that no corresponding arrow or menu exists for the **Action** column. Therefore, if you want to change the action that an event triggers for a certain tag, you must delete the existing behavior and create a new one. You can change an action's settings, however, by double-clicking the behavior to bring up the action dialog box (K).

H move up

A single event can trigger multiple actions. This button moves the selected behavior up in the sequence when you've defined more than one behavior for the same action (such as, say, **OnMouseOver**). Upper behaviors occur before lower ones.

I move down

The same as (H), only in the opposite direction.

J events column

Here's where the events appear.

K actions column

Here's where the corresponding actions appear.

L help

Click the question mark icon to bring up context-sensitive help.

M expander arrow

This arrow does nothing, although it has the function of displaying a pop-up menu in other panels.

> **tip** If neither the **Move Up** nor **Move Down** arrow shows active (that is, black-on-grey rather than dark-grey-on-grey), then you haven't defined multiple behaviors for the same event and the same tag. Dreamweaver dims these arrows if they don't apply.

Behaviors & JavaScript

Behaviors are JavaScript programs. However, what if a user who visits your site has decided to disable script processing on his machine, for example, to reduce the likelihood of getting infected with script-based viruses? In that situation, your behaviors won't work, so you may want to provide a link ("No JavaScript? Click Here") on any page that makes extensive or important use of behaviors, pointing to a non-JavaScript version of that page.

An alternative would be to include a Web page explaining how to turn JavaScript processing on in IE and Navigator; for example, in IE, choose **Tools➡Internet Options**, click the **Security** tab, click the **Custom Level** button, scroll down to the **Scripting** category, and click the **Enable** box next to **Active Scripting**. You may also want to include a note that when you enable Active Scripting in IE, you enable not only JavaScript processing but also VBScript processing.

Because JavaScript is a programming language, people who know how to write JavaScript code can create their own behaviors, and some have done just that. The command is **Get More Behaviors** from the **Actions** menu (the plus sign) of the **Behaviors** panel, which takes you to the Macromedia Exchange site. As of this writing,

there's even a tool on that site to help you create your own behaviors.

If you want to check out the JavaScript code that corresponds to a behavior you've designed, it's easy (and a great way to learn JavaScript). The behavior code resides in the **<head>** content at the top of the document, and the actual behavior exists as an attribute of the tag you selected. You can see both in code view or the Code inspector. For example, in the document shown here, a popup message action is associated with the **<body>** tag for the **onLoad** event. The JavaScript code is very simple and is the **MM_popupmsg** function toward the top; the actual text of the message, and the behavior that activates it, occurs inside the **<body>** tag, just below the head area.

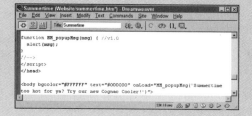

The JavaScript Debugger

If you decide to start writing your own JavaScript behaviors (or other JavaScript code), then you'll appreciate Dreamweaver's new JavaScript debugger facility. The debugger does two things for you: It checks your script code for syntactical validity and then allows you to execute the code, optionally setting breakpoints (places where you want the script to stop) and creating a "watch list" of variables whose values you want to monitor as the script executes. I can't provide a lot of detail in this book on how to write and debug JavaScript, but here's an introduction to the new debugger so that you can have a sense of what it does.

A *syntax error dialog box*

B *debugger window*

C *run*

D *stop debugging*

E *set/remove breakpoint*

F *remove all breakpoints*

G *watch list*

A syntax error dialog box
Here's what you'll see if you choose the **File➡ Debug In Browser** command and your script has a syntax error, such as (in this case) a missing opening brace. You can double-click the error, and Dreamweaver will take you to the offending line.

B debugger window
If your script has no syntax errors, Dreamweaver opens the debugger window. The window title lists the HTML file you're debugging.

C run
The **Run** button lets you begin the script execution; the keyboard shortcut is **F8**.

D stop debugging
The **Stop Debugging** button tells Dreamweaver to close the debugger window.

E set/remove breakpoint
This command sets or removes a breakpoint at the present cursor location; the shortcut is **F7**. You'd place a breakpoint at a place in the script where you'd like execution to stop, so you can either take a look at the browser window or examine the values of any variables you're watching (see G).

F remove all breakpoints
This button clears all breakpoints from the debugger.

G watch list
The lower part of the debugger window contains any variables whose values you'd like to watch. Add a variable to the list by highlighting it in the main code window and clicking the + button.

The Check Browser Action

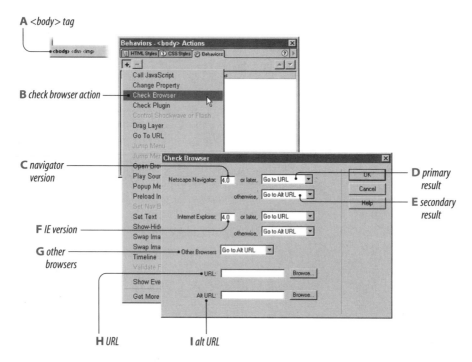

A *<body> tag*

B *check browser action*

C *navigator version*

D *primary result*

E *secondary result*

F *IE version*

G *other browsers*

H *URL*

I *alt URL*

One of the more popular uses of Dreamweaver's built-in behavior library is to check the user's browser version. You could use the **Check Browser** action in association with the **<body>** tag of your Web site's home page, for example, to redirect the visitor to a different URL if he has a pre-Version-4 browser. Such a technique avoids user frustration with Version 4 features that don't work for him. You could also use the **Check Browser** action in association with a null link tag to send a user to one URL if he has a Version 4+ browser or to another URL if not. (For more on creating a null link, see Attach A Behavior To Text on page 200.)

> **tip** A related action, **Check Plugin**, is really only useful in Netscape Navigator, so I don't discuss it in this book. If your audience is Netscape-only, the **Check Plugin** action can be useful in determining whether the user has a required plug-in, and in redirecting the user to an alternate page or a plugin download site if the answer is no.

Be aware that the **Check Browser** action doesn't work for versions of Internet Explorer prior to 3.0, or for versions of Navigator prior to 2.0. Those browser versions don't support JavaScript, the technology on which Dreamweaver behaviors are built.

> **tip** If you need more sophisticated browser sniffing than the Dreamweaver behavior provides—for example, to detect specific browsers other than Navigator and IE— and you don't mind getting your fingernails dirty with some HTML coding, check out the "practical browser sniffer" posted on *developer.netscape.com*.

A <body> tag

The **<body>** tag is what you'd probably select if you want to perform a browser check immediately upon having the page load. Click this tag in the tag selector (lower left of the document window) before adding a behavior. After you set the action to **Check Browser** and set the various options (C and following), you'd associate this tag with the **onLoad** event, which occurs when a user loads the page into a browser. (You don't have to do things this way; for example, you could associate the **Check Browser** action with the **onClick** event of an **<a>** tag, that is, a link. The nice thing about **onLoad**, though, is that it's automatic.).

B check browser action

The **Check Browser** action appears in the menu when you click the **Add Action** button (the one with the + sign) in the **Behaviors** panel. Select this action, and Dreamweaver displays the **Check Browser** dialog box, offering settings unique to this action.

C navigator version

The **Netscape Navigator** field is where you'd enter the minimum version of Navigator for which you want the primary result (D) to occur. Any version less than the one you enter here will activate the secondary result (E). In the most typical application of the Check Browser action, you would enter 4.0 here, because so many browser features become available as of Version 4.0 and higher. However, if all you're interested in is support for frames, Navigator 2.0 and higher can handle them.

D primary result

The primary result field lets you specify one of three things that can happen if the Navigator version is equal to or greater than the number you typed (C): **Stay On This Page**, **Go To URL**, or **Go To Alt URL**. Typically, the primary result would be **Stay On This Page**, because if the user has a Version 4 browser, you don't need to redirect him to a different page that's compatible with earlier browsers.

E secondary result

The secondary result field lets you specify what happens if the Navigator version is less than the number you type (C). It offers the same choices as the primary result field. Normally, you'd specify a secondary result that redirects the user to a different page that's 3.0-friendly, so you'd choose **Go To URL**. This result would direct the user to the URL specified in the lower part of the dialog box.

F IE version

The **Internet Explorer** field works just like the **Netscape Navigator** field but targets the IE browser instead. Again, you'd normally set this field to 4.0, and specify the IE primary result of **Stay On This Page**. (Frame support in IE starts a bit later than in Navigator; 3.0 is the minimum IE version.) The primary and secondary results associated with IE work just like they do in (D) and (E).

G other browsers

If someone's using a browser other than Navigator or IE, you can send that person somewhere very safe indeed. Common practice is to use the **Alt URL** result here and point to a text-only page. (You don't get to choose a version number here because this setting is a catchall for many browsers.)

H URL

In the **URL** field, type (or better yet, use the **Browse** button to find) the file path for the Web page that you specified in one or more of the earlier result fields. Typically this would be a page that would work well with Version 3 browsers of both stripes.

I alt URL (optional)

In the **Alt URL** field, type or **Browse** to the file path for an alternative Web page, if you specified one.

> **tip** What if you are getting very fancy with a certain page on your Web site, and you actually make four versions of it: One for Navigator less than Version 4, one for Navigator 4 and higher, one for IE less than Version 4, and one for IE 4 and higher? You obviously can't set that up with the **Check Browser** dialog box, because you can only define two URLs. However, you can certainly create two behaviors for the same tag and event! You'd create one behavior that stays on the page for all versions of Navigator but distinguishes between **URL** and **Alt URL** for IE. Then you'd create a second behavior that stays on the page for all versions of IE but distinguishes between **URL** and **Alt URL** for Navigator. (Then hire some extra help to maintain all those pages.)

The Open Browser Window Action

You will encounter situations where you'd like to give the user some formatted information— maybe some text with one or more images—but without closing the current page. You can certainly accomplish this goal with *framesets* (see Chapter 7, Create Frames, for details), but you may not need that much power or complexity.

In this example, the human resources director for Acme Cognac created a

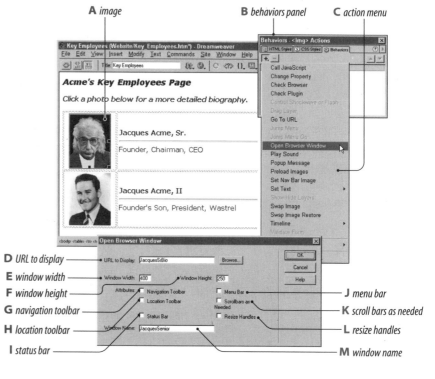

A *image*   **B** *behaviors panel*   **C** *action menu*

D *URL to display*

E *window width*

F *window height*

G *navigation toolbar*

H *location toolbar*

I *status bar*

J *menu bar*

K *scroll bars as needed*

L *resize handles*

M *window name*

Web page listing key employees. When a user clicks a low-res employee photo on the main page, a behavior associated with that low-res photo causes a new, "floating" browser window, containing a high-res photograph and brief biography, to appear. The main page stays open underneath, so when the visitor is done learning about one employee, she can close the detail window and click someone else's low-res photo on the main page. The result is quicker and less jarring than using a regular hyperlink. You'd implement a solution like this when you feel the visitor is likely to choose more than one item from the same main page.

A image

Here's the low-res photo on the main page. Because it's an image, and therefore has an image tag, you can associate it with a behavior.

B behaviors panel

You would typically open the Behaviors panel with **Window➡Behaviors**.

> *tip* As a style point, don't go overboard with opening new browser windows. You've probably visited one or more sites that opened so many windows, you spent two minutes just closing them all when you leave the site. If all you want to do is give the user a brief, textual chunk of information, consider using the Popup Message behavior instead, as described on page 203. Consider, too, that some Web surfers have become so disenchanted with pop-up windows—and their annoying "pop-under" variant—that they have applied software (from vendors like Panicware) that suppresses all commands that open a new browser window.

C action menu

When you click the **Add Action** button (with the plus sign), the **Action** menu appears, listing the **Open Browser Window** action. Select it, and you open the **Open Browser Window** dialog box.

D URL to display

In this field, type (or, better still, browse to) the path specifying the file whose contents you want to appear in the pop-up browser window. If you use the **Browse** button, you reduce the risk of a typo. The URL is document-relative by default.

E window width

You have quite a bit of control over the appearance of the "child" browser window. Here, specify the width of the window in pixels. I generally like to make the child window noticeably smaller than the main window is likely to be, so the user can still see the main page underneath.

F window height

Here, specify the height of the child window in pixels.

G navigation toolbar

You'll probably want to leave the **Navigation Toolbar** check box cleared, because you don't normally want the user trying to click the browser's **Back** button (or **Forward**, **Home**, **Refresh**, and so on). The simple act of closing the child window is enough to restore the main page to the display's foreground. The more you can do to prevent visitors from going down an unintended (and unproductive) path, the more those visitors will enjoy your site.

> **tip** The **Navigation Toolbar** check box is one of a group of "attributes" that also includes H, I, J, K, and L. If you don't specify any of these attributes, and you also don't specify window width (E) or height (F), then Dreamweaver makes the child window assume the size and attributes of its parent window. However, if you specify even one attribute or a width or height value, Dreamweaver sets the other listed attributes from their values in the **Open Browser Window** dialog box.

H location toolbar

In a similar vein, you're likely to leave the **Location Toolbar** disabled as well. (It's the browser toolbar that contains the address field.)

I status bar

The **Status Bar** check box lets you display (by checking) or inhibit (by clearing) the browser's bottom status bar. For a clean pop-up window, leave this check box cleared.

J menu bar

The browser's text menu bar (**File**, **Edit**, and so forth) is either visible or not, depending on this check box. I usually leave it off.

K scroll bars as needed

The **Scrollbars As Needed** check box requires a little thought. Ask yourself if the width (E) and height (F) settings are always adequate to contain the objects in the HTML files you plan to load. If so, you can clear this check box and lose the ugly scroll bars. However, in my example, some employee bios run longer than others, but the Webmaster wants a uniform width and height for aesthetic reasons, so you'd want to check the box.

> **tip** Even with this option checked, the browser won't show scroll bars unless the file's content exceeds the specified width and/or height.

L resize handles

Check this box if you want to let visitors resize the child window by any method, such as clicking and dragging the lower-right corner. If you're going for a clean look and consistent window sizes, clear it so that users can't resize the window.

M window name

Always give the child window a name (no spaces) as a matter of good design practice, but be aware that the name you specify here is not the title that the user will see in the browser window. That will be the document title as defined in the HTML file you specified in (D). Be sure that file has a title defined, so your site doesn't look amateurish!

steps Attach A Behavior To Text

At the start of this chapter, I noted that behaviors attach to tags. It's easy to attach a behavior to an image, therefore, or to an entire page (via the **<body>** tag). But how do you attach a behavior to a word or phrase of plain text? If the text is a link, you're okay, because links use tags. But say that you don't want the text that initiates a behavior to act like a link.

The secret is to create a link that purposely does nothing. This link creates a tag pair around the text so that you can attach a behavior to it, but the link has a special name that tells the browser to basically ignore it. (You can actually use two kinds of links, *null* and *script*, as you'll see.)

In the example that follows, I create a page that includes several "glossary" terms in italics. I don't want the user to have to click the terms to see their definitions, but rather just mouse over them. Tricky? Yes. Difficult? Not with behaviors and "nonlink links." This example is also a nice illustration of how you can use behaviors to change text dynamically in a layer.

such as "Definition," because you'll need to reference the layer when you create the behavior (8).

2 highlight word
Select the word or phrase you want to make into a glossary entry by clicking and dragging over it.

3 open properties
Choose **Window➞Properties**, or press **ctrl+F3** (Win) or **command-F3** (Mac). The property inspector for the selected text appears.

4 create do-nothing link
You can create a do-nothing link one of two ways. First, you can simply type the pound sign (#) into the **Link** field of the property inspector and press **Enter**. This method creates a so-called null link; the # sign tells the user's browser not to go anywhere when the user clicks the link.

Well, that's not quite true; the browser will stay at the same page, but it jumps to the top of the page, which may be inconvenient in different circumstances. For example, if you were creating a long page, you may not want to force a visitor who'd scrolled down to go back

1 create message layer
The first step is to create a place for the glossary definition to appear when the user mouses over a defined word. A layer is a natural choice for this sort of thing. You can click the **Draw Layer** icon on the objects panel and draw a rectangular area where the text that it contains will be legible. Make sure that you give the layer a name,

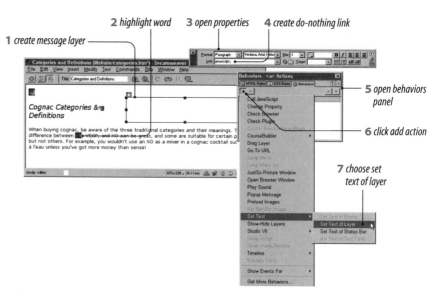

2 *highlight word* 3 *open properties* 4 *create do-nothing link*

1 *create message layer*

5 *open behaviors panel*

6 *click add action*

7 *choose set text of layer*

up to the top after clicking a null link; the user would then have to scroll back down to find his place again.

Therefore, I prefer the second method, which is to create a *null script link*. Enter **javascript:;** in the **Link** field (that's the word **javascript** followed by a colon and a semicolon, no spaces) and press **enter**. This method gets the browser ready to run a JavaScript program, but it doesn't provide the name of a program, so nothing happens. The benefit is that the page position doesn't change.

> **tip** When you create the do-nothing link, notice that it appears as a link in the document window— that is, it will be underlined and have the link color specified in the **Page Properties** dialog box. You may or may not want your text to have this appearance; toward the end of this example, I'll show you how to change it, but just leave it for now.

5 open behaviors panel

With the link still selected, open the **Behaviors** panel. The command is **Windows➛Behaviors** or **shift-F3**.

6 click add action

It's the button with the plus sign, and clicking it opens the **Action** pop-up menu.

7 choose set text of layer

Actually, you first choose **Set Text** and then, from the cascading submenu, **Set Text of Layer**.

> **tip** Notice the other options on the submenu: **Set Text of Frame**, **Set Text of Status Bar**, and **Set Text of Text Field**. (One or more of these may appear dimmed, depending on the type of object to which you're attaching the behavior.) You can and should experiment with these actions; I used a layer here because of its positioning flexibility, but I'm limiting myself to Version 4 browsers in doing so. Bear in mind, though, that many users ignore the status bar, so anything you put there via the **Set Text of Status Bar** action should probably be repeated someplace more prominently unless you include specific instructions to "look at the status bar."

8 *select layer*   **9** *type HTML*   **10** *click OK*   **11** *choose event*

12 *create cleanup behavior*

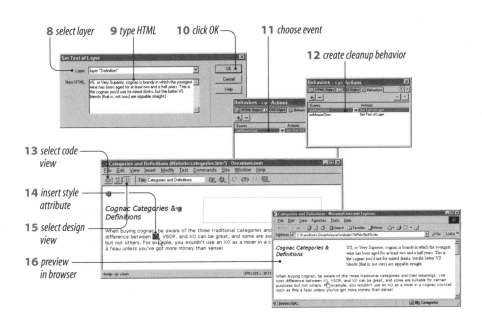

13 *select code view*

14 *insert style attribute*

15 *select design view*

16 *preview in browser*

8 select layer

In the **Set Text of Layer** dialog box, from the **Layer** drop-down list, choose the layer you created in (1). If you don't see it, then you may have neglected to name the layer, and you'll have to go back and do that now.

9 type HTML

The **New HTML** field is where you enter the HTML code for what you want to appear in the layer; I just put in a simple definition, but you could get fancier by creating some formatted HTML in another document and then copying and pasting it into this field. Any valid HTML formatting is allowed here.

10 click OK

Click the **OK** button to close the **Set Text of Layer** dialog box.

11 choose event

Click the down arrow and choose **onMouseOver** as the event to trigger the **Set Text of Layer** action. In a different context, you may prefer a different event, such as **onClick** or **onDblClick**.

12 create cleanup behavior

Next, you should basically repeat steps 6 through 11, but use the **onMouseOut** event and don't type anything in the **New HTML** field of the **Set Text of Layer** dialog box. By doing so, you instruct the browser to clear the definition window when the user moves the cursor away from the glossary item. This step prevents any user confusion that may arise from seeing a definition that no longer applies to the object under the cursor.

13 select code view

Now assume that you don't want your link to look like a link. What are your options? You could just modify the way links look by choosing **Modify➡Page Properties**, but that's not a very elegant solution, because your page may have some "real" links and you'd like them to appear as links would normally. A better solution may be to modify the appearance only of the non-link links. The first place to start is to switch to code view by clicking the **Show Code View** icon on the toolbar or by choosing **View➡Code** from the menu.

tip If you leave the glossary item selected in design view, the **<a href>** tag defining the "non-link link" will remain selected when you switch to code view.

14 insert style attribute

Type the attribute **style="text-decoration:none"** inside the **<a href>** tag. What this does is to deactivate the underline characteristic of the tag so that it no longer looks like a link (although it retains the link color so that the user knows there's something special about it and a reason to mouse over it). However, because you haven't modified the way links normally appear in the **Page Properties** dialog box, "regular" links will appear as they usually would.

15 select design view

Click the **Show Design View** icon on the toolbar or choose **View➡Design** from the menu. You should see your glossary item colored, but with no underline.

tip If you want to use a different color for your glossary items, use an attribute like **style="text-decoration:none;color:green"** instead of the simpler one in the preceding paragraph. You can also use the other styles than **text-decoration**; for example, you can use **font-weight** to change character thickness (values are **bold**, **bolder**, **lighter**, **normal**, and numeric values from 100 to 900). Just remember to separate each style setting by a semicolon and keep 'em all inside the double-quotes. See the CSS Reference guide (**Help➡Reference**, and choose **O'Reilly CSS Reference** in the **Book** pop-up menu) for details on the various styles you can set.

16 preview in browser

Click the **Preview/Debug In Browser** toolbar icon and choose the appropriate subcommand to preview your page in the target browser(s). Test the glossary item's behavior and see whether it works. The definition should appear when you mouse over the glossary item and disappear when you mouse out.

The Popup Message Action

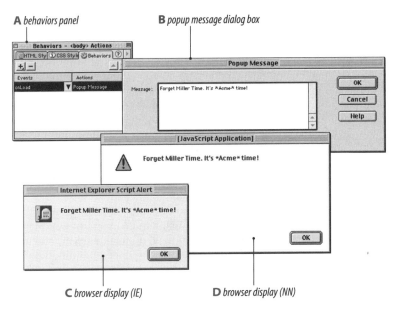

A *behaviors panel* **B** *popup message dialog box*

C *browser display (IE)*   **D** *browser display (NN)*

One of the simplest actions you can use in a behavior is also one of the most fun: Popping up a simple message. You can use this action in combination with images or null text links to provide feedback to users who click those objects; one application might be to tell a user whether she's right or wrong when clicking the answer to a multiple-choice question in a Web-based quiz, for example.

> **tip** The **Popup Message** action requires a user response. Don't use this action so frequently that you run the risk of irritating users who may tire of clicking OK before proceeding.

You can use this action to display information to users who first load your Web page (via the **onLoad** event for the **<body>** tag) or who depart the page (via the **onUnload** event for the **<body>** tag). That is, you can create "hello" and "goodbye" messages. One nice thing about the **onLoad** and **onUnload** events is that they work in Version 3, or greater, browsers.

> **tip** Don't use the **Popup Message** action to prompt the user to select whether or not to proceed based on the provided information. The only button that appears is an OK button.

A behaviors panel

Here's what the **Behaviors** panel would look like for a **Popup Message** action associated with the **<body>** tag and the **onLoad** event.

B popup message dialog box

The **Popup Message** dialog box, which you'd see upon first creating a behavior using this action (or upon editing an existing behavior), is quite simple. However, you JavaScript jockeys will enjoy being able to include any valid JavaScript expression within the text area; when you do, make sure that you remember to enclose such an expression with curly braces.

> **tip** The browser controls the formatting of alert messages. You can use the **Open Browser Window** action (see pages 198 and 199) if you want or need formatting control.

C browser display (IE)

Here's what Internet Explorer would display based on the content in the dialog box (B).

D browser display (NN)

And here's how Navigator would display the alert.

Let Users Drag Layers

If you're targeting 4.0-Version browsers and above, use the **Drag Layer** behavior to create interesting and unusual Web page interactivity. In this example, an Acme sales executive wants to design a slider control that lets the user move a pointer along a horizontal scale until reaching the value indicating year-to-date sales. The pointer should snap into place when it's at the correct position, and a pop-up message should then inform the user of the sales figure. The example begins with the horizontal scale already present as a GIF image.

1 draw new layer

For example, choose **Insert▸Layer** and then draw a small rectangle about where you'd like the slider pointer to be. The layer that you create will be the one that the user will be able to drag.

2 open context menu

Right-click (Win) or **control**-click (Mac) the layer's selection handle at the upper-left corner and choose **ID**.

3 name layer

Give the layer a descriptive name, such as **Pointer**, and click **OK**.

4 insert image

Click inside the new layer and choose **Insert▸Image** to place a graphical up-arrow into the layer. This image will be the pointer that the user will drag along the horizontal scale.

5 click body tag

In the document window's tag selector, click the **<body>** tag. It's the tag to which you'll attach the **Drag Layer** behavior. I know, it seems like you should attach the behavior to the **<div>** tag denoting the layer, but it doesn't work that way. Remember, not all tags allow you to attach behaviors to them.

6 open behaviors panel

Click the **Show Behaviors** icon on the mini-launcher.

7 choose add action

Click the button with the **+** sign to bring up the **Action** menu.

8 choose drag layer

When you choose the **Drag Layer** action, Dreamweaver opens the **Drag Layer** dialog box, featuring a **Basic** tab and an **Advanced** tab. The **Basic** tab appears first, and that's where you should start.

9 choose layer

Select the **Pointer** layer from the drop-down menu in the **Layer** field.

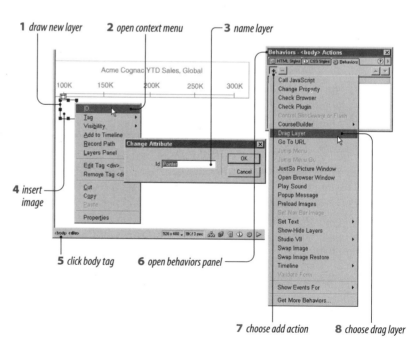

1 draw new layer 2 open context menu 3 name layer
4 insert image 5 click body tag 6 open behaviors panel
7 choose add action 8 choose drag layer

10 set constraints

You want the user to be able to move the layer in a horizontal direction only. Therefore, choose **Constrained** in the **Movement** field, place zeroes in the **Up** and **Down** fields, place 1 in the **Left** field, and the pixel width of the horizontal scale graphic in the **Right** field.

11 click get current position

The **Get Current Position** button loads the current pixel coordinates of the layer's upper-left corner into the **Left** and **Top** fields of the **Drop Target** area.

12 specify drop target

Now, tell Dreamweaver where the drop target is (that is, the pixel coordinates of the upper-left corner of the draggable layer when it has reached its desired position). In this example, the **Top** coordinate isn't going to change, because the user can move the slider arrow only horizontally. So, you'd enter the **Left** pixel value corresponding to the position at which the pointer points to the correct number on the horizontal scale graphic. (A little trial and error with the browser preview function may be necessary to get this just right.)

13 set snap if within

When the user releases the layer after dragging it, Dreamweaver can snap it to the drop target (12) if it's within the number of pixels you enter here. The larger this value, the easier it is for the user to find the target.

14 click advanced tab

It's time to tell Dreamweaver to do something when the pointer has snapped to its target. Do so on the **Advanced** tab.

15 enter JavaScript

Fill in an appropriate JavaScript command, such as that shown, in the **When Dropped Call**

JavaScript field. If all you want is an alert message, you don't have to be a JavaScript programmer; just pattern your command after mine.

16 click only if snapped

Select the **Only If Snapped** check box to indicate that you only want to display the alert message if the user has found the target.

17 click OK

Click the **OK** button to close the **Drag Layer** dialog box (finally!).

18 verify event

If the event showing in the Behaviors panel for the **Drag Layer** action isn't **onLoad**, click the down arrow to display the **Event** menu and choose **onLoad**. Now you're ready to try out your new interactive slider with the **File➡Preview In Browser** command.

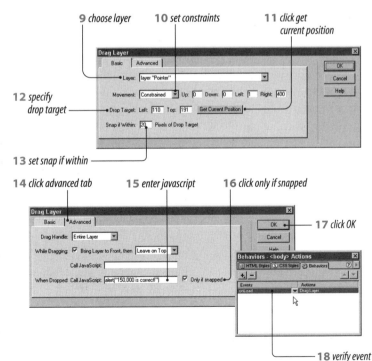

9 *choose layer* 10 *set constraints* 11 *click get current position*

12 *specify drop target*

13 *set snap if within*

14 *click advanced tab* 15 *enter javascript* 16 *click only if snapped*

17 *click OK*

18 *verify event*

⬬steps⬬ Control Multimedia Content

Although you can place multimedia content on your Web page for control by the user, you may occasionally want to activate or control multimedia objects via some other method. Using behaviors, you can have the browser play a sound or control a Flash or Shockwave movie when the user clicks a custom graphic or null text link. This example shows you how you can make a single button start a Flash movie and play a sound file simultaneously. (I assume that you've already placed the Flash movie on the page and set Autoplay off; for details, see The Insert Flash Movie Command on page 234 in Chapter 15.)

1 click button graphic
Select the image in the document window to which you want to attach the behaviors.

2 open behaviors panel
The menu command is **Window▸Behaviors**; the shortcut is **shift+F3**, but the easiest method is to click the **Show Behaviors** icon on the mini-launcher.

3 click add action
This opens the **Action** menu.

4 choose play sound
This opens the **Play Sound** dialog box.

5 browse to sound file
Click the **Browse** button to locate the sound file and click **OK**.

6 set event
If the event listed in the **Events** column isn't **onClick**, click

the down arrow and choose **onClick** from the **Events** menu.

7 click add action
To add the next action, click the button with a plus sign once more and choose **Control Shockwave or Flash**.

8 choose movie
Select the movie from the **Movie** drop-down list. (If you haven't named the Flash movie, Dreamweaver will chide you and prompt you to cancel and do so.)

9 click play
In the **Action** field, click the **Play** radio button and then click **OK**.

10 set event
Repeat step 6 to make sure that the event is **onClick**.

11 preview in browser
Click the **Preview/Debug In Browser** icon on the toolbar and choose the appropriate command to preview your handiwork. If it works as you want, close the preview window and save your file.

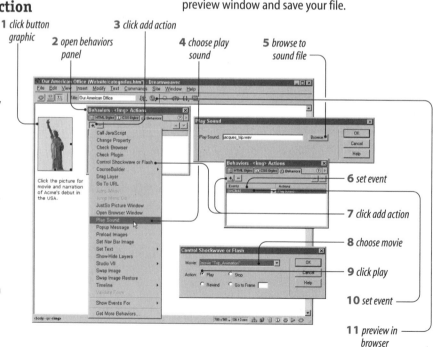

1 *click button graphic*

2 *open behaviors panel*

3 *click add action*

4 *choose play sound*

5 *browse to sound file*

6 *set event*

7 *click add action*

8 *choose movie*

9 *click play*

10 *set event*

11 *preview in browser*

chapter

Integrate Video & Sound

Sections @ A Glance

Add video and sound to create a multimedia experience.

As media compression efficiencies and Internet connection speeds increase, more Web designers are discovering that adding sound and video is more practical than ever. However, Dreamweaver's online help and user manual don't give you much to go on in these areas, so this chapter gets you started on how to add media clips to your site.

Mastering Web-based multimedia is a lot of fun but requires some experimentation and Web research. So, don't plan to whip through this chapter quickly, even though it's a relatively short one!

Terminology note: As the term appears in this book, *video* means a media clip taken from film, or contained in a traditional video file format (AVI, Quick-Time, MPEG, and so on). Keep in mind that this chapter does not deal with Flash and Director animations unless they've been exported into one of these video file formats. (Chapter 15 deals with Flash and Director animations.)

The Plugin Property Inspector

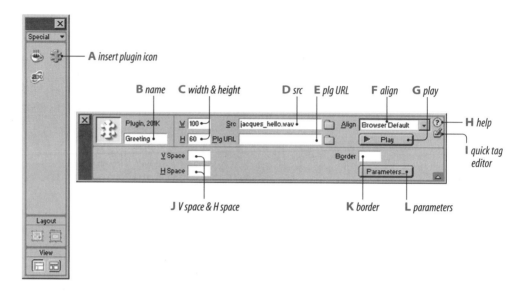

A insert plugin icon

B name **C** width & height **D** src **E** plg URL **F** align **G** play

H help

I quick tag editor

J V space & H space **K** border **L** parameters

A *plugin* is nothing more than a chunk of software that "plays" a file that isn't a standard HTML file type (such as HTM, GIF, or JPEG). For example, a browser may not have the built-in ability to display a digital video, but the browser can pass control to a plugin, which does have that ability.

Plugins are sometimes also called *helper applications*, because they help the browser deal with foreign data types; technically, though, a helper application is a program that can run on its own (such as the QuickTime player), whereas a plugin must run in the context of a browser.

Nowadays, popular browsers ship with many popular plugins already installed. However, if you want compatibility with the widest variety of browser versions, you need to consider providing your users information on how to obtain and install a plugin that they may not have but that your site demands.

Display the plugin property inspector with the **Window⇒Properties** command. When you click the plugin to select it, the inspector reflects attributes of the plugin and lets you change those attributes.

tip As the term was used originally, plugins are programs that work with Netscape Navigator. (*ActiveX controls*, on the other hand, are analogous programs that work with Internet Explorer.) However, the term "plugin" has become somewhat generic, and you'll use the **Insert Plugin** command to add sounds and videos to your Web pages even if your intended audience uses Internet Explorer.

When you tell Dreamweaver you want to insert a plugin, the program creates an **<embed>** tag pair in your HTML code. IE interprets this tag in a similar manner to Navigator, although the program that IE uses to deal with a particular kind of media object may well be different than the program Navigator uses.

A insert plugin icon

Click this icon on the **Special** objects panel to add a plugin-controlled media clip at the current insertion point. Or, use the **Insert⇒Media⇒Plugin** command from the menu. (Dreamweaver uses the **<embed>** tag for plugins.)

B name (optional)

Add a name if you want to refer to the plugin in a script.

C width & height

Set the dimensions for the plugin in the **W** and **H** fields. For example, if you want to add a sound file, make sure that these dimensions are large enough to display the plugin's user interface (typically, a control bar). Typical units are pixels, but you can also specify picas (pc), points (pt), inches (in), millimeters (mm), centimeters (cm), or percentage of parent object's dimensions (%). You can also change a plugin's size by clicking and dragging the resize handles.

D src

The **src** field contains the data file that you want the plugin to play. For example, you'd specify a sound or video clip here.

E plg URL

Add the URL of the public Web site where a user could go get the appropriate plugin if it's not already on the user's system. For example, enter *www.apple. com/quicktime/download/* if you are embedding a QuickTime movie into your Web page.

F align

Set the object's alignment on the page with this drop-down menu. The alignment options are the same as those presented on page 57, Place An Inline Image, in Chapter 4.

G play

This button previews the media clip. For details on previewing, see The View Plugins Command on page 218 of this chapter.

H help

The question mark activates context-sensitive help.

I quick tag editor

Click this icon to see the HTML code for the plugin's **<embed>** tag.

J V space & H space

Specify the number of pixels of white space Dreamweaver should surround your object with here.

K border

Here's the width of the border around your plugin, should you want one.

L parameters

This button brings up the Parameters dialog box, where you can set plugin-specific behaviors; see page 214, The Parameters Dialog Box, for more.

Plugins & Navigator 4.75

Macromedia bundles Netscape Communicator 4.75 with Dreamweaver 4. The Communicator suite includes the browser component Navigator, which comes with plug-ins including Shockwave Flash (SPL and SWF files), RealPlayer G2 (RPM sound files), Headspace Beatnik (RMF sound files), NPAVI32 (AVI video files), and LiveAudio (AU, AIFF, WAV, MIDI, LA, and LMA sound files).

A user can change the plugins that Navigator associates with different file types by opening Navigator, choosing **Edit➡Preferences**, and clicking **Navigator** and then **Applications** in the **Category** window. In the figure, Netscape associates MP3 audio files with the WinAmp plugin, but the **Edit** button lets users alter this behavior.

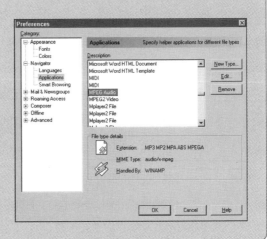

The ActiveX Property Inspector

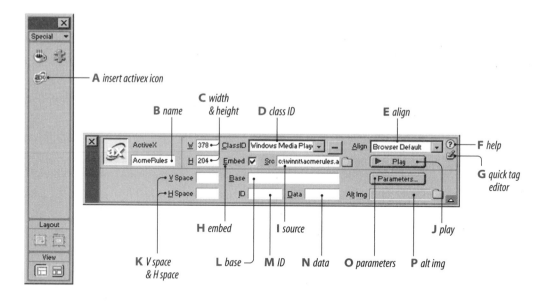

A insert activex icon

B name   **C** width & height   **D** class ID   **E** align   **F** help   **G** quick tag editor

H embed   **I** source   **J** play

K V space & H space   **L** base   **M** ID   **N** data   **O** parameters   **P** alt img

ActiveX controls are programs designed to work in the Microsoft Windows environment. Many ActiveX controls can function in the same way that plugins, or helper applications, do; however, keep in mind that they typically only work in the Internet Explorer browser and on the Windows platform. If your target audience works in this environment, you can add ActiveX objects to your Web page for displaying sound and video content, as well as for other purposes.

> **tip** You can add ActiveX support to Navigator 4.*x* with the ActiveX Plugin from Esker Software (*www.esker.com*). As I write this, Esker is working on a version for Navigator 6.0. This plugin may be useful if you work in a closed environment (say, a corporate intranet) and you must have ActiveX support across browsers. The older ScriptActive plugin from NCompass Labs is no longer available from NCompass, which is now a subsidiary of Microsoft.

You can display the ActiveX property inspector by choosing the **Window→Properties** command.

A insert activex icon
Click this icon on the **Special** objects panel to add an ActiveX object at the current insertion point. Or, use the **Insert→Media→ActiveX** command from the menu. Dreamweaver uses the **<object>** tag for ActiveX objects, as opposed to the **<embed>** tag, which it uses for plugins.

B name (optional)
Add a name if you want to refer to the control in a script.

C width & height
Set the dimensions for the control here. Appropriate values will depend on the specific control. For example, if you want to install a movie to be played using Windows Media Player, make sure that these dimensions are large enough to display the movie and the control bar.

D class ID
The *class ID* is a unique code (such as *CFCDAA03-8BE4-11cf- B84B-0020AFBBCCFA*, the code for RealPlayer, or *22D6F312-B0F6-11D0-94AB-0080C74C7E95*, for Windows Media Player) specifying the precise control you want to add. You may have to

visit the Web to get the proper class ID for the ActiveX control you want to use (or search the Windows Registry, if you know how to do that while taking the proper precautions).

> **tip** The drop-down list takes its content from the file **ACTIVEXNAMES.TXT**. Dreamweaver updates this file when you add a new class ID and nickname via the ActiveX property inspector; you can also edit the file with your favorite text editor to add nicknames and class IDs. Make your new entries using the same format as the existing entries.

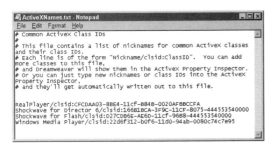

E align
Set the object's alignment on the page with this drop-down menu. The alignment options are the same as those presented on page 57, Place An Inline Image, in Chapter 4.

F help
Click the question mark whenever you need to activate context-sensitive help.

G quick tag editor
Click this icon to see the HTML code for the plugin's **<embed>** tag.

H embed
Remember that you can click here if a Navigator plugin provides equivalent functionality to the ActiveX control. Checking **Embed** activates the **Src** field (I). Dreamweaver places an **<embed>** tag, which it uses for plugins, inside the **<object>** tag pair so that Navigator has a way of playing back the media clip.

I source
If you click **Embed** (H), you can specify your media file in the **src** field, so the media clip will play in Navigator as well as IE. Note, however, that the file type of the media clip must be one that Navigator recognizes and associates with a particular plugin or helper application.

J play
This button is supposed to preview the media clip if a Netscape plugin exists for the clip, but it doesn't always work, so you're better off previewing the page with the **File➡Preview In Browser** command.

K V space & H space
Specify the number of pixels of white space Dreamweaver should surround your object with here.

L base
Similar to the **Plg Url** field on the plugin property inspector, the **Base** field tells the browser where on the Internet to go looking for the specified ActiveX control if it isn't already resident on the user's PC.

M ID
The **ID** parameter is not one you'll use often; it transfers data between two or more controls.

N data
Some ActiveX controls look to this field for the media clip's data file. However, many popular ActiveX controls don't use this field. For example, Windows Media Player uses the *FileName* parameter instead.

O parameters
This button brings up the **Parameters** dialog box, where you can set control-specific behaviors, such as *autostart* and *showstatusbar*. See page 214, The Parameters Dialog Box, for more.

P alt img
Some browsers can't handle the **<object>** tag pairs that Dreamweaver creates for ActiveX controls, and you can use the **Alt Img** field to specify an image the browser will display if that's the case. Watch out, though: If you check the **Embed** field (H), **Alt Img** isn't available to you.

Add A Sound To A Page

Adding a sound file to a page is one way to make it more interesting, personal, and dynamic. However, keep a few factors in mind, first being the size of the file. Many good tools (such as Sonic Foundry's Sound Forge) can compress sound files so that they don't take as long to download. Second, if you want both Navigator and Internet Explorer users to be able to play your sounds, choose a format such as WAV, MIDI, MP3, or RealAudio that enjoys broad cross-platform support (see Sound & Video File Formats on page 217). Third, don't assume that a visitor to your site is using the usual, or default, sound controller. Browser users can change which controllers handle different types of sound files, for example, using the **Preferences** dialog box of Netscape Navigator or the **Folder Options** dialog box of a Windows system running IE.

tip You can add sound to a page in three ways. This example shows you how to *embed* a sound file—that is, make it an integral part of your Web page. To create a sound *link*, see the sidebar on the next page, Linking Versus Embedding. To play a sound in response to a user action, such as mousing over a link, use the **Play Sound** Javascript behavior (see Chapter 12's section Control Multimedia Content on page 206). Experiment with all three methods, so you'll develop an instinct for when to use which one.

1 place insertion point

Click to position the insertion point where you want the sound to reside. (If you plan to make the sound object hidden, it doesn't matter where you place the insertion point, but you still have to place it somewhere on the page.)

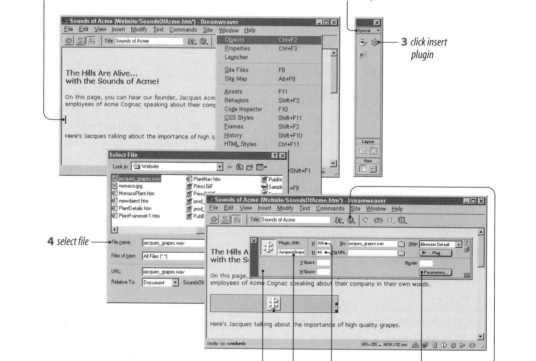

1 *place insertion point*

2 *choose special*

3 *click insert plugin*

4 *select file*

5 *display property inspector*

6 *name plugin*

7 *set width & height*

8 *set parameters*

9 *preview in browser*

2 choose special

Click the pop-up menu on the objects panel and choose **Special**.

3 click insert plugin

Click the Insert Plugin icon on the **Special** objects panel. As an alternative to this step and step 2, you could choose the menu command **Insert➡ Media➡Plugin**.

4 select file

In the **Select File** dialog box, navigate to the sound file and click the **Select** button (**Open** button on the Mac). If you choose a sound file outside your site root folder, Dreamweaver will offer to copy it into that folder.

5 display property inspector

The command is **Window➡Properties**, or **ctrl+F3** (Win) or **command-F3** (Mac).

6 name plugin (optional)

If you think you may want to refer to the sound object in a script, give it a name.

7 set width & height

If you want the user to be able to see the sound's helper application, size the plugin object appropriately. You can use the resize handle, or the **W** and **H** fields. Watch out: A size that may work just fine for one helper application, such as Netscape's LiveAudio controller, may be too small for another one, such as WinAmp or Windows Media Player.

8 set parameters

Click the **Parameters** button on the property inspector to add parameters that control your sound file's playback. Common parameters for sound objects include **hidden** (true or false), **autoplay** (true or false), **loop** (true, false, or a number indicating how many times to play the file), and **volume** (0 to 100, expressed as a percentage of system volume).

9 preview in browser

Click the **Preview/Debug In Browser** button on the toolbar, or use **File➡Preview In Browser**. For sound files, this step is a must. Change the width and height of the object, or modify its parameters as needed.

Linking Versus Embedding

The embedding method gives you the most control over how and when the sound plays. However, you may want to *link* to a sound file on your Web page instead.

The difference is that the user controls whether to download and play the sound if you provide it by means of a link, whereas you control the sound's behavior if you embed it onto the page. For example, you would probably use linking rather than embedding if you want to make several sound clips available to your user, or if you want your site to work with browsers that don't support embedded sound files.

The technique is the same as for creating any other sort of link: Simply highlight the text or image and specify the sound file in the **Link** field of the property inspector for that text or image. To be considerate, provide the user with information about the size and format of the sound file, for example, in the linked text. You may even want to provide multiple versions of the linked file in different formats, again, with an appropriate description.

You can't predict exactly what will happen when a user clicks a link to a sound file. The resulting action depends on the platform (Windows or Macintosh), operating system, browser, installed plug-ins, and user preference

settings. For example, clicking a linked .WAV file opens the LiveAudio controller, shown here, in Navigator 4.75:

But clicking the same file in Internet Explorer 5 could open the Windows Media Player, shown here:

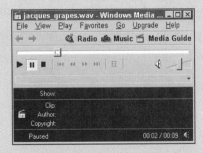

The Parameters Dialog Box

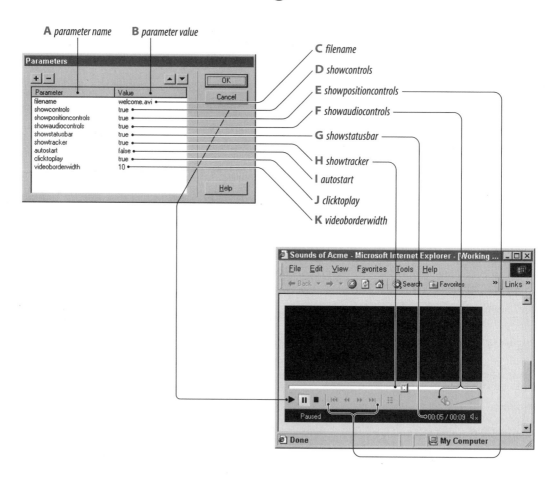

A *parameter name* **B** *parameter value*

C *filename*
D *showcontrols*
E *showpositioncontrols*
F *showaudiocontrols*
G *showstatusbar*
H *showtracker*
I *autostart*
J *clicktoplay*
K *videoborderwidth*

Whether you insert a media clip as a plugin or as an ActiveX control, you control the clip's behavior primarily through the **Parameters** dialog box. A parameter is just a setting that Dreamweaver provides to the plugin or ActiveX control telling it how to act. (Parameters also apply to Java applets, small programs that you can insert onto a Web page via the **Insert➟Media➟Applet** command. Why Macromedia put applets in the category of media elements, I'm not sure, because you don't typically use Java to control sound and video clips.)

You need to know a parameter's name, and its possible values, in order to properly control a plugin or control. The difficult thing about the **Parameters**

dialog box, which you access via the **Parameters** button on the property inspector or by choosing **Parameters** from the object's context menu (right-click in Windows, **control**-click on the Mac), is that Dreamweaver doesn't give you much assistance in this regard, and neither does the online help system or the user manual.

This figure shows you some parameters for Windows Media Player and their effect. For more details, check out *developer.netscape.com* (for Netscape plugins), *msdn.microsoft.com* (for ActiveX controls), *www.apple.com/quicktime/authoring* (for QuickTime parameters), or fire up an Internet search engine with search terms, such as **plugins, activex, browser,** and **parameters**.

A parameter name

Every plugin or ActiveX object that takes parameters looks for a parameter name and a parameter value. The name generally describes the parameter's function, such as *filename* or *autostart*, but you have to know the name in advance; Dreamweaver doesn't prompt you with a list, nor does it warn you if you enter an invalid name.

B parameter value

Each parameter can have one of at least two values. For example, *autostart* is either true or false. Some other parameters, however, may have values that are harder to guess, in which case you'll need a definitive reference for the control or plugin that you want to embed. Again, Dreamweaver expects you to know the correct values in advance.

C filename

Here's where you would enter the name of the video or audio clip you want Windows Media Player to play. The value is a filename.

D showcontrols

The *ShowControls* parameter specifies whether Windows Media Player should display its control bar, with VCR-like buttons for play, pause, and stop. This parameter has values of true or false. (You can also use 1 for true and 0 for false.) The exact content of the control bar also depends on the values for *ShowPositionControls* (E) and *ShowAudioControls* (F).

E showpositioncontrols

The position controls are buttons for *skip back*, *rewind*, *fast forward*, and *skip forward*. This parameter is either true or false and controls whether the position controls appear on the control bar. The *ShowControls* parameter must be true for this parameter to have any effect.

F showaudiocontrols

The audio controls consist of a mute icon and a volume slider. This parameter is either true or false and controls whether the audio controls appear on the control bar. As with the *ShowPositionControls* parameter, the *ShowControls* parameter must be true for this setting to work.

G showstatusbar

The *status bar* displays information such as elapsed time and clip duration. Values are true and false.

H showtracker

The *tracker* is a slider that appears above the buttons on the control bar and lets the user move immediately to any place in the sound or video clip. Values are true and false.

I autostart

A common parameter, *AutoStart* can be true or false and determines whether the browser should begin running the media clip immediately upon loading its containing page. To give the user control over playback, set this to false.

J clicktoplay

If the *ClickToPlay* parameter is true, the user can start and stop video playback by clicking on the image. If you set this parameter as true, you should add some text to your page advising the visitor how to use this feature.

K videoborderwidth

This parameter takes a pixel value indicating the size of the border to display around the media clip.

Add A Video To A Page

The procedure for adding a video to a page is similar to that for adding a sound, with two key differences. First, if you're embedding a video object, you must size the object so that the movie (and its associated helper application's control bar, if desired) can appear at the correct size. (You don't need to worry about the object's size if you're adding a hidden sound file, but a hidden video doesn't make much sense.) Second, because video clips are typically much larger in size than sound clips, the file format decision becomes much more important.

> **tip** As with sound files, you can provide a link to a video, or embed the video. This example uses the embedding technique; see Linking Versus Embedding on page 213 for more.

1 place insertion point

Open the page you want and click on it in the document window using design view so that you can position the insertion point where you want the video to appear.

2 choose insert media plugin

Use the menu command **Insert➡Media➡Plugin**. If you know your audience will only be using Internet Explorer on the Windows platform, then choose **Insert➡Media➡ActiveX** and specify the Windows Media Player class ID in the ActiveX property inspector; here, I'm going for maximum cross-platform compatibility, so I use the plugin command instead. Internet Explorer can usually interpret the **<embed>** tag that the plugin command creates, but you can't depend on Navigator to interpret the **<object>** tag that Dreamweaver uses for ActiveX objects.

3 select file

In the **Select File** dialog box, navigate to the video file and click the **Select** button (**Open** button on the Mac). If you choose a file outside your site root folder, Dreamweaver will offer to copy it into that folder.

4 display property inspector

The command is **Window➡Properties** or **ctrl+F3** (Win) or **command-F3** (Mac).

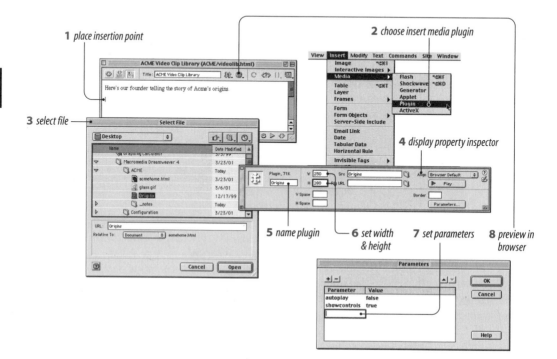

1 *place insertion point*

2 *choose insert media plugin*

3 *select file*

4 *display property inspector*

5 *name plugin*

6 *set width & height*

7 *set parameters*

8 *preview in browser*

5 name plugin (optional)

If you think you may want to refer to the video clip in a script, give it a name.

6 set width & height

Size the video clip so that it appears at the desired size on the page, either using the resize handles or the **W** and **H** fields. If you want the user to be able to control the video, leave room for the controller. (If you were linking to a video clip instead of embedding it, the helper application or plugin would automatically set itself to the correct size.)

7 set parameters

Click the **Parameters** button on the property inspector to add parameters to control playback. For example, if you want to give the user control, you

might set *AutoPlay* to false and *ShowControls* to true. I typically set automatic playback off with video clips because if the user has a slow Internet link, he or she may prefer to decide whether the video is worth the wait; a line of text near the video clip, informing the user of the file format and file size, is always a good idea. (See The Parameters Dialog Box on page 214 of this chapter for more details on parameters.)

8 preview in browser

Click the **Preview/Debug In Browser** button on the toolbar, or use the menu command **File➡ Preview In Browser** and then choose the **Preview** command for your primary or secondary browser from the menu. Change the width and height of the object, or modify its parameters, to taste.

Sound & Video File Formats

The Web is a public, open technology space, which has its pros and cons. One of the cons is that no hard-and-fast rules exist for which sound or video file format you should use. So, before you start adding sound and video to your site, get familiar with the different formats so you know which is best for a specific situation. Here are common sound formats:

AIFF

Audio Interchange File Format features good quality and compatibility. The tradeoff is large file sizes. Lots of Mac sound files use this format, and the QuickTime player supports it (along with MIDI, MP3, and WAV).

MIDI

Musical Instrument Digital Interface files can have very good quality and offer very low file sizes. The drawbacks are 1) you need a computer and/or synthesizer to create them and 2) they're for instrumental music only.

MP3

Motion Picture Experts Group Audio Layer-3 files have very good quality, small size, and can "stream" (play while downloading). This format requires a plugin or helper program, but it's so popular that most systems now support it (for example, via QuickTime, WinAmp, and Windows Media Player).

RealAudio

RealAudio files, like MP3 files, offer small size and the ability to stream, but MP3 still has the edge in quality at this writing.

RMF

Rich Music Format provides good quality and good compression. It requires the Beatnik plugin, which you can download from *www. beatnik.com*.

WAV

Waveform Extension files offer good quality and compatibility. As with AIFF, the tradeoff is large file sizes. Popular on Windows PCs.

As for video, here are some common formats:

AVI

AVI is not a streaming format, but it's very popular, especially on the Windows platform.

QuickTime

Probably the most popular video format on the Macintosh, PCs can also play QuickTime movies, which offer a variety of quality and compression settings. These files have the type MOV. Note that "Quick-Time" can also refer to the plugin and the standalone player.

MPEG

MPEG video provides a great combination of high quality and high compression ratios, making it a popular format. It's also excellent in terms of cross-platform compatibility.

WMF

Windows Media Format is another popular PC video format, but it isn't cross-platform.

The View Plugins Command

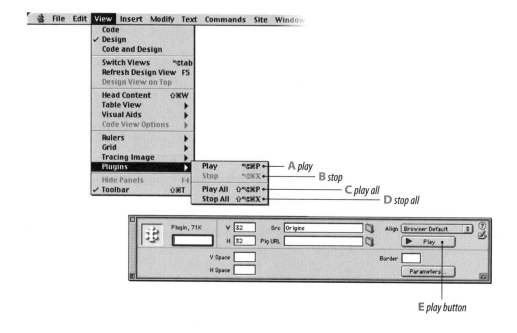

A play
B stop
C play all
D stop all
E play button

You can use Dreamweaver's document window to preview videos or sounds that rely on Netscape plugins, as long as Dreamweaver can find the plugin code in the **Netscape/Communicator/Program/Plugins** folder or in the **Dreamweaver 4/Configuration/Plugins** folder. In fact, if you have multiple media elements on the page, you can play them one by one, or all at the same time.

> **tip** Don't be discouraged if you get an error message when trying to preview ActiveX content. To preview a video that relies on the Windows Media Player control, for example, you have to fire up a browser; you can't preview the video in the document window. Use **F12,** or the menu command **File→Preview In Browser**, to preview the current page in the primary browser.

A play
Choose **View→Plugins→Play** (keyboard shortcut **ctrl+alt+P** in Windows, **command-option-P** on the Mac) to preview the selected media clip.

B stop
Choose **View→Plugins→Stop** (**ctrl+alt+X** in Windows, **command-option-X** on the Mac) to stop the playback of the currently playing media clip.

C play all
Choose **View→Plugins→Play All** (**ctrl+alt+shift+P** in Windows, **command-option-shift-P** on the Mac) to play all the media clips in the current document.

D stop all
Choose **View→Plugins→Stop All** (**ctrl+alt+shift+X** in Windows, **command-option-shift-X** on the Mac) to stop the playback of all currently playing media clips.

E play button
Another way to preview a plugin is to click the green **Play** button on the plugin's property inspector. When you click it, it turns into a red **Stop** button that you can click to stop the preview.

Create & Use Style Sheets

While writing this book, I used several preformatted *styles* in my word processor. (For example, a headline style might be defined as using the Arial font, size 20 point, and boldface.) The *Cascading Style Sheet (CSS)* specification lets you do the same sort of thing with HTML text instead of a word-processing document. You can even go beyond regular HTML, for example, by specifying precise indents and pixel-based font sizes.

Like templates (Chapter 9), CSS *style sheets* save you time in two ways. When creating a page, applying a style to a section of text saves you from having to set each attribute individually. Later, if you decide to change the style's look, Dreamweaver automatically updates any pages that use the style.

The drawback of CSS styles is that they only work with Version 4.0 and newer browsers. If you want broader compatibility, consider using *HTML styles* (discussed in Chapter 3), but you sacrifice the automatic updating feature that makes CSS styles so appealing.

The CSS Styles Panel

The **CSS Styles** panel is somewhat less evolved than other panels in Dreamweaver 4. You can't detach a style from a page here, for example, nor can you directly view or edit all types of styles. Further, you don't get a preview window. However, you'll need to work around this panel's quirks and limitations, and I'll try to help you do just that.

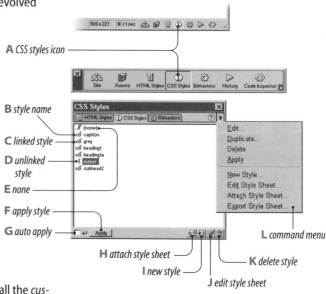

A *CSS styles icon*
B *style name*
C *linked style*
D *unlinked style*
E *none*
F *apply style*
G *auto apply*
H *attach style sheet*
I *new style*
J *edit style sheet*
K *delete style*
L *command menu*

A CSS styles icon

Click the **CSS Styles** icon in the launcher bar or the mini-launcher in the status bar, or choose **Window→CSS Styles,** to display the **CSS Styles** panel. You can also press **shift+F11**.

B style name

The panel's only window lists the names of all the *custom* styles (that is, ones you can apply yourself; see Custom & Redefinition Styles on page 221 for details) that are available to the currently open document. These custom styles may reside in the document's **<head>** content area, or in an external style sheet.

> *tip* To edit a single style quickly, double-click its name to display the **Style Definition** dialog box. Then make your changes and click **OK.**

C linked style

A style with a chain link icon is a *linked* style, meaning that the code for the style's specification resides in an external document, not the current document.

D unlinked style

A style with no chain link icon is an *unlinked* style, meaning that its code lives in the **<head>** content of the current document. Unlinked styles work only in the current document, while linked styles can work in multiple documents.

E none

Click this pseudo-style and click the **Apply** button (F) to remove CSS style formatting in the selected text. See also (G).

F apply style

Click a style name (B) and then click **Apply** to apply that style to the current text selection. See also (G).

G auto apply

Check this check box to have Dreamweaver apply a style as soon as you click it, without your having to click the **Apply** button.

> *tip* The program applies a style to selected text. If you haven't selected any text, style applies to the entire paragraph around the insertion point. Or, you can select a tag from the status bar's tag selector and then apply a style to the tag.

H attach style sheet

Click this button or choose **Text→CSS Styles→ Attach Style Sheet** to bring up the **Select Style Sheet File** dialog box, where you can specify (or browse to) an external style sheet containing styles you want to use in the current document. Be aware that it *links*, rather than *imports*, the style sheet; your **<head>** section simply specifies a link to the external file. For details, see Attach A Style Sheet on page 227.

I new style

Click here or choose **Text➡CSS Styles➡New Style** to open the **New Style** dialog box, which lets you create a new unlinked or linked style specification, as explained in Create A CSS Style on pages 222 through 224.

J edit style sheet

This button brings up the **Edit Style Sheet** dialog box, which is a bit misnamed because you can edit an unlinked style (D) as well as a linked style (C). You can also display the dialog box by choosing **Text➡ CSS Styles➡Edit Style Sheet** or by pressing **ctrl+shift+E** (**command-shift-E** on the Mac).

K delete style

Click the trash can button to remove a selected unlinked style from the list.

> **tip** Although Dreamweaver *appears* to let you delete a linked style, it doesn't really do so, nor does it give you any error message to that effect. Next time you open the **CSS Styles** panel, the style you thought you deleted will reappear. (I told you this panel had some glitches.) If you want to delete a style from an external style sheet, you must use the **Edit Style Sheet** command, double-click the name of the style sheet in the **Edit Style Sheet** dialog box, click the style you want to delete, and click the **Remove** button.

L command menu

Click the arrow at the panel's upper right to see the pop-up command menu. This menu duplicates the panel's buttons and includes three additional commands: **Edit**, which lets you edit the selected style; **Duplicate**, which creates a copy of the selected style (handy if you're making multiple similar styles), and **Export Style Sheet**, which saves all the styles defined in the document to an external file.

Custom & Redefinition Styles

CSS style sheets come in two basic types: *custom* and *redefinition*. A custom style is one that you must apply; redefinition styles are applied automatically.

Custom styles

When you define a custom style, you control what text you want the style to affect. Apply a custom style by highlighting a text selection and applying the style from the **CSS Styles** panel (which shows *only* custom styles). Dreamweaver implements the style in HTML with a **class** attribute or a **<span>** tag, depending on whether you choose

a complete or partial block of text . These styles appear with a leading period when you edit a style sheet.

Redefinition styles

Redefinition styles redefine how the browser interprets standard HTML tags. If you redefine a single tag, then the redefinition style is called a *tag style*; if you redefine the appearance of a combination of tags, or if you want the redefinition to occur only in tags containing a specific **ID** attribute, then the redefinition style is called a *selector style*. In both cases, Dreamweaver (and the user's browser) changes the appearance

of the page automatically, which is the stated reason why the **CSS Styles** panel doesn't show redefinition styles. (You can still edit them, though, so I wish the panel displayed them.) These styles appear with the name of the HTML tag they redefine when you edit a style sheet.

Which should you use? If you intend your styles to apply only to a small percentage of the total text in your site, or if you don't want to risk an unintended automatic application, use custom styles. Otherwise, use redefinition styles.

✦steps✦ Create A CSS Style

The following steps show you how to create a style that lives entirely within the current document. The code for the style resides in the page's **<head>** content. You may create such an *unlinked* or *internal* CSS style if you need to use a particular text format many times on the same page, but you don't anticipate using it on other pages. To find out how to create an *external* style sheet that you can use for multiple documents, see Create An External Style Sheet on pages 225 and 226.

1 open document
Choose **File➟Open** or press **ctrl+O** (**command-O** on the Mac) to open the document in which you wish to define the CSS style.

2 open CSS styles panel
If it isn't already showing, you can display the **CSS Styles** panel by choosing **Window➟CSS Styles**, by pressing **shift+F11**, or by clicking the **CSS Styles** icon on the launcher or mini-launcher.

3 click new style
The **New Style** button at the panel's lower right has a plus sign for easy identification. You can also click the pop-up menu arrow at the panel's upper right and choose **New Style**. Either way, the **New Style** dialog box appears.

4 choose style type
Even though the **Type** area isn't at the top of the **New Style** dialog box, you should choose it first,

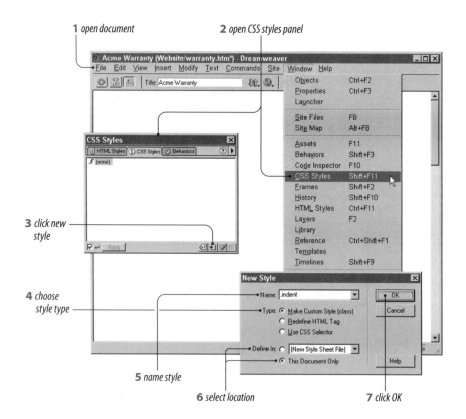

1 *open document*

2 *open CSS styles panel*

3 *click new style*

4 *choose style type*

5 *name style*

6 *select location*

7 *click OK*

because it will determine whether and how you name the style (5). If you want the style to take effect only when you explicitly apply it, as in this example, choose **Make Custom Style (Class)**; if you want the style to replace an existing HTML tag or tag combination, choose **Redefine HTML Tag** or **Use CSS Selector**, respectively. See the sidebar Custom & Redefinition Styles on page 221 for details.

5 name style

If you chose **Make Custom Style (Class)** in step 4, then you must name the style. (If you chose **Redefine HTML Tag** in that step, then you don't need to name the style because it effectively takes the name of the HTML tag it redefines; you just pick the tag.) When naming a custom style, begin with a period and a letter and then use any combination of letters and numbers, such as **.indent** for example.

tip Change your mind? You can't rename a style in the **CSS Styles** panel. The workaround is to right-click (Win) or **control**-click (Mac) the style, choose **Duplicate**, give the duplicate the name you want, and then delete the original. Or you can drop into code view and edit the HTML manually.

6 select location

If you want to create an internal (unlinked) style, click the **This Document Only** radio button, as in this example. Or you can click the radio button by the pop-up menu and make a choice from that list to create an external style, either in a new style sheet or an existing one.

7 click OK

When you click the **OK** button, Dreamweaver displays the **Style Definition** dialog box.

8 *choose attributes*

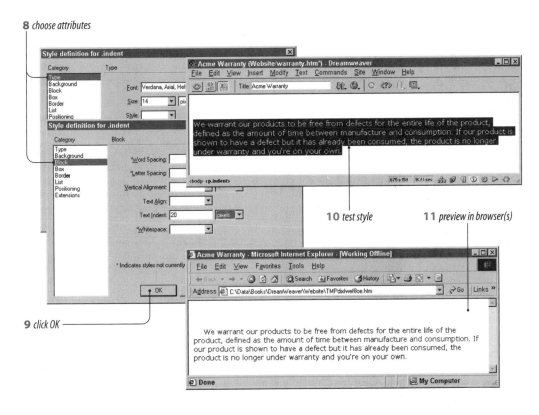

9 *click OK*

10 *test style*

11 *preview in browser(s)*

8 choose attributes

The **Style Definition** dialog box offers several dozen attributes you can select to define your style. The eight choices in the **Category** column on the left correspond to different choices in the details part of the dialog box on the right. In this example, I chose a **Font** and **Size** in the **Type** category, and a value for **Text Indent** in the **Block** category. This style will only apply to paragraphs, because the **Block** category doesn't work with text snippets. (See Style Definitions on page 228 for details of the different categories.)

9 click OK

When you've gone through all the attributes you want to specify for your new style, click the OK button in the **Style Definition** dialog box. Dreamweaver places the style's name in the **CSS Styles** panel, and it also appears in the upper part of the **Text▸CSS Styles** menu. The code for the style appears in the **<head>** content of the current document if you chose to create an internal (unlinked) style, as in this example; you can verify this by switching to code view from the toolbar, as shown here.

10 test style

Test your style by applying it to a portion or block of text in the current document. For details on how to do this, see Style Application Methods on this page.

11 preview in browser(s)

Merely applying a style to a text selection doesn't mean that you'll see it in the document window as it will appear in a browser. For example, applying this example's **.indent** style doesn't actually indent a paragraph until you view it in a browser preview window. Click the **Preview/Debug In Browser** icon on the toolbar and choose the target browser. By default, the keyboard shortcuts are **F12** for the primary browser, and **ctrl+F12** (Win) or **command-F12** (Mac) for the secondary browser.

Style Application Methods

So how do you apply a custom style, once you've created it? The methods depend on whether you're selecting a portion of text or a text block. (Note that you don't apply redefinition styles; Dreamweaver applies them for you automatically.)

Select Text Portion

If you want to apply the style to a portion of a text block, such as a word or phrase, simply select it with the mouse using click and drag. Then click a name in the **CSS Styles** panel. If the **Auto Apply** check box is selected, Dreamweaver applies the style; otherwise, click the **Apply** button.

Select Text Block

Sometimes you'll want to apply a style to an entire block of text, such as a list or paragraph. (The block definition attributes apply only to text blocks; see Style Definitions on page 228.) You can select the block using click and drag, but you may not always get the block tags with this method, which is why I prefer clicking a tag on the tag selector part of the document window's status bar. For example, to select a paragraph, click the **<p>** tag. Then click a name in the **CSS Styles** panel or click the name and click **Apply** if Auto Apply is off.

Although it's handy for most folks, you don't have to use the **CSS Styles** panel if you don't want to. You can select a text portion or text block as described and then use the menu command **Text▸CSS Styles▸** **stylename** where **stylename** appears in the menu's upper group.

Finally, you can use the context menu to apply a style. Select the text, right-click it (Win) or **control**-click it (Mac), click **CSS Styles**, and select the style from the submenu's upper group.

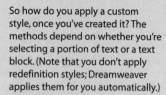

Create An External Style Sheet

Most of the time you work with CSS styles, you'll want to create external styles rather than internal ones. The main reason is convenience: With an external *style sheet*, as the file is called, you can apply styles to multiple documents instead of just to one document, yet you maintain the style definition in only one place.

> **tip** The following method varies from that given in the Dreamweaver program manual, but it's faster!

1 open document
Open the document in which you wish to define the first CSS style in your new style sheet.

2 click new style
Click the **New Style** button on the **CSS Styles** panel to bring up the **New Style** dialog box.

How can you create a new style without having created an external file for it first? That's the clever aspect of this method. Dreamweaver creates the CSS file for you as a byproduct of your creating the first style that it will contain. Two birds, one stone.

3 choose style type
Choose a type as discussed in step 4 on page 222.

4 name style
Name the style as discussed in step 5 on page 223.

5 select new style sheet file
Click the radio button by the pop-up menu showing **(New Style Sheet File)**.

6 click OK
When you click the **OK** button, instead of displaying the **Style Definition** dialog box as it would if you were creating an internal style, Dreamweaver displays the **Save Style Sheet File As** dialog box.

7 enter filename
Give your style sheet file a descriptive name, such as **newsltr**. Dreamweaver will append the **.css** extension automatically. You can also choose a different folder in which to save the file, if Dreamweaver guessed wrong on that point.

8 click save
Dreamweaver saves your new style sheet, and the **Style Definition** dialog box appears. The rest of the

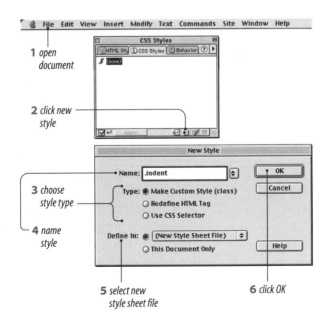

1 open document

2 click new style

3 choose style type

4 name style

5 select new style sheet file

6 click OK

procedure simply finishes the definition of the first style in that sheet.

> *tip* You can create multiple style sheets for your Web site, each of which contains a group of styles that apply to a particular type of page. This may be more efficient than creating one gargantuan style sheet file.

9 choose attributes

Select attributes to define your style. See Style Definitions on page 228 for details.

10 click OK

Dreamweaver places the style's name in the **CSS Styles** panel, and it also appears in the upper part of the **Text⇒CSS Styles** menu. The **<head>** content of the current document now contains nothing more than a link to the external file, as shown here.

11 test & preview

Test your style by applying it to a portion or block of text in the current document. Click the **Preview/Debug In Browser** icon on the toolbar and choose the target browser.

At this point, you can define more styles for inclusion in your style sheet by clicking the **Edit Style Sheet** button on the **CSS Styles** panel and then clicking the **New** button in the **Edit Style Sheet** dialog box.

> *tip* If you already *have* a document in which you've defined one or more CSS styles, you don't have to recreate them laboriously by following the preceding steps.
>
> Instead, you can open the document (you must be in design view, for some odd reason) and choose **Text⇒CSS Styles⇒Export Style Sheet** (or the equivalent command **File⇒Export⇒Export CSS Styles**). Dreamweaver asks you to give the new style sheet a name and saves it for you, by default, in the root of the site folder. You can then link to that style sheet from any other document and apply its styles.
>
> Watch out, though: The export process doesn't export linked styles, just unlinked ones—that is, styles whose definitions reside in the **<head>** content of your document.

7 enter filename

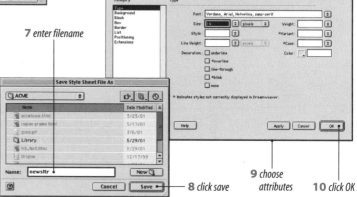

8 click save   *9 choose attributes*   *10 click OK*

11 test & preview

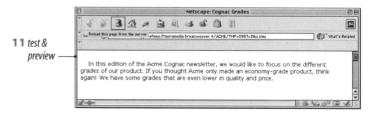

〈steps〉 Attach A Style Sheet

Once you've created one or more external style sheets, you will frequently want to use those styles in existing documents. However, when you open a document and open the **CSS Styles** panel, you don't see anything. To make the styles in an external file available to a given document, you need to attach the style sheet to the document.

1 open document
Open the document to which you want to attach the CSS style sheet.

2 click attach style sheet
The **Attach Style Sheet** button at the lower right of the **CSS Styles** panel is the fastest way to attach an external style sheet to a document.

3 select file
In the **Select Style Sheet File** dialog box, select the file you want; it will have the extension **.css** and (usually) will reside in the site's root folder.

〈tip〉 This command uses the "link" method of attaching a style sheet. An alternative method, "import," does not work as consistently, but if you want to use it for some special reason, you have to go through this sequence: Click the **Edit Style Sheet** button; click **Link**; specify the file in the **Link External Style Sheet** dialog box; click the **Import** radio button; click **OK;** and click **Done.**

4 click select or open
Under Windows, click the **Select** button; on the Mac, click **Open.** Dreamweaver attaches the style sheet to the open document. You can now apply styles from the **CSS Styles** panel to selected objects on the document page (see Style Application Methods on page 224). Also, be aware that any redefinition styles defined in the CSS file will automatically apply to your document's HTML tags after you attach the style sheet.

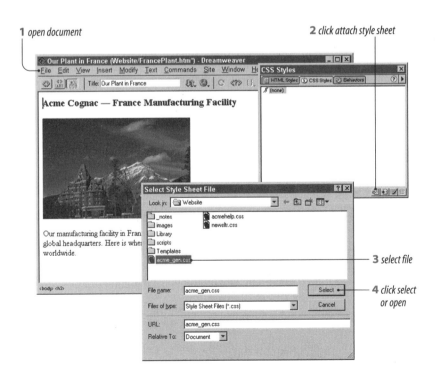

Style Definitions

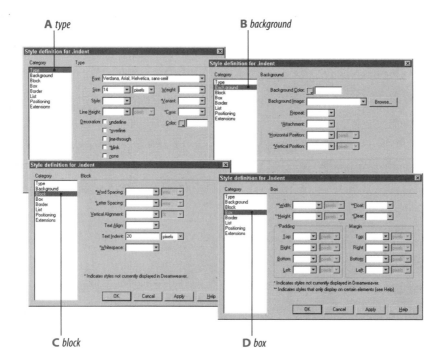

A *type*
B *background*
C *block*
D *box*

The **Style Definition** dialog box offers dozens of attributes from which you can choose when defining a CSS style. This section provides an overview of the eight attribute categories and discusses a subset of the attributes in each one. Experiment with them, and always remember that Internet Explorer and Navigator treat many of these attributes differently.

> **tip** You'll see a number of attributes with an asterisk (*) next to them. The asterisk denotes an attribute that won't show up in the Dreamweaver document window. Some of these attributes won't show up in a user's browser, either, depending on what flavor and version it is. When using CSS styles, be extra careful to check the appearance in target browsers before publishing your site.

A type

Lots of typographic settings live in the **Type** category. For example, you can set font **Size** to a specific pixel value, rather than a relative value as in HTML.

You can also specify **Line Height**, or what print professionals call *leading*, which isn't an option in regular HTML. As a **Decoration**, you can specify underline, overline, strikethrough, or blinking attributes. If you want to control how bold your bold is, enter a value in the **Weight** field.

B background

The **Background** category lets you specify a **Background Color** and **Background Image**, but the really cool part of this category is the **Repeat** options. You can specify **no-repeat**, **repeat**, **repeat-x**, and **repeat-y** to control the exact behavior of a tiled background image. The **Attachment**, **Horizontal Position**, and **Vertical Position** attributes aren't supported by all versions of Netscape Navigator, so be wary of these.

C block

All the **Block** category attributes apply only to a block of selected text—that is, a complete paragraph or a complete list. Many of these settings are typographical in nature, like **Word Spacing** and **Letter Spacing**. **Text Indent** lets you indent the first line of a paragraph but not subsequent lines (you can't achieve this effect, even with layers). **Text Align** works like it does in regular HTML, but if you're going to use CSS styles, you should make the specification here rather than with the usual HTML attributes.

D box

The **Box** category works fairly similarly to a "text box" structure in a word-processing program. You can specify the size of the text box via the **Width** and **Height** attributes. **Float** can be left, right, or none, and determines whether the text box is part of the page's flow or outside of it. **Padding** works much like the cell padding attribute of a table cell and specifies how much white space should exist between the box's border or margin and the text itself.

E border

The attributes in the **Border** category are **Width**, **Color**, and **Style**. You can specify different widths and colors for each of the four borders (although I can't imagine too many cases in which that would look good!).

> **tip** If you want borders to display consistently across a range of browsers, consider putting the text into a table rather than using a CSS style.

F list

One of my favorite CSS attribute categories is **List**, mainly because you can use any custom image you want as a bullet. The **Position** field lets you specify how far to the left a list item wraps.

G positioning

The **Positioning** category actually turns your selected text into a layer. The various attributes here, which Netscape Navigator 4.x does not fully support, are best understood by reading Chapter 8, Make & Manipulate Layers. They include **Visibility**, **Z-Index**, **Overflow**, **Placement**, and **Clip**.

H extensions

The **Page Break** extension attribute lets you specify a page break to occur before or after the selected text when the user prints the page. This attribute isn't yet widely supported by common browsers.

To minimize problems with conflicting styles and make downloads faster, set only the attributes that you definitely want the styly to apply.

E border

F list

G positioning

H extensions

* Indicates styles not currently displayed in Dreamweaver.

Edit A Style

One of the main benefits of using CSS styles is that when you change a style, the change automatically applies to all occurrences (or *instances*) of that style. In the case of an unlinked or internal style, the changes will apply only to the document hosting the style. With a linked style that lives in an external style sheet, the changes will apply to all documents that both link to that style sheet and use the specific style.

The procedure for editing an internal style varies somewhat from editing an external style; this section shows you the fastest way to do both operations.

1 open document

Choose **File→Open** to load a document that contains or links to the style you want to edit. You must use this method to edit an unlinked, internal style. If you want to edit a linked style, it's easier to open the **Site Files** window (**F8**), double-click the style sheet, and skip to step 3.

> *tip* If you're editing an external style, I strongly recommend backing up your entire site before making the change. The nature of external style sheets is such that they can modify many, even all, of your HTML pages in one fell swoop. Yes, Dreamweaver has an **Undo** command, but what if the program crashes before you can choose **Edit→Undo Edit CSS Style**?

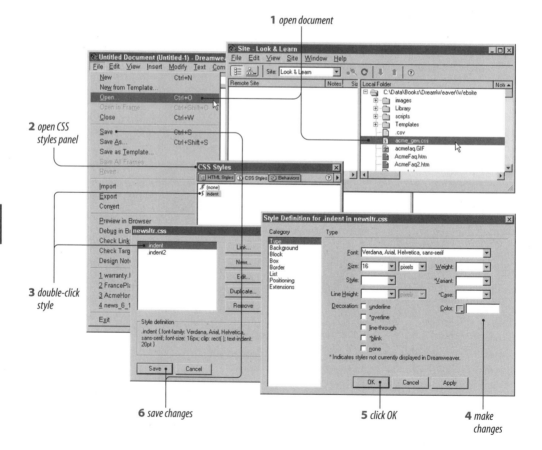

1 open document

2 open CSS styles panel

3 double-click style

6 save changes

5 click OK

4 make changes

2 open CSS styles panel

This step is necessary only if you're editing an unlinked style. Choose **Window→CSS Styles**, press **shift+F11**, or click the **CSS Styles** icon in the launcher or mini-launcher.

3 double-click style

If you're editing an unlinked style, make sure that the **Auto Apply** check box is off and double-click the style's name in the **CSS Styles** panel. If you're editing a linked style, double-click its name in the dialog box whose title is the name of the CSS file (such as **newsltr.css**). In either case, the **Style Definition** dialog box will appear.

For the sake of thoroughness, I will mention that if you have a document open that uses the style you want to edit, you can also click the **Edit Style Sheet** button at the bottom of the **CSS Styles** panel, select the style from the **Edit Style Sheet** dialog box, and click the **Edit** button. That's the method the program manual recommends, but my method is a lot faster and easier! (If you want to edit an internal redefinition style, however, you have to use the manual's method, as Dreamweaver doesn't list such styles in the panel.)

4 make changes

In the **Style Definition** dialog box, make whatever changes you want to the style. Click in the **Category** column at the left to display different sets of attributes in the right part of the dialog box.

5 click OK

Click the OK button to indicate you're happy with your changes and to close the **Style Definition** dialog box.

> **tip** Note that the **Apply** button applies your changes but leaves the dialog box open; this button is pretty useless here, because you can't always see style changes until you preview your file in a browser window.

6 save changes

If you're editing an external CSS style, click the **Save** button in the CSS file dialog box. If you're editing an internal style, choose **File→Save** to save your document, whose code contains the updated style.

Style Conflicts

You need to be concerned about two categories of style conflicts: CSS styles versus other kinds of formatting, and CSS styles with other CSS styles. Here's what you should know.

CSS versus HTML

When a text selection contains both HTML formatting, either manual or via an HTML style, that HTML formatting trumps CSS style formatting. Therefore, before applying a CSS style to a text selection, make sure that no HTML formatting of any kind applies to that selection if you want the CSS style to be in total control of all formatting options.

Custom CSS versus custom CSS

When two custom CSS styles apply to the same text selection, several things can happen. If none of the attributes specified in the two CSS styles conflict, then the user's browser applies all of them (what you'd call a *union* operation in set theory). If an attribute does conflict, then whichever style definition is inside the other (check this out in code view) is the one that takes precedence.

Custom CSS versus redefinition CSS

When a custom CSS style contains an attribute that conflicts with a redefinition CSS style applied to the same text, the custom CSS style attribute wins.

My personal view is that you should never apply multiple styles to any text selection. That way, you don't have to clutter your mind with these rules!

⟨steps⟩ Convert CSS to HTML

Say that you've spent a fair amount of time creating some wonderful CSS styles, and your manager calls up and says that priorities have changed and it is now top priority that the Web site you're working on be compatible with Version 3 browsers. Dreamweaver anticipates this situation, and although the conversion is by no means perfect, it gets you off to a fast start.

1 open document
Use **File➤Open** to load the page you want to convert in the document window. (Unfortunately, no simple way exists to convert a number of documents in a batch procedure; you have to go through this drill one page at a time.)

2 choose 3.0 browser compatible
The actual menu command is **File➤Convert➤3.0 Browser Compatible**. You can run this command whether you're in design view, code view, or split view.

Dreamweaver displays the **Convert to 3.0 Browser Compatible** dialog box.

3 select CSS styles to HTML markup
Click the **CSS Styles to HTML Markup** radio button to tell Dreamweaver you want to attempt a style conversion. Or if your document uses layers, and you also want to convert layers to tables, click **Both**.

4 click OK
Dreamweaver performs whatever conversions it can to imitate your CSS styles using standard HTML and opens a new document window containing the converted file.

> ⟨tip⟩ Some CSS attributes, like the **Text Indent** attribute I've mentioned in this chapter, don't have an HTML equivalent. Dreamweaver silently discards such attributes, so the only way you know they didn't convert is to proceed to step 5.

5 preview in browser
Click the **Preview/Debug in Browser** icon and make the appropriate selection to preview your converted file in a browser window.

Close the browser window when you've identified the manual work you must do to clean up the document further.

6 save file
Save the new document, preferably with a different name so as not to overwrite the original document and its CSS styles.

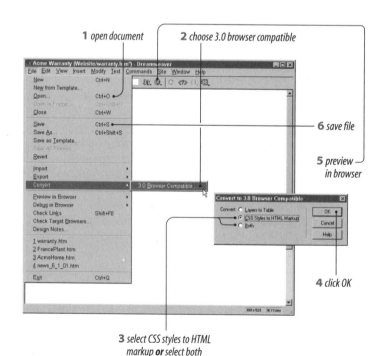

1 *open document*   2 *choose 3.0 browser compatible*

6 *save file*

5 *preview in browser*

4 *click OK*

3 *select CSS styles to HTML markup **or** select both*

Work With Other Programs

Much of the information on any given Web page probably wound its way through several different programs before landing at that URL. The Web is not just weblike in its hyperlinked structure, it's also weblike in its ability to integrate data from different sources (although its designers didn't necessarily have that thought in mind!).

Dreamweaver is particularly adept at weaving in files from other Macromedia products, such as Flash and Director, but it can also work with spreadsheets such as Excel and databases such as Access. Dreamweaver and Fireworks play well together, too, but see Chapter 4 for more on that subject.

Another way to use Dreamweaver with other programs is when you use those programs to modify HTML created by Dreamweaver, as you might do if you don't like (or aren't familiar with) the Code Inspector. In addition, some organizations use code management systems for version control, and Dreamweaver 4 supports those as well.

The Insert Flash Movie Command

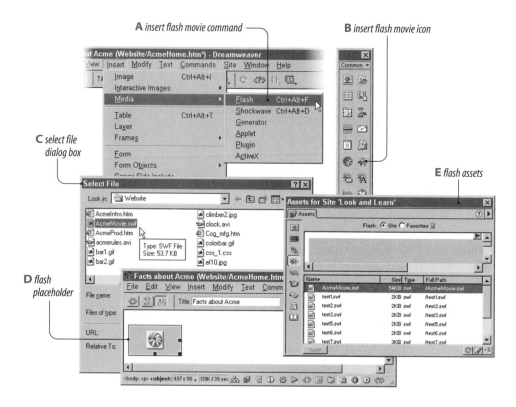

A *insert flash movie command*

B *insert flash movie icon*

C *select file dialog box*

D *flash placeholder*

E *flash assets*

Macromedia's Flash product has become enormously popular for all manner of vector-based imagery, but most of all for animations. The compact vector format (which identifies lines and shapes by endpoints, instead of defining every dot) is a boon for designers who must consider dial-up users but still want to deliver attention-grabbing mini-movies. Most popular browsers now include the Flash Player plugin or "helper" application, so compatibility isn't a big problem. (However, see the sidebar Download Shockwave & Flash Players, on page 239 for details on how the browser can automatically download the player if it's missing.)

When you insert a Flash movie, Dreamweaver adds whatever HTML code is required to "host" that movie on the page, including both the **<object>** and **<embed>** tags so that both Navigator and Internet Explorer can play the movie.

tip Flash is also capable of exporting bitmap versions of Flash animations, for example, in Quick-Time or AVI format. The possible benefit of using such a format is greater cross-platform compatibility, but file sizes will be much larger and playback speeds slower than if you use the Flash vector format. For more on these types of movies, see Chapter 13, Integrate Video & Sound.

A insert flash movie command

The menu command, **Insert➛Media➛Flash**, has the keyboard equivalents **ctrl+alt+F** (Win) and **command-option-F** (Mac). Place the insertion point (that is, click the mouse) in the document window where you'd like your movie to go, before you execute the menu command or keyboard equivalent. (You can move it later if you need to, however.) Note that this command distinguishes Flash movies from the more limited and "prefabricated" Flash objects,

Flash text and *Flash buttons*, which you insert using the **Insert→Interactive Images** command.

If you want to know more about inserting Flash Text, please see Chapter 3, page 53, Insert Flash Text. If you want to know about Flash buttons, see Chapter 11, page 178, The Insert Flash Button Command.

B insert flash movie icon

My preferred method for inserting a Flash movie is to click the **Insert Flash** icon on the **Common** objects panel.

C select file dialog box

For some weird reason, on both the PC and Macintosh, choosing either the menu command (A) or the objects panel icon (B) opens a rather generic **Select File** dialog box, instead of a specific **Select Flash File** dialog box. It's incumbent on you to choose a proper Flash file format; usually that will be SWF (Flash File Types, on this page, for more). If you choose some other file type, Dream-weaver won't present any sort of error message, but your movie obviously won't work.

D flash placeholder

When you insert a Flash movie, as opposed to a Flash text object or Flash button, Dreamweaver places a gray box (called a *placeholder)* where the movie will go. The dimensions of the placeholder are those of the original Flash movie, but you can change them by using the property inspector or by manually altering the HTML code.

E flash assets

After you've added a Flash movie to your site folder (and, as usual, Dreamweaver prompts you to copy it there if you select the movie from a different folder), it will show up in your **Assets** panel, assuming that you've set up your site to create a local site cache. (For more on the site cache, see Chapter 10, Manage Your Site.) Click the Flash icon at the left of the **Assets** panel to change to the Flash category and list your movies at the lower right.

> **tip** Flash text and Flash buttons also appear in the **Flash** category of the **Assets** panel, because the panel goes by file suffix (in this case, SWF). For this reason, it's not a bad idea to name Flash text objects with "text" or "txt" and Flash button objects with "button" or "btn." Otherwise, you don't have an easy way to tell them apart in the **Assets** panel.

Flash File Types

There's not just one "Flash file," but four! Here's a brief explanation of the different formats.

SWF

The *SWF (ShockWave Flash)* format is the one you'd use when creating a Web page object. You couldn't edit an SWF file in the native Flash program, but that doesn't matter to browser users whom you simply intend to watch the movie, and doing away with editability means the SWF format can be a lot smaller than the native FLA format. Think of SWF as "read-only Flash."

FLA

The *FLA* type is the native Flash file format. That is, when you create a movie in Flash, you'll save it as an FLA file, and then you'll open it as an FLA file if you want to edit it later. This format isn't suitable for use on a Web page, though, because the user's browser won't know what to do with it unless the full Flash program is on her system.

SPL

This is the FutureSplash player format, an earlier form of the SWF format. You should consider converting SPL files to SWF if you have

Flash 5, because it's not clear how long Macromedia will continue to support SPL files.

SWT

SWT, for *ShockWave Template*, is also known as the *Generator template* file type. This special format lets you identify parts of a Flash movie (usually text, but possibly graphics and sound) that can change. Dream-weaver uses the SWT format for Flash buttons. You start with an SWT format, which Dreamweaver loads automatically, and then save your customized button as SWF.

The Flash Property Inspector

A *property inspector icon*

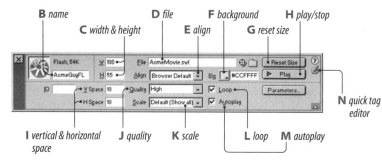

B *name*

C *width & height*

D *file*

E *align*

F *background*

G *reset size*

H *play/stop*

I *vertical & horizontal space*

J *quality*

K *scale*

L *loop*

M *autoplay*

N *quick tag editor*

After you insert a Flash movie, your next step is generally to display the property inspector in order to set various attributes of that movie. By using the property inspector, you don't have to worry about modifying the **<embed>** and **<object>** tags' attributes separately to ensure compatibility with both primary types of browsers. This section explains the settings you're likely to modify, some of which aren't obvious.

> *tip* You'll see some of these same settings in the property inspector for Flash buttons and Flash text objects, but differences do exist. For example, some properties, such as **Autoplay** and **Loop**, are unique to Flash movies.

A property inspector icon

As usual in Dreamweaver, you can open the property inspector window by choosing **Window➡ Properties**, pressing **ctrl+F3** (Win) or **command-F3** (Mac), or clicking the **Show Properties** icon on the mini-launcher or launcher (assuming that you've added this to the usual launcher bar icons via **Edit➡Preferences**).

B name

Add a name (optional) in this mysterious unmarked field if you want to refer to the plugin in a script, or if you want to attach a behavior to it (such as **Control Shockwave or Flash**; see Chapter 12, Add Interactivity, for details).

C width & height

Set the dimensions for the movie in the **W** and **H** fields. Most Flash movies are *scalable*, meaning that they don't lose quality when you change their size (although some Flash movies do contain bitmap images, which don't scale well). Typical units are pixels, in which case you don't need to specify units. However, you can also specify picas (pc), points (pt), inches (in), millimeters (mm), centimeters (cm), or a percentage of the parent object's dimensions (%) by putting the appropriate symbol right after the number (no spaces!). You can also change the movie's size by clicking and dragging the resize handles.

> *tip* If you use the percentage method of specifying width and height, and the movie is not inside another HTML object, Dreamweaver will interpret that percent value to mean "percentage of browser window size," and the browser will adjust the movie size accordingly whenever the user resizes the browser window. Better test your movie in a browser and resize the browser window to make sure that everything looks okay. If not, consider specifying fixed pixel dimensions in the **W** and **H** fields.

D file

The **File** field contains the path to the Flash movie that you want to play. You can click and drag the **Point-to-File** icon (for example, over the **Site Files** window) to select a movie, or you can click the folder icon to browse your system, but most of the time you don't need to modify this value because Dreamweaver updates it when you move the movie file.

> **tip** Notice that, unlike the Plugin property inspector, no **plg url** field appears. Macromedia already knows where to point the user's browser if she doesn't have the Flash plugin and adds that information to the HTML code automatically.

E align

Here's where you set the movie's alignment on the page. The alignment options are the same as those presented on page 57, Place An Inline Image, in Chapter 4.

F background

The background color, which the user only sees when the movie is not playing, goes in the **Bg** field; you can pick it with the Dreamweaver color picker by clicking the color box, or you can enter a hexadecimal value in the white text field.

G reset size

If you changed the size of the movie and made it ugly, you can click **Reset Size** to bring the movie back to its original dimensions.

H play/stop

This button previews the movie in the document window when it's stopped and also stops the movie when it's playing. It's very handy in that you don't have to fire up a browser preview to see the movie play, although that should always be your last step.

> **tip** If you have multiple Flash movies on the same page, use **ctrl+shift+alt+P** (Win) or **command-shift-option-P** (Mac) to play 'em all at the same time.

I vertical & horizontal space

Specify the number of pixels of white space Dreamweaver should surround your object with here.

This setting is analogous to the *cell padding* setting in a table cell (see Chapter 5, Design Tables).

J quality

One way to make text, line art, and vector animations look good on a computer screen is to *anti-alias* them. Anti-aliasing is a nerd word for fuzzing up edges to eliminate the stairstepping that would otherwise remind you that you're looking at a display with discrete pixels. On slow computers, you can't have both anti-aliasing and fast playback, so the **Quality** pop-up menu lets you specify where you want to compromise. **High** means you want to do anti-aliasing even if it slows things down; **Low** means you want to run your movie fast even if it means no anti-aliasing. **Auto High** is like **High**, but if things slow down a lot, the browser will reduce the anti-aliasing; **Auto Low** is like **Low**, but if the computer isn't breathing hard, the browser will increase the anti-aliasing.

K scale

The **Scale** pop-up menu is confusing, and although I'll try to explain it here, you really have to experiment to make a good decision. **Default (Show All)** fits the movie into the width and height values (C) you've specified and maintains its proportions. **No Border** also keeps the movie's proportions but fits one dimension first and then crops the other one to fit. **Exact Fit** forces the movie's playback area into the dimensions you specified, at the risk of losing proportionality.

L loop

Check here to make the movie play in an endless loop.

M autoplay

Check this box to make the movie play automatically once the page loads into the browser window.

N quick tag editor

Click this icon to see the HTML for the movie's **<object>** tag. To see the **<embed>** tag, too, you have to switch to code view.

The Insert Shockwave Command

Shockwave is a plugin or "helper application" that lets a browser play movies (potentially interactive ones, at that) created in Macromedia Director. You can think of Director as Flash's older, bigger brother; Director can do just about everything Flash can do, and then some. Director has its own full-fledged programming language called *Lingo*, and a wealth of third-party extensions called *Xtras*. Although Director is harder to learn than Flash (even though Flash is no picnic), there's not much you can't do in terms of Web animation and multimedia once you master it.

As with Flash, Director is capable of exporting files in bit-oriented formats such as AVI and QuickTime, but keep in mind that you get the best download speed and playback performance with the Shockwave player and the DCR compressed Web-delivery format.

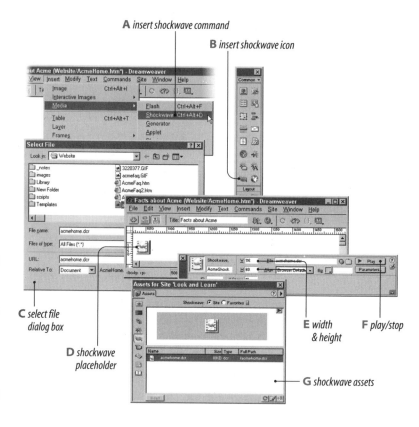

A *insert shockwave command*

B *insert shockwave icon*

C *select file dialog box*

D *shockwave placeholder*

E *width & height*

F *play/stop*

G *shockwave assets*

A insert shockwave command

Choose **Insert→Media→Shockwave** or press **ctrl+alt+D** (**command-option-D** on the Mac). Place the insertion point where you want your Director movie to go and then execute the menu command or keyboard equivalent.

B insert shockwave icon

If you like using the objects panel, click the **Insert Shockwave** icon as an alternative to choosing the menu command **A**.

C select file dialog box

As is the case with Flash movies, Dreamweaver tosses you out in the middle of the pool's deep end when it comes to selecting a file. You need to know ahead of time that Shockwave movies have the extension .DCR, because Dreamweaver will let you make a mistake in the file type selection without warning you about it.

> *tip* The DCR file format is to Director movies as SWF is to Flash movies: a compressed format suitable for delivery via the Web and for playback by a browser. If you bump into files with the DIR type, these are like FLA files in Flash: fully editable, uncompressed files that you create and edit in the Director application but that you don't put on a Web page. The DXR format is a variant of DIR that's not editable.

D shockwave placeholder

You'd think that because Macromedia makes Director, Dreamweaver would be able to recognize the default size of a Shockwave movie, as it can with a Flash movie; but this didn't work in Dreamweaver 3 and it still doesn't work in Dreamweaver 4. So, the movie will come in at 32 pixels by 32 pixels, almost certainly the wrong size. You'll need to get the proper size from the movie's creator or play the movie, watch it change size, and make your best guess. Turning on the rulers helps (**View➥Rulers➥Show**).

E width & height

In the property inspector for a Shockwave movie, you'll need to key in the correct width and height values for the movie. Some Shockwave movies are fully scalable, but others aren't; experiment with different sizes and make your own judgment.

F play/stop

This button works like it does in the Flash property inspector, with the exception that you'll notice more of a delay while the larger Shockwave player loads into memory.

> **tip** Note the conspicuous absence of the **Autoplay** and **Loop** check boxes in the Shockwave property inspector. You can simulate the **Autoplay** action by attaching the **Control Shockwave or Flash** behavior to the Shockwave object and associate the **Play** action with the **onLoad** event. For more on behaviors, see Chapter 12, Add Interactivity.

G shockwave assets

Director movies in your site folder will show up in the **Assets** panel (accessible from the mini-launcher) if your site's local object cache is on. The **Shockwave** icon at the left of the **Assets** panel displays the Shockwave movie category with your files in the asset list at the lower right.

Download Shockwave & Flash Players

Unlike the Flash player, you can't assume that the *Shockwave Player* (which nowadays also incorporates the Flash player) is likely to show up preinstalled on most browsers. It may not even be present on the PC or Mac where you run Dreamweaver. However, if you have access to the Dreamweaver 4 CD-ROM, then you can install Version 8 of the *Shockwave Player* onto your computer by navigating to the CD's **Other Macromedia Software\Shockwave Player** folder and running the installer program. Otherwise, you can download it from the Macromedia Web site.

What about your users? Well, if you take a look at the code inspector view of the document window after you've inserted a Shockwave animation, you may notice an attribute of the **<object>** tag called **codebase**. This tells the browser where to get the Shockwave Player if the user either doesn't have it at all or has a version that's too old to work properly. (The version information shows up after the pound sign (**#**) in the codebase URL.) FYI, the **classid** attribute is what identifies the Shockwave Player as opposed to other ActiveX controls.

But isn't the **<object>** tag just for Internet Explorer? Yep, Navigator uses the **<embed>** tag for objects such as Director and Flash movies. With the **<embed>** tag, the attribute that points the browser to where it can download the player is **pluginspage**, not codebase. Dreamweaver uses both the **<object>** and **<embed>** tags, and the respective download attributes, to make sure that the Flash and Director movies you add to your page not only display properly in both browsers, but trigger the automatic download operation if necessary, too. (So don't believe it if you read in another book about Dreamweaver that the Flash and Shockwave players are just Netscape plugins. They're also ActiveX controls that work with IE.)

Note that if you're designing a site for a private intranet, and you can put the Shockwave and/or Flash players on a local server so that users don't have to connect to the public Internet to get them, you'd want to modify the **codebase** and **pluginspage** attributes accordingly.

🄢steps Add A Shockwave Design Note

Design Notes are notations you attach to the objects on your Web pages. Thankfully, you're not limited to using Design Notes for objects that you created inside Dreamweaver; you can create notes for objects you created in other programs, too, such as a Shockwave or Flash object. For example, you may attach a Design Note to a Director or Flash animation, saying "Playback looks choppy on a PowerMac 7300/200."

1 open context menu
The easiest way to open an object's context menu is to right-click it (Win) or **control**-click it (Mac) in the document window. If you happen to have the site window open instead, the same technique works there, too.

2 choose design notes
Simply choose **Design Notes** from the menu, and the **Design Notes** dialog box appears for you.

3 set status
If you want to indicate the object's status, choose from the **Status** menu. Your options are **draft**,

revision 1, **revision 2**, **revision 3**, **alpha**, **beta**, **final**, and **needs attention**.

4 click date icon
If you click the little date icon to the right, Dreamweaver inserts the current date, a colon, and a carriage return in the **Notes** area, saving you a couple of seconds.

5 add note
Click in the **Notes** area and type whatever notation you want to attach to the object. The note will remain with the object until you turn off the Design Notes feature and clean up.

6 show when file is opened
This check box tells Dreamweaver to display the note whenever you open the file. However, because you don't open Flash or Shockwave movies within Dreamweaver, this option doesn't have any effect when you attach it to such a movie; it's really designed for Design Notes that you attach to HTML pages. Click **OK** to finish up.

> *tip* For more on Design Notes, see Chapter 10's section titled *Create A Design Note* on page 166.

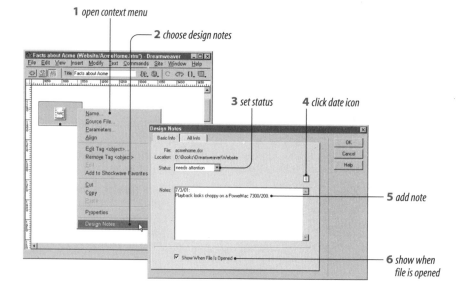

1 *open context menu*

2 *choose design notes*

3 *set status*

4 *click date icon*

5 *add note*

6 *show when file is opened*

The Insert Generator Command

A buzz-phrase these days in Web design is *dynamic content*, which simply means pages that change. For example, a Web page with a back-end database connection will present different information whenever the data in the database changes.

Macromedia Generator is a program that enables you to marry dynamic content with Flash delivery. For example, if you create a Flash movie that incorporates a short quotation, say on a waving flag, you could use Generator to make a template file that a Web server could use to change that quotation daily, without your having to rebuild the SWF file by hand.

If this sounds cool to you, get a copy of Flash 5 (which is required) and install the Generator 2 development software that comes on the Dreamweaver 4 CD-ROM in the folder **Other Macromedia Software\Generator 2 Developer Edition**. (There's different software for authoring Generator templates, and for deploying on the Web server that will serve up the dynamic content; the read-me files explain which is which.) This page simply lays out how to add a Generator object to your Web page in Dreamweaver after you've already created the object using Flash and Generator.

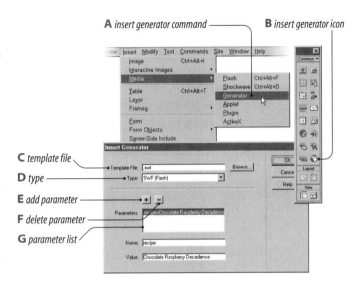

A *insert generator command*   B *insert generator icon*

C *template file*
D *type*
E *add parameter*
F *delete parameter*
G *parameter list*

A insert generator command
The menu command is **Insert➤Media➤ Generator**. No keyboard shortcuts for this one.

B insert generator icon
There is, however, an **Insert Generator** icon on the **Common** objects panel. (If you don't anticipate using Generator, this icon's a good candidate for removing, as I explain how to do in Chapter 16, Personalize Dreamweaver.)

C template file
You can either type in the name and (if necessary) path to the SWT template file that you created with Flash and Generator or browse to it; I prefer the latter to reduce the chance of errors.

D type
You'll most likely use Generator with Flash, but you can also use it with other types of HTML objects; choose the one you want here.

E add parameter
Click the + button to add a parameter. Parameters, which tell the Generator Web server how to generate the served dynamic content, have two parts: a name and a value. Enter these in the fields of the same name, not in the parameter list (G). (The Generator documentation tells you more about parameters than I can begin to explain here.)

F delete parameter
Click the – button to remove the highlighted parameter.

G parameter list
Here's where the parameters (name and value pairs) for the Generator object appear.

Convert Excel Data To Tables

Many Web sites convey tabular information, explaining why HTML tables have been staples of the layout language since the Web's early days. However, organizations often already have charts and tables in spreadsheet format, not HTML table format. You can't open a spreadsheet directly in Dreamweaver (although that would be a nice feature), but you *can* use your spreadsheet program to create a generic file in row-and-column format and import that into Dreamweaver.

When I say "generic file," I mean a file that leaves out all the pretty text formatting (bold, italics, colors, centering) and all the complex calculation formulas and just contains the meat-and-potatoes text and numbers, separated by carriage returns for the rows and a special *delimiter* character, such as a comma, for the columns. (These generic files sometimes have special names depending on the delimiter used; for example, a CSV file is a "comma-separated-value" file.)

In this example, I show you how to create a generic file from Microsoft Excel and then import that intermediate file into Dreamweaver. The procedure is much the same for other spreadsheet programs,

just as long as the spreadsheet can create a generic export file.

> **tip** In addition to spreadsheets, another likely source for tabular data in companies both large and small is the *database*. Databases range in type from simple flat-file systems to more complex relational databases; they can be small in scale, like Microsoft Access, or large, like Oracle. As long as they can create generic export files, or even (less preferably) HTML files, you can import database information into Dreamweaver, just as you do with spreadsheet information. I say HTML files are less preferable because it's usually faster to bring in table data "clean" and then format it inside Dreamweaver.

1 choose save as

In Excel 2000, for example, open the file containing data that you'd like to import into Dreamweaver. The command **File➡Save As** brings up the **Save As** dialog box with the option for you to specify the file format.

2 specify CSV

Choose **CSV (comma delimited) (*.csv)** in the **Save As Type** drop-down list. (You could choose from

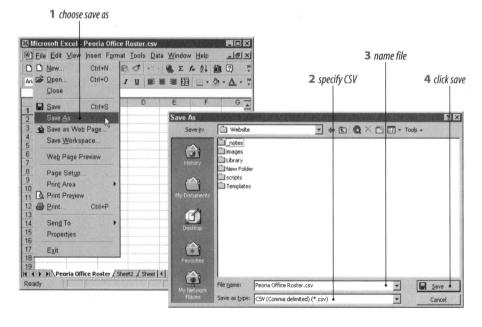

1 *choose save as*

3 *name file*

2 *specify CSV*

4 *click save*

a variety of other generic export formats, and they'd work just as well. You could even choose **Web Page (*.htm, *.html)**, but that would include some extraneous HTML code that you'd rather not deal with later.

> *(tip)* You can't just export part of a spreadsheet; Excel exports the whole thing, and most other spreadsheet programs do the same. To save some time, you may want to trim any unnecessary rows and columns and then save your spreadsheet under a new name. Do leave in the header row with column titles, though.

3 name file

Give the export file a name, here, **Peoria Office Roster**, which is the same name as the original XLS file.

4 click save

Click the **Save** button to actually export the file. If you see a message like the one shown here, stating

that you're going to lose some formatting information with the CSV format, acknowledge the fact by clicking the **Yes** button.

You can put it in whatever folder you like; I choose the Web site's root folder just so the file will be easy to find when I move to Dreamweaver and perform the import operation.

> *(tip)* Because a file like a CSV file doesn't contain formulas, you must re-export the CSV file from your spreadsheet program whenever the numbers or formulas change and then re-import it into Dreamweaver, if you want your Web page to reflect the changed data. There are ways to make Web pages update tabular data dynamically through what are called *back-end database connections*, but that topic is beyond the scope of this book.

5 *open dreamweaver document*

6 *place insertion point*

7 *choose insert tabular data*

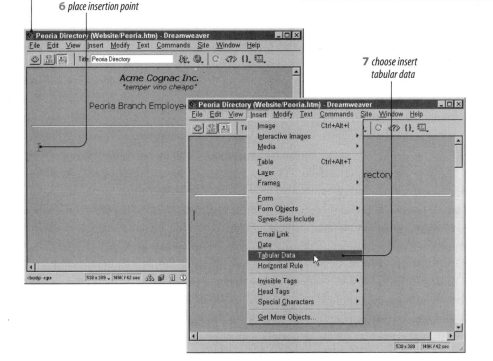

For the curious, here's what a typical CSV file looks like "raw."

5 open Dreamweaver document

Now, open Dreamweaver and load the document into which you plan to import the tabular data.

6 place insertion point

Position the cursor in the document window where you'd like the table to appear. You can always move it later, but at least get it into approximate position here.

7 choose insert tabular data

The menu command is **Insert→Tabular Data**. If you prefer, you can use the alternative command **File→Import→Import Tabular Data**; the result is exactly the same with the exception of the ensuing dialog box's title, which is **Import Table Data** in the latter case and **Insert Tabular Data** in the former. (The dialog boxes themselves are otherwise identical.)

8 specify file

You can specify the file containing the generic export data either by typing its name into the **Data File** field or clicking the **Browse** button and navigating to the file. If you click **Browse**, you'll see the **Open** dialog box; browse to the CSV file and click **Open**. Dreamweaver returns you to the **Insert Tabular Data** dialog box, but notice that it's filled in the **Delimiter** field with the value **Comma**. Dreamweaver helps you out by taking a look at the file and makes an educated guess about the character in the file that separates one data element from another.

9 set delimiter

If Dreamweaver guessed right about the delimiter character, leave this setting alone;

otherwise, change it to fit the file you saved in (4). Your choices are **Tab**, **Comma**, **Colon**, **Semicolon**, and **Other**. If you choose **Other**, you must specify the character in a new field that appears just to the right of the **Delimiter** menu, as shown.

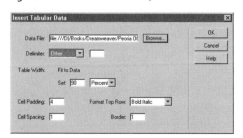

> **tip** By the way, if you get the delimiter character wrong, Dreamweaver doesn't give you a warning, it just slavishly goes through the file and builds the table according to your instructions. You'll have to delete the table and start over at step 6.

10 set table width

You have a few different choices about how to format the incoming data. If you choose **Fit to Data**, then Dreamweaver creates columns that are only as wide as the widest data element in each column. This approach is fairly safe in that it ensures you'll be able to see all the data after Dreamweaver imports it; you can adjust table dimensions later if you want. If you choose **Set**, then you must specify a value in the empty field and whether that value is in pixels or percent.

8 *specify file*   9 *set delimiter*   10 *set table width*

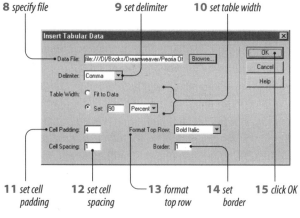

11 *set cell padding*   12 *set cell spacing*   13 *format top row*   14 *set border*   15 *click OK*

11 set cell padding

Cell Padding lets you input a value for the number of pixels you want Dreamweaver to insert between cell contents and the cell boundary. If you leave this at zero, your data will butt up against the cell walls, which may not look good. I suggest putting a value of 2 to 4 in this field as a starting point; you can adjust it later if you like.

12 set cell spacing

The **Cell Spacing** value specifies the number of pixels between each cell. No data can appear in the space between cells.

13 format top row (optional)

If your original spreadsheet file included a top row with column titles, Dreamweaver lets you treat that row as cosmetically different from all subsequent rows in the **Format Top Row** menu. Your options are **Bold**, **Italic**, and **Bold Italic**.

14 set border

If you want a border for your table, choose its width by typing a pixel value here. You'll have to set other border options, such as color, later using the Table property inspector.

15 click OK

When everything in the **Insert Tabular Data** dialog box is to your liking, click the **OK** button to close it and tell Dreamweaver to perform the export. Lo and behold, the table appears on your page, although probably not exactly as you'd like it to look, which is why I include (16) as your final design step.

16 format more

Now that the table data is on the page, you can format the table further so that it looks and acts the way you want. For example, you may want to apply one of the several predefined table designs via the **Commands➡Format Table** command. You can also format columns and rows individually, using the various table-related property inspectors. Chapter 5, Design Tables, offers a lot of information on table formatting.

16 *format more*

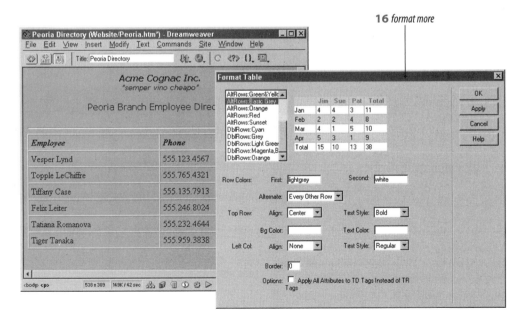

steps Connect To A Code Management System

For large, complex, or long-duration projects, *code management systems* provide specialized benefits. For example, you may need to maintain multiple versions of a Web design project, just in case the boss says, "Let's go back to the way we did it six months ago." Also, you may have multiple versions of many of the component files that go into your Web site, and you need to keep track of what version of which component goes with what version of the published site. Finally, you may work for a company that manages multiple sites, each with their own project management needs.

Code management systems (also called *version management* and *source control* systems) help you deal with all these situations with a minimum of redundant and manual effort. Dreamweaver supports two types of code management systems: those that comply with *WebDAV*, which stands for *Web Distributed Authoring and Versioning*, and Microsoft *Visual SourceSafe* (*VSS*). Some of the most popular Web servers on the market, such as Apache and Microsoft's *IIS* (*Internet Information Server*), support WebDAV, so that's the kind of code manager this example shows you how to set up.

1 choose define sites

The menu command is **Site→Define Sites**, which brings up the **Define Sites** dialog box. There's no keyboard shortcut here, which is fine because you won't be using this command every day.

2 choose site

Choose the site you want to connect to the WebDAV server from the list by clicking it. You can tell

Dreamweaver to use a code management system for one site and not for other sites; the settings you're about to make will only apply to the site you choose here.

3 click edit

Click the **Edit** button to bring up the **Site Definition for <sitename>** dialog box.

4 click remote info

In the **Category** column at the left of the **Site Definition** dialog box, click **Remote Info**. This category tells Dreamweaver how you want to connect to the remote server that publishes your Web site.

5 choose webDAV access

Click the arrow at the **Access** drop-down list and choose **WebDAV**. Your other choices are **None**, **FTP**, **Local/Network**, and **SourceSafe Database**; you'd choose the latter if you were using Microsoft Visual SourceSafe as your code management system.

6 decide about check out

As soon as you choose WebDAV in (5), some information about the supported version appears, as does a new check box titled **Check Out Files when Opening**. This option, which is checked by default,

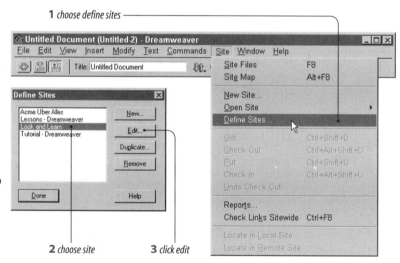

1 *choose define sites*

2 *choose site*   3 *click edit*

means that when you open the site, Dreamweaver automatically marks the files as checked out on the server, so nobody else can modify them while you're working on them.

7 click settings

The **Settings** button takes you to the **WebDAV Connection** dialog box, where you'll provide details that the WebDAV server needs for you to connect to it.

8 enter URL

In the **URL** field, type the full Uniform Resource Locator of the WebDAV server (including the http:// part and any subfolder path). The WebDAV administrator should be able to supply this URL if you don't know it.

9 enter username & password

In the **Username** and **Password** fields, you must enter information that the WebDAV server recognizes as a known account with server access privileges. Again, see your WebDAV administrator if you don't know these details.

10 enter e-mail address

If someone else needs to work on a page that you've checked out, they need to know how to contact you, so enter your e-mail address in the **Email** field.

11 save password

If you don't want to have to re-authenticate every time you connect to the WebDAV server, select this check box.

12 click OK

When you click the **OK** button, you save the settings and are now ready to connect to the WebDAV server, assuming that it's online and you have a physical connection to it.

13 connect to webDAV server

Do this just as you would to any remote server, by clicking the **Connect** icon on the Site window toolbar. You can now get and put files as you would do through any other kind of connection, such as FTP or local area network. The code management system tracks your activities in an effort to keep everything organized.

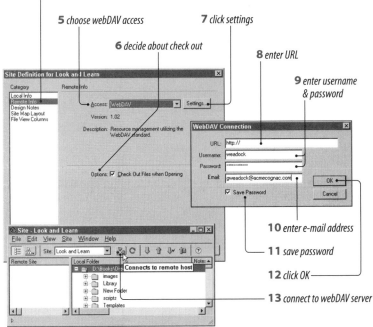

4 *click remote info*

5 *choose webDAV access*

6 *decide about check out*

7 *click settings*

8 *enter URL*

9 *enter username & password*

10 *enter e-mail address*

11 *save password*

12 *click OK*

13 *connect to webDAV server*

External HTML Editors

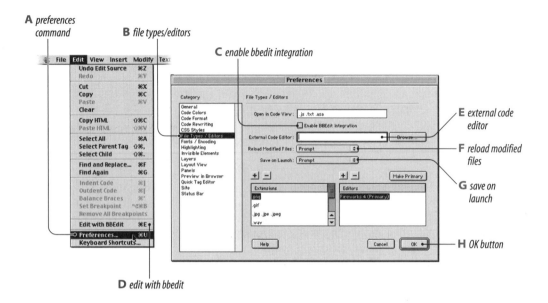

A preferences command

B file types/editors

C enable bbedit integration

E external code editor

F reload modified files

G save on launch

H OK button

D edit with bbedit

Dreamweaver includes a reasonably capable HTML editor in the form of the Code Inspector (as a separate window) or the "code view" of the document window. The Code Inspector offers syntax coloring, line numbering, word wrap, auto indent, real-time error checking, and other handy features that programmers expect. (Users of earlier Dreamweaver versions were not quite so fortunate.)

However, Macromedia recognizes that Web designers may already be very familiar and comfortable with another HTML editing tool, such as BBEdit on the Macintosh, or HomeSite on the Windows platform. In fact, Macromedia even includes these programs on the respective CD-ROMs. In Windows, open the **Dreamweaver 4** folder, then the **HomeSite 4.5** folder, and double-click **homesite451retail.exe** to install the program. On the Mac, open the **Dreamweaver 4** folder, then the **BBEdit 6.1** folder, and then the **BBEdit 6.1 Demo** folder; finally, double-click the **BBEdit 6.1 Demo** file. (You can copy this file to your hard drive for better speed.)

tip The version of BBEdit provided on the Dreamweaver PowerMac CD-ROM is a trial version that only launches 24 times. To get the full version that does not expire, you have to pay some dollars to Bare Bones Software. The version of Allaire HomeSite provided on the Dreamweaver Windows CD-ROM is a full version that never expires.

A preferences command
Whichever platform you use, set up an external HTML editor via the **Edit➥Preferences** command. The shortcut is **ctrl+U** (Win) or **command-U** (Mac).

B file types/editors
Clicking the **File Types/Editors** option in the **Category** column at the left of the **Preferences** dialog box displays the details you need to change in the detail area to the right.

C enable bbedit integration (Mac)
Macromedia has made things very simple for those Mac users among you who want to use BBEdit as your external HTML editor: Just select the **Enable BBEdit Integration** check box. This option buys you several handy features.

First, you don't have to make any other settings (E, F, G) in the **Preferences** dialog box. Second, when you have both Dreamweaver and BBEdit loaded and active, switching between programs in the Finder causes the Mac to save any data you've changed and update the other program's window. Third, you can switch between programs and the code or text that you highlighted in the first program stays highlighted in the second.

> *tip* If you use BBEdit, you don't have to close it when you return to Dreamweaver; instead, click the Dreamweaver button on the **HTML Tools** palette, shown here. BBEdit saves the file and switches you over to Dreamweaver, updating the display, but BBEdit remains in memory, ready to spring into action again at the next **Edit with BBEdit** command. (By the way, display the HTML Tools palette in BBEdit with the **Markup➡HTML Tools Palette** command.)

D edit with bbedit

After you've set your external editor in the **Preferences** dialog box, you'll notice that the **Edit** menu looks different. Specifically, you have the **Edit➡Edit with <editor>** command, where <editor> is the program you specified in (E). This command lets you edit any HTML file that Dreamweaver has open with the editor of your choice. On the Mac, you can use the simple command **Edit➡Edit with BBEdit**, as long as you've enabled BBEdit integration (C).

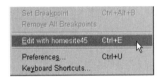

E external code editor

You would use the **External Code Editor** field in one of two circumstances: You're running Windows, or you're running a Mac but you don't want to use BBEdit. Either type the full path and filename directly into the text field, or click the **Browse** button and go find the program you want to use as your external HTML editor in the **Select External Editor** dialog box. In the example shown here, I'm about to choose HomeSite.

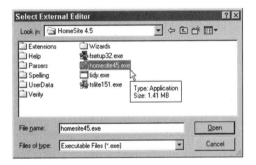

F reload modified files

The **Reload Modified Files** option lets you tell Dreamweaver whether and when it should reload an open document that an external code editor has changed. Your options are **Always**, **Never**, and **Prompt** (which means Dreamweaver asks you what to do).

G save on launch

The **Save on Launch** check box lets you tell Dreamweaver whether to save your documents just before launching an external editor. To me, this is always a good idea.

> *tip* Ignore the **Extensions** and **Editors** columns at the lower right of the **Preferences** dialog box; you don't need these to designate an external HTML editor.

⬭steps Edit A Page In HomeSite

The previous section discussed setting up an external HTML editor for use with Dreamweaver; this section shows you what the editing process looks like when you actually perform code editing in the Allaire HomeSite program, which Macromedia bundles with the Windows version of Dreamweaver. (I don't walk you through the steps of how to use BBEdit on the Mac platform because the procedure is both similar to, and simpler than, the procedure presented here.)

1 open document

Open your document in Dreamweaver's document window with **File➞Open** or by double-clicking it in the site window (which you can display with **F8**).

> *tip* If you already know exactly which document you want to edit and you don't need to look at it in the document window first, right-click (Win) or **control**-click (Mac) the file in the site window, choose **Open With** to open a submenu, and choose your external editor from that submenu, to the right below. Saves a bit of time, and you can skip (2) below.

2 choose edit with <program>

To edit the code for the open document in the external editor you've already set up (see External HTML Editors on page 248), you can choose the menu command **Edit➞Edit with <program>** where, in this example, **<program>** would be **homesite45**. However, I'm going to suggest that you use the keyboard shortcuts here: **ctrl+E** (Win) and **command-E** (Mac). Finally, a shortcut you can remember!

When you execute the edit command, Dreamweaver launches the external editor, whose window appears in the foreground. If the editor isn't already open, you may notice a few seconds' delay while Windows loads its code into memory, but if it's already open, the HomeSite window appears right away.

1 *open document*   **2** *choose edit with <program>*

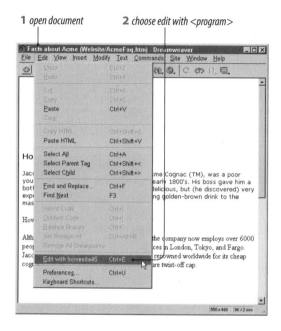

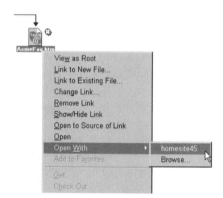

3 edit in homesite

Perform whatever edits you want to the document in the HomeSite workspace. By default, the code editing window's on the right, and your hard drive's folder hierarchy and file list are on the left. Common HTML tags appear at the upper right, broken out by category. If you have multiple Dreamweaver documents open in the HomeSite window, you'll see their names on tabs that appear at the bottom of the code editing window.

4 save changes

Save your edits with **File➡Save** in HomeSite, if you think you might come back and edit the file some more. Otherwise, choose **File➡Close** and answer **Yes** to save the changes.

5 return to Dreamweaver

You can navigate back to Dreamweaver one of two ways: by clicking the Dreamweaver document's taskbar icon, or by pressing **ctrl+D**, the shortcut for the HomeSite command **View➡Open in Macromedia Dreamweaver**.

6 choose to reload

If you set up your external editor preferences dialog box to prompt you when returning to Dreamweaver after a file's been modified outside of Dreamweaver, you'll see a dialog box asking you if it's okay to reload the changes; click **Yes**. (If that gets too annoying after a while, you can turn it off, but then you run the risk of

accepting edits that you may have made unintentionally in your external HTML editor.)

7 repeat as necessary

You can bounce back and forth between the two programs as often as you like, repeating steps (3) through (6) to tweak the HTML in HomeSite, and then look at the results in Dreamweaver. You can use your operating system's task switching facility (**alt+tab,** or the taskbar, in Windows) rather than the **ctrl+E** and **ctrl+D** commands supplied by the two programs; it's up to you.

> **tip** Just remember that you must save the edits you make in the external editor before Dreamweaver can reflect those edits in its document window.

8 save document

When you're happy, save the document and move to the next one.

3 edit in homesite

4 save changes

5 return to dreamweaver

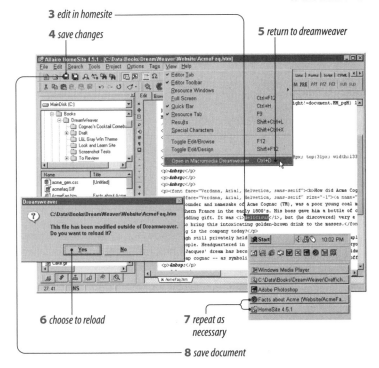

6 choose to reload

7 repeat as necessary

8 save document

Code Rewriting Preferences

When Dreamweaver opens an HTML file from an external editor, Dreamweaver performs a few automatic cleanup operations. Normally, these operations don't affect the vaunted *Roundtrip HTML* capability whereby Dreamweaver can open and resave a file from an external editor without disturbing code that it doesn't understand. However, you'll be happy to know that you can restrict even these cleanup operations if you find circumstances where they create problems with an external HTML editor. You can also tell Dreamweaver it's okay to rewrite code for certain file types it doesn't normally touch.

A *preferences dialog box*
B *code rewriting category*
C *fix invalidly nested/ unclosed tags*
D *remove extra closing tags*
E *warn when fixing/ removing tags*
F *never rewrite code*
G *special characters*

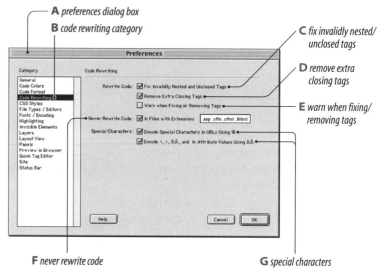

A preferences dialog box

Choose **Edit➥Preferences** from the menu to bring up the multifaceted **Preferences** dialog box.

B code rewriting category

Click **Code Rewriting** in the **Category** column on the left to display the code rewriting options in the details area on the right.

C fix invalidly nested/unclosed tags

When checked, Dreamweaver nests overlapping tags so that the tag pairs nest from the inside out, symmetrically, instead of from left to right; and the program also supplies any missing close quotes or right brackets. (Are "invalidly" and "unclosed" really words? Never mind; you know what they mean!)

D remove extra closing tags

Where a closing tag exists but no corresponding opening tag exists, Dreamweaver nukes the closing tag.

E warn when fixing/removing tags

Normally cleared, check this box if you want Dreamweaver to give you the real scoop all about the behind-the-scenes code rewriting operations that occur when opening a document.

F never rewrite code

If you want Dreamweaver to rewrite HTML in specific file types that it doesn't normally modify, change the list of types in the white text field. The default types that Dreamweaver doesn't touch are ASP, CFM, CFML, IHTML, JS, JSP, PHP, and PHP3. These files contain tags that Dreamweaver doesn't understand and doesn't want to mess up. If you want Dreamweaver to rewrite HTML for all types, clear the **Never Rewrite Code** check box.

G special characters

Dreamweaver normally encodes special characters (basically, those other than numbers and letters) in the HTML for maximum browser compatibility. If either type of encoding listed produces problems, which is rare, clear the relevant check box.

chapter

16

Personalize Dreamweaver

Unless you look at Web design tools that cost thousands of dollars, you won't find another program that offers as much customizability as Dreamweaver. Kudos and huzzahs to Macromedia for allowing users to personalize virtually every aspect of the user interface.

Don't like the way the objects panel lays out? Change it. Don't use certain menu commands? Remove 'em. Prefer different keyboard shortcuts? Specify your own. Want to make a custom command out of a sequence of actions you perform repeatedly? You can do that, too.

Many personalizations are easy, involving nothing more than a check box. Some are more complex, involving moderately tedious text file edits. A few you must program in JavaScript.

If you use Dreamweaver frequently, the time that you invest learning exactly what you can change—and how—can pay you back many times in the long run. (Besides, it's fun looking under the hood of this complex software engine.)

The Preferences Command

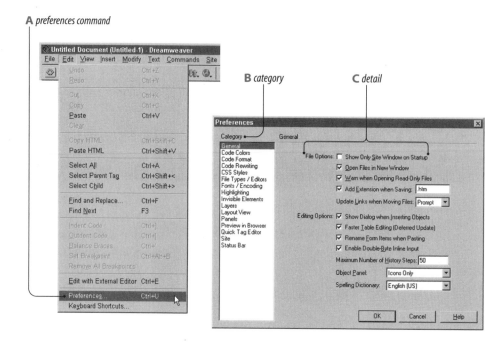

A *preferences command*

B *category*

C *detail*

The nexus for most of Dreamweaver's customizable options is the **Preferences** command. Macromedia has actually packed several dialog boxes into one.

The following pages explore a few of the Preferences dialog boxes. This page describes features common to all, while some of the dialog boxes receive attention in the appropriate context in other chapters.

A preferences command

Bring up the **Preferences** dialog box with the menu command **Edit➞Preferences**, or with the keyboard shortcut **ctrl+U** (Win) or **command-U** (Mac).

B category

Click the category of interest to display the options that Dreamweaver lets you customize for that category. Some categories overlap a little, and some you'll probably never need; it's a great idea to go through each one, however, so that you become aware of what you can change and what you can't.

C detail

The detail part of the dialog box is what changes when you choose a different category. Typically, this area contains check boxes, radio buttons, and drop-down lists to help minimize opportunities for error. For example, when a choice consists of mutually exclusive options, Dreamweaver presents a group of radio buttons, which don't let you choose more than one item.

> **tip** On a Windows computer, Dreamweaver writes many of the **Preferences** settings to the Registry. I heartily recommend against using a Registry editor to change these settings; the **Preferences** dialog box is much safer! (Incorrectly editing Registry values can render your PC unbootable.)
>
> Additionally, Dreamweaver saves some preferences to plain-text files on disk. In the same vein, don't use a text editor to modify a file like **SourceFormat.txt** unless you just can't find a **Preferences** dialog box that can do the job for you.

Preferences, Code Format

D code format

D *code format*

The **Code Format** preferences dialog box presents settings pertaining to the way the code view (or the **Code Inspector**) window appears when you're working with raw HTML. When you make changes here, Dreamweaver modifies SourceFormat.txt, which lives in the Configuration folder under the main Dreamweaver program folder.

E *indent*

F *tab size*

G *automatic wrapping*

H *line breaks*

I *case*

J *case override*

K *centering*

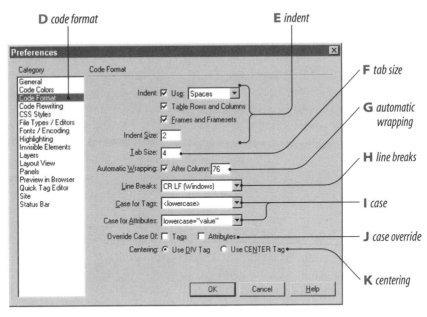

E indent

The **Indent** check box tells Dreamweaver whether you want to use automatic indenting. If checked, you can then specify the character you want to use for indenting (space or tab) in the **Use** field and whether you want to indent **<tr>**, **<td>**, **<frame>** and **<frameset>** tags in the **Table Rows and Columns** and **Frames and Framesets** check boxes. The **Indent Size** field specifies how many spaces or tabs Dreamweaver should use when indenting.

> *tip* To see which tags automatically indent, use a text editor to search for occurrences of "indent" in **SourceFormat.txt**.

F tab size

This setting specifies how many spaces to insert when you press the **tab** key.

G automatic wrapping

The **Automatic Wrapping** option here is different from the **Word Wrap** option you see in code view's **Options** menu. This one tells Dreamweaver to put a permanent carriage return in the code at the position you specify. The **Word Wrap** option puts temporary carriage returns in the code for that viewing session only.

H line breaks

Different computing platforms use different combinations of line feed (LF) and carriage return (CR) characters to signify a line break. Tell Dreamweaver what type of server hosts your Web site so that the program can produce line breaks appropriate for that platform.

I case

The **Case For Tags** and **Case For Attributes** fields let you specify how Dreamweaver generates the underlying HTML code when you create or modify an object in design view.

J case override

Check either or both of the **Tags** and **Attributes** boxes to force the capitalization preference you set in (I) to change documents created in the past, when you open them in Dreamweaver.

K centering

Specify which tag you prefer to use for centering, **<div>** or **<center>** (**<center>** works with more browsers).

Preferences, Code Colors

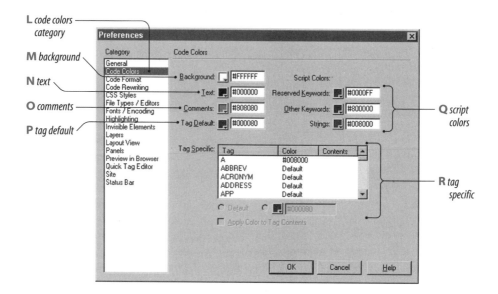

L code colors category

M background

N text

O comments

P tag default

Q script colors

R tag specific

L code colors category

The **Code Colors** dialog box lets you set color options for code view (and the separate-window **Code Inspector**). You can get very detailed in this dialog box and even set colors for specific HTML tags. In each case, you can change a color either by clicking the color box and choosing from Dreamweaver's standard color picker or by entering a hexadecimal value into the white data field directly.

> *tip* You can set colors for design view, too. I don't show them here, but the **Highlighting** dialog box offers color options for documents that use templates and library items. In addition, the **Layout View** dialog box lets you set colors for table cell outlines, as well as highlights and backgrounds.

M background

Change the background color of the code view or **Code Inspector** window. Careful: Changing the color radically renders many of the text, comment, and tag colors illegible, so you'll have to change them, too.

N text

The **Text** color setting affects text that appears between HTML tag pairs. You can override this for specific tags using the **Tag Specific** controls (R).

O comments

The **Comments** color affects comment text and the enclosing comment tags.

P tag default

Set the **Tag Default** color for all tags that are neither comments nor have other colors assigned in the **Tag Specific** area (R).

Q script colors

If your code includes JavaScript or VBScript, the **Script Colors** area lets you set colors for **Reserved Keywords**, **Other Keywords** (nonreserved), and text **Strings**.

R tag specific

You can scroll down the **Tag Specific** area to see any tag-specific colors that Dreamweaver has assigned. To change any of these colors, you simply click the radio button next to the color box and to the right of **Default**.

Check the **Apply Color to Tag Contents** box if you want your change to include the text between tags; otherwise, the default behavior is for Dreamweaver to change the color of the tag elements only.

Preferences, Panels

S panels category

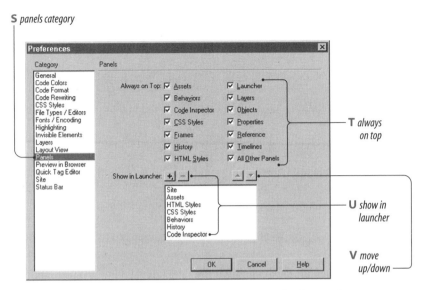

S panels category

Dreamweaver's floating panels (Dreamweaver 2 called them *palettes*) offer you a fair degree of flexibility, given that you can "tear away" individual panels to make them stand on their own or combine them into a tabbed window via drag and drop. The **Panels Preferences** dialog box affords even greater control, and I'm a particular fan of customizing the mini-launcher area to include extra icons.

T always on top

Check the boxes next to the panels you want to float over the document window. Clear a check box, and the panel will only float over the document window if it's active. If it's not active, the document window will cover the panel.

> *tip* Okay, how do you make a panel active if you can't see it? For one thing, you can choose it in the **Window** menu. Even though the panel will appear checked, select it and it comes to the foreground. Another method is to click the icon corresponding to the panel on the mini-launcher at the lower right of the document window. Here again, the icon will appear to be depressed because the panel is on the screen, even though it's obscured. It seems counter-intuitive, but clicking the depressed icon actually does bring the panel to the foreground.

U show in launcher

The lower part of the **Panels** category of the **Preferences** dialog box controls the icons that appear in the launcher (**Window→Launcher**) and its more recent (and more useful) sibling, the mini-launcher. Add icons to the list with the **+** button; remove them with the **-** button.

> *tip* On today's typical 17"-and-larger monitors, you've got a lot of room in the mini-launcher area. Here's what it looks like with all possible panel icons added to it; the additions are (starting in the middle, just to the right of the **Code Inspector**): **Frames**, **Layers**, **Objects**, **Properties**, **Timelines**, and **Reference**. This is how I like to work; I hate going to the **Window** menu all the time, and I can't remember all those silly shortcuts.

V move up/down

The up and down arrows move the selected launcher icon up or down in the sequence (on the mini-launcher, "up" translates to "left" and "down" to "right"). Rearrange the order to suit you.

Preferences, Site

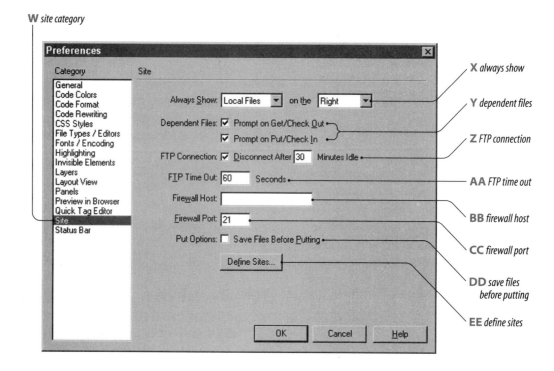

X *always show*

Y *dependent files*

Z *FTP connection*

AA *FTP time out*

BB *firewall host*

CC *firewall port*

DD *save files before putting*

EE *define sites*

W site category

Most Web site designers don't modify files directly on the Web servers where they will ultimately reside; instead, they modify files on a local computer and then periodically upload files to the "live" server once the pages all work properly (at least you hope so).

The **Site** category of the **Preferences** dialog box is where you supply Dreamweaver with information about how you want the **Site** window to look, when you want Dreamweaver to prompt you to transfer dependent files, and the computer-specific FTP and proxy server settings that apply globally to all sites you define on a given machine.

On the other hand, you make *site*-specific connection settings, such as remote access ID's and

passwords, in the **Define Sites** dialog box, which you can also access from the **Site** category of the **Preferences** via a handy button.

X always show

Here's an instance where you can see what happens when user interface designers get just a tad too clever. The left drop-down menu indicates whether you want the **Site** window to always show the local site or always show the remote site upon opening. This setting could stand on its own. The right drop-down menu, on the other hand, lets you specify whether you want the window that Dreamweaver always shows you to appear in the left window pane or the right one.

You might have figured that much out on your own, but here's another wrinkle. The site (local or remote) that's *not* selected in the left drop-down list can show a list of files or a map of the file structure. The site that does appear in the left drop-down menu can display only the file list. Got that?

Y dependent files

You have two check boxes in this area: **Prompt on Get/Check Out**, and **Prompt on Put/Check In**. The first deals with the situation when you are downloading a page, and the second deals with the upload scenario. When one of these boxes is checked, Dreamweaver will present a dialog box asking whether you want to include any dependent files when you up- or download a page. (Dependent files are, for example, templates, libraries, scripts, images, and styles to which the page you're transferring refers.) The factory default is for both to be checked, which is how I like to work. Most of the time, I decline the option when prompted, but sometimes I have modified one or more dependent files, and it's nice to let Dreamweaver select them instead of me having to do it.

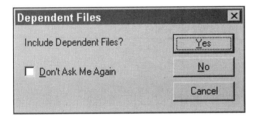

Z FTP connection

Check the box if you want Dreamweaver to disconnect an FTP (File Transfer Protocol) session that has been idle for the number of minutes you specify in the numeric field to the right.

> *tip* This feature is helpful for dial-up Internet users without an "unlimited use" plan, so that they don't connect to upload their site, forget to disconnect, and then needlessly run up their connection time.

AA FTP time out

This setting is completely different from the disconnect interval in (W). Here, you specify how long Dreamweaver should wait after querying a remote FTP host without getting a response, before popping up a dialog box alerting you that the remote system doesn't seem to be awake.

BB firewall host

Here's where you'd enter the *IP address* of the *proxy server* through which your computer connects to the remote Web server. (A proxy server, a term that you can take as synonymous with *firewall*, is a computer that limits the traffic that can pass back and forth between the public Internet and a private intranet (like most corporate networks). It's pretty risky to work without a firewall of some sort if you're on a local area network that connects to the Internet, but if your LAN doesn't have one, leave this field empty.

CC firewall port

Typically, you'd enter 21 here; that's the default port for the FTP protocol in the TCP/IP scheme of things. If your network administrator advises you differently, key in the number you're given.

> *tip* Just setting the firewall address and port here isn't enough. For each site, you also need to check the **Use Firewall (in Preferences)** box in the **Site Definition** dialog box's **Remote Info** category. Ask your network administrator if you should also check **Use Passive FTP** in the same dialog box.

DD save files before putting

Check this box if you want Dreamweaver to save any unsaved documents to disk before uploading them to the remote server. I can't think of a good reason why you wouldn't want this feature activated.

EE define sites

This little button opens the **Define Site** dialog box, which itself has several categories, specifying site details such as the root folder, remote access ID and password, and site name. Use the **Define Site** dialog box to set details on a site-by-site basis. For more details, see Define A Site in Chapter 10.

steps Redesign The Objects Panel

All through this book, you've seen that the quickest way to perform many Dreamweaver operations is to click icons in one of the various objects panels. After you spend some time working with Dreamweaver, you'll notice that you use some of these icons more than others. You'll also notice that some of the objects panels are really under-populated, like **Invisibles** and **Special**.

You can save yourself beaucoup time by redesigning the objects panel so that the **Common** category contains every command you use on a regular basis. In this example, you move the icons from the **Invisibles** and **Special** categories into the **Common** category and then delete the **Invisibles** and **Special** categories. Simplify, simplify.

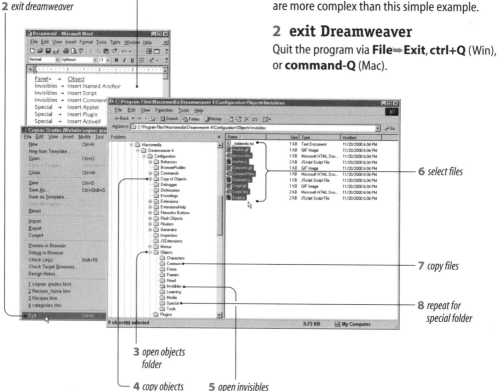

1 *make list*

2 *exit dreamweaver*

3 *open objects folder*

4 *copy objects folder*

5 *open invisibles folder*

6 *select files*

7 *copy files*

8 *repeat for special folder*

tip Your **Common** objects panel is likely to grow considerably if you follow the steps in this section. Heck, I know some people who put all their icons into the **Common** panel! If you have a two-monitor setup, you may find it handy to put the newly reconstructed panel on a second monitor, where it can be available at all times. You could also place the property inspector and all of your panels on this second monitor, leaving the primary monitor for the uncluttered current document.

1 make list

Take note of the icons you use in the various objects panels and make a list of them. The list should include the name of the icon and the panel on which it normally lives. Such a list guides you when moving files and folders to reconfigure the objects panel (3 through 10) and is especially useful if your needs are more complex than this simple example.

2 exit Dreamweaver

Quit the program via **File➞Exit**, **ctrl+Q** (Win), or **command-Q** (Mac).

3 open objects folder

Using your computer's file management facilities (such as Finder on the Mac, Windows Explorer on the PC), open the **Objects** folder. It typically lives in the main Dreamweaver program folder under the **Configuration** folder. The **Objects** folder has subfolders corresponding to each of the different specific objects panels.

4 copy objects folder

Before you make any changes, copy the entire **Objects** folder to another location. This way, you can copy it back if you decide you don't like your changes (or if you get a new computer and somebody else inherits yours!).

5 open invisibles folder

When you open the **Invisibles** folder, you'll see the support files for the **Anchor**, **Script**, and **Comment** icons. Each icon has three support files: a GIF graphic, an HTML file, and a JS (JavaScript) file. (Some other icons in the objects panels don't have the JS file, but all have GIF and HTML files.)

6 select files

Select all nine support files, for example, by dragging a rectangle around them. Do not select the file **_folderinfo.txt**, which contains the category name and ordered list of icons for the specific objects panel.

7 copy files

Copy the files to the **Common** folder under the **Objects** folder.

8 repeat for special folder

Repeat steps 5 through 7 for the **Special** folder.

9 modify _folderinfo.txt (optional)

In the **Common** folder, open the plain text file **_folderinfo.txt** in any text editor (Notepad, SimpleText, and so on). You can probably just double-click the file to fire up your computer's default text editor. The first line

of this file is the name of the panel (**Common**); any subsequent lines list the HTML filenames (no full paths, just the names of the files themselves) for each of the icons in that folder, in the order in which they will appear in the **Common** objects panel. You can rearrange these names, or add them, if they're not present, to define the order that you like best. When you're done, close the text editor and save the file with the same name.

10 delete invisibles & special folders

You don't need 'em anymore as you've moved their icons and support files to the **Common** folder.

11 reopen dreamweaver

The objects panel should still be on display from your last work session; if not, display it with **Window➞ Objects**. You should see a newly beefed-up **Common** category and no more **Invisibles** or **Special** categories.

> *tip* You can also add a new object that you create yourself. See Create An Object Extension on page 275 of Chapter 17 for details.

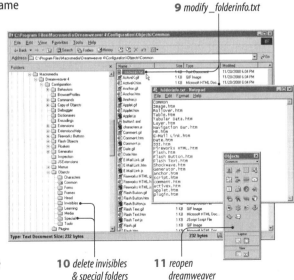

9 modify _folderinfo.txt

10 delete invisibles & special folders

11 reopen dreamweaver

The Configuration Folder

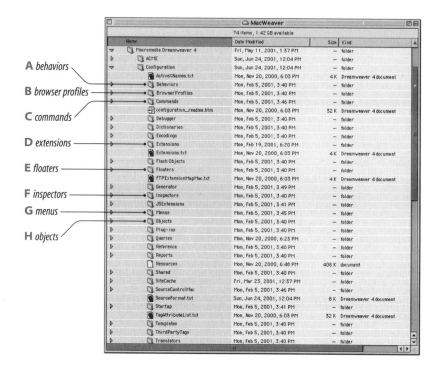

A *behaviors*

B *browser profiles*

C *commands*

D *extensions*

E *floaters*

F *inspectors*

G *menus*

H *objects*

The Dreamweaver program comes in two big chunks. One chunk is the monolithic file (**Dreamweaver.exe** on the PC, **Dreamweaver 4** on the Mac), which lives in the Dreamweaver program's main folder. (For example, on a Windows machine, the main folder would typically be **C:\Program Files\Dreamweaver 4**.) You can't change anything in **Dreamweaver.exe** unless you want to fire up a disk utility that edits files bit by bit—not something I'd ever recommend!

The other big chunk is the **Configuration** folder, directly beneath the main program folder in the directory hierarchy. You can change almost anything in this folder and in its various subfolders, although you should only modify JavaScript code if you have a solid knowledge of that programming language. This section presents a few of the folders beneath the **Configuration** folder and tells you what they contain.

> **tip** Be very, very careful when modifying files and folders inside the **Configuration** folder. One slip, and you could easily delete much of the code that Dreamweaver needs in order to launch and run correctly. You'd be very smart to back up the entire **Configuration** folder to another location before making any changes to it. By doing so, you give yourself a graceful fallback position in case you make a slip.

A behaviors

The **Behaviors** folder contains two subfolders, **Events** and **Actions**, that contain files describing 1) the events that various browsers can generate and 2) the Dreamweaver actions (generally JavaScript code) that you can have the program perform when a browser detects one of those events. Each action has an associated JavaScript file and an HTML file. You normally associate actions with events via the **Behaviors** panel and don't need to access files in the **Behaviors** folder, but if you're proficient in

JavaScript, you could write your own actions and place them in the **Actions** subfolder.

B browser profiles

The **BrowserProfiles** folder contains text files that the **File➡Check Target Browsers** command consults when determining whether the tags you use in a particular document receive support in a given browser. You'll add documents to this folder when updating Dreamweaver to support newer browser versions.

C commands

You might think that this folder would contain only commands that appear on the **Commands** menu, but it contains many more than that. Most of the commands that live here have an associated HTML file that specifies how the user interacts with the command's dialog box, and a JavaScript file that contains the code to execute the command.

D extensions

Here's where any extensions that you download from Macromedia Exchange, or other Dreamweaver-related Web sites, live after you install them; these files use the **MXI** format. (The downloaded extension packages in **MXP** format typically live in the **Downloaded Extensions** folder under the main program folder.)

E floaters

If you download (or write) code for custom floating panels, that code would appear in this folder.

F inspectors

You'll be disappointed if you think you can go to this folder and open files that will let you personalize the various property inspectors that are so much a part of Dreamweaver's user interface. This folder contains but a few inspectors; most of them live within the actual Dreamweaver program file and are out of the customizer's reach.

G menus

This hugely important folder hosts **menus.xml**, the file that defines Dreamweaver's menu structure. See The Menus.xml File on page 266 for details on personalizing program menus.

H objects

Here's where the files that support the myriad objects panels and their icons live. Subfolders of the **Objects** folder parallel the different objects panels you can select from the panel's pop-up menu. Again, this is such an important folder that I give it a two-page spread starting on page 260, in the section Redesign The Objects Panel.

Text Configuration Files

The **Configuration** folder contains a few text files that include customizable information. Here's a bit of info on some of the ones you may want to explore or change. You can modify them with a simple text editor, but, as always, make a backup first!

TagAttributeList.txt

The **Edit➡Find and Replace** command gets its list of specific tags and attributes from this file, which also feeds the Quick Tag Editor's hints menus.

SourceFormat.txt

This file stores settings you specify in the **Code Format** category of the **Preferences** dialog box, but you have to edit the file directly to change some of the tag-specific settings.

Extensions.txt

This file specifies which extensions Dreamweaver can open with the **File➡Open** command and which file format appears as the default type in the **File Open** dialog box.

If you're working with code files having a nonstandard file suffix, you should specify it here to let Dreamweaver list and open those files more conveniently than by choosing the **All Files** option in the dialog box.

ActiveXNames.txt

This file contains the list of ActiveX class identifiers, a list which feeds the **Class ID** menu in the ActiveX property inspector.

The Keyboard Shortcuts Command

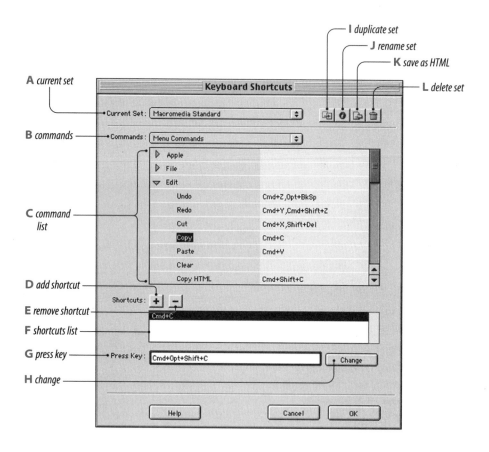

A *current set*

B *commands*

C *command list*

D *add shortcut*

E *remove shortcut*

F *shortcuts list*

G *press key*

H *change*

I *duplicate set*

J *rename set*

K *save as HTML*

L *delete set*

As you've figured out by now if you've read any chapters prior to this one, Dreamweaver makes extensive use of keyboard shortcuts for the benefit of those who use the product daily. Some of the shortcuts make sense, but many of them seem pretty arbitrary, and after you work with the program for awhile you're likely to want to redefine at least a few of these. You can do just that via the **Edit→Keyboard Shortcuts** command. In addition, you may want to load an entirely different *set* of shortcuts to make Dreamweaver work more like BBEdit, Dreamweaver 3, or HomeSite; you can do that with this command, too.

One of Dreamweaver's little ironies is that there is no keyboard shortcut for the **Edit→Keyboard Shortcuts** command.

tip I've occasionally run into problems with this command; especially on a system where the **menus.xml** file has been customized, you may see a JavaScript error and the shortcut data may refuse to load. If that happens, my experience is that the shortcuts usually load properly if you try the command again. Also, be aware that Dreamweaver often takes a few seconds to load the keyboard shortcut data after you select **Edit→Keyboard Shortcuts**. Give it some time, and if the dialog box doesn't show up 30 seconds or so, press **esc** and try again.

A current set

The **Current Set** menu does two things: It displays the current set of keyboard shortcuts, and it lets you select a different set if you'd rather work with shortcuts that feel more like the ones used in Dreamweaver 3, BBEdit, or HomeSite. This pop-up menu will also show any custom sets you (or someone working on your computer) may have set up in the past.

> **tip** Choosing a different shortcut set usually causes the program to pause for a few seconds. This is normal.

B commands

Start your keyboard shortcut editing session at the **Commands** pop-up menu, which lets you pick a command category from the following list: **Menu Commands**, **Site Menu Commands**, **Code Editing**, **Document Editing**, and **Site Window**.

C command list

In this large central list area, Dreamweaver displays the commands associated with the category you select in (B). If you chose **Menu Commands** or **Site Menu Commands**, you'll see a hierarchy that you must expand by clicking the + symbols in order to see actual commands and their related shortcuts.

D add shortcut

If you want to add a shortcut to a command, first highlight it in the command list (C) and then click the + button to tell Dreamweaver you want to make a new shortcut. You then type the shortcut into the **Press Key** field (G) and click the **Change** button (H). If you don't get that far and you see the error message shown here, you must duplicate the current set and give it a new name, because the program maintains the integrity of the original shortcut sets in case you ever need or want to return to them.

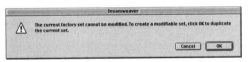

> **tip** You can enter up to two keyboard shortcuts per command, although I don't usually recommend defining more than one.

E remove shortcut

The – button will remove the currently highlighted shortcut in the shortcuts list (F).

F shortcuts list

Here's the list of shortcuts defined for the currently highlighted command in the command list (C).

G press key

You can type a new shortcut when the **Press Key** field is activated, and you'll see your keystrokes mirrored on screen. If you type a shortcut that already exists in the set, Dreamweaver warns you of the fact, but you can continue if the existing shortcut is one that you don't use.

H change

When you're happy with the new shortcut, click the **Change** button to make it take effect.

I duplicate set

You'll need to click this button before you can make any customizations. Pick a set and duplicate it, giving it a new and descriptive name. Then edit the shortcuts in that duplicate set to customize Dreamweaver's shortcuts. You can always go back to the original set.

J rename set

Click this button to rename the currently highlighted shortcut set.

K save as HTML

I love this command. It saves the current set (which can be your customized set) to an HTML table, which you can then open in Dreamweaver or in a browser window, print, and laminate to keep by your computer until you've memorized all the shortcuts you use frequently.

L delete set

If you want to delete an entire shortcut set, click this trash-can icon, but bear in mind that the program won't let you delete one of the original sets, only the one that you've created in order to create your own customizations.

The Menus.xml File

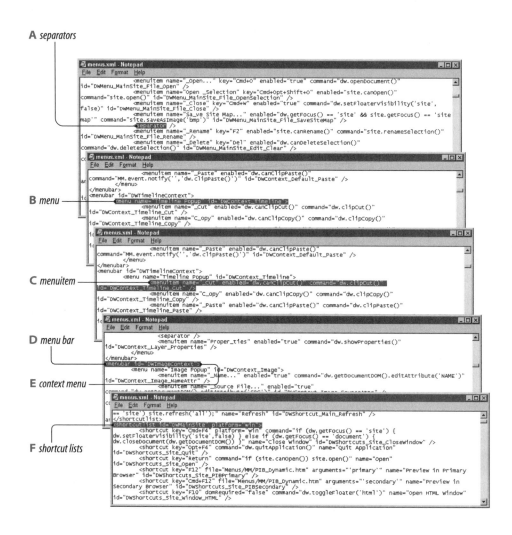

A separators

B menu

C menuitem

D menu bar

E context menu

F shortcut lists

Dreamweaver lets you personalize its menu structure as well as its keyboard shortcuts. However, because Macromedia doesn't think many of you will want to do this, the company has not provided a user-friendly interface for changing menus around, as it has for changing keyboard shortcuts. Menu modifications require loading **menus.xml** (which resides in the Configuration\Menus folder under the Dreamweaver program folder) into a text editor, such as Notepad, HomeSite, or BBEdit, and performing surgery on that file.

tip Always, always make a backup copy of **menus.xml** before modifying it directly. Dreamweaver keeps a backup of the file in the **Menus** folder, but that copy isn't likely to be recent. This file is very dense, and it's extremely easy to make a mistake that could render an entire menu invisible. If you're reading this page because you made such a mistake and want to get out of the woods, your options are two: Get a good copy of **menus.xml** from another machine or reinstall Dreamweaver.

A separators

Don't like those annoying horizontal lines dividing up sections of your menus? Get rid of them by deleting the **<separator />** tags. Or, if you love them and want more, add **<separator />** between two **<menuitem>** tags.

B menu

The **<menu></menu>** tag pair surrounds a menu definition, not just for a top-level menu such as **File** or **Edit** but also for *submenus* such as **File→ Import** and for *context menus* such as the **Time- lines** panel menu (accessible via the right-arrow at the panel's upper right corner). The **<menu>** tag has at least two attributes: **name** and **id**. Macromedia urges you not to edit the **id** attribute, which other parts of the program (scripts and so on) expect to stay constant, but you can certainly change the name of a menu, if you want.

> *tip* Notice the underscore character, which pre- cedes the letter in the menu name that will appear with an underline in Windows for hotkey purposes.

C menuitem

The **<menuitem />** tag and its attributes (again, don't monkey with **id**) define a menu item—that is, a "leaf node" in the menu hierarchy. To remove an item from a menu, first find it in **menus.xml** (don't forget the underscore when you're searching) and then delete the enclosing **<menuitem />** tag. To rename it, change the **name** attribute. You'll see various other attributes for this tag, including key, which specifies the command's keyboard shortcut, and enabled, which specifies whether the item should appear active or dimmed (inactive).

> *tip* If you just want to delete the menu entry for a personalized command that you create with the **History** panel, see page 270's section, The Edit Command List Command, for an easier method than editing **menus.xml**.

You can copy a menu item from one location to another by highlighting the **<menuitem />** tag, including all its attributes, cutting the selection with **Edit→Cut**, clicking the cursor at the new location (which must be inside a **<menu></menu>** tag pair), and choosing **Edit→Paste**.

D menu bar

A *menu bar* is one or more menus grouped in a stand-alone bar. For example, the main Dreamweaver menu bar consists of the menus **File**, **Edit**, **View**, **Insert**, and so on. Each context menu has its own separate menu bar, although context menu bars typically consist only of a single menu. Menu bars appear in **menus.xml** bracketed by the tag pair **<menubar>** and **</menubar>**. Each menu bar tag pair must contain at least one menu tag pair.

E context menus

menus.xml contains complete definitions of actions in the context menu of every floating panel and every object type. For example, the context menu for the "image" object resides after the **<menubar id="DWImageContext">** tag and would appear when you right-click (Win) or **control**-click (Mac) an image in the document window. You can also change these menus around to your liking, deleting and adding menu items and renaming menu items so that they're more convenient for you.

F shortcut lists

The top half of **menus.xml** contains several sets of shortcut lists, each surrounded by the tag pair **<shortcutlist></shortcutlist>**. While you can change keyboard shortcuts here, by modifying the **key** attributes, it's easier and safer to change key- board shortcuts with the keyboard shortcut editor (see The Keyboard Shortcuts Command on page 264).

> *tip* If you use Dreamweaver to edit **menus. xml** in code view or the **Code Inspector**, you must close Dreamweaver and restart it before you will see your changes take effect.

One of the best things about computer software is that it can save you time when you need to perform repetitive actions. Today's applications typically offer a macro record-and-playback feature, a macro being a logically related series of steps to perform a common action. Happily, Dreamweaver is no exception.

You can define your own personal macros and save them as new commands with the help of the **History** panel. The only caveat is that Dreamweaver is unable to record certain commands, nor is it able to record motions you make with the mouse (such as drag and drop operations). You'll see a black line or a red X in the **History** panel whenever you do something that Dreamweaver can't record.

> **tip** Always try using keyboard equivalents of mouse operations, such as arrow keys. Dreamweaver can record most keyboard operations. There are still a few it doesn't understand, unfortunately; the only advice I can give is use trial-and-error to discover which ones work.

In this example, which presumes that you have a document already open, you create a macro to make a raised initial cap—that is, an initial letter in a paragraph with a larger point size and bold, colored formatting.

1 open history panel

Choose the command **Window➡History**, or press **shift+F10** for the shortcut. Doing so causes the **History** panel to create a new line every time you perform an action in the document window.

> **tip** Don't confuse creating a command by using the **History** panel with creating a command via the **Commands➡Start Recording** command. The latter is only useful for creating an unsaved command that you never intend to use in the future.

2 click in first line

Click anywhere in the first line of the paragraph you want to format with a drop cap.

1 *open history panel*

2 *click in first line*

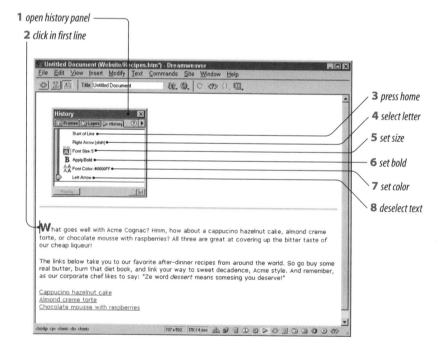

3 *press home*

4 *select letter*

5 *set size*

6 *set bold*

7 *set color*

8 *deselect text*

3 press home

Tap the **home** key to move the insertion point to the beginning of the line. The reason to do things this way is to make it easier for you in the future. You can invoke the **Raised Initial Cap** command after clicking anywhere in the first line of the paragraph, because the macro will automatically move the insertion point to the start of the line.

4 select letter

The way to select a single letter from the keyboard is to press **shift** and click the right-arrow key one time.

5 set size

Choose **Text⟶Size⟶5** from the menu to set the drop cap size. You could also make the size setting via the **Text** property inspector, if you have it open.

6 set bold

Press **ctrl+B** (Win) or **command-B** (Mac) to set the bold attribute. It would also be okay to perform this task via the property inspector or by choosing **Text⟶Style⟶Bold**.

7 set color

Choose **Text⟶Color** and click a nice blue from the color picker.

8 deselect text

Tap the left arrow key to deselect the text. This is the final step in your macro, completing the sequence of steps in the **History** panel that you will select and save as a new command.

9 click start of line

In the **History** panel, scroll up and click the **Start of Line** item, corresponding to step 3. This is the first command in your macro sequence.

10 shift-click left arrow

Scroll down in the command list and **shift**-click the **Left Arrow**

command, corresponding to step (8). This operation selects all the intervening commands.

11 click save as command icon

The lower right of the **History** panel sports a disk icon that saves your selected steps as a command. It's the equivalent to the panel's context menu command **Save As Command**, just faster.

12 name command

Give your command a descriptive name ("Raised Initial Cap" in this example) and click **OK**. The new command will appear at the bottom of the **Commands** menu. Try it out on another paragraph in the document by clicking in the paragraph's first line and choosing **Commands⟶RaisedInitialCap**.

> *tip* Use your file management utility to see the new file, **RaisedInitialCap.htm**, in the **Configuration\Commands** folder. Open the HTML file in Dreamweaver or any text editor to see the JavaScript code that Dreamweaver generated to create the command.

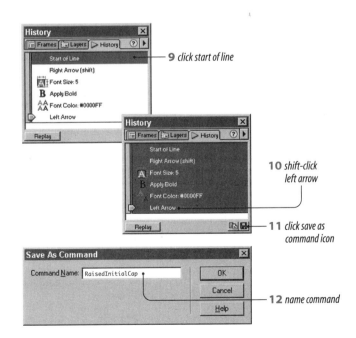

9 *click start of line*

10 *shift-click left arrow*

11 *click save as command icon*

12 *name command*

The Edit Command List Command

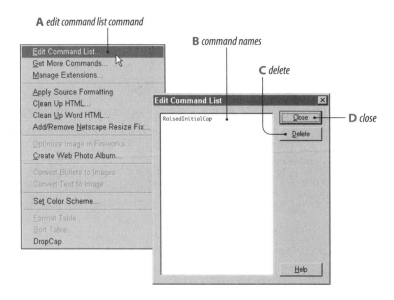

A *edit command list command*

B *command names*

C *delete*

D *close*

If you create a command using the **History** panel, as described in the preceding section, but you later decide you'd like to delete it, you can do so with **Edit Command List**.

A edit command list command
Choose **Commands➡Edit Command List**. The **Edit Command List** dialog box appears.

B command names
In the main part of the dialog box with the white background, Dreamweaver displays the list of commands that have been defined by users on the computer you're using. The "standard" elements that appear on the **Commands** menu after a clean installation of Dreamweaver aren't available on this list.

You can rename a command by clicking its name, waiting a couple of moments, and then clicking again to position the text-editing cursor at the command name.

> *tip* To rename or delete standard Dreamweaver commands, you need to edit the **menus.xml** file located in the **Configuration\Menus** folder inside the Dreamweaver program folder. See The Menus.xml File on pages 266 and 267 for complete details.

C delete
Click a command to highlight it and then click the **Delete** button to remove the command and its associated code.

> *tip* I don't like deleting commands that I've created, even if I don't expect to use them again. The moment you make that assumption, a situation will arise when you'll wish you'd kept the code.
>
> A simple solution is to locate the HTML file corresponding to the command you want to take off the **Commands** menu; it'll reside in the **Configuration\Commands** folder under the main Dreamweaver program folder. Now, just rename it, for example from **raisedinitialcap.htm** to **raisedinitialcap.sav**. Because it no longer has the HTM extension, it won't appear in the **Commands** menu, but you can still resurrect the file easily be changing its extension back to HTM.

D close
Click the **Close** button to close the dialog box.

chapter 17

Extend Dreamweaver

Extending a program (as opposed to customizing it) means adding software that gives the program new or enhanced capabilities. Happily, Macromedia has designed Dreamweaver to be highly extensible by independent programmers. Many such programmers have shared the fruits of their labors with the public, either freely or for a fee.

Most of this chapter focuses on how to stretch Dreamweaver's feature set with publicly available extensions. These extensions include behaviors, commands, objects, translators, and property inspectors.

If you happen to program in JavaScript or C, then you can create your own extensions, either for your own use or for sharing. This chapter won't teach you how to write such code, but it will introduce you to the Dreamweaver programming interfaces and provide hints about the possibilities that are open to you.

271

The Extension Manager

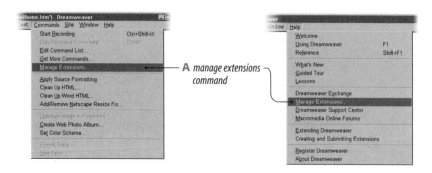

A *manage extensions command*

B *install new extension* C *remove extension* D *program selector* E *macromedia exchange* F *help* G *extension list*

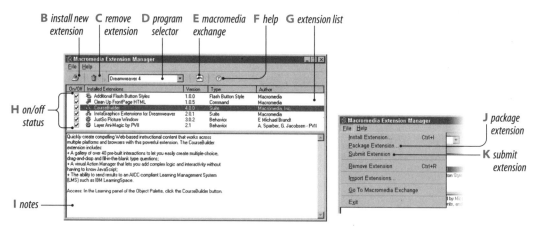

H *on/off status*

I *notes*

J *package extension*

K *submit extension*

The **Extension Manager**, a.k.a. *Package Manager* (Macromedia documentation uses both terms interchangeably), is the tool you use to keep track of extensions you download and/or create. Unlike previous versions of Dreamweaver, Version 4 doesn't make you download the **Extension Manager** as a separate tool: It's part of the package you install from CD. (Don't believe the user manual if it advises otherwise!)

A manage extensions command

One way to open the **Extension Manager** is to choose **Commands➡Manage Extensions**. Another way is to choose the **Manage Extensions** command from the **Help** menu. This command appears in a group along with related commands: **Dreamweaver Exchange**, **Dreamweaver Support Forum**, and **Macromedia Online Forums**.

tip To reduce redundancy in the user interface, you may want to remove one of the two **Manage Extensions** commands. (I removed the one on the **Commands** menu, because the one on the **Help** menu lives next to three related commands; another good approach is to move the three related commands from the **Help** menu to the **Commands** menu and group them with the **Manage Extensions** command there.) See The Menus.xml File on page 266 of Chapter 16 for details on how to edit Menus.xml to accomplish this task; look for the string _Manage Extensions... in that file.

B install new extension

This toolbar button brings up the **Select Extension To Install** dialog box, where you navigate to the extension you want to add. Alternatively, you can choose **File➡Install Extension** from the **Exten-sion Manager** menu bar or press **ctrl+I** (Win) or **command-I** (Mac).

To use this command, you must have one or more extensions files (*.MXP) on an accessible local or network drive, preferably on the local drive in the **Downloaded Extensions** folder under the main Dreamweaver program folder.

C remove extension

Click this button to remove the extension that shows as selected in the extension list (G). You can also choose **File➡Remove Extension** or press **ctrl+R** (Win) or **command-R** (Mac).

When you remove an extension, you physically remove its code from your hard drive, as opposed to merely disabling it (H).

D program selector

Use this pop-up menu to select the Macromedia program for which you want to manage extensions. For example, if you have Flash installed on the same computer, you can choose that program to manage Flash extensions from the same interface.

E macromedia exchange

Click this button or choose **File➡Go To Macrome-dia Exchange** to open a browser window pointing to the Macromedia Exchange for Dreamweaver Web site, *www.macromedia.com/exchange/dreamweaver/*. You can download extensions from this Web site (see Download & Install An Extension on page 276). You must have an Internet connection to use this command.

F help

As in many other Dreamweaver dialog boxes, the question mark opens the context-sensitive Help system.

G extension list

The upper window is the *extension list*, where the name of each installed extension appears along with its version number, type, and author. You can sort

extensions in the list by clicking a column header, such as **Type**.

H on/off status

The check boxes in this column indicate whether the extension is active. An extension must be active for you to use it. However, if you don't want to use an extension for a given project but you want to keep it around for the future, you can clear the status check box to disable the extension without deleting it from your hard drive. If you really want to delete it, use the **Remove Extension** command (C).

I notes

The lower window is the notes area, where you can view more details about the extension, such as what it does and where to learn more about it. You must click an extension in the extension list (G) to see notes about it.

J package extension

If you're a programmer and you've created a cool extension, the menu command **File➡Package Extension** tells Dreamweaver to look at your exten-sion installation file, which has the type *.MXI, and create a package suitable for submitting to Macro-media. The details are beyond the scope of this book, but at this writing, you can get details for creating an MXI file at *download.macromedia.com/pub/exchange/mxi_file_format.pdf*.

K submit extension

After you've created an extension package (J), upload it to Macromedia's Dreamweaver Exchange by choos-ing this command, which requires a connection to the Internet.

> *tip* If you're developing extensions, you should consider signing up for the Macromedia Dreamweaver Extensibility Newsgroup. Point your browser to www.macromedia.com/support/dreamweaver/extend/form and fill out the appli-cation for membership. Macromedia will e-mail you the URL and password.

Types of Extensions

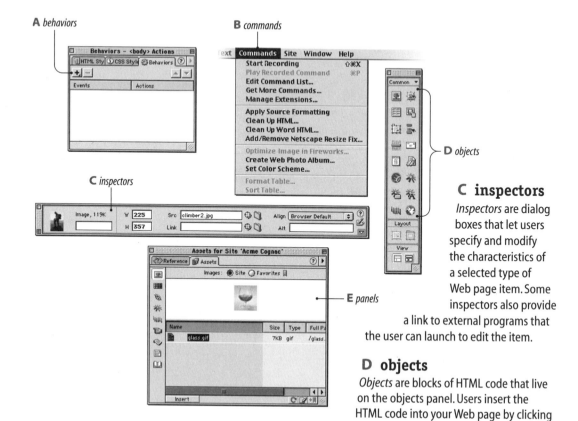

A *behaviors*

B *commands*

C *inspectors*

D *objects*

E *panels*

C inspectors

Inspectors are dialog boxes that let users specify and modify the characteristics of a selected type of Web page item. Some inspectors also provide a link to external programs that the user can launch to edit the item.

D objects

Objects are blocks of HTML code that live on the objects panel. Users insert the HTML code into your Web page by clicking the panel icon representing the object. You can generate object extensions even if you're not a programmer (see Create An Object Extension on page 275). Object extensions live in **Configuration/Objects/ <subfolder>**, where <subfolder> is the specific objects panel into which you want to add the new object.

E panels

Panels provide information about the current document or site. These contain HTML and JavaScript. Panel extension files reside in the **Configuration/ Floaters** folder.

F translators

Translators can convert certain types of non-HTML code into HTML, prevent Dreamweaver from attempting to interpret the HTML as it would "normal" HTML, or control how this code appears in the Document window in design view.

This page lists the different specific types of extensions that you can download (or create) for Dreamweaver 4.

A behaviors

Behaviors are actions that happen as a result of a browser event, such as a user moving the cursor over a graphic. These live in the **Configuration/ Behaviors/Actions** folder; you access them via the + button in the **Behaviors** panel.

B commands

A *command* is a menu item that fires up a JavaScript program. Commands that appear on the **Com- mands** menu have extension files that reside in the **Configuration/Commands** folder; modify MENUS.XML if you want the command to appear on a different menu.

Create An Object Extension

Some extensions are easier to create than others. Nonprogrammers can create a type of extension called the *object*, which is a simple chunk of HTML code used often enough to warrant placing it onto the objects panel. This example shows you how to create a "designed by" section that you may want to place on Web sites that you build. Because you'd use this section of code in multiple sites, you may prefer to make it a Dreamweaver object rather than a library item, given that library items are site-specific.

1 create HTML

Open a new document and create a chunk of HTML that you'd like to turn into a new object. This example is a simple text heading.

2 switch to code view

Click the **Code View** toolbar icon or choose **View➡ Code** to switch to code view.

3 prune default tags

Remove the default tags that Dreamweaver normally adds to all new documents (html, head, and body) to leave only the code that you want in your new object.

4 save file

Choose **File➡Save**, name the HTML file, and save it into the folder corresponding to the objects panel where you'd like the new object to appear.

5 create icon

Using your favorite image editor, create an 18x18-pixel GIF file to use as the icon for your new object. Give the file the same name as the HTML file (except the suffix) and save it to the same folder. (If you want it to look cool, give it a gray background like all the other panel icons have.)

6 test object

Restart Dreamweaver and test your new object to make sure that it works just as you want it to. (Your new object also appears at the bottom of the **Insert** menu, in addition to the objects panel.)

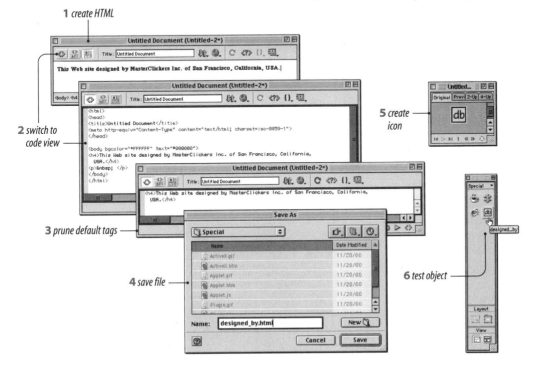

steps Download & Install An Extension

Downloading and installing a Dreamweaver extension is a lot easier than it used to be. For one thing, you already have instant access to the **Extension Manager**, a component that you had to download separately in earlier versions of Dreamweaver. For another, Macromedia provides a convenient online clearinghouse, **Macromedia Exchange For Dreamweaver**, that provides access to hundreds of extensions in one well-organized location.

1 connect to exchange for dreamweaver

I can think of at least six ways to connect to the **Macromedia Exchange For Dreamweaver** Web site. You can point your browser to the site directly (it's *www.macromedia.com/exchange/ dreamweaver/*). Within Dreamweaver, you can choose

Commands➡Get More Commands or **Help➡ Dreamweaver Exchange** or **Insert➡Get More Objects**. You can also open the **Behaviors** panel, click the **+** icon, and choose **Get More Behaviors**. Finally, you can use **File➡Go To Macromedia Exchange**.

2 search name/category/criteria

The Web site provides several different ways to navigate its contents. You can search for a particular name or key word using the **Search Extensions** field, browse by category using the pop-up menu, or click **Advanced Search** to specify a combination of very specific search criteria.

3 click download arrow

Once you find the extension you want, click the relevant download arrow for a Windows or Macintosh system. If

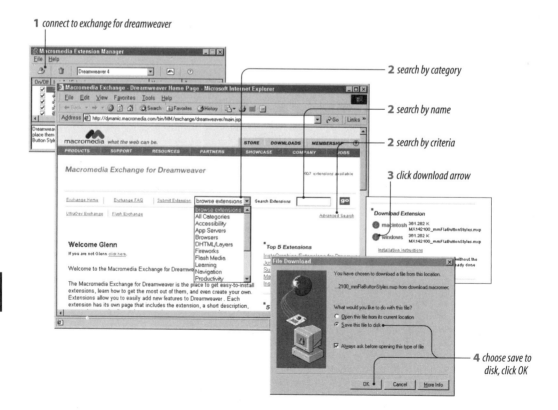

1 *connect to exchange for dreamweaver*

2 *search by category*

2 *search by name*

2 *search by criteria*

3 *click download arrow*

4 *choose save to disk, click OK*

you get a message telling you that you must be logged in to download an extension, then you need to create an account for yourself on the Exchange site; the site provides full instructions for doing so.

4 choose save to disk, click OK

In the **File Download** dialog box that may appear (depending on your browser), always choose **Save This File To Disk** rather than **Open This File From Its Current Location**. You want to have the extension package (of type *.MXP) on your hard drive should you ever need to reinstall it. Then click **OK**, which brings up the **Save As** dialog box.

5 specify location, click save

The normal procedure is to save extensions in the **Downloaded Extensions** folder in the Dreamweaver program folder. Use a consistent location in any case. The exact steps depend on your browser and platform.

6 install extension

Click back to Dreamweaver and the **Extension Manager**, where you can now install the

downloaded package by clicking the **Install New Extension** toolbar button or by pressing **ctrl+I** (**command-O** on the Mac).

7 select extension

Navigate to the folder you specified in step 5 and double-click the extension you want to install.

8 accept legalese

If you see a dialog box of legal jargon, read it and click the **Accept** button if it seems reasonable.

9 read notes

After Dreamweaver has installed the extension, read any notes that appear about it in the **Extension Manager**'s lower window.

10 reload extensions

Finally, you can either exit and relaunch Dreamweaver, or (to save a minute or two) **ctrl-click** (Win) or **option-click** (Mac) the drop-down menu on the objects panel and choose **Reload Extensions**.

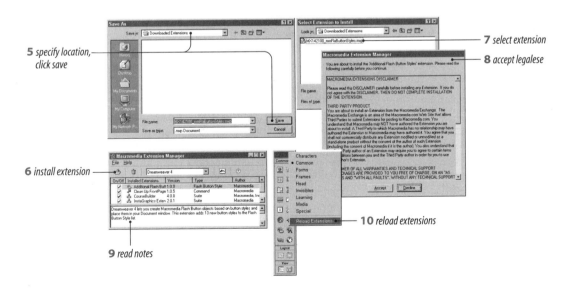

5 specify location, click save

7 select extension

8 accept legalese

6 install extension

10 reload extensions

9 read notes

The Dreamweaver API

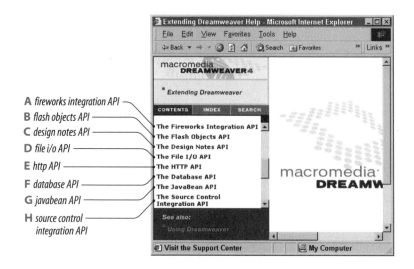

A *fireworks integration API*
B *flash objects API*
C *design notes API*
D *file i/o API*
E *http API*
F *database API*
G *javabean API*
H *source control integration API*

An *API*, or *Application Programming Interface*, is a specification detailing how a programmer can make things happen within a certain software environment. For example, the Dreamweaver API lists all the commands and syntax necessary for a programmer to create a property inspector, menu command, or behavior that will work happily within Dreamweaver, just like the built-in inspectors, commands, and behaviors.

The starting point for the Dreamweaver API is the *Document Object Model*, or *DOM*. This API is a standard adopted by the *World Wide Web Consortium* (known as *W3C*). However, Macromedia has dramatically extended the DOM API by providing over 400 additional JavaScript functions that programmers can use in designing Dreamweaver extensions.

So, the Dreamweaver API consists primarily of the JavaScript API. However, the Dreamweaver API also includes several "mini-APIs" that list built-in commands for specific situations. These include the following:

A Fireworks integration API

Fireworks integration is a significant feature in Dreamweaver 4, and the FWLaunch library lets

the developer perform actions such as switch to Dreamweaver, switch to Fireworks, execute a script in Fireworks, launch an image optimization session in Fireworks from Dreamweaver, and determine whether a specific version of Fireworks exists on the user's machine.

B flash objects API

Two of the cooler features in Dreamweaver 4, **Insert Flash Text** and **Insert Flash Button**, use the *Flash Objects API*. The provided commands let you define parameters for a Generator template (Generator is a tool for automating the creation of Flash content) and create a new Flash file based on that template and those parameters.

C design notes API

Design Notes enable and enhance collaborative Web design projects by providing files in which developers can write and read comments about their work. Macromedia built a shared C library (see JavaScript & C on the following page) called *MMNotes* that contains commands for opening, closing, reading, and writing Design Notes files. Dreamweaver includes a JavaScript API for MMNotes in addition to the C API, so that extension developers can easily access these functions.

D file i/o API

The shared library that contains file input/output commands is written in C and called *DWFile*. This library contains commands for creating, removing, reading, and writing files and folders, as well as for detecting file attributes.

E HTTP API

Need to communicate with a remote Web server in the extension you're writing? The *HTTP API* contains commands to let you do so. These commands typically take a URL as a parameter and return both a status code and a data result. You can retrieve a file from a remote Web server and save it onto the local disk. You can also retrieve a text document and even post form-encoded data to a Web site.

F database API

Integrating Web sites with back-end databases is a hot topic these days as organizations try to provide customers and vendors with more, and more useful, online transaction options. An important element of the Dreamweaver API is the *database API*, which lets developers work with server-hosted SQL (*Structured Query Language*) databases while creating Web-based database applications. This API, which requires Macromedia's companion Dreamweaver Ultradev product, includes functions to get details of a database's structure; establish an authenticated connection to a database; and retrieve the results of a SQL query.

G JavaBean API

This API (which also requires Dreamweaver Ultradev) provides JavaBeans support. (JavaBeans are software components very much like Java applets.)

H source control integration API

Dreamweaver 4 offers connectivity with so-called *source control systems*, programs (such as Microsoft's Visual SourceSafe) that help developers manage multiple versions of the code necessary to run one or more large Web sites. Once you specify that you want to use an SCS, via the Site Definition dialog box, you can use Dreamweaver's file transfer features to upload content to the SCS database. This API lets developers access source control systems that Dreamweaver supports and define an interface to systems that Dreamweaver does not support "out of the box."

JavaScript & C

So what are these languages, and how are they different?

C is a full-fledged programming language that lets the programmer perform just about any imaginable task on the computer. For example, Microsoft Windows is written in C. Programmers create C *source code* and then *compile* it, or translate it, into machine-readable code that the computer can execute. Big software projects often use C or one of its variants.

JavaScript, on the other hand, is a more limited programming language, called a *scripting* language. You can't do certain things with JavaScript that you can do with C

(for example, read a file from the disk). Another difference is that JavaScript is *interpreted* rather than compiled. That means that the computer reads each line of JavaScript and then interprets its intention.

Think of a C program as a translated book, which is ready to read in its entirety, while a JavaScript program is like a live speech at the United Nations, which a person has to translate sentence by sentence in real time. JavaScript is better suited for smaller and more specialized programs than C.

So say that you're a developer and you want to create a Dreamweaver extension that needs the

capabilities of the C language. What you'd do is to create a function in C that does what you need the C language to do. Then you'd compile that function and save it on disk in a file. (Incidentally, this is just what Macromedia did with its shared C library *DWfile*, which provides a number of general-purpose file I/O commands.) Finally, you'd write a JavaScript program that called upon the C function when necessary. This method works because JavaScript programs can execute functions written in C. Macromedia calls this ability *C-level extensibility* and if you want to know more about it, check out **Help➡Extending Dreamweaver**.

Third-Party Image Filters

Those of you who use the Dreamweaver/ Fireworks studio, Macromedia's Web and graphic design bundle, can extend this dynamic duo's graphics ability by adding third-party filters to Fireworks. Such extensions are a real boon, as Fireworks doesn't ship with many filters—you get bevels, embosses, drop shadows, and blurs, but not

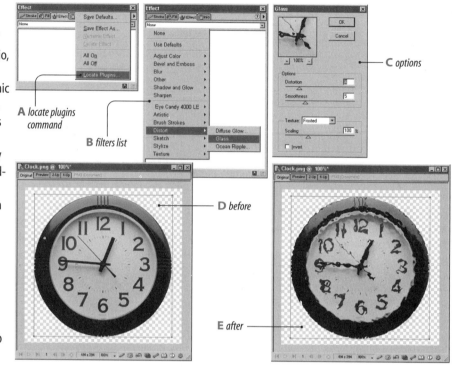

A *locate plugins command*

B *filters list*

C *options*

D *before*

E *after*

much more. The third-party filters that you add to Fireworks become available whenever you edit a Web page image from within Dreamweaver.

A locate plugins command

If you have Adobe Photoshop Version 5.0 or earlier, just open Fireworks, open the Effect panel, click the arrow to open the pop-up menu, choose **Locate Plugins**, and navigate to your Photoshop plugins folder. You have to exit and restart Fireworks for the program to find the filters.

> *tip* This method works with Photoshop Version 5.0 and earlier but not with Version 6.0, at which point Adobe changed its filter format.

Many Photoshop-compatible filters from companies other than Adobe also work in Fireworks. Examples are Kai's Power Tools, sold by Corel, and Xenofex and Eye Candy 4000, from Alien Skin Software.

B filters list

To apply a third-party filter to an image, simply open the image in Fireworks, select an area to modify, and select a filter from the drop-down list in the Effects panel. If you see a dialog box (C), choose your options and click **OK** to apply them.

C options

Depending on the filter you choose, you may see an options dialog box, and you may not. The contents of the dialog box vary depending on the filter, too. The example shown applies to the **Glass** filter from Photoshop.

D before

Here's an image before applying the **Glass** special effect.

E after

Here's the same image after applying **Glass**.

The Instagraphics Extensions

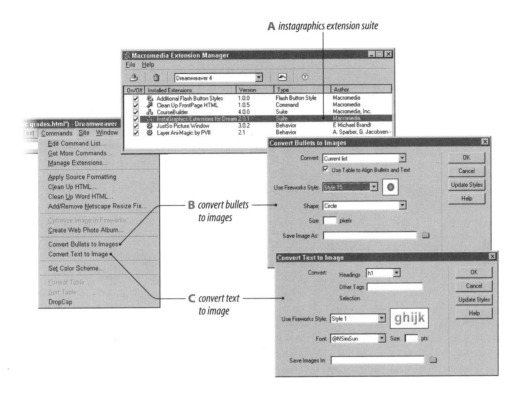

A *instagraphics extension suite*

B *convert bullets to images*

C *convert text to image*

To start you on your way toward discovering the nifty things that extensions can do for you, I mention some that I've found very useful. The first provides handy commands for metamorphosing text objects into more interesting graphical ones and is available at Macromedia Exchange for Dreamweaver as I write this.

A instagraphics extension suite

After you install this extension, it appears as a "suite" in the **Type** column. Suites contain multiple commands; this one includes two of special interest (B and C).

B convert bullets to images

This command converts a boring old unordered list into a table containing jazzy graphical buttons and aligned text. You can choose from 30 different button styles and 10 different shapes. The command is **Commands⇒Convert Bullets To Images**.

C convert text to image

The **Convert Text To Image** command on the **Commands** menu enables you to convert a selected block of text to a graphic. You can specify a Fireworks style and font to create a GIF file from the selected text. Although your formatting choices are wider if you create a GIF image containing text via an image editing program like Fireworks or Photoshop, I don't know of a quicker way than this extension to create a reasonably good-looking GIF file containing text you specify.

> **tip** Speaking of graphics, another great extension I just had to squeeze in here is *Additional Flash Button Styles*. After installing it, click the Flash Buttons icon on the Common Objects panel to display the Insert Flash Button dialog box. The new buttons that the extension installs appear in the list of styles.

The CourseBuilder Extension

A *insert coursebuilder interaction*   B *multiple choice dialog box*   C *drag & drop dialog box*

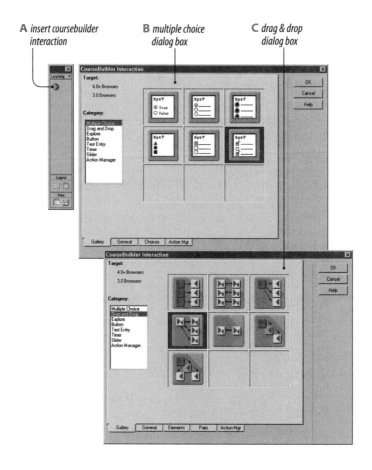

A good example of an incredibly deep extension is Macromedia's own free *CourseBuilder for Dreamweaver*, which helps you create an instructional Web site suitable for distance learning.

> **tip** After you install CourseBuilder via the Extension Manager, you must exit and restart Dreamweaver.

A insert CourseBuilder interaction
Get to CourseBuilder via this new icon on the also-new **Learning Objects** panel.

B multiple choice dialog box
If you click **Multiple Choice** in the **Category** list after clicking the **Insert CourseBuilder**

Interaction icon on the **Learning Objects** panel, you can see a variety of styles that CourseBuilder can create to place a multiple-choice question onto your Web page. Once you choose a style on the **Gallery** tab, you can define details of the question (text of choices, time delays, actions to perform based on user input) on the **General** and **Choices** tabs.

C drag & drop dialog box
Another example of a CourseBuilder object is a drag and drop area, in which the user interacts with the Web page by dragging and dropping one or more graphics onto a designated target area. Display the possible styles by clicking **Drag and Drop** in the **Category** list. Click on a style and then define its details on the **General**, **Elements**, and **Pairs** tabs.

Essential Shortcuts

Every time your hand has to leave the keyboard and grab the mouse, you lose a couple of seconds. Fortunately, Dreamweaver provides a wide variety of timesaving shortcuts that let you perform many operations directly from the keyboard.

Some of Dreamweaver's keyboard shortcuts are likely to be familiar. For example, **ctrl+S** (Win) or **command-S** (Mac) saves the current document, just as it does in most Windows and Macintosh applications. Dreamweaver also offers many program-specific shortcuts that you may want to learn if you're a frequent weaver.

This chapter presents many standard Dreamweaver keyboard shortcuts. You're likely to use some shortcuts so often that you'll want to commit them to memory—such as the keys that display panels, choose common menu commands, and modify tables. For all the others, you can let this chapter be your handy reference (the program manual and online help aren't always correct). If you want to use a different set of shortcuts, or even make your own, check out The Keyboard Shortcuts Command on page 264 in Chapter 16.

Panel Shortcuts

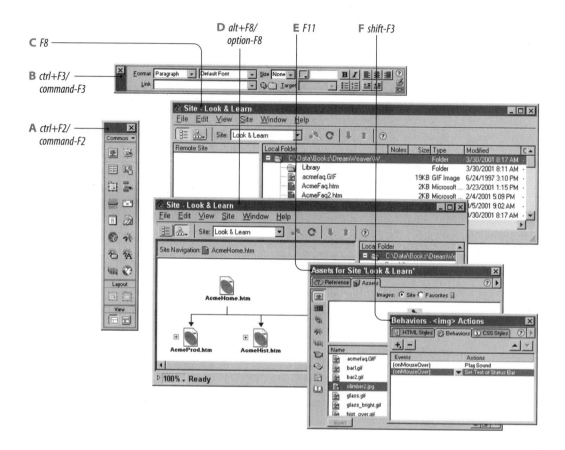

The handiest keyboard shortcuts by far in Dreamweaver are those that let you display or hide the program's many panels. As you work with the program, you'll come to appreciate the value of having several panels open at once — and the value of navigating between them quickly.

These shortcuts (all of which, by the way, appear on the **Window** menu) behave differently depending on what's on screen. If a panel isn't open, then the shortcut displays it and puts it on top of any other open panels or documents. If a panel is open, but it's not on top, then the shortcut puts it on top. Finally, if a panel is open and on top of the stack, then the shortcut closes the panel.

A ctrl+F2/command-F2

Displays or hides the objects panel.

B ctrl+F3/command-F3

Displays or hides whichever property inspector is relevant for the currently selected page object.

C F8

Displays or hides the **Site Files** window. (Okay, it's not really a panel, but it has the character of a panel.) If the **Site Map** window is open, this shortcut leaves it open, but activates the file view in the right windowpane.

> 🄣 If you have a multiple-display setup (Windows 98, Windows 2000, or MacOS), you can reduce the need for these shortcuts by putting your panels on the secondary display and leaving them there. The panels won't overlap your document window, so you won't need to hide the panels that you aren't using.

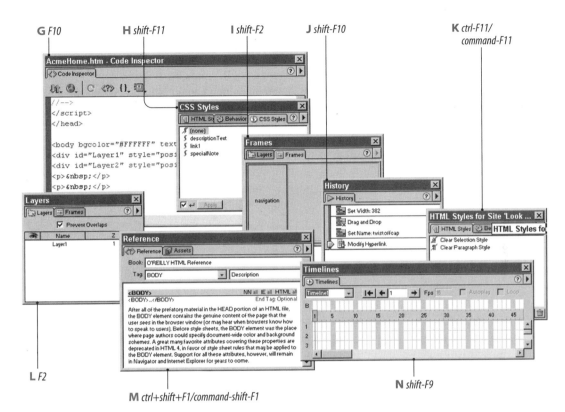

G *F10* **H** *shift-F11* **I** *shift-F2* **J** *shift-F10* **K** *ctrl-F11/command-F11*

L *F2*

M *ctrl+shift+F1/command-shift-F1*

N *shift-F9*

D alt+F8/option-F8

This combination displays or hides the **Site Map** window. If the **Site Files** window is already open, this shortcut leaves it open but activates the map view in the left window pane.

E F11

Display or hides the **Assets** panel.

F shift-F3

Display or hides the **Behaviors** panel.

G F10

Display or hides the **Code Inspector**.

H shift-F11

Display or hides the **CSS Styles** panel.

I shift-F2

Use this combination to display or hide the **Frames** panel.

J shift-F10

This keyboard combination displays or hides the **History** panel—one of the more important ones to leave on the desktop.

K ctrl-F11/command-F11

Displays or hides the **HTML Styles** panel.

L F2

Displays or hides the **Layers** panel.

M ctrl+shift+F1/command-shift-F1

Displays or hides the **Reference** panel.

N shift-F9

Displays or hides the **Timelines** panel.

> 💡 The **F4** key lets you hide all open panels at one fell swoop; tapping **F4** again brings them all back. If you press **shift+F4** in Windows, you minimize *all* windows, including the current document.

Menu Command Shortcuts

The following table lists keyboard shortcuts for common menu commands, in alphabetical order by command. These commands either don't neatly fit into any of the other categories in this chapter, or they span multiple categories. If a command you need doesn't appear here, see whether it appears in the relevant section—for example, the Insert Column command is in the Table & Frame Shortcuts section on page 288.

On the Windows platform, you also have a wealth of *alt-key equivalent* shortcuts for menu commands

menu command	windows shortcut	macintosh shortcut
add keyframe	F6	F6
add object to library	ctrl+shift+B	command-shift-B
add object to timeline	ctrl+shift+alt+T	command-shift-option-T
check links	shift+F8	command-F8
check links sitewide	ctrl+F8	command-F8
check spelling	shift+F7	shift-F7
clear	delete	delete
close	ctrl+W or ctrl+F4	command-W
copy	ctrl+C or ctrl+ins	command-C
cut	ctrl+X or shift+del	command-X or shift-del
debug in primary browser	alt+F12	option-F12
debug in secondary browser	ctrl+alt+F12	command-option-F12
edit in external program	ctrl+E	command-E
edit style sheet	ctrl+shift+E	command-shift-E
exit	ctrl+Q or alt+F4	command-Q
find & replace	ctrl+F	command-F
find next	F3	command-G
help	F1	F1 or Help
insert Director movie	ctrl+alt+D	command-option-D
insert Flash movie	ctrl+alt+F	command-option-F
insert image	ctrl+alt+I	command-option-I
insert named anchor	ctrl+alt+A	command-option-A
insert table	ctrl+alt+T	command-option-T
layout view	ctrl+F6	command-F6
make link	ctrl+L	command-L
modify page properties	ctrl+J	command-J
modify selection properties (toggle)	ctrl+shift+J	command-shift-J
new document	ctrl+N	command-N
new editable region	ctrl+alt+V	command-option-V
open document	ctrl+O	command-O
open in frame	ctrl+shift+O	command-shift-O

containing an underlined character; to save trees, and because they're obvious on the screen anyway, I won't list those shortcuts here.

Parallel traditions sometimes dictate that more than one shortcut work for a given command (a PC example is **ctrl+V** and **shift+ins**, both of which perform a paste operation). In those cases, I list both. Also, when the same shortcut turns something on or off, depending on whether that something was on or off to begin with, I've added **(toggle)** after the command name.

menu command	windows shortcut	macintosh shortcut
open quick tag editor	ctrl+T	command-T
paste	ctrl+V or shift+ins	command-V
play all plugins	ctrl+shift+alt+P	command-shift-option-P
play plugin	ctrl+alt+P	command-option-P
play recorded command	ctrl+P	command-P
preferences	ctrl+U	command-U
preview in primary browser	F12	F12
preview in secondary browser	ctrl+F12	command-F12
redo	ctrl+Y or ctrl+shift+Z	command-Y or command-shift-Z
refresh design view	F5	F5
remove keyframe	shift+F6	shift-F6
remove link	ctrl+shift+L	command-shift-L
save	ctrl+S	command-S
save as	ctrl+shift+S	command-shift-S
select all	ctrl+A	command-A
show context menu	right-click	control-click
show site files	F8	F8
show site map	alt+F8	option-F8
show/hide grid (toggle)	ctrl+alt+G	command-option-G
show/hide head content (toggle)	ctrl+shift+W	command-shift-W
show/hide panels	F4	F4
show/hide rulers (toggle)	ctrl+alt+R	command-option-R
show/hide toolbar (toggle)	ctrl+shift+T	command-shift-T
show/hide visual aids (toggle)	ctrl+shift+I	command-shift-I
snap to grid (toggle)	ctrl+shift+alt+G	command-shift-option-G
standard view	ctrl+shift+F6	command-shift-F6
start/stop recording (toggle)	ctrl+shift+X	command-shift-X
stop all plugins	ctrl+shift+alt+X	command-shift-option-X
stop plugin	ctrl+alt+X	command-option-X
switch between code & design view	ctrl+tab	command-tab
undo	ctrl+Z	command-Z

Table & Frame Shortcuts

Tables and frames are probably the two most popular Web page design elements, so you're likely to make frequent use of the following shortcuts. Read Chapter 5, Design Tables, for the complete lowdown on designing and modifying tables.

Chapter 7, Create Frames, contains full details on building and editing framesets.

Note that some of the table-related shortcuts listed below don't work in layout view, but they all work in standard view.

table or frame task	windows shortcut	macintosh shortcut
add new last row	tab in last cell	tab in last cell
decrease column span	ctrl+shift+[	command-shift-[
delete current column	ctrl+shift+-	command-shift--
delete current row	ctrl+shift+M	command-shift-M
disable cell snapping	hold down alt while drawing cell	hold down option while drawing cell
increase column span	ctrl+shift+]	command-shift-]
insert column	ctrl+shift+A	command-shift-A
insert row above	ctrl+M	command-M
insert table	ctrl+alt+T	command-option-T
layout view	ctrl+F6	command-F6
merge selected cells	ctrl+alt+M	command-option-M
next cell	tab	tab
previous cell	shift+tab	shift-tab
select cell containing cursor	ctrl+A or click and drag down or to right	command-A or click and drag down or to right
select column	click top column border	click top column border
select multiple adjacent cells	select first cell, shift+click other cells	select first cell, shift-click other cells
select multiple nonadjacent cells	select first cell, ctrl+click other cells	select first cell, command-click other cells
select row	click left row border	click left row border
select table	click top, right, or bottom edge of table	click top, right, or bottom edge of table
select table containing cursor	ctrl+A twice	command-A twice
split cells	ctrl+alt+S	command-option-S
standard view	ctrl+shift+F6	command-shift-F6
update layout	ctrl+spacebar	command-spacebar
add new frame	alt+ctrl-drag border	command-option-drag border
open in frame	ctrl+shift+O	command-shift-O
select first child frame	alt+↓	command-↓
select frame containing cursor	alt-click	option-shift-click
select next frame	alt+→	command-→
select parent frameset	alt+↑	command-↑
select previous frame	alt+←	command-←
show/hide Frames panel (toggle)	shift+F2	shift-F2

Layer & Image Shortcuts

Layers give you great flexibility in page design as long as you don't mind restricting your viewing audience to Version 4+ browsers. Read Chapter 8, Make & Manipulate Layers, to learn everything you need to know to create and edit layers like a pro.

Most of the shortcuts listed in the table below have to do with moving and resizing layers. Note that you can't resize a layer below the minimum size required to hold the text and graphics the layer contains. Also, some of the shortcuts move layers or layer boundaries by the current *snap increment*, a

pixel value that you can modify by choosing **View⟶Grid⟶Edit Grid**. For operations that depend on layer anchor points being visible, you need to display the anchor points (if they aren't already visible) in order for the shortcuts to work. You can do so by pressing **ctrl+shift+I** (**command-shift -I** on the Mac).

Just for good measure, the bottom of the following table contains a handful of image-related shortcuts that you may find handy as well. For more information on using images in your Web site, see Chapter 4, Add & Edit Graphics.

layer or image task	windows shortcut	macintosh shortcut
align selected layer to edge of last selected layer	ctrl+arrow key	command-arrow key
draw multiple layers	hold down ctrl after clicking Draw Layer on objects panel	hold down command after clicking Draw Layer on objects panel
insert layer	sorry, you have to use the menu!	sorry, you have to use the menu!
make layer active	click inside layer	click inside layer
make selected layers same height	ctrl+shift+]	command-shift-]
make selected layers same width	ctrl+shift+[	command-shift-[
move selected layer by 1 pixel	arrow keys	arrow keys
move selected layer by 1 snap increment	shift+arrow keys	shift-arrow keys
resize selected layer by 1 pixel	ctrl+arrow keys	option-arrow keys
resize selected layer by 1 snap increment	ctrl+shift+arrow keys	shift-option-arrow keys
select & move layer	shift+ctrl-drag	shift-command-drag
select layer	ctrl+shift+click inside layer or click layer anchor or click edge of layer	command-shift-click inside layer or click layer anchor or click edge of layer
select multiple layers	select first layer and then shift+click other layers	select first layer and then shift+click other layers
show/hide Layers panel (toggle)	F2	F2
snap layers to grid (toggle)	ctrl+shift+alt+G	command-shift-option-G
change image source	double-click image	double-click image
duplicate image	ctrl+click and drag	command-click and drag
edit in external program	click image & press ctrl+E	click image & press command-E
edit image with external program	ctrl+double-click image	command-double-click image
insert image	ctrl+alt+I	command-option-I

Code Editing Shortcuts

Some of you reading this book are either now, or will be soon, HTML code jockeys. This page, which mainly contains shortcuts you would use in code view or in the code inspector, is for you. Weavers who have no desire to muck about with HTML code can skip this page in its entirety; all the shortcuts

you need to know for regular text entry and editing appear on the following page.

Chapter 2, Build & Edit HTML, offers a quick introduction to HTML editing, and the HTML Reference Guide (**shift+F1**) contains more details on specific HTML tags and attributes than you'd ever want to know.

code editing task	windows shortcut	macintosh shortcut
balance braces	ctrl+'	command-'
breakpoint (toggle)	ctrl+alt+B	command-option-B
copy	ctrl+C	command-C
cut	ctrl+X	command-X
find & replace	ctrl+F	command-F
find next	F3	command-G
indent code	ctrl+]	command-]
move to end of code	ctrl+end	command-end
move to end of line	end	end
move to page down	page down	page down
move to page up	page up	page up
move to start of line	home	home
move to top of code	ctrl+home	command-home
open Quick Tag Editor	ctrl+T	command-T
outdent code	ctrl+[	command-[
paste	ctrl+V	command-V
select 1 character left	shift+←	shift-←
select 1 character right	shift+→	shift-→
select 1 line down	shift+↓	shift-↓
select 1 line up	shift+↑	shift-↑
select all	ctrl+A	command-A
select child tag	ctrl+shift+>	command-shift->
select parent tag	ctrl+shift+<	command-shift-<
select to end of code	ctrl+shift+end	command-shift-end
select to page down	shift+page down	shift-page down
select to page up	shift+page up	shift-page up
select to top of code	ctrl+shift+home	command-shift-home
select word left	ctrl+shift+←	command-shift-←
select word right	ctrl+shift+→	command-shift-→
switch to design view (toggle)	ctrl+tab	option-tab

Text Editing Shortcuts

Web pages consist mainly of text and graphics, so the shortcuts on this page are almost all worth memorizing. Happily, some of them may be familiar to you from work with other programs. Chapter 3, Create & Edit Text, contains further details on the operations laid out in the following table.

text editing task	windows shortcut	macintosh shortcut
add selected text to library	ctrl+shift+B	command-shift-B
align selected text center	ctrl+shift+alt+C	command-shift-option-C
align selected text left	ctrl+shift+alt+L	command-shift-option-L
align selected text right	ctrl+shift+alt+R	command-shift-option-R
boldface selected text (toggle)	ctrl+B	command-B
check spelling	shift+F7	shift-F7
copy selected text	ctrl-drag	option-drag
cut selected text	ctrl+X	command-X
edit style sheet	ctrl+shift+E	command-shift-E
end list	enter twice	return twice
find & replace	ctrl+F	command-F
find next	F3	command-G
format none	ctrl+zero	command-zero
format paragraph	ctrl+shift+P	command-shift-P
heading 1	ctrl+1	command-1
heading 2	ctrl+2	command-2
heading 3	ctrl+3	command-3
heading 4	ctrl+4	command-4
heading 5	ctrl+5	command-5
heading 6	ctrl+6	command-6
indent	ctrl+]	command-]
insert line break	shift+enter	shift-return
insert nonbreaking space	ctrl+shift+spacebar	option-spacebar
italicize selected text (toggle)	ctrl+I	command-I
make hyperlink for selected text	ctrl+L	command-L
make new paragraph	enter	return
move selected text	drag	drag
move to end of line	end	end
move to start of line	home	home
outdent	ctrl+[	command-[
paste text	ctrl+V	command-V
select word	double-click	double-click
switch to code view (toggle)	ctrl+tab	option-tab

Site Management Shortcuts

Dreamweaver's full power isn't evident until you start managing one or more moderate to large Web sites. In fact, many users begin appreciating the program's page layout features only to shift later in their careers to working mainly with the site management tools.

This page sets forth the shortcuts you're most likely to need if your site has more than just a few pages, or if you update it frequently over an FTP connection. For the full briefing on this subject, see Chapter 10, Manage Your Site.

site management task	windows shortcut	macintosh shortcut
change selected link	Ctrl+L	command-L
check in	ctrl+shift+alt+U	command-shift-option-U
check links in entire site	ctrl+F8	command-F8
check out	ctrl+shift+alt+D	command-shift-option-D
check selected links	shift+F8	shift-F8
find & replace	ctrl+F	command-F
get (download) selected files from remote site	ctrl+shift+D	command-shift-D
link to existing file	ctrl+shift+K	command-shift-K
make new file	ctrl+shift+N	command-shift-N
make new folder	ctrl+shift+alt+N	command-shift-option-N
open assets panel	F11	F11
open linked-to document	ctrl+double-click	command-double-click
open page	double-click	double-click
open selection	ctrl+shift+alt+O	command-shift-option-O
put (upload) selected files to remote site	ctrl+shift+U	command-shift-U
refresh current pane	shift+F5	shift+F5
refresh remote site	alt+F5	option-F5
refresh site window	F5	F5
remove selected link (document window)	ctrl+shift+L	command-shift-L
remove selected link (map view only)	delete	delete
rename selected file	F2 (or click twice, slowly)	click twice, slowly
select adjacent pages (file view only)	click first page and then shift-click	click first page and then shift-click
select all	ctrl+A	command-A
select nonadjacent pages (file view only)	click first page and then control-click	click first page and then command-click
show page titles/filenames (toggle)	ctrl+shift+T	command-shift-T
show site files	F8	F8
show site map	alt+F8	option-F8
show/hide link	ctrl+shift+Y	command-shift-Y
view as root (map view only)	ctrl+shift+R	command-shift-R
zoom in site map	ctrl++	command-+
zoom out site map	ctrl+-	command--

Look It Up & Learn

 A

<a href> tag, 25, 202
<a> tag, 29
absolute links, 54, 179

🚫 action denied cursor, 7
action menus, 139
actions, 262
   buttons, 98
   changing settings, 194
   events triggering multiple, 193
   listing, 192–193, 194
   recent, 18
   removing, 193
   unable to perform, 7
Actions folder, 262
active
   documents, 3
   links color, 35
ActiveX class identifiers, 263

ActiveX controls, 10, 210
   adding, 212
   aligning, 211
   alternative images, 212–214
   behaviors, 212
   class ID, 210
   context-sensitive help, 212
   dimensions, 211
   names, 210
   space around, 211
   transferring data between, 213
   where on Internet to find, 212
ActiveX Plugin, 210
ActiveX property inspector, 210–211, 263
ActiveXNames.txt file, 211, 263
Add Keyframe command, 183, 188
Add Object to Library keyboard shortcuts, 149
Add Timeline command, 190
Additional Flash Button Styles extension, 179, 281

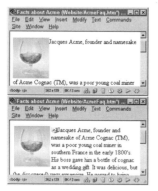

continued
(begins on page 294)

Balance Braces command, 31

\<base> tag, 35

\<base target="framename"> tag, 114

\<b> tags, 29

BBEdit, 248–249

behaviors, 191, 274
   ActiveX controls, 212
   adding, 193
   animation, 187
   associating images with, 198
   attaching to text, 200–202
   changing events, 193
   changing text dynamically in
      layer, 200–202
   hotspots, 66
   JavaScript, 194
   keyboard shortcuts, 105, 192
   listing, 192
   Popup Message action, 203
   removing, 193
   tags, 192
   timeline, 181
   Timelines panel, 182
   trying to link to missing file, 171

Behaviors channel, 182

Behaviors folder, 262

Behaviors panel, 115, 177, 181,
      193–194, 198, 201, 274

   Action button, 192
   Add Action button, 192
   keyboard shortcut, 287
   Popup Message action, 203

bitmap graphics, 53–57

_blank frame, 62

_blank predefined target, 114

blockquote tag, 43

body, 34–36

body content, 29

\<body> tags, 29, 34, 194, 196–197,
     203–205

Bold keyboard shortcuts, 15, 269

bold text, 29, 42

borders, 62

\
 tag, 29, 36, 43

Breakpoint keyboard shortcut, 195

breakpoints, 20, 31, 195

broken links, 159, 170–171

Broken Links report, 171

BrowserProfiles folder, 262

browsers
   checking version, 196–197
   CSS border attributes, 229
   debugging pages, 19
   Flash support, 178
   formatting alert messages, 203

browsers *continued*
   HTML tags, 262
   layers, 123, 127
   opening window in, 198–199
   plugins, 208
   previewing pages, 19, 48
   testing with compatibility, 168
   text-only page, 197

built-in help system, 22

bulleted lists, 42

Here are our product grades:

- Truly Superb
- Good
- Better-than-Nothing

And what the names mean:

Truly Superb
   Aged for 250 years
Good
   Aged for 250 days
Better-than-Nothing
   Aged for 250 minutes

bullets, converting to images, 281

Button inspector, 98

buttons, 16, 95, 98

 C

C API, 278

C programming language, 279

Call JavaScript behavior, 102

capitalization, 14

caps lock key, 14

cell boundary, 9

cell padding, 81

Cell property inspector, 83

cell spacing, 81

 Look It Up & Learn: B–C   **295**

Index

Which of our products have you tried?
☐ *Gallic Gold*
☐ *American Amber*

Index

 continued
(begins on page 295)

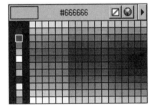

Index

 continued
(begins on page 298)

debugging
    HTML code, 31
    pages, 19
    stopping, 195
default text size, 42
Define HTML Style dialog box, 49
Define Site dialog box, 259
Define Sites command, 163
Define Sites dialog box, 155–156, 246, 258
definition list, 45
deleting
    commands, 270
    files, 157
    keyboard shortcuts, 265
    linked style, 221
    styles, 49
    tags, 37
    unlinked style, 221
delimiter character, 92, 242, 244
dependent files, 159, 258
descenders, 58
description <meta> tag, 35
descriptor, 101
Design Notes, 163, 240
    case-sensitivity, 167
    creation of, 166–167
    custom name/value pair, 167
    maintaining, 163
    showing when document
        opens, 167
    uploading for sharing, 163
Design Notes API, 278
Design Notes command, 166
Design Notes dialog box,
        19, 166–167, 240
Design Notes reports, 172, 174

design view
    options, 20
    refreshing, 19, 27
    View Options button, 27
 Design View button, 19
Design View On Top command, 27
desktop

    close button, 4
    context menus, 5
    cursor, 5
    document window, 3
    Macintosh, 2–5
    maximize button, 4
    menu bar, 2
    mini-launcher, 5
    minimize button, 4
    objects panel, 2
    panels, 5
    property inspectors, 5
    restore button, 4
    scroll arrow, 4
    scroll bars, 4
    scroll box, 4
    size and download time, 5
    size box, 5
    status bar, 5
    tag selector, 5
    title bar, 2
    toolbar, 3
    window size pop-up menu, 5
    Windows, 2–5
    zoom icon, 4
DHTML (Dynamic HTML), 183
 diagonal resize cursor, 6

dialog boxes, 2, 14, 16
DIR file format, 238
disjoint rollover, 66, 177
<div> tag, 125, 127, 130
document area, 8
document windows, 2, 3

    cell boundary, 9
    document area, 8
    form elements, 9
    grid, 9
    as guide to Web page view, 8
    hyperlinks, 9
    insertion point, 9
    object border, 8–9
    objects automatically changing
        shapes, 8
    resize handles, 9
    resizing, 21
    rulers, 9
    scrolling, 4
    status bar, 5, 21
    table boundary, 9
    tag selector, 32
    Title field, 34
    toolbar, 19, 59
document-relative links, 54, 179
document-relative path, 57
documents
    active, 3
    attaching templates, 144
    background, 3
    closing, 3, 4
    comments, 163
    estimated download time, 21
    foreground, 3

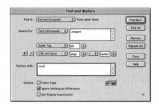

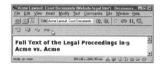

Index

 continued
(begins on page 304)

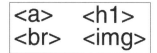

Index

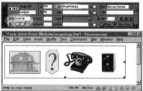

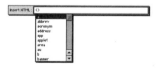

"An Apple a Day"

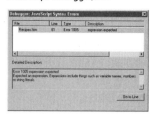

continued
(begins on page 308)

Index

Index

named anchors, 10, 24, 66
navigating to inline images, 57–58
navigation, 107
navigation bar, 67–68, 68, 107, 199

 , 43
nested frames, 118
nested layers, 125, 126, 131
nested lists, 43
nested tables, 79, 82
nesting layers, 122, 130–132
Netscape Developer Web site, 196

Netscape Navigator
ActiveX support, 211
events, 193
media clip, 212
minimum version, 197
plugins, 209
pop-up message, 203
Preferences dialog box, 213
turning on JavaScript
processing, 194
Version 4.0, 123
Version 4.75 and plugins, 218
Netscape plugins, 10
Netscape Web site, 216
New Document keyboard
shortcuts, 112
new documents, 3
New Editable Region dialog box, 142
New Folder command, 157
New HTML window, 116
New Style command, 222
New Style dialog box,
221, 222–223, 225

Next (tab) keyboard shortcut, 16, 99
<noframes> tags, 120
noframes content, 120
Nonbreaking Space keyboard
shortcuts, 43
None action, 98
nonlayer CSS styles, converting to
HTML styles, 134
Notes window, current date in, 167
NPAVI32 plugin, 218
null links, 115, 196, 200, 201
numbered list, 43

object extension, creation of, 275
object panels, files supporting, 263
<object> tags, 212–213, 234
codebase attribute, 239
Flash movies, 237
objects, 274, 275
adjusting settings, 5
aligning, 9, 136, 210, 212
aspect ratio, 6
automatically changing shapes, 8
border, 8–9
code, 275
collections of, 2
comments, 163
file name, 159
horizontally resizing, 6
icon creation for, 275
inserting, 24
JavaScript behaviors, 20
modifying, 33
moving, 6
naming, 17
notations, 240
operating performable on, 5
placing, 9

objects *continued*
positioning, 135–136
renaming, 159
resize handles, 9
resizing, 6
selecting, 8–9
selecting all, 30
snapping to guidelines, 9
status, 240
testing, 275
vertically resizing, 6
white space, 210
Objects folder, 261, 263
Objects panel, 2, 24, 35, 274, 275

Draw Layer icon, 41, 59, 122, 125,
128, 131, 132, 184, 200
Draw Layout Cell icon, 40, 46, 86
Draw Table Layout icon, 46
hiding, 10
icons, 10
Insert Image icon, 57, 59, 132, 184
Insert Navigation Bar icon, 67
Insert Table icon, 88
keyboard shortcut, 15, 284
layout commands, 10
Layout View icon, 40, 46, 78, 86
listing icons, 260
redesigning, 260–261

Index

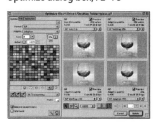

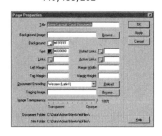

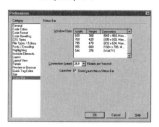

Index

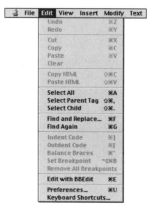

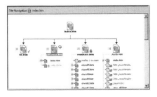

Index

 S *continued*
(begins on page 315)

Site➡Site Map View➡Show
Dependent Files command, 159
Site➡Site Map View➡Show Files
Marked as Hidden
command, 159
Site➡Site Map View➡Show Page
Titles command, 159
Site➡Site Map View➡Show/Hide
Link command, 159
Site➡Site Map View➡View as Root
command, 158
site-specific assets, 165
Site➡Undo Check Out command, 156
size box, 5
Snap to Web Safe command, 63
snapping cells into place, 79
snapping to grid, 134
sorting, 91
    list of files, 156
    table data, 90–91
sound files, 213–215, 217
    Assets panel, 164
sound object, 215
Source Control Integration API, 279
source control systems, 246, 279
SourceFormat.txt file, 254, 255, 263
spacer GIFs, 82
spacer images, 86–87
spacer.gif file, 87
<span> tag, 125, 127, 221
special characters, 43, 48, 253
special object panel, 10
Special Objects panel
    ActiveX icon, 211
    Insert Plugin icon, 209, 214
Spell Check keyboard shortcut, 14
spell-checking, 52
SPL file format, 235

Split Cell keyboard shortcuts, 83
split view, 27

splitter bar, 27
splitting
    cells, 83
    screen, 19
spreadsheets
    delimiter character, 242, 244
    formatting data, 244
    trimming unnecessary
        elements, 243
SQL (Structured Query Language)
    databases, 279
stacking, 41
standard view, 10, 40, 41, 47, 59, 77,
    78, 90
    cell properties, 83
    Cell property inspector, 83
    Clear Column Widths button, 82
    Column property inspector, 83
    column width, 80–81
    inserting tables, 79
    keyboard shortcuts, 88
    naming tables, 80
    number of rows and columns, 80
    Row property inspector, 83
    selecting columns, 83
    table height, 81
    Table property inspector, 80–82
    tables, 88–89
Start menu, 15
Start of Line command, 269
status bar, 5
    <form> tag, 102
    mini-launcher, 20

status bar *continued*
    modifying, 21
    pop-up browser window, 199
Style Definition dialog box, 220,
    223–224, 225–226, 228, 231
style sheets
    attaching, 227
    external, 225–226

styles, 43, 219
    applying, 49, 220
    conflicts, 231
    CSS, 220–221, 231
    custom, 221
    default ordered or unordered lists,
        45
    deleting, 49
    editing, 49, 221
    glossary items, 202
    HTML, 231
    linked, 220
    minimalist definitions, 229
    naming, 49
    new, 49
    quickly editing, 220
    redefinition, 221
    unlinked, 220
submenu arrow, 12
submenus, 12
Submit button, 95, 98, 102
Submit form action, 98
Swap Image behavior, 177
Swap Image Restore behavior, 177
.swf file extension, 54
SWF (ShockWave Flash) file format, 235

Index

Index

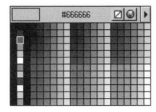

Index

 continued
(begins on page 323)

windows, 4, 21
Windows 2000, 13
windows key, 15
Windows Media Player, 215, 216, 218

Window➡Site Files command, 154
Window➡Site Map command,
154, 158
Window➡Templates command,
138, 144
Window➡Timelines command, 180,
185, 188, 189
WMF (Windows Media Format), 217
Word documents, 38
workflow, 172
wrapping text in text fields, 96
wristwatch, 7

WYSIWYG (What You *See* Is What You
Get), 93

XML files, 173
Xtras, 238

z-index, 124–125, 126
zooming foreground documents, 4